Volkswagen Beetle Owners Workshop Manual

by J H Haynes
Member of the Guild of Motoring Writers
and K F Kinchin

Models covered

UK: 1303 Super Beetle, 1285 cc, 1972 on
1303S Super Beetle, 1584 cc, 1972 on
GT Beetle, 1584 cc, 1972 on
USA: Super Beetle, 96.7 cu in., 1972 on
Sports Bug, 96.7 cu in., 1972 on
Basic Beetle, 96.7 cu in., 1970 on

ISBN 978 0 85733 648 4

(159-11P3)

J H Haynes & Co. Ltd.
Haynes North America, Inc

www.haynes.com

Acknowledgements

Thanks are due to Brian Horsfall who took the vehicle to bits and put it together again; to Les Brazier who took the photographs and to Tim Parker and Rod Grainger for advice and encouragement.

The assistance of the VW Organization and their provision of some of the illustrations is most appreciated.

About this manual

Its aim

The long history of the VW Beetle has been told many times before and it is not our intention to tell it again here. This universally loved 'people's car' is brilliant in concept, very well made, extremely hardy and long-lived and generally badly written about! We have taken one to pieces, renovated it, assembled it, run it and written about it here. We trust that you will find it a well illustrated and practical service/repair manual, the like of which cannot be found elsewhere for the do-it-yourself motorist. The main problem is producing a book about such an 'over-exposed' car, which has been produced in such large numbers, in a profusion of different models, is deciding what to leave out. Our first task has, of course been to the fundamentals throughout. We have also included all those modifications of any significance including those still being made in retrospect by Volkswagenwerk. Such is our confidence in this superbly constructed and long running car that we are sure that any minor details not specifically mentioned are only minor details.

We have found that most VW owners and agencies are enthusiasts first and foremost. (We are now too!). They will give more help and advice then most. At certain points in the repair of a Beetle, 'professional' help is necessary. It is true that the use of special tools is desirable for ease, speed and accuracy and essential in some tasks. This manual assumes that the owner has no such tools but it does assume in certain applications that a part or assembly can be taken to a Volkswagen workshop where the tools are available with competent staff to use them. Tales are heard of frustrated looking (without this book) men arriving at VW workshops carrying suitcases, which when opened, reveal an engine dismantled down to the last carburettor jet. No instance has been heard yet of anyone being turned away!

Although this manual describes how to service, how to check for safety, repairs, replacement of parts and general maintenance of the VW Beetle you will find that the frequency of doing these tasks is less than in more 'conventional' cars. Nevertheless we do assume that the enthusiastic owner does, himself, possess a reasonable set of good quality tools.　　　　Much of

Much of the work involved in looking after a car and carrying out repairs depends on accurate diagnosis in the first place. Where possible, therefore, a methodical and progressive way of diagnosis is presented. The time that can be wasted in hopping from one possible source of trouble to another, suggested at random quite often by self styled 'experts' must have been experienced by many people. It is best to say at the start; 'this could be one of several things - let's get the Haynes manual out'.

We trust that you continue to receive as much trouble free and pleasurable motoring in your VW Beetle as we have in ours, and it's not very often we can say that!

Its use

The book is divided into thirteen Chapters. Each Chapter is divided into numbered Sections which are headed in bold type between horizontal lines. Each section consists of serially numbered paragraphs.

Procedures, once described in the text, are not normally repeated. If it is necessary to refer to a particular paragraph in another Chapter the reference is eg; 'Chapter 1/5:5'. Cross-references given without the use of the word 'Chapter' apply to Section in the same Chapter, eg; 'See Section 8' means also 'in this Chapter'.

All illustrations carry a caption. Where the illustration is designated as a Figure the reference is merely a sequence number for the Chapter. Where the illustration is not designated as a Figure (i.e. photographs) the reference number pinpoints the Section and paragraph in that Chapter to which the picture refers.

When the left or right side of a car is mentioned it is as if looking forward.

Whilst every care is taken to ensure that the information in this manual is correct no liability can be accepted by the authors or publishers for loss, damage or injury caused by any errors in, or omissions from, the information given.

Introduction

This book is about the VW Beetle in its latest forms. The models covered are the 1303/1303S Super Beetle and GT Beetle (UK) and the Super Beetle (113), basic Beetle 1600 (111) and Sports Bug (USA).

The vehicle used to take to pieces was a UK 1303 Super Beetle; where the other vehicles differ this is pointed out (eg Disc brakes on the 1303s and GT, Torsion bar front suspension on the USA basic Beetle and UK GT Beetle.

A lot of changes have taken place even in the short life of the current Super Beetle (carburettor, petrol pump, generator) as it has evolved from the earlier 'longnose, flat screen' Super Beetle of 1970 to 1972 to its present state.

The interior has been much improved, and the steering now has a new safety factor built in. Nevertheless, it is still the cheerful Beetle willing to go flat out, all the way, if necessary and not get fussed.

However, even Beetles have accidents or wear out, and should this happen it is hoped that the owner may be helped by "getting out the book".

Contents

	Page
Acknowledgements	2
About this manual	2
Introduction	2
Safety first!	5
Buying spare parts and vehicle identification numbers	6
Recommended lubricants and fluids	7
Routine maintenance	8
Chapter 1 Engine	12
Chapter 2 Cooling, heating and exhaust systems	43
Chapter 3 Fuel system and carburation	53
Chapter 4 Ignition system	65
Chapter 5 Clutch	75
Chapter 6 Transmission and final drive	82
Chapter 7 Automatic stick-shift transmission	100
Chapter 8 Rear suspension, wheels, bearings and driveshafts	106
Chapter 9 Braking system	119
Chapter 10 Electrical system I : charging and starting systems	134
Chapter 11 Electrical system II : lighting system, facia board and electrical accessories	144
Chapter 12 Steering mechanism, front suspension and wheels	174
Chapter 13 Bodywork and underframe	195
Conversion factors	210
Use of English	211
Index	212

1974 Super Beetle

Safety first!

Professional motor mechanics are trained in safe working procedures. However enthusiastic you may be about getting on with the job in hand, do take the time to ensure that your safety is not put at risk. A moment's lack of attention can result in an accident, as can failure to observe certain elementary precautions.

There will always be new ways of having accidents, and the following points do not pretend to be a comprehensive list of all dangers; they are intended rather to make you aware of the risks and to encourage a safety-conscious approach to all work you carry out on your vehicle.

Essential DOs and DON'Ts

DON'T rely on a single jack when working underneath the vehicle. Always use reliable additional means of support, such as axle stands, securely placed under a part of the vehicle that you know will not give way.

DON'T attempt to loosen or tighten high-torque nuts (e.g. wheel hub nuts) while the vehicle is on a jack; it may be pulled off.

DON'T start the engine without first ascertaining that the transmission is in neutral (or 'Park' where applicable) and the parking brake applied.

DON'T suddenly remove the filler cap from a hot cooling system – cover it with a cloth and release the pressure gradually first, or you may get scalded by escaping coolant.

DON'T attempt to drain oil until you are sure it has cooled sufficiently to avoid scalding you.

DON'T grasp any part of the engine, exhaust or catalytic converter without first ascertaining that it is sufficiently cool to avoid burning you.

DON'T allow brake fluid or antifreeze to contact vehicle paintwork.

DON'T syphon toxic liquids such as fuel, brake fluid or antifreeze by mouth, or allow them to remain on your skin.

DON'T inhale dust – it may be injurious to health (see *Asbestos* below).

DON'T allow any spilt oil or grease to remain on the floor – wipe it up straight away, before someone slips on it.

DON'T use ill-fitting spanners or other tools which may slip and cause injury.

DON'T attempt to lift a heavy component which may be beyond your capability – get assistance.

DON'T rush to finish a job, or take unverified short cuts.

DON'T allow children or animals in or around an unattended vehicle.

DO wear eye protection when using power tools such as drill, sander, bench grinder etc, and when working under the vehicle.

DO use a barrier cream on your hands prior to undertaking dirty jobs – it will protect your skin from infection as well as making the dirt easier to remove afterwards; but make sure your hands aren't left slippery. Note that long-term contact with used engine oil can be a health hazard.

DO keep loose clothing (cuffs, tie etc) and long hair well out of the way of moving mechanical parts.

DO remove rings, wristwatch etc, before working on the vehicle – especially the electrical system.

DO ensure that any lifting tackle used has a safe working load rating adequate for the job.

DO keep your work area tidy – it is only too easy to fall over articles left lying around.

DO get someone to check periodically that all is well, when working alone on the vehicle.

DO carry out work in a logical sequence and check that everything is correctly assembled and tightened afterwards.

DO remember that your vehicle's safety affects that of yourself and others. If in doubt on any point, get specialist advice.

IF, in spite of following these precautions, you are unfortunate enough to injure yourself, seek medical attention as soon as possible.

Asbestos

Certain friction, insulating, sealing, and other products – such as brake linings, brake bands, clutch linings, torque converters, gaskets, etc – contain asbestos. *Extreme care must be taken to avoid inhalation of dust from such products since it is hazardous to health.* If in doubt, assume that they *do* contain asbestos.

Fire

Remember at all times that petrol (gasoline) is highly flammable. Never smoke, or have any kind of naked flame around, when working on the vehicle. But the risk does not end there – a spark caused by an electrical short-circuit, by two metal surfaces contacting each other, by careless use of tools, or even by static electricity built up in your body under certain conditions, can ignite petrol vapour, which in a confined space is highly explosive.

Always disconnect the battery earth (ground) terminal before working on any part of the fuel or electrical system, and never risk spilling fuel on to a hot engine or exhaust.

It is recommended that a fire extinguisher of a type suitable for fuel and electrical fires is kept handy in the garage or workplace at all times. Never try to extinguish a fuel or electrical fire with water.

Note: *Any reference to a 'torch' appearing in this manual should always be taken to mean a hand-held battery-operated electric lamp or flashlight. It does NOT mean a welding/gas torch or blowlamp.*

Fumes

Certain fumes are highly toxic and can quickly cause unconsciousness and even death if inhaled to any extent. Petrol (gasoline) vapour comes into this category, as do the vapours from certain solvents such as trichloroethylene. Any draining or pouring of such volatile fluids should be done in a well ventilated area.

When using cleaning fluids and solvents, read the instructions carefully. Never use materials from unmarked containers – they may give off poisonous vapours.

Never run the engine of a motor vehicle in an enclosed space such as a garage. Exhaust fumes contain carbon monoxide which is extremely poisonous; if you need to run the engine, always do so in the open air or at least have the rear of the vehicle outside the workplace.

If you are fortunate enough to have the use of an inspection pit, never drain or pour petrol, and never run the engine, while the vehicle is standing over it; the fumes, being heavier than air, will concentrate in the pit with possibly lethal results.

The battery

Never cause a spark, or allow a naked light, near the vehicle's battery. It will normally be giving off a certain amount of hydrogen gas, which is highly explosive.

Always disconnect the battery earth (ground) terminal before working on the fuel or electrical systems.

If possible, loosen the filler plugs or cover when charging the battery from an external source. Do not charge at an excessive rate or the battery may burst.

Take care when topping up and when carrying the battery. The acid electrolyte, even when diluted, is very corrosive and should not be allowed to contact the eyes or skin.

If you ever need to prepare electrolyte yourself, always add the acid slowly to the water, and never the other way round. Protect against splashes by wearing rubber gloves and goggles.

When jump starting a car using a booster battery, for negative earth (ground) vehicles, connect the jump leads in the following sequence: First connect one jump lead between the positive (+) terminals of the two batteries. Then connect the other jump lead first to the negative (–) terminal of the booster battery, and then to a good earthing (ground) point on the vehicle to be started, at least 18 in (45 cm) from the battery if possible. Ensure that hands and jump leads are clear of any moving parts, and that the two vehicles do not touch. Disconnect the leads in the reverse order.

Mains electricity and electrical equipment

When using an electric power tool, inspection light etc, always ensure that the appliance is correctly connected to its plug and that, where necessary, it is properly earthed (grounded). Do not use such appliances in damp conditions and, again, beware of creating a spark or applying excessive heat in the vicinity of fuel or fuel vapour. Also ensure that the appliances meet the relevant national safety standards.

Ignition HT voltage

A severe electric shock can result from touching certain parts of the ignition system, such as the HT leads, when the engine is running or being cranked, particularly if components are damp or the insulation is defective. Where an electronic ignition system is fitted, the HT voltage is much higher and could prove fatal.

Buying spare parts
and vehicle identification numbers

Buying spare parts

Spare parts are available form many sources, for example: VW garages, other garages and accessory shops, and motor factors. Our advice regarding spare part sources is as follows:-

Officially appointed VW garages - This is the best source of parts which are peculiar to your car and are otherwise not generally available (eg complete cylinder heads, internal gearbox components, badges, interior trim etc). It is also the only place at which you should buy parts if your car is still under warranty-non-VW components may invalidate the warranty. To be sure of obtaining the correct parts it will always be necessary to give the storeman your car's engine and chassis number, and if possible, to take the 'old' part along for positive identification. Remember that many parts are available on a factory exchange scheme - any parts returned should always be clean! It obviously makes good sense to go straight to the specialists on your car for this type of part for they are best equipped to supply you.

Other garages and accessory shops - These are often very good places to buy materials and components needed for the maintenance of your car (eg oil filters, spark plugs, bulbs, fan belts, oils and greases, touch-up paint, filler paste etc). They also sell general accessories, usually have convenient opening hours, charge lower prices and can often be found not far from home.

Motor factors - Good factors will stock all-of the more important components which wear out relatively quickly (eg clutch components, pistons, valves, exhaust system, brake cylinders/ pipes/hoses/seals/shoes and pads etc). Motor factors will often provide new or reconditioned components on a part exchange basis - this can save a considerable amount of money.

Vehicle identification plate

The VW organization refer to this as the vehicle's 'birth certificate'. On the Super Beetles and Sports Bug it is under the luggage boot lid fastened at the front near the lock. On the USA basic Beetle and UK GT Beetle it is in the spare wheel well.

Chassis number: The 'FAHRGEST' is the chassis number of the car which is stamped on the frame tunnel under the rear seat.

Engine number: The engine number is stamped on the generator pedestal under the 'ZUNDFOLGE' (firing order). The engine number has two letters which tell the storeman what type of engine, and the figures which give him the batch number

and modification state. The 1285 cc (78.3 cu in) is AB or AR. The 1600 cc (96.7 cu in) engine may be AD (7.5:1 compression ratio) AE (exhaust emission control fitted) AF (6.6:1 compression ratio) AH (exhaust recirculation systems USA) or AS (fitted with 1973 modifications).

If these numbers are recorded correctly then the VW storeman will give uou the part for your particular VW. It may be a modified piece - but he will be up-to-date.

If you are buying gasket sets and oil seals check that you have ALL the ones you need before you leave the store. There may be too many, and there may be some missing (oil cooler seals for instance).

Finally, check that the spares are available before you take the vehicle to pieces. Some pieces may not be on the schedule and have to be obtained from the factory. This can take time. Again some items are not serviced. You can get a CV joint, but not the pieces for it. The spares organisation is very efficient but they are obviously not going to let stocks fall so low that their own workshops have to wait, and you may have to accept waiting time if their stocks are low.

All the same if you treat them as allies and not business rivals they will help, and advise you.

Engine number

Frequencies are based on an average monthly
mileage of 1000

ENGINE

Weekly: Check level and if necessary replenish with Castrol

3 Months: Drain off old oil while
warm and refill with fresh, clean,
Castrol.
Owners are advised that more
frequent sump draining periods
are derivable if the operation of
the car involves:-
1) Frequent start/stop driving.
2) Operation during cold weather,
especially when appreciable engine
idling is involved, i.e. town operating conditions.
Capacity — 4.4 pints (2.5 litres).

TRANSMISSION

3 Months: Check level and if
necessary top up to the edge or
the filler plug hole with Castrol
Hypoy Gear Oil.

2 Years: Drain off old oil while
warm from the drain plug and
refill with fresh Castrol Hypoy
Gear Oil to the edge of the filler
plug hole.
Capacity — 4.4 pints (2.5 litres).
5.25 pints (3 litres)
from dry.

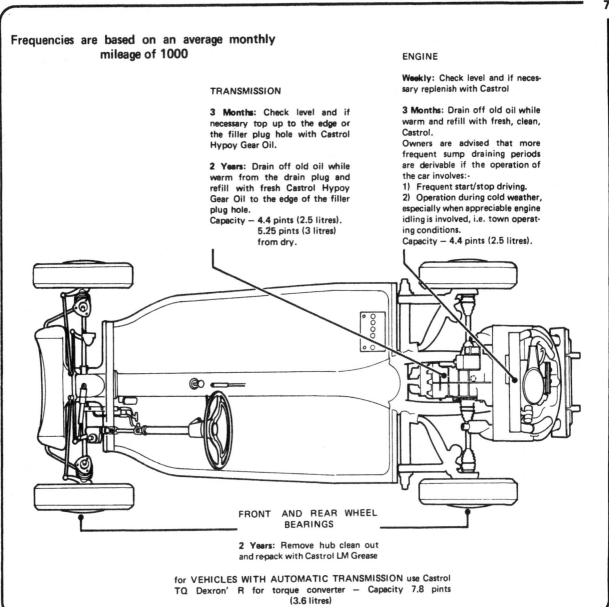

FRONT AND REAR WHEEL
BEARINGS

2 Years: Remove hub clean out
and re-pack with Castrol LM Grease

for VEHICLES WITH AUTOMATIC TRANSMISSION use Castrol
TQ Dexron' R for torque converter — Capacity 7.8 pints
(3.6 litres)

Recomended lubricants and fluids

Item	Type	Recommended
Engine lubricant	Multigrade engine oil*	CASTROL GTX
Transmission	SAE 90 gear oil	CASTROL HYPOY
Transmission with limited slip differential	SAE 90 gear oil	CASTROL HYPOY LS
Wheel bearings	Lithium based multipurpose grease	CASTROL LM
Contact breaker cam	Petroleum jelly	VASELINE
Battery terminals	Petroleum jelly	VASELINE
Brake hydraulic fluid	SAE 70 R3	CASTROL GIRLING UNIVERSAL BRAKE AND CLUTCH FLUID
Torque converter (automatic transmission)	Dexron	CASTROL TQ, DEXRON R

* In view of the small engine oil capacity and the heavy strains imposed on the oil
none but the best quality should be used. Do not mix oils of different types.

Routine maintenance

Introduction

Because of their inherent toughness and reputation for reliability and long life there is a tendency for owners to be a bit sketchy on Beetle maintenance - particularly with vehicles not in the first flush of youth.

The Beetle will put up with neglect for a much longer time than most cars but when the crunch eventually does come it is likely to be drastic.

Regular maintenance therefore, is just as important as on any other vehicle. If it is not neglected the Beetle is very much a long term investment with a low rate of depreciation value.

The service procedures listed hereafter cover all the points of required regular service. The frequency of service tends to vary according to changes in design of various components, the conditions under which the vehicle is used, and the way in which it is driven. The frequencies given are based on a mileage of 12000 per year in a temperate climate which is mainly non dusty. Variations from this will be taken into account by VW service agencies in different conditions. Variations in driving style must be the responsibility of the driver where servicing requirements could be affected.

Where maintenance is solely a matter of inspection (rather than lubrication, cleaning or adjustment) the findings from such inspections will determine whether or not further action is required. Such further action is no longer within the scope of Routine Maintenance. It is a workshop procedure requiring repair or renewal. How to do the maintenance is detailed after the schedules. If the details are already in the main chapter then reference is made appropriately.

1 Safety Maintenance

a) Steering

Steering tie-rod ball joints - check for wear	3 months
Steering gear - check worm to roller play and worm shaft bearings. Adjust if necessary	3 months
Front wheel bearings - check end play and adjust if necessary	3 months
Suspension strut upper and lower pivots - check for wear	3 months

b) Brakes

Hydraulic fluid reservoir level	1 month
Efficiency and foot pedal free play - check and adjust as required	3 months
Handbrake efficiency - check and adjust as required	6 months
Brake friction lining material - check thickness	6 months
Hydraulic lines, hoses, master cylinder, wheel cylinders and calipers - examine exteriors for leaks or corrosion	6 months
Renew all seals and fluid	3 years

Note: A significant drop in fluid reservoir level or any other indication of fluid leakage is a danger signal. A complete and thorough examination of the hydraulic system should be made

c) Suspension

Tyres - inflation pressure check	weekly
Tyres - wear and damage check	As suspect
Dampers - check for leakage and malfunction	3 months

d) Vision

Lights functioning
Screen washer operative

2 Safety Maintenance Procedures

a) Steering
See Chapter 12

b) Brakes
Hydraulic fluid reservoir level - Raise the front compartment lid. The fluid reservoir is mounted at the left-hand side. Clean round the filler cap before removing it and top up to the indicated level with approved fluid as required.
Remaining items - See Chapter 9.

c) Suspension
See Chapters 8 and 12

d) Vision
Lights - See Chapter 11
Screenwasher reservoir - See Chapter 11
The screenwasher reservoir should be full of clean water with an additive of anti-smear compound as wished. The tank should be pressurized from an ordinary type inflator to the maximum pressure of **42 lbs psi** which is marked on the tank. If it is overinflated it will split and require renewal. If the jets do not direct water on to the screen as they should; refer to Chapter 11.
In the United Kingdom correctly functioning screenwashers are a legally obligatory fitment to all cars.

3 Efficiency and performance maintenance

a) Engine

Lubricating oil - top up to level	Weekly
- drain, clean filter and refill with fresh oil	3 months
Fan belt - check tension and adjust if required	1 month
Air cleaner - clean out bowl and refill with oil	1 month
- check correct operation of warm air control flaps	1 month
Battery - check electrolyte level	Weekly
Distributor - check contact points gap. Adjust and/ or renew - lubricate cam	3 months
Valve clearances - check and adjust as required (renew rocker cover gaskets)	6 months
Spark plugs - remove, clean and reset	6 months
- renew	12 months
Fuel pump - clean filter	6 months
Carburettor - check setting of throttle cable and lubricate linkage	16 months
Cover plates and fan housing - check security of all screws and grommets	3 months

b) Suspension

Front wheel bearings - repack with grease	2 years
Rear wheel bearings - repack with grease	2 years

c) Transmission and final drive

Gearbox oil - check level and top up as needed	3 months
- drain and refill with fresh oil	2 years
Clutch pedal free play - check movement and adjust	As necessary
Axle shaft flexible gaiters - check for splits	3 months

d) Automatic transmission
Refer to Chapter 7

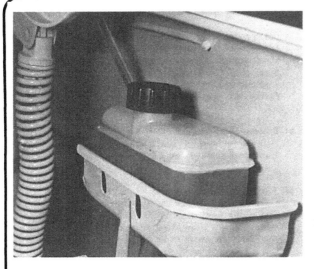

Brake fluid reservoir

Adding oil to the engine

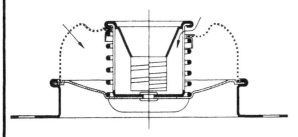

Cross section of engine oil filter screen showing normal oil flow (arrowed left), and relief flow (arrowed right), in the event of a blocked filter screen

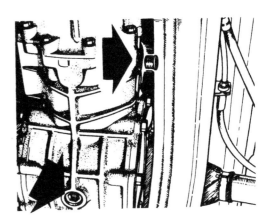

Underside of transmission showing drain and level plugs - the latter removed

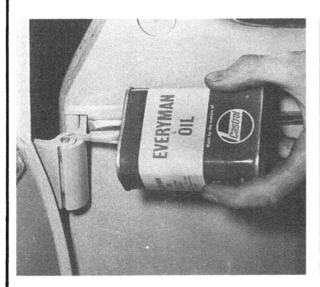

Oiling the door hinge

Lubricating the carburettor linkage

4 Efficiency and performance maintenance procedures

a) Engine

Lubricating oil

To top up the oil, remove the filler cap from the filler pipe at the right-hand side of the engine. Remove the dipstick to prevent possible blow back up the filler pipe when pouring oil in. A funnel is necessary sometimes if spillage is to be avoided.

When changing the engine oil the filter screen - which is simply wire gauze - should also be flushed out with paraffin to clear the gauze. This entails removing the circular retaining plate in the centre of the bottom of the crankcase. Before starting, you must obtain two new gaskets for it, and it is also desirable to get six new copper washers for the stud nuts.

First drain the oil by removing the centre plug and then remove the cover plate. Take care when removing the strainer. Do not distort it.

The oil suction pipe which goes into the centre of the strainer gauze must be quite firm. If it is loose then it is likely that suction is being lost and the oil circulation is not 100% efficient. (The engine needs completely stripping to put this right).

The strainer incorporates a relief valve in case the filter mesh should get completely blocked up

Having thoroughly cleaned everything refit the strainer with a gasket on each side of the flange. See that the suction pipe is properly located in the strainer. Fit new copper washers followed by the cap nuts. Do not overtighten the cap nuts - otherwise the threads may strip.

Replace the drain plug and refill with 4½ imperial pints of approved engine oil.

Fan belt - see Chapter 2
Air cleaner - see Chapter 3

Battery - see Chapter 10
Distributor - see Chapter 4
Valve clearances - see Chapter 1
Spark plugs - see Chapter 4
Fuel pump - see Chapter 3
Carburettor - see Chapter 3

b) Suspension

Front wheel bearings - see Chapter 12
Rear wheel bearings - see Chapter 8

c) Transmission and final drive

Gearbox oil - To check the level stand the car on level ground and undo the level plug which is halfway up the side of the casing on the left - just ahead of the axle shafts. This plug is a recessed hexagon which could be very difficult to undo.

Use a tubular spanner or bolt head which fits snugly. If the plug is burred by makeshift methods it will get progressively difficult to remove. Add oil from a suitable oil gun or squeeze pack with flexible filler spout. Add oil slowly until it runs out from the filler/ level hole. Clean the plug and replace it tightly.

When changing the transmission oil it is best to run it warm first. Then undo the magnetic drain plug in the bottom of the casing. Let the oil drain out for at least 15 minutes. Clean the magnetic drain plug and replace it. Before beginning to refill get the exact amount of oil needed ready, and then start to fill up through the filler/level plug. It is possible that oil will overflow before you have put it all in. Wait so that the air pockets have time to bubble out and then continue until all the oil is put in.

Clutch pedal free play - see Chapter 5.
Axle shaft gaiters - see Chapter 8.

See next page for 'VW Computer Diagnosis'

VW COMPUTER DIAGNOSIS

As part of the VW service at 6000 miles (or 6 months) intervals a diagnosis check is carried out covering all aspects of maintenance. This system is described in more detail in Chapter 11. The diagnosis check list of 88 items is given below and covers all models of Beetle which are built.

1 Steering/ignition lock, warning lights*
2 Brake pedal pushrod, clearance
3 Brake pedal, free travel
4 Clutch pedal, clearance
5 Play at steering wheel rim
6 Handbrake, free play
7 Windscreen washer operation
8 Windscreen wiper mechanism (mechanical)
9 Windscreen wiper blade rubber
10 Windscreen wiper blade assembly
11 Low beam
12 Fog lights*
13 High beam
14 Lights operating with ignition switched on
15 Reversing lights*
16 Instrument panel illumination
17 Fuel gauge*
18 Warning lamp, emergency warning system*
19 Control lamp, brake warning system*
20 Battery voltage, engine switched off
21 Condition of battery
22 Side, rear and number plate lights
23 Brake lights
24 Battery, electrolyte level
25 Indicator (left) - control light
26 Indicator (right) - control light
27 Heated rear window (operation)*
28 Tyre pressures, adjusted
29 Spare wheel tyre (pressure)
30 Spare tyre for damage
31 Level of brake fluid
32 Engine oil level
33 Front wheels, total toe   + degrees/minutes
34 Front wheels, total toe   - degrees/minutes
35 Front wheels left, camber   + degrees/minutes
36 Front wheel left, camber   - degrees/minutes
37 Front wheel right, camber   + degrees/minutes
38 Front wheel right, camber   - degrees/minutes
39 Upper torsion arm axial play*
40 Brake lines, inside vehicle
41 Engine oil temperature   (°C)

42 Starter motor current   (amps)
43 Compression pressures: cylinder 1   (units)
44 Compression pressures: cylinder 2   (units)
45 Compression pressures: cylinder 3   (units)
46 Compression pressures: cylinder 4   (units)
47 Horn operation   Voltage
48 Voltage control regulator, function at 2000 rpm
49 Distributor (dwell angle) degrees
50 Generator current (maximim output) amps
51 Kick down switch*
52 Kick down solenoid*
53 Coolant level, antifreeze content
54 Cooling and heating system
55 Engine, upper part
56 Pre-heating circuit and restrictor*
57 V-belt tension and condition
58 Ignition timing, adjust
59 Headlights
60 King pin and link pin, play*
61 Ball joint, axial play (upper left)*
62 Ball joint, axial play (lower left)*
63 Ball joint, axial play (upper right)*
64 Ball joint, axial play (lower right)*
65 Ball joint, dust covers and sealing plugs
66 Tie rod ends, play
67 Tie rods, mounting and dust covers
68 Steering rack bellows*
69 Steering gear
70 Brake lines and hoses (front)
71 Brake linings: thickness (front)
72 Suspension strut upper ball joints and dust covers*
73 Tyre (front left)
74 Tyre (front right)
75 Dust sleeve (CV joints)*
76 Final drive
77 Transmission
78 Engine lower part
79 Torque converter and lines (automatic, stick shift)*
80 Exhaust system
81 Brake lines and hoses (rear)
82 Brake regulator valve, linkage and dust seal*
83 Intake ducts, water drain flaps
84 Shift clutch (automatic, stick shift) play
85 Brake linings: thickness(rear)
86 Tyre (rear left)
87 Tyre (rear right)
88 Wheel bolts torque

*These test operations do not apply to all vehicles

Chapter 1 Engine

Contents

Ancillary components removal - engine - general 6	Engine - removal 4
Ancillary components - engine - refitment 37	Engine - dismantling - general 5
Camshaft and tappets - removal and renovation ... 16	Engine - reassembly - general 22
Camshaft and tappets - replacement 25	Engine - replacement and starting up 38
Connecting rods and bearings - removal and renovation ... 15	Fan housing - removal 6
Connecting rods - reassembly to crankshaft 24	Fan housing - replacement 35
Crankcase - examination and renovation 21	Fault diagnosis - engine 39
Crankcase, crankshaft, camshaft and tappets - reassembly ... 25	Flywheel - removal and renovation 17
Crankshaft and main bearings - removal and renovation ... 19	Flywheel - replacement 32
Crankshaft - assembly of gears and Nos. 3 and 4 main	General description 1
bearings 23	Oil cooler - removal and renovation 8
Crankshaft - oil seal - removal 18	Oil cooler - replacement 34
Crankshaft - oil seal - replacement 31	Oil pressure relief and control valves - removal and
Crankshaft - pulley wheel - removal and replacement ... 10	renovation 9
Cylinders, pistons and rings - removal and renovation ... 14	Oil pump - removal and renovation 11
Cylinders - replacement 27	Oil pump - replacement 33
Cylinder heads - removal 12	Pistons and rings - removal and renovation 14
Cylinder heads - overhaul of rocker gear, valves and springs 13	Pistons and rings - reassembly of rings and to connecting
Cylinder heads - reassembly of valves and springs ... 28	rod 26
Cylinder heads - replacement 29	Rocker gear - dismantling and renovation 13
Distributor driveshaft - removal 20	Rocker gear - reassembly (including pushrods and
Engine - removal - preparation 3	tubes) 30
	Valve/rocker - clearances and adjustment 37

Specifications

Engine specifications and data:

1285 cc (78.3 cu in.)	44 DIN bhp
1584 cc (96.7 cu in.)	50 DIN bhp

Engine general:

	1300 (Code AB, AR)	1600 (Code AD, AE, AS)
Type	4 cylinders flat horizontally opposed	Pushrod ohv
Weight	115 kg/253 lbs	
Bore	77 mm	85.5 mm
Stroke	69 mm	69 mm
Cubic capacity	1285 cc (78.3 cu in.)	1584 cc (96.7 cu in.)
Compression ratio (normal)	7.5 : 1	8 : 1
- low	6.6 : 1 (Code AC)	6.6 : 1 (Code AF)
Power output (Standard)	44 DIN bhp @ 4100 rpm	50 DIN bhp @ 4000 rpm
(Low compression)	40 DIN bhp @ 4000 rpm	46 DIN bhp @ 4000 rpm
Max torque (Standard) DIN	63 ft lbs/8.7 mkg @ 3000 rpm	77 ft lbs/10.7 mkg @ 2600 rpm
(Low compression) DIN	58 ft lbs/8.0 mkg @ 3000 rpm	72 ft lbs/10 mkg @ 2600 rpm
Fuel octane required - Standard	91 RON	91 RON
- Low compression	83 RON	83 RON
Compression pressure - Standard	92 psi/6.5 kg/cm^2 minimum	100 psi/7.0 kg/cm^2 minimum
- Low compression	71 psi/5 kg/cm^2 minimum	71 psi/5 kg/cm^2 minimum
Location of No. 1 cylinder	Right-hand pair - front	
Firing order	1 (r. front) 4 (l. rear) 3 (l front) 2 (r. rear)	
Engine mounting	Bolted direct to transmission casing	

Camshaft and camshaft bearings:

Camshaft drive	Lightweight alloy gear direct from crankshaft
Camshaft bearings	Steel backed white metal shells
Camshaft journal diameters	24.99 - 25.00 mm (0.9837 - 0.9842 in.)
Journal/bearing radial clearance	0.02 - 0.12 mm (0.008 - 0.0047 in.)
Endfloat	0.04 - 0.16 mm (0.0016 - 0.0063 in.)
Gear backlash	0.0 - 0.05 mm (0.- 0.002 in.)

Connecting rods and bearings:

Type	Forged steel
Big end bearings	3 layer thin wall shells
Crankpin (big end) diameter	54.98 - 55.00 mm (2.1644 - 2.1648 in.)
Small end bush	Lead/bronze coated steel - pressed in
Undersize big end shells available	0.25 mm, 0.50 mm, 0.75 mm
Crankpin to bearing clearance limits	0.02 - 0.15 mm (0.0008 - 0.006 in.)
Crankpin endfloat	0.1 - 0.7 mm (0.004 - 0.028 in.)
Gudgeon pin/bush radial clearance limit	0.01 - 0.04 mm (0.0004 - 0.0016 in.)
Gudgeon pin diameter	21.996 - 22 mm (0.8658 - 0.8661 in.)
Connecting rod weight - brown or white	580 - 588 grams
grey or black	592 - 600 grams
Maximum crankpin ovality	0.03 mm (0.0011 in.)

Crankshaft and main bearings:

Number of bearings	4
Main bearing journal diameters Nos. 1, 2 and 3	54.97 - 54.99 mm (2.164 - 2.1648 in.)
No. 4	39.98 - 40.00 mm (1.5739 - 1.5748 in.)
Regrind diameters undersize	0.25 mm, 0.50 mm, 0.75 mm
Bearing shells - type Nos. 1, 3 and 4	Aluminium, lead coated 1 piece
No. 2	Split - 3 layer steel backed
Journal/bearing radial clearance limit	
Nos. 1 and 3	0.04 - 0.18 mm (0.0016 - 0.007 in.)
No. 2	0.03 - 0.17 mm (0.0011 - 0.0066 in.)
No. 4	0.05 - 0.19 mm (0.0019 - 0.0074 in.)
Crankshaft endfloat	Taken by flange of No. 1 main bearing and adjusted by shims
Endfloat limits	0.07 - 0.13 mm (0.0027 - 0.0051 in.)
Main journal maximum ovality	0.03 mm (0.0011 in.)

Crankcase:

Main bearing bore diameters Nos. 1, 2 and 3	65.00 - 65.03 mm (2.559 - 2.5601 in.)
No. 4	50.00 - 50.04 mm (1.9685 - 1.9700 in.)
Oil seal bore diameter (flywheel end)	90.00 - 90.05 mm (3.5433 - 3.5452 in.)
Camshaft bearing bore diameter	27.5 - 27.52 mm (1.0825 - 1.0852 in.)
Oil pump housing bore diameter	70.00 - 70.03 mm (2.756 - 2.758 in.)
Tappet (cam follower) bore diameters	19.00 - 19.05 mm (0.748 - 0.750 in.)

Cylinders:

Type	Single barrels - finned - cast iron
Distance between pair centres	112 mm (4.41 in.)

Cylinder heads:

Type	Aluminium - 1 per pair of cylinders
Port arrangement	Each head has two inlet ports and two exhaust ports. The inlet ports are side by side being fed from a twin branch induction manifold to each head.

Gudgeon pins:

Type	Fully floating, steel tube retained by circlips
Diameter	21.996 - 22.00 mm (0.8658 - 0.8661 in.)

Lubrication system:

Type	Wet sump - pressure and splash
Oil filter	Wire gauze suction strainer in sump
Sump capacity	2½ litres (4.4 Imp pints)
Oil pump type	Twin gear
Oil pressure (SAE 30, 70° C at 2500 rpm)	42 psi (min. 28 psi)
Oil pressure warning light	Comes on between 2 - 6 psi
Oil cooler	Pressure fed multitube type in cooling fan housing
Oil dipstick	Upper mark indicates full capacity. Lower mark indicates half full

Oil pump:

Gear/body end clearance (no gasket)	0.1 mm (0.004 in.) max
Gear backlash	0 - 0.2 mm (0.008 in.)

Oil pressure relief valve:

Spring length loaded at 7.75 kg (17 lbs)	23.6 mm (0.928 in.)
Oil pressure regulating valve	Maintains oil pressure at bearings at 28 psi

Pistons:

Type	Light alloy with steel inserts
Clearance in cylinder limits	0.04 - 0.02 mm (0.0015 - 0.008 in.)
Number of rings	3 — Two compression, one oil control
Ring/groove side clearance - Top compression	0.07 - 0.12 mm (0.0027 - 0.0047 in.)
- Lower compression	0.05 - 0.10 mm (0.0019 - 0.0039 in.)
- Oil control	0.03 - 0.10 mm (0.0012 - 0.0039 in.)
Piston oversizes available	0.5 mm and 1.0 mm (0.020 and 0.040 in.)
Piston pin bore offset	1.5 mm (0.060 in.)

Piston rings:

Top compression:	
Thickness	2.5 mm (0.10 in.)
Gap limit	0.3 - 0.9 mm (0.012 - 0.035 in.)
Bearing face	Bevelled, angle facing top of piston
Lower compression:	
Thickness	2.5 mm (0.10 in.)
Gap limit	0.3 - 0.9 mm (0.012 - 0.035 in.)
Bearing face	Parallel, lower edge cut back
Oil control:	
Gap	0.25 - 0.95 mm (0.010 - 0.037 in.)

Tappets - (cam followers):

Type	Cylindrical flat based
Diameter	18.96 - 18.89 mm (0.7463 - 0.7471 in.)

Pushrods and rocker arms

Pushrod type	Tube with hemispherical ends
Pushrod length	272.5 mm
Rocker arm bore size limits	18.00 - 18.04 mm (0.7086 - 0.7093 in.)
Rocker shaft diameter size limits	17.97 - 17.95 mm (0.7073 - 0.7066 in.)

Valves:

Inset - head diameter	35.6 mm
- stem diameter	7.94 - 7.95 mm
- seat width	1.3 - 1.6 mm
- seat angle	44°
- guide bore diameter	8.00 - 8.06 mm
- maximum rock in guide	0.8 mm
Exhaust - head diameter	32.1 mm
- stem diameter	7.92 - 7.94 mm
- seat width	1.7 - 2.0 mm
- seat angle	45°
- guide bore diameter	8.00 - 8.06 mm
- maximum rock in guide	0.8 mm
Seat width correction angle - inner	75°
- outer	15°
Rocker arm/valve clearance	0.15 mm (0.006 in.) all cold

Note: Rocker arm to valve clearances are set at 1 mm (0.040 in.) for the purpose of valve timing only

Valve springs:

Type	Single coil spring
Loaded length	31 mm at 53 - 61 kg (116 - 134 lbs)

Torque wrench settings:

		lb ft	kg m
Crankshaft pulley nut		33	4.5
Oil pump nuts		14	2.0
Oil drain plug		33	4.5
Oil strainer cover nuts		5	0.7
Cylinder head nuts		23	3.2 (See text)
Flywheel screw		253	35
Crankcase nuts and screws:	M8	14	2.0
	M10	25	3.5
Connecting rod cap nuts		24	3.3
Engine securing nuts		22	3.0
Rocker shaft nuts		18	2.5

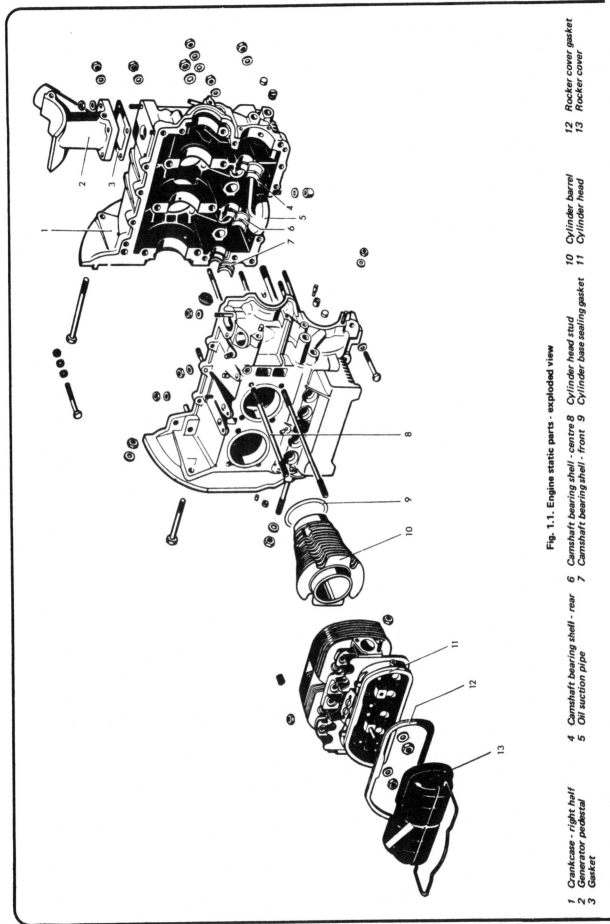

Fig. 1.1. Engine static parts - exploded view

1 Crankcase - right half
2 Generator pedestal
3 Gasket
4 Camshaft bearing shell - rear
5 Oil suction pipe
6 Camshaft bearing shell - centre
7 Camshaft bearing shell - front
8 Cylinder head stud
9 Cylinder base sealing gasket
10 Cylinder barrel
11 Cylinder head
12 Rocker cover gasket
13 Rocker cover

1 General description and engine numbers

The Beetle models covered by this manual are fitted with a 1285cc (78.3 cu in) or 1584cc (96.7 cu in) engine (only the latter is presently available in the USA). They are both direct descendants of the original flat four air cooled design, incorporating modifications to improve cooling and bearing lubrication pressures.

As a guide to identification the engines have prefix letters in front of the 7 figure serial numbers, viz:

1285 cc	AB, AR
1584 cc 7.5 : 1 cr	AD, AS
1584 cc exhaust emission control	AE, AS
1584 cc 6.6 : 1 cr	AF
1584 cc USA and Canada	B

The engine is an air-cooled horizontally opposed flat four cylinder design. The short crankshaft runs in aluminium alloy shell bearings located between the two halves of a magnesium alloy crankcase which join vertically. The camshaft runs centrally below the crankshaft and is gear driven from the rear end of the crankshaft. The camshaft is also located between the crankcase halves and runs in removable split shell bearings.

The distributor is driven by a removable shaft from a gear mounted on the rear end of the crankshaft. The same shaft incorporates a cam which operates the fuel pump operating plunger rod.

The gear type oil pump is mounted in the rear of the crankcase, held between the two halves and driven by a horizontal shaft. A tongue on the inner end of the shaft engages in a slot in the end of the camshaft.

The four, finned cylinder barrels are separately mounted and each pair has a common cylinder head containing the valves and rocker gear. The pushrods locate in cylindrical flat faced cam followers at the camshaft end and pass through sealed cylindrical tubes clamped between the head and crankcase outside the cylinder barrels. Each rocker cover is held to the head by spring hoops locating in a recess in the cover.

The flywheel is located on the front of the crankshaft by four dowel pegs and secured by a single central bolt which also incorporates needle roller bearings for the gearbox input shaft. The front crankcase oil seal bears on the centre hub land of the flywheel. The rear end of the crankshaft has an oil thrower plate and a helical groove machined in the pulley wheel hub to contain the oil. An oil filter screen is mounted in the bottom centre of the crankcase and the oil suction pipe for the pump comes from the centre of it. There is no other form of oil filter incorporated. The generator, which is mounted on a pedestal above the engine, is driven by a 'V'- belt from the crankshaft pulley. On the forward end of the generator shaft the cooling fan is mounted. This runs in a sheet steel housing which ducts air down to the cylinder barrels.

On the latest type engine the dynamo has been replaced by an alternator. This has been designed to fit on to the pedestal and drive the fan. The petrol pump has been modified to make room for the alternator (see Chapter 3).

There is no separate oil sump - the crankcase acting as an oil reservoir with a capacity of just under 4½ imp pints. Engine cooling is regulated by a bellows type thermostat which is mounted in the air flow under the right-hand pair of cylinders. The thermostat operates two linked control flaps in the fan housing lower duction section at left and right.

The car heating system is integral with the engine cooling and is achieved by directing air through ducts which shroud the exhaust pipes. Two flexible ducts lead from the fan housing to the heat exchangers - and then, via two more ducts, to the car interior.

The cooling system also incorporates an oil cooler which is a multitube heat exchanger mounted vertically on the crankcase. Air from the cooling fan is ducted past it.

2 Repair and maintenance procedures - dismantling

The VW beetle engine has always been easier to work on when removed from the car. It has been possible in the past to do a certain amount of work, however, with the engine in place. With the various design developments there are now fewer opportunities, in the Beetle for this. Apart from routine maintenance tasks the parts or sub-assemblies which can be repaired and/or removed with the engine in place are:

Fan housing)	
Oil pressure relief valve)	
Oil cooler)	
Oil pressure control valve)	
Crankshaft pulley wheel)	Details in Chapter 2
Oil pump)	
Thermostat)	
Exhaust manifold)	
Heat exchangers)	
Fan (with generator))	
Carburettor)	
Fuel pump)	Details in Chapter 3
Inlet manifold)	
Distributor)	
Distributor drive shaft)	Details in Chapter 4
Coil)	
Generator (with fan))	
Starter)	Details in Chapter 11

For any other work on the engine to be carried out it must be removed from the car.

3 Engine removal - preparation

Removal of the Beetle engine is quite straightforward and speedy; provided that the correct tools and lifting tackle are assembled beforehand. The engine is held to the transmission unit by two studs and two bolts - nothing more. It has to be drawn back from these and lowered out of the car. If you have a pit or raised ramp a firm stand or platform will be needed to support the engine as soon as it is detached. It weighs 240 lbs (109 kg) and attempts to draw it off without providing support under the ramp or in the pit will result in disaster.

Without a pit or ramp a method must be devised to support the engine as soon as it is detached so that the supports may then be removed and the engine readily lowered to ground level. The car body is then lifted up at the rear and the engine drawn out from under - or the car rolled forward over the engine. Four strong men can lift the car the required three feet to clear the engine. Alternatively a conventional hoist can be used to lift the car with the sling fastened between the rear bumper support brackets. If no hoist is available then at least two conventional scissor jacks or hydraulic jacks will be needed together with suitable wooden or concrete blocks, to raise and support the car at each side near the jacking points.

A 17 mm ring spanner - of the non-cranked sort you get on a combination - is essential for undoing the mounting nuts and bolts as there is no space to get a socket on.

If the car is very dirty underneath it would be well worthwhile getting it thoroughly cleaned off, away form the removal area, first. The lower mounting stud nuts are exposed to the elements and the tip bolts and nuts call for a certain amount of reaching around. If you are working on your back at floor level, dirt falling in the eyes can be a major irritation.

It is possible to get the engine out and clear single-handed if all the foregoing equipment is available but the trickiest part is lowering the engine to floor level. Assistance is insurance against dropping it. Even a few inches fall could crack the aluminium

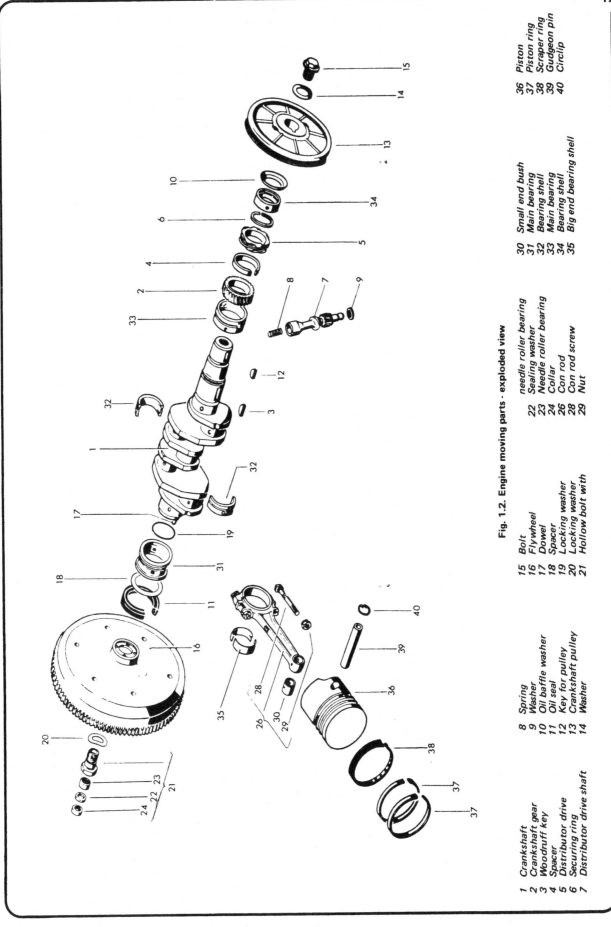

17

Fig. 1.2. Engine moving parts - exploded view

1 Crankshaft
2 Crankshaft gear
3 Woodruff key
4 Spacer
5 Distributor drive
6 Securing ring
7 Distributor drive shaft

8 Spring
9 Washer
10 Oil baffle washer
11 Oil seal
12 Key for pulley
13 Crankshaft pulley
14 Washer

15 Bolt
16 Flywheel
17 Dowel
18 Spacer
19 Locking washer
20 Locking washer
21 Hollow bolt with

22 Sealing washer
23 Needle roller bearing
24 Collar
26 Con rod
28 Con rod screw
29 Nut

needle roller bearing

30 Small end bush
31 Main bearing
32 Bearing shell
33 Main bearing
34 Bearing shell
35 Big end bearing shell

36 Piston
37 Piston ring
38 Scraper ring
39 Gudgeon pin
40 Circlip

crankcase (there being no conventional sump). Note that the engine is back-to-front as compared with a conventional layout so that the flywheel is at the front. All references to front and rear of the engine will, therefore, be in relation to its position in the car.

4 Engine - removal

1 Stand the car on a level hard surface with sufficient room to roll it forward about six feet if you wish to lift the car over the engine rather than drag the engine back from under the car. Disconnect the battery (photo). Now is the time to drain the engine oil into a container - whilst you are disconnecting the ancillaries described next.

2 Open the engine compartment and have a good look round. It may be some time before it looks like this again. Mark any leads or hose connections that may seem difficult to remember. Coloured adhesive tape is a useful marker. Remove the air cleaner and the air cleaner hoses (Chapter 3).

3 Remove the heat insulating plates from round the intake manifold pre-heater pipe at each side (photos). Undo the screws securing the small cover plate over the crankshaft pulley (photo). Then remove the remaining screws and the large rear cover plate (photo).

4 Some vehicles are fitted with a generator, later ones with an alternator. Whichever is fitted, disconnect the leads - noting their terminals and colours. Take care over this and it will save you trouble and worry on reassembly.

5 Undo the connectors to the auto-choke and solenoid cut-off valve (one each side of the carburettor), from the oil pressure sender switch and coil (photos). The loom containing all these wires may then be taken from the clips and tucked to one side of the engine compartment.

6 Remove the distributor cap and then slacken the clamping screw which holds the distributor in position. Lift the distributor out (photo).

7 The accelerator cable connected to the carburettor is the next item to be detached. This is somewhat unusual arrangement as the cable has to pass through the fan housing en route to the carburettor. First undo the locking screw which clamps the end of the cable to the link pin on the operating lever (photo). Pull the cable out and do not lose the link. The cable itself need not be pulled through from the back of the fan housing until the engine has been disengaged from the transmission.

8 Now jack up the car, using the vehicle jack to enable you to get underneath the rear end comfortably, but keep the tyres touching the ground. Replace the oil drain plug. From underneath, first disconnect the control wires that run to the heater flaps, one on each side. They are held to the flap control arms by cable clamps as used on the carburettor but are quite likely to be dirty and rusted up so be prepared with penetrating oil and suitable self-grip wrenches as necessary. If you have difficulty in identifying them get someone to operate the heater control while you are underneath. You will see them move. The fuel pipe runs along on the left side of the engine and if you feel around you will be able to locate the point where the flexible hose connection occurs (photo). This should be pulled off at the end of the hose nearest the engine so that the end of the flexible pipe can be clamped, or plugged with a pencil stub, to prevent the fuel leaking out. If the fuel level in the tank is fairly low it may not be necessary to do this. Next unclip and pull off the flexible hoses which fit onto the heat exchangers on each side of the engine.

9 The two lower mounting nuts can now be removed and this is where the 17 mm ring spanner mentioned earlier is needed. The nuts are positioned about four inches from each side of the engine centre line and about two inches up from the bottom of the flange where the engine joins the transmission unit. Remove the two nuts and washers (if any), (photo).

10 Then remove the left-hand top mounting bolt, also from underneath. This is best done with a socket and extension with a universal joint (photo).

11 Lower the vehicle to the ground once more.

12 The fourth mounting bolt is in front of the fan housing to the right. The nut can be felt so put an arm around and undo it (photo). Strictly speaking, it is safer to support the engine underneath now before the last mounting bolt is removed, although the likelihood of the engine moving 3 to 4 inches (7.5 to 10 cm) rearward and falling down of its own accord is fairly remote. The bolt head has a flat on it which should lock into the transmission. This enables the nut to be taken off without any difficulty provided the bolt is not pushed out.

13 Support the engine, preferably on a trolley jack with the jack head under the central circular plate in the crankcase. If another method is used bear in mind that the engine has to be drawn back about 3 inches (7.5 cm) to disengage if from the transmission. When this is done draw the accelerator cable out of the tube in the fan housing and tape it up on the bulkhead.

14 As stated earlier the engine is a tight fit in the compartment. When drawn back it should not be tilted otherwise the anti-rattle springs on the clutch release levers may get damaged by the gearbox input shaft when it is lowered. Grip the fan housing and silencer to pull the engine back. It may need a bit of jiggling to get it clear. Lower carefully until it rests on the ground. All that remains is to raise the rear of the car sufficiently to enable it to be rolled forward over the engine or achieved by four strong men or by hoisting the rear of the car with a sling stretched between the two rear bumper support brackets. Alternatively, the car can be raised on two jacks, one on each side, and supported progressively on blocks near the body jacking points. Great care must be taken to chock the front wheels securely when using this latter method and the blocks used must be perfectly square and large enough to provide a stable 'pillar' when stacked up. Each support under the body at each side will have to be at lease 2 ft 6 ins (76 cm) high so collect sufficient blocks beforehand. Do not use odd bits and pieces. The base blocks should be at least 9 inch x 12 inch (22.5 x 30 cm) square. When the car is raised sufficiently the engine can be pulled out from the rear. It is a little more work to lower the car to the ground at this stage but if you are going to leave it then the extra effort is worthwhile. It is better to be sure than sorry, particularly if there are children about.

5 Engine dismantling - general

1 Unlike the majority of conventional engines the Volkswagen is one which does not make it easy to carry out most tasks with the engine still in the car. In view of the relative ease with which it can be taken out and lifted on to a bench this manual does not, in general, recommend that engine repair work of any significance is carried out with the engine still in the car. If you have a pit or ramp that enables you to work conveniently under the car there are instances when is is justifiable. Otherwise the inconvenient 'flat on you back' method is far too risky in view of the likelihood of dirt getting into the wrong places and mistakes occurring.

2 For an engine which is obviously in need of a complete overhaul the cost of this against that of a replacement engine must also be carefully considered. The dismantling and reassembly of the Volkswagen engine is more complex that for a conventional four cylinder block. Each cylinder is separate and the crankshaft and camshaft run in bearings mounted between the two halves of a precision faced, split crankcase. The number of individual parts is far greater. It is not our intention to put you off - far from it - but we must, in fairness to the owner, point out that it is much easier to make an assembly mistake than on a conventional engine.

3 The dismantling, inspection, repair and reassembly as described in this Chapter follows the procedure as for a complete overhaul.

4 Before starting work on any part it is strongly recommended that time is spent in first reading the whole Chapter. It would be too cumbersome and confusing to cross reference the implications of each and every activity. So if you think that the

4.1 Disconnect the battery

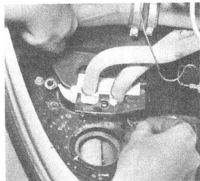

4.3a Remove the plates from the pre-heater pipes ...

4.3b ... and the gasket

4.3c Remove the small plate over the crankshaft pulley ... (this is not fitted to later models)

4.3d ... then take out the screws and the large plate

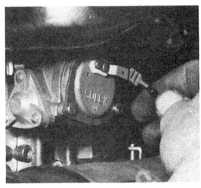

4.5a Disconnect the automatic choke lead ...

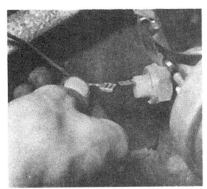

4.5b ... the oil pressure switch lead ...

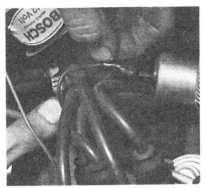

4.5c ... and the solenoid valve and coil leads

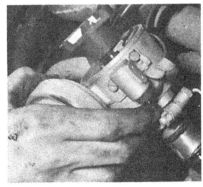

4.6 Remove the distributor

4.7 Disconnect the throttle cable

4.8 Disconnect the fuel pipe and block it

4.9 Remove the lower engine mounting nuts

4.10 Remove the left upper engine mounting bolt

4.12 Remove the right upper engine mounting bolt

9.1 Undo stubborn oil pressure plugs with an improvised screwdriver

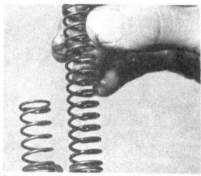

9.4 The relief valve spring is longer than the regularor valve spring

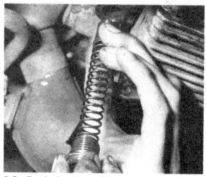

9.6a Replacing the relief valve piston, spring, & plug

9.6b Replacing the regulator valve piston, spring and plug

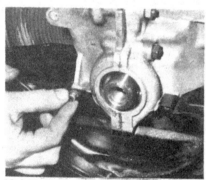

10.4 Fitting the lower cover before the crankshaft pulley

10.5a Replace the pulley nut

10.5b Tightening the pulley nut

big-end bearings are your problem, for example, do not think that by turning to the heading 'Big-end bearings' all the implications of repairing them will be contained in that single

section. Mention will be made in brief of the operations necessary which may lead up to it and the   details of these should be read first.

5 Whatever degree of dismantling is carried out, components can only be examined properly after they have been thoroughly cleaned. This is best carried out using paraffin and a stiff bristled brush. Some engines can be particularly bad, with a stubborn

coating of hard sludgy deposits - generally denoting neglect of regular oil changing - and it can take some time and effort to get this off. Afterwards, the paraffin can be hosed off with a water jet. Cleaning may sometimes seem to take a disproportionate amount of time but there is no doubt that it is time well spent.

6 Engine ancillary components removal - general

Having removed the engine from the car it may be assumed that all the tinware will have to come off before any major overhauls are carried out. Once the fan housing assembly is removed together with the manifolds and heat exchangers, the dismantling of the other components is dealt with in this chapter.

7 Fan housing - removal

Although the removal of the fan housing forms an integral part of the total dismantling procedures of the engine, it is possible to remove it with the engine still in position in the car. As it is part of the cooling system it is therefore dealt with in detail in Chapter 2.

8 Oil cooler - removal and renovation

1   It is possible to remove the oil cooler with the engine installed provided the fan housing is first completely removed as described in Chapter 2.
2   Undo the three nuts holding the oil cooler mounting adaptor to the crankcase.
3   Undo the nuts holding the cooler to the adaptor.
4   It will be fairly obvious if the cooler leaks severely but if there is no apparent damage it may be difficult to decide whether it functions correctly. If suspect it should be subjected to a pressure test by a Volkswagen agent equipped with the proper equipment. If there is any doubt about it the only sure remedy is a new one. If the cooler is found to be leaking the oil pressure relief valve should also be checked as it could have caused the failure of the cooler.
5   It is rare for the fins of the cooler to get clogged up but if they have, soak them in a solvent such as 'Gunk' and then flush and blow them through with a high pressure air line. Do not try and poke dirt out with sharp pointed instruments.

9 Oil pressure relief and control valves - removal and renovation

1   These may be removed from underneath with the engine in the car. They are spring loaded pistons held into the left-hand half of the crankcase at front and rear by large screw plugs (photo).
2   It is not necessary to drain the engine oil but be prepared to catch a small quantity when either of the valves is removed.
3   When the plugs are removed the springs and plungers should drop out. If a plunger sticks in the bore in the crankcase it may need a little assistance and poking with a screwdriver.
4   If a piston seems seized and will not move it may be necessary to start the engine. Oil pressure should blow it out. Such drastic action being necessary would indicate serious neglect in the matter of regular oil changes. Note that the plungers and springs are not interchangeable; so do not mix them up (photo).
5   Both pistons should be a sliding fit in the crankcase bores. Minor signs of seizure may be cleaned up. If there is severe scoring in the piston it may be renewed but if the crankcase bore is damaged the consequences could be serious and expensive, calling for a new one also.
6   The larger of the two springs is for the oil pressure relief valve and goes into the rear bore near the oil pump (photo). The shorter spring is for the pressure regulating valve and goes into the front bore near the transmission mounting (photo).
7   When refitting ensure that the springs locate in their recesses in both piston and plug and that a new plug seal is used. The relief valve serves to relieve excessive oil pressure from the oil cooler when the oil is cold and thick. The regulating valve serves to maintain oil pressure at the crankshaft bearings when the oil is hot and thin.

10 Crankshaft pulley wheel - removal and replacement

1   Take off the cover plate held by three screws.
2   The pulley wheel is a straight keyed fit on the end of the crankshaft. It is secured by a single, central bolt. To lock the pulley when undoing or tightening the bolt push a suitable article through one of the holes in the pulley and jam it against the crankcase flange.
3   If, when the nut has been removed, the pulley is a very tight fit, do not apply force at the edges or you are likely to distort it. Soak the boss with penetrating oil and hook something through the two holes if any leverage is necessary.
4   If the pulley has been removed during the course of an overhaul remember that the lower rear engine plate has to be re-fixed before the pulley (photo). There is no access to the two securing screws after the pulley is in position.

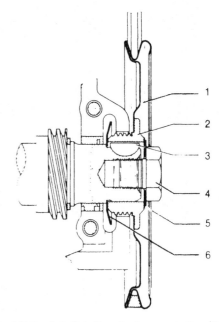

Fig. 1.3. Crankshaft pulley wheel - cross section (Sec. 10)

1   Pulley
2   Oil return scroll
3   Woodruff key
4   Securing bolt
5   Lockwasher
6   Oil thrower disc

5   The nut should be tightened to a torque of 33 ft/lb (4.5 kg m) when the pulley has been replaced (photos)

11 Oil pump - removal and renovation

1   Remove the crankshaft pulley wheel and the lower rear cover plate.
2   The oil pump gears may be removed relatively easily because once the oil pump cover plate has been released by removing the four retaining nuts, the gears may be drawn out of the pump body.
3   The pump body itself is mounted over the same four studs as the cover plate and is clamped between the two halves of the crankcase. To remove the pump body from the engine without splitting the crankcase is best done with a special tool which fits over the studs, locks to the inside of the body and draws it out. If you do not have such a tool then the best way is first to slacken the crankcase clamping stud nuts above and below the pump. This relieves the pressure on the body. A suitable tool can then be tapped against the edge of the pump body and, in easy stages it can be eased out over the studs. Do not force a tool into the gap between the pump body and the crankcase as this could damage the mating faces and upset the correct alignment of the pump on replacement.
4   If the crankcase is to be split anyway leave the pump body to be taken out then.
5   It is possible to check the pump fairly comprehensively without removing the body from the crankcase but it is, of course, far less convenient and liable to cause measurement inaccuracies.
6   First check the cover plate. If it is very badly scored it should be renewed anyway. Light scoring can be ground out using carborundum paste on a piece of plate glass.
7   Check that the driving spindle is a good fit in the body. Any apparent rocking indicates that the inside of the pump body must also be worn. The driven gear spindle should be tight in the body. The gear should be a good fit on it with no play.
8   Provided both gear spindles are in good shape refit the gears and measure the end clearance between them and the end of the

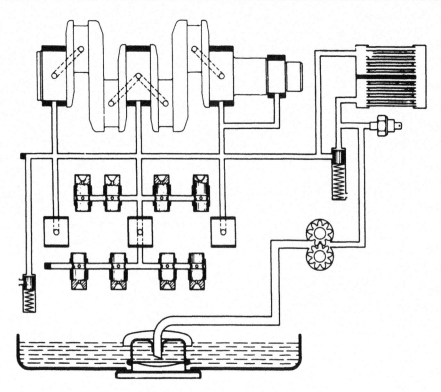

Fig. 1.4. Lubrication system - diagrammatic

pump body. This is done by putting a straight edge across the body and using a feeler gauge to measure the gap between the straight edge and the gears. Make sure no traces of gasket remain on the flange of the body when doing this. The gap should not exceed 0.1 mm (0.004 inch) or inadequate oil pressure will result. The wear is most likely to be in the pump body in this case and this will need renewal.

12 Cylinder heads - removal

1   Take the engine out of the car.
2   Remove the exhaust system, heat exchangers and upper cylinder cover plates as described in the Fuel and Cooling Chapters. The inlet manifold together with carburettor should also be taken off. See the Fuel System Chapter for details.
3   Prise off the spring clip, downwards, which clamps the rocker cover to the head. Take off the cover.
4   Undo the two nuts, evenly, which secure the rocker shaft standards and then pull off the standards, shaft and rockers as a complete assembly. Pull out the four pushrods and push them through a piece of cardboard so that the location of each one is known and which is the top and bottom end.
5   Before starting to undo the eight nuts which hold the cylinder head down onto the cylinder barrels it must be appreciated that when the head is released the four pushrod tubes will be freed and the cylinder barrels also. If the cylinder barrels are not being taken off the pistons they will rest in position but the engine must not be turned. If the engine is to be turned the barrels should be temporarily tied down to the crankcase with string or wire.
6   Using a socket spanner, the cylinder head stud nuts should be slackened 1/4 to 1/2 turn each only, in the reverse order of the final tightening sequence as given in Fig 1.12. Continue releasing each nut a little at a time until they are all slack. When all are removed the head may be drawn back a little way.
7   Remove the pushrod tubes from between the head and crankcase and make sure the cylinders are disengaged from the head before pulling the head right off.

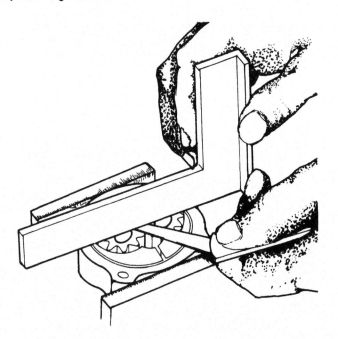

Fig. 1.5. Measuring oil pump gear end clearance (Sec. 11)

13 Cylinder heads - overhaul of rocker gear, valves and springs

1   To remove the rocker arms from the shaft the spring clips at each end should be removed and the thrust washers and wave washers taken off. The end rocker: may then be removed. The rocker shaft support standards may need tapping off if they are tight in order to remove the two inner rocker arms, clips and washers. If possible lay out the parts in the order in which they were dismantled in a place where they need not be disturbed.

2 To remove the valves it is necessary to use a proper tool to compress the valve springs. The tops of the springs are almost level with the edge of the head casting. If you are unable to obtain a G clamp with extended ends (to clear the edge of the head when the spring is compressed) it will be necessary to use a short piece of tube, with an aperture cut in the side, in conjunction with a conventional spring compressor. The aperture is to enable one to get at the split collars on the valve stem.

3 Compress the spring using the clamp and if the tubular spacer is being used make sure that the pressure is applied squarely and that the tube cannot slip. As soon as the two split conical collars round the valve stem are revealed, use a small screwdriver through the aperture to hook them off the valve stem. It is advisable to maintain one's hold on the spring clamp while doing this to prevent anything from slipping. When the collars are clear release the spring clamp.

4 The spring retainer collar and spring may then be lifted off. There will be small sealing rings round the valve stems and these too should be taken off. The valve can now be pushed through the guide and taken out. If it tends to stick then it will be because of carbon or sludge deposits on the end of the valve stems and these should be cleaned off as necessary. The end of the valve stem could also be burred due to the 'hammering' action of the rocker arm; in which case the burrs should be carefully stoned off. Do not force a tight valve through the guide or you will score the guide. Keep valves in order so that they may be replaced in the same port. Push them through a piece of cardboard to avoid getting them mixed up.

5 After the cylinder head has been removed and the valves taken out, the head itself should be thoroughly cleaned of carbon in the combustion chambers and examined for cracks. If there are any visible cracks the head should be scrapped. Cracks

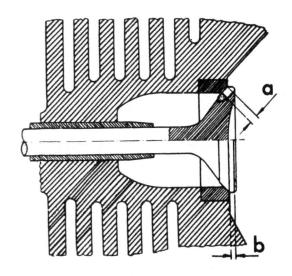

Fig. 1.6. Valves - cross section of seat (Sec. 13)

a = seat width 1.7 - 2 mm exhaust and 1.25 - 1.65 mm inlet

b = 1 mm minimum, all valves

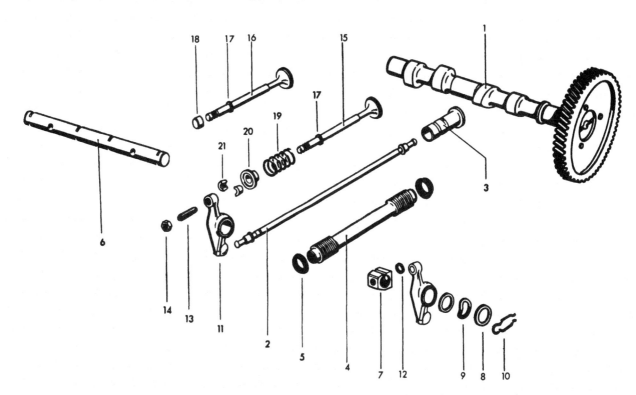

Fig. 1.7. Camshaft and valves - exploded view (Sec. 13)

1 Camshaft and gear assembly	6 Rocker shaft	12 Sealing ring	17 Oil wiper
2 Pushrod	7 Shaft support bracket	13 Tappet adjusting screw	18 Valve cap
3 Tappet	8 Thrust washer	14 Locknut	19 Valve spring
4 Pushrod tube	9 Corrugated washer	15 Inlet valve	20 Valve spring seat
5 Pushrod tube seal	10 Securing clip	16 Exhaust valve	21 Valve cotter halves
	11 Rocker arm		

are most likely to occur round the valve seats or spark plug holes. Bearing in mind that one head will cost (new) nearly 20% of the cost of a complete replacement engine economies should be considered as well as the likelihood of obtaining a used head from a breaker's yard. If the latter, make sure that the head you get is the same type as the old one - and in better condition!

6   The valve seats should be examined for signs of burning away or pitting and ridging. If there is slight pitting the refacing of the seats by grinding in the valve with carborundum paste will probably cure the problem. If the seat needs re-cutting, due to severe pitting, then the seat width should not exceed specification. Fitting new valve seat inserts is a specialist task as they are chilled and shrunk in order to fit them. Check with the nearest Volkswagen dealer because you could have difficulty in getting this problem solved cheaply.

7   The rocker gear should be dismantled and thoroughly cleaned of the sludge deposits which normally tend to accumulate on it. The rocker arms should be a smooth fit on the shaft with no play. If there is any play it is up to the owner to decide whether it is worth the cost of renewal. The effect on engine performance and noise may not be serious although wear tends to accelerate once it is started. The domed ends that bear on the valve stems tend to get hammered out of shape. If bad, replacement is relatively cheap and easy.

8   The valves themselves must be thoroughly cleaned of carbon. The head should be completely free of cracks or pitting and must be perfectly circular. The edge which seats into the cylinder head should also be unpitted and unridged although very minor blemishes may be ground out when re-seating the valve face.

9   Replace the valve into its guide in the head and note if there is any sideways movement which denotes wear between the stem and guide. Here again the degree of wear can vary; if excessive the performance of the engine can be noticeably affected and oil consumption increased. The maximum tolerable sideways rock, measured at the valve head with the end of the valve stem flush with the end of the guide, is 0.8 mm (0.031 inch). Wear is normally in the guide rather than on the valve stem but check a new valve in the guide if possible first. Valve guide renewal is a tricky operation in these cylinder heads and you may find it difficult to get it done. Check with the nearest Volkswagen dealer first. Do not attempt it yourself. One final part of the examination involves the end of the valve stem where the rocker arm bears. It should be flat but often gets 'hammered' into a concave shape or ridged. Special caps are available to put over the ends. Alternatively the ends can be ground off flat with a fine oil stone. Remember that it is difficult to set the valve clearances accurately with the adjusting screw and valve stem in a battered condition.

14 Cylinders, pistons and rings - removal and renovation

1   The cylinders may be removed, after the cylinder heads are off, simply by drawing them from over the pistons. Make sure that the piston and rings are not damaged after the cylinder has been removed. It must also be remembered that if the crankshaft is turned after removing the cylinder the piston skirts can foul the crankcase unless they are guided at the bottom of the stroke.

2   The piston rings may be removed from the pistons by carefully spreading the ends of each ring so that it comes out of its groove and then drawing it off over the top of the piston .

3   To remove the piston it is necessary to separate it from the connecting rod as it is not possible to get at the connecting rod bolts with the piston fitted.

4   Remove the circlip from one side of the piston boss where the gudgeon pin is retained and it will be possible to push out the gudgeon pin.If it resists then warm up the piston with an electric light bulb held next to it for a while. Do not try and drive out the gudgeon pin from a cold piston. You will possibly bend a connecting rod. It is only necessary to push out the pin far enough to enable the connecting rod to be released from the piston. If the pistons are to be put back make sure that each one

is marked suitably so that you know (a) which number cylinder it came from and (b) which way faces forward. A good way is to scratch the number and an arrow, pointing forward, on the crown before removal. If you do make a nonsense and forget how it came off then carefully clean the top of the crown and look for identifying marks which indicate the front or flywheel side. Volkswagen pistons are stamped with an arrow at the edge of the crown pointing towards the flywheel. British made pistons have the word 'flywheel' stamped on in that position.

5   Piston and cylinder bore wear are contributory factors to excessive oil consumption (over 1 imperial pint to 300 miles) and general engine noise. They also affect engine power output due to loss of compression. If you have been able to check the individual cylinder pressures before dismantling so much the better. They will indicate whether one or more is losing compression which may be due to cylinders and pistons if the valves are satisfactory.

6   The piston rings should be removed from the pistons first by carefully spreading the open ends and easing them from their grooves over the crown of the piston. Each one should then be pushed into the cylinder bore from the bottom using the head of from the bottom edge. The gap between the ends of the ring can then be measured with a feeler gauge. For the two compression rings it should not exceed 0.90 mm (0.035 inch) and for the oil scraper ring 0.95 mm(0.037 inch). If the gaps are greater you know that new rings at least are required.

7   Determining the degree of wear on pistons and cylinders is complementary. In some circumstances the pistons alone may need renewal - the cylinders not needing reboring. If the cylinders need reboring then new pistons must be fitted. First check the inside walls about 1/2 inch (10 mm) down from the top edge. If a ridge can be felt at any point then the bores should be measured with an inside micrometer or calipers to see how far they vary from standard. The measurement should be taken across the bore of the cylinder about 15 mm (0.6 inch) down from the top edge at right angles to the axis of the gudgeon pin. Then measure the piston, also at right angles to the gudgeon pin across the skirt at the bottom. The two measurements should not differ by more than 0.20 mm (0.008 inch).

8   Further measurement of the cylinder across the bore will indicate whether or not the wear is mostly on the piston. If the cylinder bore is uniform in size fitting new pistons alone is possible. However, it is a very short sighted policy. If new pistons are needed the cylinders must be worn considerbly and it is better to do the job properly while the engine is dismantled. Although rebored cylinders are not cheap the extra cost will be small compared with the overhaul total cost and you will not have to do the job again.

9   Another feature of the pistons to check is the piston ring side clearance in the grooves. This should not exceed 0.12 mm (0.0047 inch) for the top ring and 0.10 mm (0.004 inch) for the other two. Usually however, this wear is proportionate to the rest of the piston wear and will not occur in a piston which is otherwise apparently little worn. If you think that only a new set of rings is required it would be a good idea to take your pistons to the supplier of the new rings and check the new rings in the gaps. You may change your mind about how worn the pistons really are! Once a cylinder has been rebored twice it must not be rebored again. New cylinders must be obtained.

15 Connecting rods and bearings - removal and renovation

1   Connecting rods may be removed only after the pistons have been taken off. It is not necessary to split the crankcase although if you are going to do so anyway it will be simpler to take the connecting rods off the crankshaft afterwards. Start with No1 and, using a socket with an extension, slacken the two connecting rod cap nuts by inserting the extension into the crankcase. It is important to have the crankshaft positioned so that the socket spanner fits squarely and completely onto the head of each nut.

2   Once both are loose, carefully undo each one and keep them captive in the socket when undoing them so as not to drop them in the crankcase. The cap will be left behind and may be awkward to retrieve. Tip the engine to shake it out if necessary. Retrieve both halves of the bearing shells also. Loosely refit the cap to the connecting rod noting the two matching numbers on the shoulders of the rod and cap which must line up on replacement. It is a good idea to note on a piece of paper which serial number applies to which cylinder number. This avoids the need to mark the connecting rod further . If the same rods and pistons are being put back it is very desirable that they should go back in the same position as they came out.

3   It is unlikely that a connecting rod will be bent except in cases of severe piston damage and seizure. It is not normally within the scope of the owner to check the alignment of a connecting rod with the necessary accuracy so if in doubt have it checked by someone with the proper facilities. It is in order to have slightly bent connecting rods straightened - the manufacturer's provide special jigs for the purpose. If a rod needs replacement, care should be taken to ensure that it is within 10 grams in weight of the others. If too heavy, connecting rods may by lightened by removing metal from the shoulders near the big end of the wider parts where the bearing cap mates up to it.

4   The small end bushes are also subject to wear. At a temperature of 70°F (21.1°C) the piston (gudgeon) pin should be a push fit. No axial or rocking movement should be apparent. The fitting of new bushes is a specialist task and although the bushes themselves may be easily pressed in it is necessary to ream them ot fit the gudgeon pins. Unless you have reamers readily available and the knowledge of how to use them this should be done by a firm (or individual) specialising in engine reconditioning. Remember that if you are fitting new pistons it may be necessary to fit new connecting rod bushes. If you are lucky the new gudgeon pins may fit the old bushes properly. However make sure that the new bushes have been drilled to match the oil holes in the connecting rod. This should be done before reaming so that there are no burrs on the bush bore.

5   The shell bearings from the big end are matt grey in colour when in good condition. If the engine has done a considerable mileage it is good policy to renew them anyway when the opportunity presents itself. To make sure you get the correct replacement size make a note of the numbers on the back of the bearing shell or take it along to the supplier.

6   If the crankshaft is being reground new bearing shells will be required anyway and these are normally available from the firm which does the regrinding and will be matched to the degree of regrinding carried out.

16 Camshaft and tappets - removal and renovation

1   The camshaft and tappets can be removed only after splitting the crankcase and this procedure is described in the section on crankshaft removal.

2   Having split the crankcase the tappets should be checked in their bores in the crankcase and no excessive side-play should be apparent. The faces of the tappets which bear against the camshaft lobes should also have a clear, smooth, shiny surface. If they show signs of pitting or serious wear they should be renewed. Refacing is possible with proper grinding facilities but the economics of this need investigating first. The lobes of the camshaft should be examined for any indications of flat spots, pitting or extreme wear on the bearing surfaces. If in doubt get the profiles checked against specification dimensions with a micrometer. Minor blemishes may be smothed down with a 120 grain oilstone and polished with one of 300 grain. The bearing journals also should be checked in the same way as those on the crankshaft. The camshaft bearings are renewable.

3   The gear wheel which is riveted to the end of the camshaft must be perfectly tight and the teeth should be examined for any signs of breakage or excessive wear. It may be possible to have a new gear wheel fitted to the existing camshaft - much depends on the facilities available in your area. It is not a job to be attempted by the owner.

17 Flywheel - removal and renovation

1   With the engine removed from the car the flywheel may be removed after the clutch cover has been taken off (as described in Chapter 5).

2   The flywheel is held by a single centre bolt which is tightened up to 253 ft/lbs (35 kg m) so do not think you can get it undone just like that. It was necessary to obtain a piece of angle iron to lock the flywheel by putting the angle iron across two of the clutch bolts which were put back into the flywheel. If by yourself the other end of the angle iron (or flat bar will do) can then be held in the vice with the engine on the bench.

3   A 36 mm socket is then put on the bolt with the handle from the socket set (do not under any circumstances try to use anything other than a correct sized socket - you could easily cause serious damage or even hurt yourself). A piece of steel pipe is then put over the socket handle and leaned on with considerable weight. The bolt slackens with no fuss at all. It may cost you a little money to get the stuff to do this job properly but we cannot recommend any other way.

4   Remove the bolt and large washer and before going any further make an identifiable mark on the flywheel hub so that you can re-locate the flywheel in the same place. The matching mark on the crankshaft cannot be made until the flywheel is off, so remember not to move the flywheel when it has come off until you can make a corresponding line up mark on the crankshaft flange. This is important as there may be no other way of knowing the correct position of balance.

5   The flywheel is now located only by four dowel pegs which fit into holes in the crankshaft flange and flywheel boss. Put a piece of wood under the edge of the flywheel starter teeth to

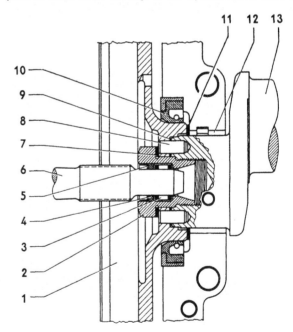

Fig. 1.8. Cross section view of the flywheel end of the crankshaft (Sec. 17)

1 Flywheel	8 Dowel peg
2 Gland nut	9 'O' ring
3 Needle bearing	10 Crankshaft oil seal
4 Felt ring	11 Shims
5 Retaining ring	12 Rear main bearing
6 Gearbox input shaft	13 Crankshaft
7 Lock washer	

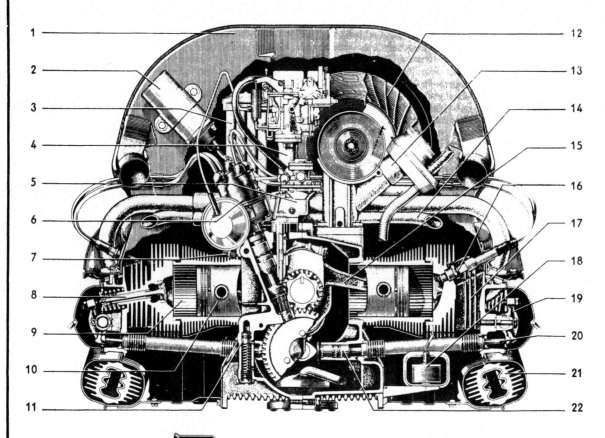

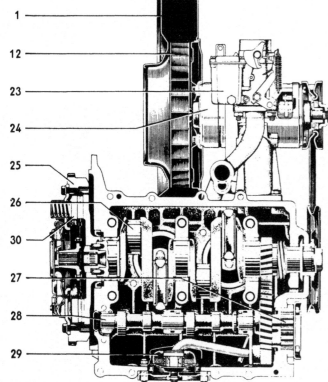

Fig. 1.9. Engine - cross section views

1	Fan housing
2	Coil
3	Oil cooler
4	Inlet manifold
5	Fuel pump
6	Distributor
7	Oil pressure switch
8	Valve
9	Cylinder
10	Piston
11	Oil pressure relief valve
12	Fan
13	Oil filler
14	Intake manifold preheater pipe
15	Connecting rod
16	Spark plug
17	Cylinder head
18	Thermostat
19	Rocker arm
20	Pushrod
21	Heat exchanger
22	Cam follower (tappet)
23	Carburettor
24	Dynamoo
25	Flywheel
26	Crankshaft
27	Oil pump
28	Camshaft
29	Oil strainer
30	Clutch

Note: This drawing does not show all the later modifications (ef: 3 section inlet manifold, one-piece fuel pump) but the basic format is the same.

support the weight and then use a soft mallet or block of wood to tap the edges of the flywheel and draw it off. Do not try and lever it off with anything against the crankcase or you are likely to crack the casting and that will be very expensive.

6 When the flywheel is free, hold it steady, and remove the metal or paper gasket fitted over the four dowel pegs in the flange. Then make the second line-up mark on the crankshaft referred to in paragraph 4.

7 The dowel pegs are a precision fit into both the flange and flywheel. If any of these should be a slack fit there is considerable risk of the flywheel working loose, despite the tightness of the securing bolt. Where a flywheel has worked loose and caused the holes to become oval a new flywheel will be needed. (The precision work of boring and fitting oversize dowel pegs would cost more).

8 Another area of wear is in the starter teeth. These are machined into the flywheel itself so there is no question of fitting a new ring gear. If the teeth have become seriously chewed up it is in order to have up to 2 mm(0.08 inch) machined off on the clutch side of the teeth. The teeth should then be chamfered and de-burred. Any good machine shop should be able to carry out this work.

9 Examine also the land on the flywheel boss where the oil seal runs. If this is severely ridged it may need cleaning up on a lathe also. Any such ridging is very exceptional.

---

18 Crankshaft oil seal - removal

---

1 The crankshaft oil seal may be removed after taking the engine from the car and removing the flywheel.

2 The oil seal may be levered out of the crankcase with a screwdriver or similar but great care must be taken to avoid damaging the crankcase where the seal seats. This means that the point of the tool used must not be allowed to dig into the crankcase.

3 When the oil seal is removed a number of shims which fit between the flywheel hub and the flange on the front main bearing will be observed. There should be three of them normally. These govern the amount of crankshaft endfloat. Make sure they are kept safely and not damaged.

4 If the crankcase is being split anyway it is simpler to wait until this is done when the oil seal may be easily lifted out.

---

19 Crankshaft and main bearings - removal and renovation

---

1 In order to remove the crankshaft, camshaft and tappets (cam followers) the two halves of the crankcase will need to be separated. Unless you are quite sure that this is essential do not do it. It is not worth opening the crankcase up just to 'have a look'. Remember also that the main bearing shells are much more expensive than on conventional cars (three of the four are not split) and before you can remove one of them two gears must be removed from the crankshaft. These gears are on very tight and are difficult to draw off.

2 Having decided to split the crankcase, remove the generator pedestal and prop the crankcase on its left side. All pistons and cylinders should already have been removed as should the flywheel. If the flywheel is left on it will add to the difficulty of controlling the weight of the crankshaft when the two halves release it. It will also be much more difficult to remove from the crankshaft afterwards. The connecting rods may be left on as these will be easier to remove after the crankcase is split.

3 The two halves are held together by large and small studs and nuts and two bolts and nuts. Slacken all the smaller nuts followed by the large nuts. Before starting to separate the two halves remember that the crankshaft and camshaft are held between them and you do not want either to fall out haphazardly. So if you keep the crankcase tilted to the left they will both rest in that half .

4 Separate the two halves by tapping lightly at the projecting lugs on the left half with a soft faced mallet or piece of wood.

Do not hit anything hard. This progressive gentle tapping at the four corners will gradually increase the gap between the two until the right-hand half will be free enough to lift off the studs. If you have a second pair of hands to help so much the better. When the right-hand half has moved out a little way there will probably be a light clatter as one or more of the four cam followers in the right-hand half fall out. If possible try and get hold of these and arrange them somewhere (in an egg box or numbered row on a shelf) so that they may be put back in the same bore.

5 Put the crankcase half in a safe place where it cannot fall or be damaged.

6 Lift out the camshaft from the other half of the crankcase. The bearing shells may be left in position. If they fall out note where they came from. If being renewed anyway take them out. One half of one shell is flanged to take the camshaft end thrust and the crankcase is suitably machined to accept it.

7 The tappets from the left-hand half of the crankcase may now be taken out. Keep them in order like the others so they may be replaced in the same bores.

8 The crankshaft can now be lifted out and should be carefully put somewhere safe. The bearing shell halves for No.2 main bearing should be removed from their locations in each half of the crankcase. Note that the location of each bearing is by a dowel peg which locates each bearing shell. These normally remain in the crankcase but if any have come out with the bearings retrieve them now before they get lost.

9 It is possible to examine the connecting rod big end journals after removing the pistons and connecting rods without splitting the crankcase, but only visually. They cannot be measured satisfactorily. Provided there is no good reason to suspect that the big end bearings were seriously worn and that the surfaces of the journal are bright and smooth with no signs of pitting or scoring then there should be no need to proceed further.

10 The main crankshaft bearing journals may be examined only when the crankcase has been split and the crankshaft taken out. An indication of serious wear in those bearings can be obtained before the crankcase is split. A wooden lever put through one of the cylinder apertures can be used to test for any indications of rocking in the bearings. If there is any then the bearing shells will almost certainly need renewal, even though the crankshaft journals themselves may be serviceable. The journals should be perfectly smooth with a bright mirror finish. They should be measured with a micrometer across the diameter for signs of ovality. If any measurement should differ by more than 0.03 mm (0.0011 inch) from any other the crankshaft should be reground. This means taking it to a specialist engineering firm who can grind it to the undersizes permissible and supply the matching new bearing shells. In view of the need to remove the two gears in order to examine No 3 main bearing journal the condition of the gears should also be checked, in conjunction with their respective mating gears on the camshaft and distributor drive spindle. The bronze worm gear which drives the distributor drive spindle is the most likely to show signs of wear. Any noticeable ridging or 'feathering' and variations in thickness of each spiral tooth indicate wear and renewal is probably justifiable.

11 Three of the four main bearings may be removed as soon as the crankshaft is taken from the crankcase. No 1 is a circular flanged shell which is drawn off the flywheel end, No 2 is the split bearing and No 4 is a narrow circular bearing which can be drawn off the crankshaft pulley end. No 3 however, is trapped by the helical gear which drives the camshaft. In front of this gear is a spacer and the distributor drive shaft worm gear, an oil thrower disc and woodruff key.

12 To remove No 3 main bearing first tap the woodruff key out of the shaft and keep it safe. Take off the oil thrower disc. The two gears are a tight keyed fit onto the shaft and the only way to get them off is by using a proper sprocket puller which has grips which will fit snugly and completely behind the helical gear so that both the gears and the spacer can be drawn off together. If you have difficulty in fitting the puller in the small gap between the bearing and gear do not try and pull off the gear

gripping only against the gear teeth. You will either chip them or break them off. If you are committed to new bearings anyhow, cut the old bearing off to enable you to get the puller properly seated behind the gear.

13 If, when you start putting the pressure on it is obvious that considerable force is going to be needed it is best to clamp the legs of the puller to prevent them spreading and possibly flying off and causing damage to the gear. Some pullers have a clamp incorporated for such a purpose. If you have press facilities available so much the better but on no account should you try to hammer the gears off. It is virtually impossible to do this without damaging the gears.

14 With the two gears removed the bearing can be taken off the shaft.

15 Having taken off the No 3 bearing it would be unwise not to renew the complete set as a matter of course. If the crankshaft needs re-grinding then the new bearings will need to be of the correct undersize to suit the amount removed during re-grinding. Such bearings will normally be supplied by the firm doing the re-grinding work. If the crankshaft is not being reground make sure that the bearings obtained are exactly the same dimensions as those removed. This can be verified by checking the numbers on the bearings which normally include an indication of whether they are standard or undersize. Do not forget that it is always possible that the crankshaft may have been re-ground already.

20 Distributor driveshaft - removal

1 The procedure for removing and replacing the distributor driveshaft from an assembled engine is given in Chapter 4. It is mentioned here because it is in order to leave it in position right up until the time when the crankcase is divided. It should, however, be removed before the crankcase is reassembled.

21 Crankcase - examination and renovation

The crankcase should be free from cracks or any other form of damage and the two mating edges must be quite free from dents, scratches and burrs which could in any way affect their precise alignment when both are clamped together. The crankshaft bearing locations should also be examined for any signs of damage or distortion. In an engine which has been permitted to run on with worn out main bearings it is possible that the bearing shells themselves will have been 'hammered' by the vibration of the crankshaft into the crankcase. This will mean that new bearings will not be a tight fit in their crankcase locations. In such instances the crankcase must be scrapped. In these circumstances the best action would be to abandon ideas of renovating the engine and obtain a complete replacement. Make sure that the camshaft bearing surfaces are in good condition.

The studs in the crankcase, both for attaching the cylinder heads and for the two halves, must be tight in their threads. Any sign of looseness which may be due to worn threads in the alloy crankcase is repairable. It will mean drilling and fitting a 'Helicoil' insert - which is a new thread in effect. This can be done at the Volkswagen agents for certain and at many other places where aluminium engines and castings are often being repaired. In any case check the economics before buying a lot of other parts.

22 Engine reassembly - general

1 As mentioned earlier, the Volkswagen engine is more complex in assembly than a conventional engine with a single cylinder block. It is therefore essential to get everything right first time and this means **do not rush it**. More than likely you will not have assembled an engine like this before so the order of assembly on other types cannot be relied upon for experience.

2 Before starting work clear the bench and arrange all the components nearby. The assembly surface must be particularly clean and it is a good idea to cover the working surface with sheets of strong paper. Have all the necessary gaskets and seals available together with clean oil in a can or convenient dispenser pack. If you are replacing bearing shells, cam followers and various other parts make sure the old parts are kept away from the assembly area in a carton or something. It is very easy to pick up an old cam follower for instance by mistake. At each stage, get the relevant batch of nuts and bolts ready - having cleaned the grit from them in a paraffin bath. A plentiful supply of clean cloths is the final requirement. Do not forget to clean the tools you will use as well. It is easy to transfer grit from a spanner to the engine with your hands and any small pieces of grit can ruin many hours and pounds worth of work. Again finally, take you time!

23 Crankshaft - assembly of gears and nos 3 and 4 main bearings

1 With the crankshaft thoroughly clean and the oilways blown out lubricate No 3 journal with clean engine oil (photo) No 3 main bearing is one of the two largest one-piece circular shells. It does not have a flange on it. This bearing goes on to the journal one way only - that is with the small dowel peg hole (which is not central) towards the flywheel end of the crankshaft (photo). Do not get this wrong or assembly will grind to a halt when you try to locate the bearing in the crankcase halves.

2 Next replace the camshaft drive gear. Before putting it on examine the surfaces of the crankshaft and key and the bore of the gear. If there are signs of slight scoring as a result of seizure when the gear was drawn off, clean them up with a very fine file. This will avoid a tendency to bind on replacement. The gear keyway should be lined up with the key in the shaft and the chamfered edge of the gear bore must face the flywheel end ie it goes on first (photo). The gear may be difficult to start on the shaft so keep it square and make sure that the keyway is precisely lined up (photo). This is most important because if wrong you will have to draw the gear off and start again. It can then be drifted on with firm evenly spaced strikes around the gear (away from the teeth). Keep it square, particularly at the start, and drive it fully home. (photo) The crankshaft should be clamped between padded vice jaws for this operation.

3 Next the spacer ring followed by the spiral distributor drive gear are fitted. They can go on either way round and the gear should be carefully drifted up to the spacer without damaging the spiral teeth (photos). Finally, fit the retaining circlip and make sure it fits snugly in its groove (photo). If it will not go in the groove then one of the gears has not been fully driven onto the crankshaft and this must be rectified.

4 Next fit the small circular bearing over the end journal, once again making sure that the offset dowel peg hole is towards the flywheel end of the crankshaft (photo). Do not confuse the dowel peg hole with the circular groove machined in the outside of this bearing. Lubricate the journal.

5 Next fit the oil thrower disc with the concave face outwards (photo). Fit the woodruff key (for the crankshaft pulley wheel) into the keyway now as this will prevent the disc from falling off inadvertently (photo).

24 Connecting rods - reassembly to crankshaft

1 If the crankcase has been split the connecting rods (without the pistons) should first be fitted to the crankshaft. Check that the gudgeon pins fit correctly in their respective small end bushes, otherwise difficulty will be encountered in fitting the pistons later. If you are refitting the connecting rods to the crankshaft in the assembled crankcase, note the additional information at the end of this Section.

2 Lay the crankshaft down on the bench with the flywheel flange end away from you.

3 Arrange the connecting rods, two on each side of the crankshaft with Nos 1 and 2 on the right, No1 nearest the

23.1a Clean the crankshaft oilways and lubricate the journal surface

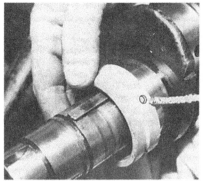

23.1b No. 3 main shell bearing showing the dowel peg hole towards the flywheel

23.2a Replace the camshaft gear with the chamfered edge inwards

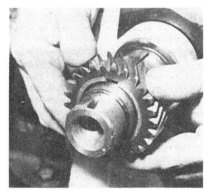

23.2b Line up the gear keyway

23.2c Drift the gear fully home

23.3a Replace the spacer collar

23.3b Replace the distributor worm drive gear

23.3c Line up the keyway before driving the gear home

23.3d Fit the circlip

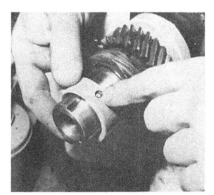

23.4 The end bearing shell locating peg hole must be towards the flywheel end of the shaft

23.5a Fit the oil thrower disc

23.5b Tap the Woodruff key into the key-way

flywheel end and No 3 and 4 on the left with No 3 nearest the flywheel end. The numbers on each connecting rod and cap must face downwards for each cylinder (photo). There is a forging mark on each rod on the opposite side which obviously faces upwards (photo). If you are fitting new connecting rods check with the supplier first about any changes which may possibly have occurred in this principle of marking. The first crank on the crankshaft from the flywheel end is No3. Pick up the connecting rod and after wiping the bearing surface perfectly clean, fit the bearing shell with the notch engaging in the corresponding notch in the rod. Fit the other half of the shell bearing to the cap in the same fashion (photo). Next, liberally oil the bearing journal with clean oil and assemble the rod to the crankshaft (photo). Match the two numbers on the shoulders and with the rod pointing to the left face them downwards. Replace the cap and nuts, finger tight so that the assembly is not loose on the crankshaft (photo).

4   Repeat this for No. 1, right, which is the second crank from the flywheel end followed by No.4, left, and No.2, right. It is easy to get confused while doing this. If your crankshaft assembly does not look like the one in Fig 1.10 rotate the crankshaft 180° but keep the connecting rods pointing the same way. Then it should look familar! Above all, think and do not rush.

5   Once the rods are correctly fitted to the crankshaft the bolts will need tightening to the correct torque of 3.3 mkg (24 ft lbs). The best way to do this is to mount the crankshaft vertical in the vice, clamping the No.4 bearing journal firmly between two pieces of wood (photo). All the connecting rod bolts can then be tightened. It is advisable to tap the shoulders of each rod with a hammer to relieve any pre-tension which can be set up between the mating surfaces of the cap and the rod. When the cap bolts are fully tightened the connecting rods should be able to rotate around the journals under their own weight. There should be no tight or 'free' spots anywhere although if you are fitting new shells to an un-reground crankshaft this is possible. If very noticeable however, it indicates that the journal is out of round. If rods on a reground crankshaft are slightly tight the engine will need running-in. If very tight then the regrinding tolerances are wrong and it should be returned to the machinists for correction.

6   Place the assembled crankshaft on the bench once more, as before, with each connecting rod facing its proper cylinder position.

7   If you are fitting the connecting rods to an assembled crankcase/crankshaft lay out the rods alongside their respective cylinder positions as already explained and fit the shells into the rods and caps. Turn the crankshaft so that the journal for the rod to be fitted is nearest its crankcase opening. The cap must then be placed on the journal and the rod fitted to it. This is easy if you have four hands and fingers ten inches long! It is helpful to have a piece of bent metal rod which can be put through from the opposite side of the crankcase to hold the cap on the journal whilst the rod and nuts are being fitted. A certain amount of patience is essential as it is more than likely that you will drop a bolt or bearing cap into the crankcase at some stage

and have to shake it out. Do not use grease to hold parts together for this assembly. It will probably affect lubrication seriously. The most important thing to ensure is that a bearing shell does not drop out unnoticed and get trapped and damaged while you are fiddling about. So if a shell drops in the crankcase go easy on rotating the crankshaft until you get it out. As soon as the first connecting rod is fitted tighten the bolts to the correct torque and check that it moves freely but without any clearance. You will be refitting new shells to the original journal sizes so if something seems amiss - bearing too tight or too loose- make sure you have bought the correct shells by comparing the numbers and oversizes (if any) with the old ones removed .

---

25 Crankcase, crankshaft, camshaft and tappets (cam followers) reassembly

1   The items in the Section heading are grouped together for the very good reason that they all have to be assembled together. None may be omitted (see Fig 1.10).

2   Both crankcase halves must be perfectly clean, inside and out. All traces of jointing compound must be removed from the mating faces, the roots of the studs, and the chamfers in the stud hole mating faces. Use a solvent such as carbon tetrachloride to remove sealing compound and not a scraper which could damage the aluminium surfaces. The distributor drive gear should have been removed. The oil pump suction pipe must be tightly fitted. If loose it must be peened in position as necessary.

3   Place the left-hand half of the crankcase on the bench with the flywheel and away from you and leaning over so that it rests on the cylinder head studs.

4   Oil the four tappets for the left half and place them in their bore. If new tappets are being fitted it is possible that their heads may be slightly thicker than the originals, so compare them (photo). If they are thicker then it is essential to check the clearance between them and the crankcase with the cam lift at its highest point. So having placed the tappets in position replace the camshaft temporarily, with its shell bearings and revolve it (photos). If any of the cam lobes should jam the tappets against the crankcase then clearance will have to be provided by relieving the crankcase by about 1 - 2 mm (1/16 inch) behind each tappet head. This can be done by a small, end face grindstone in a power drill by a competent handyman. Great precision is not important provided that there is no damage to the actual tappet bore and the resulting clearance is adequate to permit full unobstructed movement of the cam and tappet. Be sure to remove all traces of metal after such work. Repeat this check for the four cam followers in the right-hand half of the crankcase.

5   Fit the flanged No.1 bearing shell at the flywheel end of the crankshaft. Once again make sure that the off-centre locating dowel peg hole goes towards the flywheel end (photo). Look to see that the corresponding dowel pegs in the crankcase will mate up. The bearing surfaces of the journal should be well lubricated with clean oil but keep the outside surfaces of the bearing shell

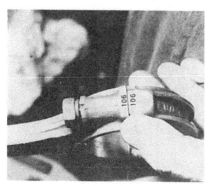
24.3a The connecting rod and cap have matching numbers

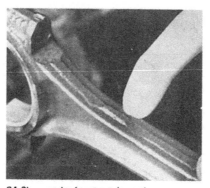
24.3b ... and a forge mark on the opposite side

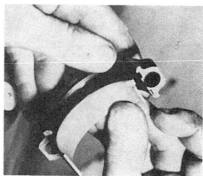
24.3c Fit the bearing shell into the cap

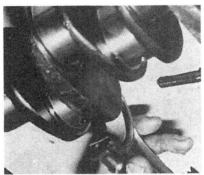

24.3d Put the rod into position on the journal ...

24.3e ... and mate up the cap

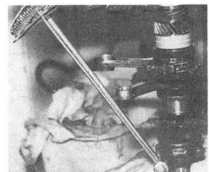

24.5 Tighten all the cap nuts

25.4a Compare new tappet flange thicknesses with the old ones

25.4b Put the tappets into the crankcase

25.4c Check the cam lobe clearances

Fig. 1.10. Crankcase, crankshaft and camshaft ready for reassembly (See Section 25)

clean and dry.

6 Place one half of the split shell in position at No.2 bearing in the crankcase, engaging the dowel pin in the hole (photo). Lubricate the bearing with clean oil.

7 The crankshaft assembly should now be placed into position in the left-hand crankcase half (photo). The three dowel holes in the circular bearings will need lining up so that they will locate snugly and Nos.3 and 4 connecting rods must pass through their respective apertures. It is a good idea to lift the assembly up by Nos.1 and 2 connecting rods for this operation. Do not force anything into place. The circular bearings may need rotating a little until you can feel the pegs engage. Ensure the thrower disc locates within the oil thrower recess in the casting. Once all the bearing pegs are located a little pressure will ensure that the assembly and bearings are completely seated. If it is stubborn for any reason lift it out, pause, look, think and have another go.

8 Next fit the camshaft bearing shells into clean locations, engaging the notches in the crankcase (photo). Then oil the bearings in readiness for the camshaft.

9 Turn the crankshaft carefully until two teeth, each marked with a centre punch, are visible and well clear of the edge of the crankcase. There is a single tooth on the camshaft gear similarly marked which must mesh between them (photo). Engage the teeth and roll the camshaft round, in mesh still, into its bearing location. Then turn the gears again to check that the timing marks are still correctly aligned.

10 Now fit the tappets (cam followers) into the right-hand half of the crankcase and if it seems as though they might fall out when it is lifted and tilted then put a dab of grease behind the lip of each one to help stick it in position.

11 Fit the other half of No.2 bearing shell into the right half of the crankcase locating it over its dowel peg correctly.

12 Now thinly coat the two clean, smooth mating surfaces of the crankcase halves with aluminium alloy jointing compound (photo). Use a good quality product such as Volkswagen themselves recommend, or 'Hylomar'. Neither is cheap but then you do not want your crankcase to leak oil when it gets hot. Make sure the two surfaces are coated completely but thinly and evenly. Take care to cover round the base of the studs. Do not let any compound get into oilways or other places where it is not wanted and may cause obstruction or binding.

13 The six larger studs have rubber sealing rings at the roots and these should all be renewed.

14 Place the right-hand half of the crankcase over the studs of the left and carefully slide it down until it just touches the crankshaft bearings (photo).

15 Coat the circular camshaft sealing plug with jointing compound and place it in position in its groove in the left-hand half at the flywheel end of the camshaft, with the recess facing inwards (photo).

16 Move the two halves together, tapping lightly with a block of wood if necessary. Use no force - none should be necessary.

17 Now stop and check:
a) Are all the connecting rods protruding from their proper holes? Cap nuts tight?
b) Are all four bearings, two gears and oil thrower disc fitted to the crankshaft?
c) Are all eight tappets in position?
d) You did not forget the camshaft? (it has been known!). Did you mesh the timing properly.
e) Camshaft sealer plug?
    All in order, replace all the nuts on the studs finger tight. Revolve the crankshaft just to make sure that everything moves freely at this stage at least.

18 It is important to tighten down the stud nuts evenly and in the correct order. Tighten first the six large nuts to a torque of 1.5 mkg (11 ft lbs) only, followed by all the smaller nuts to the same torques. Then tighten the small nut near the lower large stud clamping round No.1 main bearing to its full torque of 2 mkg (14 ft lbs).

19 Tighten the large nuts progressively to a torque of 3 mkg (20 ft lbs) and then to 3.5 mkg (25 ft lbs). Finally tighten the smaller nuts to 2 mkg (14 ft lbs) (photo).

20 Now rotate the crankshaft - it should revolve smoothly without any stiffness. If there is stiffness however, slacken all the crankcase nuts. If it then turns freely something is wrong and you should separate the crankcase again. Then check that all the bearings have been properly located on their dowel pegs and that the split bearings of the camshaft are seated properly. Any pressure spots on bearings will be visible. The cause is normally due to dirt or burrs behind them, particularly on the corners of the bearing bore corners and mating face edges. These can be chamfered lightly if necessary. Whatever happens do not press on until you have found the reason for any tightness. Start again from the beginning if necessary .

26 Pistons, rings and connecting rods - reassembly

1 If you are only fitting new rings to existing pistons make sure you have examined the pistons properly as detailed in Section 14 and checked the new ring gaps in the cylinder bores.

2 The new rings should be fitted over the piston crown replacing the bottom ring first. If you do not have a proper ring expander tool spread the ends of the ring so that it goes over the top of the piston. Then carefully ease it down over the other grooves a little at a time. The blade of a feeler gauge or some shim steel will be of great assistance in sliding it over the grooves. Do not bend the ring in any way more than necessary to move it. It breaks easily. The top two rings are different. The lower of the two has a cut-away lower edge and the top ring is chamfered on its outer face. Both rings will be marked 'oben' or 'top' which denotes which way up they go. The lower of the two is fitted first. (see Fig 1.11).

3 When new pistons are supplied for rebored cylinders the rings are already fitted and the gaps should automatically be correct. It does no harm however, to take the top ring off each piston and check it in the bore to make sure.

4 Assuming the small end bushes have been correctly sized for the gudgeon pins remove one circlip from each piston - if not already done - and push out the gudgeon pin until the piston boss is clear to permit the end of the connecting rod to be positioned (photo). If the pins are too tight to push out do not force them. Warm up the pistons in front of the fire or on a radiator or next to an electric light bulb. Do not play over them with a blow lamp or gas torch. They only need warming - not heating.

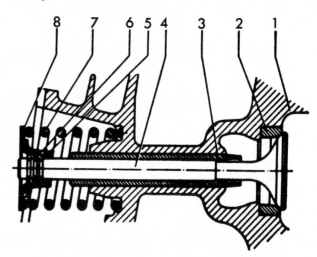

Fig. 1.11. Valve assembly - cross section (Sec. 28)

1 Cylinder head	5 Oil seal ring
2 Seat insert	6 Split collar
3 Guide	7 Valve spring
4 Valve	8 Spring retainer

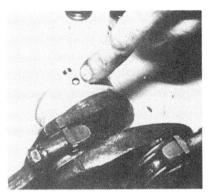

25.5 No. 1 main bearing is flanged. The dowel peg hole goes towards the flywheel

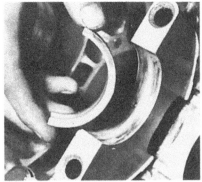

25.6 No. 2 main bearing (split). Fit each half into the crankcase halves

25.7 Fit the crankshaft and connecting rod assembly into the left hand half of the crankcase

25.8 Fit the three camshaft bearing shells. The rear one is flanged

25.9 Mesh the dot on the camshaft gear tooth between the two dots on the crankshaft gear teeth

25.12 Coat the crankcase mating surfaces with jointing compound

25.14 Fit the two crankcase halves together

25.15 Do not forget the camshaft sealing plug

25.19 Tighten the stud nuts in the correct sequence

26.4 Position the piston over the connecting rod small end

26.5a The makers put an arrow on the piston crown pointing towards the flywheel. Note the arrow pointing upwards and the No. 1 piston scratched on the crown

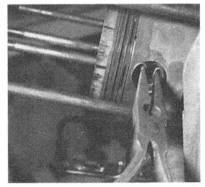

26.5b Fitting a circlip for a VW piston

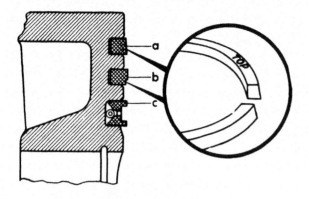

Fig. 1.12. Piston rings (Sec. 26)

(a)   Top compression ring
(b)   Lower compression ring with stepped
       lower edge
(c)   Oil control ring

5   If new pistons are being fitted they can go to any connecting rod and all that matters is that the side of the piston marked on the crown 'flywheel' or with a pointing arrow goes towards the flywheel end of the engine (photo). Push the gudgeon pin back into place and replace the circlip. Make sure that you use only the circlips supplied with the pistons. Do not use the old circlips just because they are easier to contract. (Volkswagen pistons have wire circlips with long legs (photo). English pistons have spring steel clips with small eyes needing proper circlip pliers to release them).

6   As soon as one piston has been fitted take care because when the crankshaft is rotated the skirt of the piston can foul the crankcase at bottom dead centre (bdc) unless it is guided into the cylinder aperture. This could break it. Watch too that the piston rings do not get snagged up on anything which could break them.

27 Cylinders - replacement

1   Cylinders should normally go back in their original locations unless new pistons are being fitted or they have been rebored, in which case it does not matter.

2   Before fitting the cylinders you may wish to lightly grind them into the seats in the cylinder head. This can be done using fine carborundum paste. Make sure that all traces of paste are flushed away afterwards. Light grinding in this way helps to ensure a gastight seal but do not overdo it (photo). Make sure that the mating faces at top and bottom of the cylinders are perfectly clean and clear of old gaskets. Select the new thin, cylinder base gaskets from the set and separate them. It is easy for two to stick together. Hang one over each connecting rod now so you do not forget to put them on. Alternatively they may be put in position on the cylinder base - held by a proprietary jointing compound (photo).

3   Cylinders will only go on one way, that is with the narrow fins at the base and the flat fin edges of a pair of cylinders facing each other. This should be remembered for the first cylinder of each pair. You could get it wrong and have to take it off again when the second one is ready to go on!

4   The piston ring gaps should be spaced round the upper 180° of each piston with the gap in the oil control ring facing the top of the engine.

5   The rings must be compressed into the piston grooves in order to get the cylinder over them. The type of compressor used must be such that it will split and come off round the piston because once the cylinder is on it will not be possible to lift it off over the top of the piston. A jubilee hose clip may be used quite satisfactorily. The cylinder bore is chamfered at the bottom which also facilitates assembly.

6   Fit the clip round the rings and tighten is so that all three are compressed (photo). Take care to see that no ring slips out from under the clip. This can easily happen, particularly when first tightening up the clip screw when a screw type hose clip is used.

7   Tighten the clip until the rings are flush with the piston but do not tighten it so much that the clip grips the piston tightly. Otherwise it will be difficult to slide the clip down the piston when the cylinder barrel takes over.

8   Not forgetting the lower cylinder gasket, place the cylinder over the piston crown narrow end first and with the fin flats facing the adjacent cylinder position and with the four studs aligned in the passages in the fins.

9   Press the base of the cylinder against the piston ring compressor or clip and tap it down with a wooden block or soft hammer (photo). If the clip does not move slacken it a fraction and try again. Do not let the cylinder 'bounce' off the clip when tapping it otherwise you are likely to release an otherwise captive ring. If a ring does escape it will be necessary to start again. If you break a ring you will probably have to buy a set of three for that piston - rarely can you buy a single ring unless you are lucky and a supplier has a part set or is prepared to split a set.

10 Once all rings are inside the cylinder remove the compressor. With the 'Jubilee' clip this means unscrewing it until the end can be drawn out to release it.

11 Next, carefully position the base gasket onto the bottom of the cylinder barrel. Then move the barrel down and locate it into the crankcase. It will not be a tight fit. It is important to make sure that the gasket is not dislodged and trapped incorrectly. If it is, the joint may leak and, worse the cylinder tilt fractionally out of line.

12 It will be necessary to rotate the crankshaft as each cylinder is fitted. When this is done, precautions must be taken to keep the other cylinders in position, otherwise you will have to keep checking the gasket seating. Also guard against the pistons jamming the crankcase at bottom dead centre. The cylinders may be tied down with string to prevent them moving.

28 Cylinder heads, valve and springs - reassembly

1   The valves removed should be refitted in their original positions unless, of course, new ones are being fitted.

2   If possible treat the valve stem with molybdenum disulphide or some other form of anti-scuffing paste to prevent excessive initial wear in the guide.

3   Place the valve in the guide (photo). Fit the oil ring round the valve stem and then the spring collar. Note that the close coils of the springs go against the head (photo).

4   Next arrange the valve spring compressor with the spacer tube fitted, if required, and carefully compress the spring (photos). Watch that there is no likelihood of the spring flying out. Often the spring tends to tilt on compression and this can impede the fitting of the split collars. If you can straighten the spring up without risk of releasing it all is well.

5   Compress the spring far enough to expose the grooves into which the split collars locate.

6   It will be necessary to fit the split collars through the slot in the tube if you have used this method. Fingers will be found to be too fat so put a blob of grease on the end of a screwdriver and use this to pick up the collet and put it in position with the narrow end downwards (photos). You may have difficulty with the second half because of the spring not being centrally spaced round the valve stem. This can be overcome by carefully tipping the spring with the compressor or by a little extra compression.

7   When both split collars are properly located in the grooves in the valve stems slowly release the compressor tool making sure that neither of the split collars is pushed out of positon. When the spring compressor is fully released the two halves of the split collar should be flush. If not, one is not properly bedded in the grooves of the valve stem.

8   Repeat the procedure for each valve in turn.

27.2a Grinding the cylinders into the head

27.2b Fitting the cylinder base gasket

27.6 Piston rings clamped

27.9 Fitting the cylinder over the piston

28.3a Inserting an exhaust valve into the head

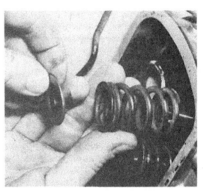
28.3b Fitting the spring and retainer

28.4a The spring compressor needs elongated ends ...

28.4b ... or use a piece of tube with a hole in it

28.6a Use grease to hold the collets on replacement

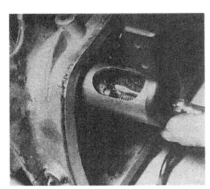
28.6b Collets in position

29.1a Stretching the push rod tubes

29.1b Fitting the push rod seals

29 Cylinders heads - replacement

1 First check the pushrod tubes. They have compressible concertina ends and these should be stretched out a little by pulling them so that the distance between the outer ends of the concertina sections is no less than 191 mm (6 15/16 inch) (photo). A new sealing ring should be fitted over each end so that the radiused face will go into the head or crankcase as appropriate (photo). When stretching the tubes pull straight so as to avoid any possibility of cracking them. If they are fractured a positive oil leak will result so check their condition carefully (Fig 1.13).

2 Next fit the sheet steel air deflector plate, of which there is one to each pair of cylinders (photo). It is a spring fit to the two centre studs and to make sure it is tight, the clip flanges may be bent out a little. Note that these deflectors (which guide air into the cooling fins) are on the lower side, ie. the same side as the pushrod tubes. They follow the contour of the cooling fins when installed so make sure they are the right way round. They cannot be fitted after putting the cylinder heads and tubes in position.

3 One head should now be put on to the eight head studs just far enough to be secure (photo). Then place the four pushrod tubes into position and hold them loosely in position by putting the pushrods back through them (photo).

4 Move the head further into position so that the tube ends locate in their respective seats at both ends. Make sure that the pushrod seals seat firm and square and that the recesses are clean. The seams in the tube should face the cylinder.

5 The cylinder head studs should not be touching any of the cylinder barrel fins so if necessary turn the barrels a little to achieve this. A piece of postcard placed behind each stud will establish the presence of a gap.

6 Replace the stud washers and nuts and tighten them lightly and evenly as far as is possible with a socket and extension using no lever bar.

7 The tightening progression of the nuts is important and is in two stages (photo). First tighten the nuts to 1 mkg (7 ft lbs) in the order shown in Fig. 1.14A. Then tighten them to 3.2 mkg (23

ft lbs) in the final diagonal pattern sequence as shown in Fig. 1.14B. There is a temptation to overtighten these head nuts. Resist it! Otherwise you will distort the head.

8 Repeat the operation for the second head.

30 Rocker gear - reassembly (including pushrods and tubes)

1 See that the lower ends of the pushrods are properly located in the recesses in the tappets (cam followers).

2 Place a new seal over each rocker assembly mounting stud (photo). Place the rocker shaft support blocks over the studs so that the socketed ends of the rocker arms will line up with the pushrods and the adjusters over the valve stems. The rocker shaft support blocks are chamfered and slotted. They are fitted with the chamfers outwards and slots upwards (photo).

3 Replace the washers and nuts and tighten the two nuts down evenly ensuring that the pushrods are properly engaged in the rocker arms. Tightening torque is 2.5 mkg (18 ft lbs). Slacken all the rocker adjuster screws for later adjustment (photo)

31 Crankshaft oil seal - replacement

1 The seal must be replaced (if it has been removed) before the flywheel is fitted. Do not fit it however, until the crankshaft endfloat has been checked as this involves temporary replacement of the flywheel and the movement of shims.

2 Before fitting the seal, place the necessary circular shims over the crankshaft flange and make sure they are perfectly clean and lightly oiled (photo).

3 Coat the outer metal edge of the new oil seal with jointing compound and place it squarely in position into the crankcase with the inner lip of the seal facing inwards (photo). It may then be tapped squarely home using a suitable mallet or piece of wood.

32 Flywheel - replacement

1 If you have taken the flywheel off you will presumably have the same equipment still available for replacing it. You will need it.

2 If you have overhauled the complete engine it will be advisable to check the crankshaft endfloat. This is governed by the gap between the inner face of the flywheel boss and the flange of the rear main bearing shell. Shims are introduced to reduce the gap and these shims need to be fitted before the oil seal. Although it is possible for them to be pushed in past the oil seal it is very difficult to get them out again without buckling or kinking them. If the main bearing shell has been renewed it is most likely that the shims originally fitted will be correct as the main wear takes place on the bearing shell flange. Three shims are always used to make up the required total thickness and they

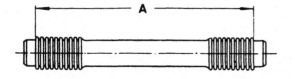

Fig. 1.13. Pushrod tube - overall length (Sec. 29)

A = 191 mm (7.5 ins) minimum before installation

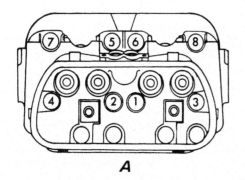

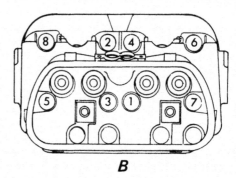

Fig. 1.14. Cylinder head nuts - tightening sequence (Sec. 29)
A — up to 7 lb ft (1 mkg)   B — up to 23 lb ft (3.2 mkg)

29.2 Fitting the lower air deflector plates

29.3a Offer up the cylinder head

29.3b Hold the push rod tubes with the push rods to start with

29.7 Tighten the head nuts in proper sequence

30.2a Fit new rocker shaft mounting stud seals

30.2b Replace the rocker shaft assembly...

30.3 ... making sure the push rods are seated correctly

31.2 Crankshaft end float shims being assembled

31.3 Replacing the oil seal

32.3 Flywheel/crankshaft dowel pegs in position

32.5 Offer up the flywheel

32.8 A piece of flat bar or angle or two clutch securing screws will hold the flywheel firm whilst the nut is tightened

come in six thicknesses (0.24 mm, 0.30 mm, **0.32 mm, 0.34 mm,** 0.36 mm, 0.38 mm). Fit two shims to start with, when the thickness of the third may then be calculated.

3 The four dowel pegs should all be placed in the crankshaft flange after having been checked for fitting in both the flange and the flywheel (photo). If any of these should be slack there is considerable risk of the flywheel working loose, despite the tightness of the nut, and this could be disastrous.

4 In the flywheel flange recess there will be the fine 'O' ring seal. Renew this before placing the flywheel in position and before measuring any crankshaft endfloat.

5 Grip the flywheel firmly and, with the marks lined up, locate it over the dowel pegs (photo). It is most important for the flywheel to be kept square. If it proves a bit of a strain and a fiddle to get in position find a piece of wood of a thickness suitable to support it at the right height. Once the flywheel is positively located on the pegs replace the centre bolt and washer and take it up as far as it will go finger tight. Then very carefully tighten the bolt to draw the flywheel on, at the same time keeping it perfectly square by tapping the rim as necessary with a soft faced mallet. If the bolt is tightened with the flywheel out of square the dowel pegs and holes will be damaged.

6 It will be necessary to tighten the centre bolt to at least 9 mkg (75 ft lbs) in order that the crankshaft endfloat may be accurately read. To do this a clock gauge micrometer is used against the face of the flywheel. The crankshaft is then moved in and out and the float measured. The thickness of the third shim is the measured float less 0.10 mm(0.004 inch). Any three shims will do, of course, provided they add up in total thickness to the sum of the two in position and the calculated third.

7 Once the correct shims have been selected the flywheel should be removed and the three shims put in position and the oil seal fitted as described in Section 31. The flywheel is then replaced in the same fashion.

8 Final tightening of the centre bolt involves a torque of 35 mkg (253 ft lbs) and the locking of the flywheel for this purpose should be arranged in the same way as for removal (photo). It is important to get this torque as accurate as possible because the flywheel may vibrate loose if it is insufficient. Too much, on the other hand, could cause unwanted stress.

9 It should also be remembered that the flywheel bolt has a built-in roller bearing which supports the transmission input shaft. This bearing should be in good condition and not over-greased.

33 Oil pump - replacement

1 Make sure that the mating faces of the crankcase and pump body are perfectly clean and unmarked.

2 Using a new gasket fit the pump body over the studs so that the fixed spindle is towards the bottom of the crankcase (photos).

3 Carefully tap the body fully home over the studs, taking care that the gasket does not get trapped incorrectly.

4 When the body is fully home tighten the two crankcase stud nuts, above and below, to the correct torque.

5 Next fit the two gears, turning the driving spindle so that the tongue engages in the slot in the end of the camshaft (photos). With both gears fully home the engine should now be turned through at least two complete revolutions. This ensures that the pump body is correctly centred by the revolving gears. The body should not be disturbed again after this has been done. Fit a new cover plate gasket followed by the cover plate (photo). Replace the four nuts. Whilst tightening up the nuts to a torque of 2 mkg (14 ft lbs) it is worthwhile rotating the engine once or twice more in case the pump body should inadvertently have moved during tightening.

34 Oil cooler - replacement

1 Using new special seals for the oilways fit the cooler over the

studs on the mounting adaptor. Fit the small sealer plate with the foam rubber strip over the same studs before fitting and tightening the nuts (photos).

2 Put two new special seals for the oilways between the adaptor and the crankcase and fit the whole assembly to the crankcase. Tighten the nuts firmly but take care not to shear the studs (photos).

35 Fan housing - replacement

The same remarks as made in Section 7 about removing the fan housing apply. For details refer to Chapter 2.

36 Valve to rocker clearances - adjustment

1 Valve clearances are important. If they should be too great the valves will not open as fully as they should. They will also open late and close early. This will affect engine performance. Similarly, if the clearances are too small the valves may not close completely, which will result in lack of compression and power. It will cause damage to valves and seatings.

2 The valve clearances should be set for each cylinder when the piston is at the top of its firing stroke. With the engine in the car this may be first found on No.1 cylinder (right, front) by removing the distributor cap and turning the engine so that the crankcase and the rotor arm points to the notch in the edge of the distributor body.

3 With the engine out of the car and distributor not yet installed the easiest method is to turn the crankshaft pulley wheel clockwise up to the mark and at the same time keep a finger over No.1 cylinder plug hole to check that there is compression. This indicates that you are on the firing stroke.

4 Both valves on No.1 cylinder may then be adjusted. First slacken the locknut on each rocker arm adjusting screw. Then put a feeler blade of the appropriate thickness between the adjuster and the end of the valve stem and turn the adjusting screw until a light drag can be felt when the blade is moved (photo). Tighten the locknut, holding the adjuster simultaneously with a screwdriver (photo). Check the gap once again.

5 Continue with the subsequent cylinders; the order is 2,3,4 and the crankshaft pulley wheel should be rotated 1/2 turn (180°) anticlockwise. The distributor rotor arm will turn 1/4 turn (90°). The valve clearances for No.2 cylinder may then be set. Continue the same way for cylinders 3 and 4 in that order.

6 Do not forget that the valve clearance settings have recently been increased. If there is a sticker on the fan housing saying the clearance is .004 inches ignore it. Put your own sticker on instead (photo).

7 *To carry out valve clearance adjustment with the engine in the car.* Take off the rear wheels and undo the valve cover clip (photo). Be careful not to get any dirt into the system. Go ahead as above. The exhaust valves are the outer ones and the inlets are in the centre.

37 Engine - refitment of ancillaries

1 In Section 2 of this Chapter details were given of items which could be removed with the engine in the car. With the exception of the distributor all these items can and should be refitted, however, before replacement of the engine. Some things have to be fitted before others and the following points should be noted:

a) As mentioned in Section 35 the inlet manifold centre section must be replaced before the fan housing assembly or before the generator/fan assembly if the two have been separated. The two outer sections of the manifold should be assembled loosely after that. Do not tighten the inlet manifold securing nuts at this stage.

b) Assemble the heat exchangers and exhaust system to the engine, to each other and to the inlet manifold with all clips, gaskets, screws and sleeves loosely put together. Do not fit

33.2a Fit a new oil pump body gasket ...

33.2b ... and replace the body in the crankcase

33.5a Replace the driving gear ...

33.5b ... and the driven gear

33.5c The oil pump cover plate gasket goes on last

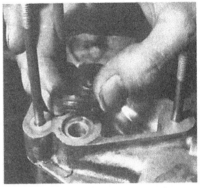

34.1a Oil cooler seals on the mounting bracket

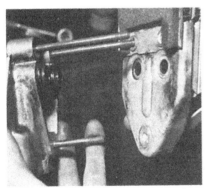

34.1b Fitting the oil cooler to the bracket

34.1c The smaller seal goes on the bracket studs

34.2a Oil cooler seals on the crankcase

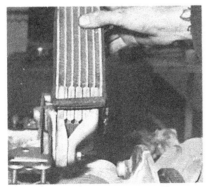

34.2b Fitting the oil cooler assembly to crankcase

34.2c Tighten the oil cooler mounting nuts

36.4a Adjust valve clearances with the screw ...

36.4b ... and tighten the locknut

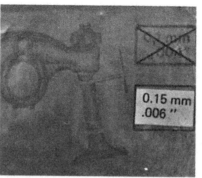

36.6 Get the valve clearance correct

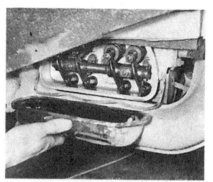

36.7 Remove the car rear wheel and access can be had to the rocker with the engine in the car

38.3 Get the accelerator cable out of the way before the engine goes back ...

38.6 ... then feed it into the tube through the fan housing before the engine is fully home

any one unit and tighten up the screws or nuts before assembling the other parts which join it. Then tighten up in the following sequence:

    Inlet manifold flange to cylinder heat nuts.
    Heat exchanger flange to cylinder head nuts.
    Exhaust manifold flange to cylinder head nuts.
    Exhaust manifold to heat exchanger pipe clamp bolts and nuts.
    Inlet manifold pre-heater pipe flange to exhaust manifold flange screws.
    Inlet manifold centre section to crankcase clamp nut.
    Heat exchanger connecting sleeve screws.
    Inlet manifold flexible connector clips.
c) Fit the fuel pump before the carburettor.
d) Attach the thermostat bellows to the pull rod and adjust the setting before fitting the lower right-hand duct plate.

38 Engine - replacement and starting-up

1 If the starter motor has been removed refit it to the transmission and connect the leads before replacing the engine. It is much easier. Put the right-hand top mounting bolt in position into the casing also and check that the nut runs easily on it.
2 Make sure the clutch assembly is fitted and the friction disc has been properly centralised.
3 Put the accelerator guide tube in position through the fan housing. Also ensure that the accelerator cable is in a position where it will not get trapped or kinked (photo).
4 With the rear of the car raised move the engine into position underneath so that it can be lifted. Ideally it will be raised on a trolley jack. Otherwise it will be necessary to raise it by some other means so that the car can be lowered to line up with it.
5 There is very little fore and aft clearance inside the engine compartment. For this reason the engine must not be tilted

otherwise the gearbox input shaft will get snagged up with the clutch cover.
6 As soon as the input shaft is lined up with the clutch centre, feed the accelerator cable through the guide tube in the fan housing (photo).
7 Push the engine forward so that the lower mounting studs engage in the holes and the crankcase moves right up to the transmission casing. It may be necessary to waggle the engine about a little to achieve this. It is important to note that any attempt to draw the engine into position with the mounting bolts when there is a considerable gap may crack the crankcase or transmission casing.
8 The upper right-hand mounting bolt should engage its head into the transmission casing and the nut can be fitted from inside the engine compartment. The two lower nuts and the upper left-hand bolt are fitted from underneath the car. The bolt goes into a captive nut in the crankcase.
9 When the engine is in position reconnect or adjust the following from underneath:
a) Fuel line.
b) Heater hoses.
c) Heater flap control wires.
d) Starter cables.
e) Adjust the clutch pedal free play.

The following items must be connected from above:
a) Accelerator cable (see adjustment details in Chapter 3).
b) Generator leads (3) brown at the fan end, red on the left D+ terminal near the pulley, and green on the D- terminal or, of course, if an alternator is fitted the alternator leeds in the same position as they where on dismantling.
c) Automatic choke lead (black).
d) Solenoid cut off valve on carburettor (black).
e) Coil - black to 15 - green from distributor to terminal 13.
f) HT leads (see Chapter 4).

g) Oil pressure switch (blue/green).

h) Fuel line at carburettor.

i) All hoses.

j) Replace distributor and set ignition timing (see Chapter 4).

k) Replace the rear cover plate, ensuring that all screws are correctly fitted and the small insulator plates secured round the inlet manifold pre-heater pipes. The edge of the plate should fit neatly in the rubber beading round the edge of the engine compartment.

l) Remove the dipstick (to prevent blow back up the filler pipe) and fill the engine to the top mark on the dipstick. Take care not to spill oil.

m) Reconnect the battery,

10 If the engine does not fire and run fairly quickly it is likely to get flooded due to the operation of the automatic choke. In such cases press the accelerator to the floor and hold it there until the engine fires. If it still fails to start go through the ignition and fuel system fault diagnosis as outlined in the respective chapters.

11 Once the engine starts see that the oil warning light goes out and then go immediately to the engine compartment to see if there is anything going on which should not. Let the engine run until normal working temperature is reached and then adjust the carburettor as necessary. Then stop the engine, let it stand for a minute or so and recheck the oil level.

12 Road test the car and if the performance is not satisfactory make small alterations to the distributor timing setting, testing on the road after each adjustment.

For 'Fault diagnosis' see next page

39 Fault diagnosis - engine

Symptom	Reason/s	Remedy
Engine will not turn over when starter switch is operated	Flat battery Bad battery connections Bad connections at solenoid switch and/or starter motor	Check that battery is fully charged and that all connections are clean and tight.
	Starter motor jammed	Rock car back and forth with a gear engaged. If ineffective remove starter
	Defective solenoid	Remove starter and check solenoid.
	Starter motor defective	Remove starter and overhaul
Engine turns over normally but fails to fire and run	No spark at plugs	Check ignition system according to procedures given in Chapter 4.
	No fuel reaching engine	Check fuel system according to procedures given in Chapter 3.
	Too much fuel reaching engine (flooding)	Slowly depress accelerator pedal to floor and keep it there while operating starter motor until engine fires. Check fuel system if necessary as described in Chapter 3.
Engine starts but runs unevenly and misfires	Ignition and/or fuel system faults	Check ignition and fuel systems as though the engine had failed to start
	Incorrect valve clearances	Check and reset clearances.
	Burnt out valves	Remove cylinder heads and examine and overhaul as necessary.
Lack of power	Ignition and/or fuel system faults	Check ignition and fuel systems for correct ignition timing and carburettor settings.
	Incorrect valve clearances	Check and reset the clearances
	Burnt out valves	Remove cylinder heads and examine and overhaul as necessary.
	Worn out piston or cylinder bores	Remove cylinder heads and examine pistons and cylinder bores. Overhaul as necessary.
Excessive oil consumption	Oil leaks from crankshaft oil seal, rocker cover gasket, oil pump, drain plug gasket, sump plug washer, oil cooler	Identify source of leak and repair as appropriate.
	Worn piston rings or cylinder bores resulting in oil being burnt by engine (smoky exhaust is an indication)	Fit new rings or rebore cylinders and fit new pistons, depending on degree of wear.
	Worn valve guides and/or defective valve stem seals	Remove cylinder heads and recondition valve stem bores and valves and seals as necessary.
Excessive mechanical noise from engine	Wrong valve to rocker clearances Worn crankshaft bearings Worn cylinders (piston slap)	Adjust valve clearances. Inspect and overhaul where necessary. Inspect and overhaul where necessary.
Unusual vibration	Misfiring on one or more cylinders Loose mounting bolts	Check ignition system Check tightness of bolts and condition of flexible mountings.

NOTE: When investigating starting and uneven running faults do not be tempted into snap diagnosis. Start from the beginning of the check procedure and follow it through. It will take less time in the long run. Poor performance from an engine in terms of power and economy is not normally diagnosed quickly. In any event the ignition and fuel systems must be checked first before assuming any further investigation needs to be made.

Chapter 2 Cooling, heating and exhaust systems

Contents

Cooling and heating system removal - general 2
Exhaust system - removal, inspection and replacement ... 9
Fan - removal and replacement 4
Fan belt - adjustment - removal and replacement 3
Fan housing - removal and replacement 5
Fault diagnosis - cooling, heating and exhaust systems ... 10

General description 1
Heat exchanger controls - checking and setting 8
Heat exchangers - removal and replacement 6
Thermostat and controls - removal, replacement, testing
and adjustment 7

Specifications

Fan capacity at 4000 rpm	600 litres (22 cu ft) of air per second, approximately
Thermostat opens at	65 — 70° C (149 — 158° F)

Torque wrench settings:

	lb ft	kg m
Fan securing nut	43	6.0
Fan/generator drive pulley nut	43	6.0

1 General description

One of the most famous and well known features of the Volkswagen Beetle engine throughout its life has been the fact that it is air cooled. The advantages are obvious - none of the problems and cost of maintaining a water cooling system with the attendant problems of extreme temperatures. There are certain disadvantages of an air cooled system however - there is greater engine noise, more engine power used to drive the cooling fan and a less precise control of engine temperatures. Air cooled engines are not at their best in dense traffic in hot weather. Great care must also be taken to ensure that the lubrication system is not neglected as the engine oil plays a more significant part in engine cooling.

The Volkswagen system is neat and simple. A multi-bladed turbo fan is mounted on the shaft which drives the generator. It rotates in a sheet steel, semi-circular housing, drawing in air through the fan centre and directing it down to each pair of finned cylinders. The cylinders are shrouded above with carefully designed sheet steel covers. Below each pair of cylinders a contoured deflection plate is mounted centrally. Thus the air is directed over the full surface area of the cylinder cooling fins.

In order to shorten the warming up time a thermostat is mounted below the right-hand pair of cylinders. This is a conventional bellows type and it operates a restriction on the through flow of air when the engine is cold. Flaps in the fan housing are opened by the thermostat when the engine warms up, so allowing the full air flow to pass round the cylinders.

The car heating system is linked with the cooling system, In addition to the cooling air circuit there are two heat exchangers mounted one below each pair of cylinders. In effect these heat exchangers consist of a finned section of exhaust pipe from the front cylinder at each side which is encased in a sheet steel 'tank'. A smaller 'tank' also encases the short piece of exhaust from the rear cylinders. The two tanks are connected together.

Air from the fan housing passes through a flexible hose to the top of the small heat exchanger and then through the larger one. Hot air then passes from the heat exchanger to the ducts in the car body. A control flap at the front of each large heat exchanger can shut off the air flow.

The heat exchangers are made from special corrosion and rust resistant metals so that under normal circumstances their life is indefinite. The exhaust silencer box also is of above average durability.

Models which are exported to Arctic climates cannot generate enough heat from this system to be effective so petrol burning heater units are fitted to supplement the interior heating system. These devices are not dealt with in this manual.

The condition and fit of all the covers is important. Sealing strips and grommets must all be properly positioned. If air leaks out the cooling capacity is reduced.

Since the introduction of the models covered by this manual some changes have been made. On the 1300 cc (78.3 cu in) engine a twin pre-heater pipe had been fitted on each side. This has also been done on the 1600 cc (96.7 cu in) engine for USA. For the European 1600 cc (96.7 cu in) engine the diameter of the pre-heater pipe had been increased from 20 mm to 24 mm.

The exhaust mufflers have been modified to suit these changes, the European 1600 cc (96.7 cu in) having an enlarged flange.

Exhaust tail pipes have also been modified with an increase from 20 mm to 23 mm in the case of the 1600 cc (96.7 cu in).

It is important that the tailpipe is not pushed too far into the muffler or back pressure will be set up with consequent overheating and damage to the engine.

On the earlier types where the pre-heater pipe extends into the tailpipe a suitable rule should be inserted into the tailpipe until it butts up against the pre-heater pipe and the measurement at the open end of the tailpipe checked. Depending on the length of the tailpipe the measurement should be:

Length of tail pipe	Measurement at open end
276 mm (10.86 inches)	270 mm (10.63 inches)
249 mm (9.80 inches)	243 mm (9.57 inches)
226 mm (8.90 inches)	220 mm (8.66 inches)

On the later models (1300 cc (78.3 cu in) from May '73, 1600 cc (96.7 cu in) from Aug '73) the pre-heater pipe does not extend into the tailpipe and the measurement is taken from the open end of the tailpipe to the clip. For a tailpipe of length 226 mm (8.90 in) the distance should be 155 mm (6.10 in).

2 Removal of cooling and heating system components - general

1 It is more difficult to dismantle the cooling and heating systems with the engine in the car than after the engine has been removed. There may be occasions when it will be necessary to remove components from the system without disturbing the engine, for example:
a) The fan and fan housing may be removed to service a damaged fan, for generator overhaul, or to give access to the oil cooler.
b) The heat exchangers may be leaking and need renewal.
2 As the cooling system is so much an integral part of the engine assembly this Chapter deals primarily with those items which are easily accessible with the engine in the car.

3 Fan belt - adjustment, removal and replacement

1 The Volkswagen fan belt needs more regular inspection than a water cooled engine fan belt usually gets because if it slips or breaks the consequences are more serious, more quickly.
2 Adjustment takes a little more time than usual. There is no tension pulley. The pulley on the generator is split into two and the gap between the two halves governs the effective diameter. The gap is regulated by spacer rings (photo). If the belt is too slack the gap between the two halves is decreased by removing one or more of the spacer rings. Spare spacers are fitted to the outside of the pulley.
3 To remove the belt and split the pulley, lock the pulley first with a screwdriver in the edge of the inner flange against the top generator bolt. Remove the nut and clamp ring. The outer half of the pulley can then be separated from the inner half. To tighten the fan belt remove one spacer from between and then replace everything (with the moved spacer now on the outside of the pulley) and try the tension again. Take care when refitting the outer half of the pulley to get it square (photo). It helps if the engine is rotated. This will get the belt into its 'running' position. The engine is easily rotated with a spanner on the crankshaft pulley wheel. Continue removing spacers until the tension is correct. If all the spacers are out and the belt is still slack it is over-stretched and must be renewed.
4 The tension of the belt is becoming increasingly critical. Too much tension and the belt wears quickly, bearings tend to suffer and even overheat. Too little tension and the belt will slip, the belt wears out and the engine overheats.
The generator has increased in output, and been replaced by an alterator with an even higher output. To cope with this a 'low stretch' or 'XDA' belt has been fitted. This belt requires very careful adjustment.
5 The older type of belt should be adjusted so that if it is pressed with the thumb midway between pulleys it should deflect about 15 mm (5/8 inch).
6 However that will not do for the 'XDA' belt. This must be checked with a spring balance of special design which is sold by a firm in Frankfurt, Germany. If you cannot get one and must use the old method the 'thumb deflection' should be 0.4 inch (10 mm) for a new belt and ½ inch (12 mm) for an old belt.
7 Assuming access to a special gauge; turn the sleeve back to 20 divisions, hook it on the belt at mid point and turn the sleeve forward until the edge of the sleeve is on the mark on the plunger. Take the gauge off the belt and read and add together the scales (black and white) and the answer for a new belt should be 16 divisions. A used belt should read 15.5 divisions.
8 If a new belt has been fitted (of either pattern) it should be rechecked for tension after 500 miles.
9 If a 'DA' or 'XDA' belt is fitted to your car then it is suggested that a visit to the VW agent is indicated either to acquire a tester (VW210) or to have the belt checked at regular intervals. It is of course done during a diagnostic service.

4 Fan and generator - removal and replacement

1 The fan and generator have a common shaft and to separate them they must first be removed together from the engine. This involves:
a) Carburettor removal (see Chapter 3)
b) Raising the fan housing, which in turn requires removal of the thermostat as described in this Chapter.
2 Remove the fan belt (Section 3).
3 Disconnect the battery to prevent accidental short circuits and then disconnect the wires from the top of the generator. Tag the wires so that you know where to replace them (photo).
4 The generator is clamped to the pedestal by means of a metal strap. Undo the clamping bolt at the right and disengage the strap. If the engine is out of the car it is a good idea to slacken the fan nut before undoing this strap. The locking notch in the fan belt pulley can then be used to hold the shaft whilst the nut is slackened off. Put the fan belt pulley back on if you have already taken it off.
5 Undo the four bolts holding the fan cover plates to the fan housing.
6 Raise the fan housing (Section 5) and remove the generator and fan assembly from out of the fan housing and off the generator pedestal.
7 With the assembly out of the car, refit the fan belt pulley and clamp the generator body in a vice. The pulley is needed so that you can use the notch to lock the shaft whilst the fan nut is undone.
8 Once the nut has been removed the lock washer may be drawn off followed by the fan. Behind the fan is the thrust washer, spacer washers and fan hub which is keyed to the shaft.
9 The fan cover plates are held to the generator by two nuts on the ends of the generator through bolts. Note that the slot in the inner cover should face downwards when fitted to the generator, and the dished side goes into the fan housing. The purpose of the two covers is to provide a better suction point into the fan housing for cooling air drawn through the generator.
10 Reassembly and replacement should be done with care to ensure that the spacers and cover plates are correctly positioned.
a) Fit the outer cover plate onto the dynamo through bolts (photo).
b) Fit the stiffening plate (photo).
c) Fit the inner cover plate so that the peripheral slot will face the bottom of the fan housing when the generator is the right way up (photo).
d) Note the spacer ring on the dynamo shaft. If it is missing the fan hub will jam into the dynamo end cover (photo).
e) Fit the fan hub and spacer washers (photo).
f) Fit the fan to the hub (photo).
g) Replace the special lock washer and nut (photo).
11 Tighten the nut sufficiently to make sure that the hub is fully home. Then measure the gap between the fan and the cover plate which should be 2 mm (0.080 in). If any alteration is needed remove the fan from the hub and increase or reduce the number of shims. Keep spare shims behind the fan nut lock washer. Tighten the fan nut to the final torque of 43 lb ft (6 kg m).
12 Replacement of the generator/fan assembly is a reversal of the removal procedure. Take care not to distort anything and get the clamp strap and fan backplate bolts all in position before any are tightened. See that the strap fits the contours of the pedestal bracket as before. When all is tightened spin the fan to ensure that nothing is touching. If it is, the fan housing is not seated correctly or something is bent.
13 The foregoing is of course for a DC generator. For vehicles fitted with an alternator the procedure is substantially the same. However, alternators should NEVER be run with the battery disconnected. Alternators also have a negative earth system. Be careful with the battery connections. The 'DA' and 'XDA' belt will have to be checked for tension with a special meter (Section 3).

3.2 The spacers between the halves of the pulley

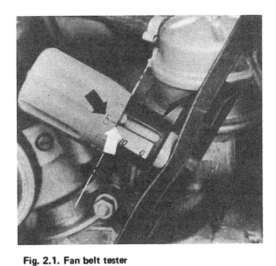

Fig. 2.1. Fan belt tester

White arrow shows leading edge in line with the mark on the plunger
Black arrow shows vernier scale

3.3 Fitting the outer half of the fan belt pulley

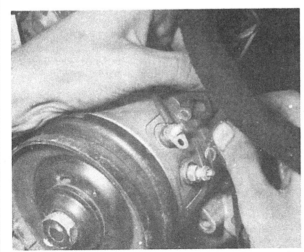

4.3 Disconnecting the rear generator connections. The second wire on the left-hand terminal goes to a radio suppressor mounted on the other end of the generator

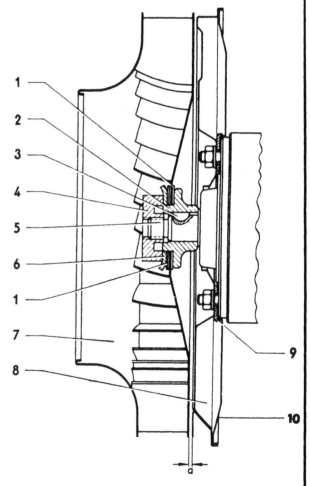

Fig. 2.2. Fan assembly - cross section

1 Spacer washers	7 Fan
2 Fan hub	8 Fan cover, inner
3 Woodruff key	9 Reinforcement flange
4 Retaining nut	10 Fan cover, outer
5 Generator shaft	A 2 mm (0.080 in.)

4.10a Fitting the fan outer cover to the generator ...

4.10b ... and the stiffening/spacer ring ...

4.10c ... and the inner cover plate

4.10d The spacer on the generator shaft

4.10e Fit the fan hub and shims ...

4.10f ... and then the fan ...

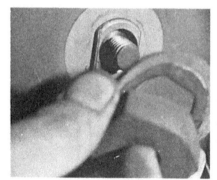

4.10g ... and secure with the lockwasher and nut

5.4 Removing the upper part of the oil cooler air duct

5.5a Removing the screw holding the lower half of the cooler outlet duct

5 Fan housing - removal and replacement

1 The fan housing may be removed with the engine installed but in addition to the items described in detail here the following must also be removed so that it may be lifted clear:

Engine compartment cover and hinges
Carburettor and air cleaner
Generator and fan

Generally speaking the only reason for removing the fan housing completely with the engine in the car would be to get at the oil cooler or the thermostatically controlled air flaps in the base of the housing. It will be appreciated that the two oil cooler cover plates and the transverse flap control rod slip will have to be removed (and replaced) blind so make yourself familiar with the layout before starting. If the fan housing is merely being raised in order to take the generator fan unit out it is not

necessary to remove the engine compartment lid and hinges

2 Slacken the generator or alternator securing strap and unscrew the thermostat bellows from the pull rod (details in next Section).

3 Slacken the two screws at each side of the fan housing.

4 Remove the nut holding the upper part of the oil cooler outlet duct to the fan housing. Once the cover is pulled clear of the stud it can be lifted out (photo).

5 The lower outlet section is held by a screw (photo). Remove this and the whole piece can be drawn out of the hole in the vertical plate through which it fits (photo).

6 Remove the fan belt.

7 Unhook the return spring on the air flap link rod across the front of the fan housing and pull off the clip holding the left end so that it can be swung clear of the oil cooler when the fan housing is raised.

8 The fan housing may be lifted partially or completely off as

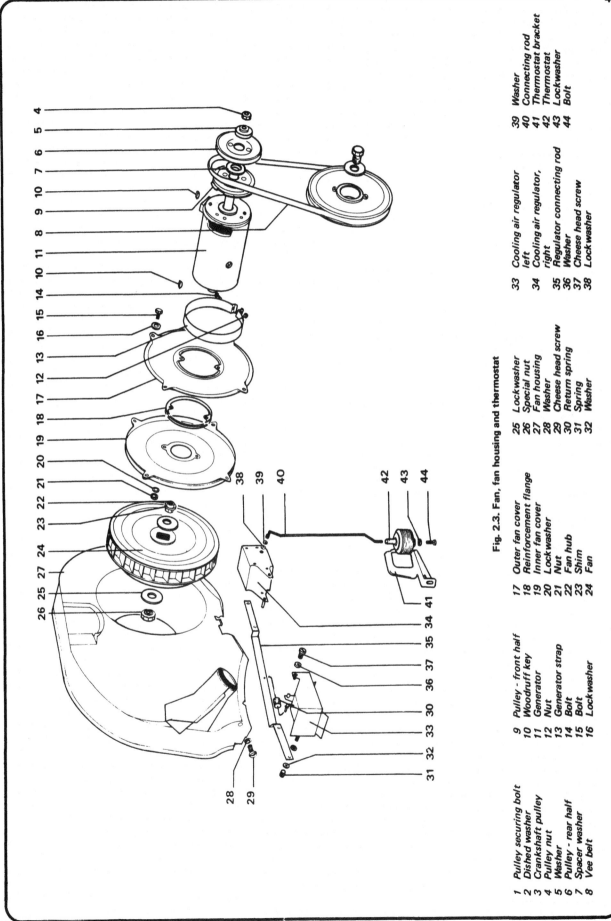

Fig. 2.3. Fan, fan housing and thermostat

1 Pulley securing bolt
2 Dished washer
3 Crankshaft pulley
4 Pulley nut
5 Washer
6 Pulley - rear half
7 Spacer washer
8 Vee belt

9 Pulley - front half
10 Woodruff key
11 Generator
12 Nut
13 Generator strap
14 Bolt
15 Bolt
16 Lockwasher

17 Outer fan cover
18 Reinforcement flange
19 Inner fan cover
20 Lockwasher
21 Nut
22 Fan hub
23 Shim
24 Fan

25 Lockwasher
26 Special nut
27 Fan housing
28 Washer
29 Cheese head screw
30 Return spring
31 Spring
32 Washer

33 Cooling air regulator left
34 Cooling air regulator, right
35 Regulator connecting rod
36 Washer
37 Cheese head screw
38 Lockwasher

39 Washer
40 Connecting rod
41 Thermostat bracket
42 Thermostat
43 Lockwasher
44 Bolt

5.5b Lifting the duct from the vertical plate

5.9 Underside of the fan housing

5.12 Lowering the fan housing into position

5.13 Guiding the thermostat rod through the cylinders

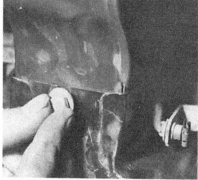

5.15 Tightening the fan housing side screws

5.16 Positioning the front plate

5.17a Replacing the rod which connects the fan housing baffle plates

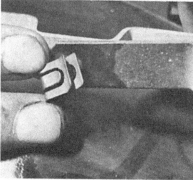

5.17b Securing the special clips ...

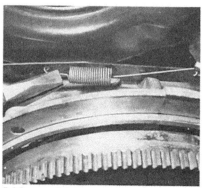

5.17c ... and the return spring

6.3 Removing the warm air duct hoses

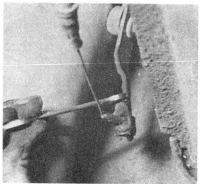

6.4 Unclamping the heat exchanger control cables

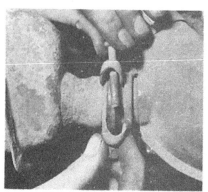

6.6a Undoing the heat exchanger rear exhaust clamp

required.

9   Whenever the fan housing is removed - for whatever reason, the opportunity should be taken to examine the condition and operation of the air flaps inside (photo). If these stick shut at any time the engine will overheat. If they are in a very poor condition and the expense of renewing them does not appeal, the best thing to do is remove them altogether. Their function is merely to shorten the warming up time and only in extremely low temperatures (well below freezing) is the engine likely to run over cold.

10 Replacement of the fan housing is the reverse of this procedure. If however, the engine is out of the car and being reassembled after an overhaul the following points should be noted.

11 Before putting the housing back onto the engine the cylinder top cover plates should be in position.

12 If the fan housing is being fitted together with the generator and fan attached, then the centre section of the inlet manifold should first be positioned. It cannot be manoeuvred between the housing and the generator pedestal afterwards (photo).

13 Continue with reassembly by carefully lowering the fan housing over the oil cooler. The pull rod for the thermostat control should go through the cylinder head aperture nearest the crankcase (photo).

14 The base of the fan housing should fit snugly inside the apertures of the cylinder cover plates. Make sure that the locating peg in the generator fits the recess in the pedestal.

15 Replace and tighten the generator or alternator securing strap and then tighten the screws at each side of the fan housing (photo).

16 If the engine is out of the car the vertical front plate should be positioned before the two oil cooler cover plates are refitted (photo). When refitting the upper oil cooler cover a little pressure will be needed to get the fixing hole over the stud.

17 Reconnect the flap connecting lever and clip. Refit the return spring (photos).

18 Refit the fan belt ensuring that it is tensioned correctly.

19 Replace the carburettor and air cleaner, and adjust the accelerator cable.

6   Heat exchangers - removal and replacement

1   Remove both the air hoses from the fan housing at the lower ends and take out the screws securing the plates round the inlet manifold pre-heater pipe. (later models have twin pipes). Take off the air cleaner pre-heater hose at the lower end.

2   Remove the securing screws and lift out the pulley cover plate (if fitted) followed by the engine rear cover plate.

3   Disconnect the warm air duct hose from the front of the heat exchanger underneath the car (photo).

4   Disconnect the control wire from the operating lever by undoing the clamping screw in the toggle (photo). This will probably be rusty and dirty so use plenty of penetrating oil otherwise you could break something which would just add to your repair list.

5   Take off the lower duct plate between the engine and the heat exchanger.

6   The front exhaust pipe flange should then be released by undoing the two nuts and the rear exhaust connection by undoing the clamp (photo). The heat exchanger inlet duct is clipped to the main exhaust silencer unit also as this has a small heat exchanger section on it. Undo this clip (photo).

7   By moving the heat exchanger forward off the front exhaust studs (photo) it will then be possible to lower and remove it.

8   Before replacing a heat exchanger it should be examined carefully for signs of splits. If it is damaged due to impact but otherwise sound it might be worthwhile having it straightened and/or welded. Otherwise fit a new one. Make sure also that the faces of the exhaust pipe flanges are perfectly flat. If they are distorted, steps must be taken to remedy the situation. Always fit new gaskets (photos).

9   The replacement of the heat exchanger is a reversal of the

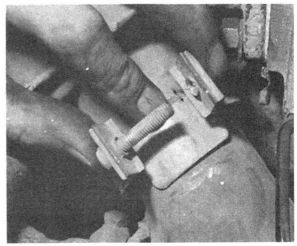

6.6b Undoing the heat exchanger sleeve clip

6.7 Drawing the heat exchanger off the front mounting studs

6.8a Fitting a new clamp gasket on the rear of the heat exchanger

6.8b Fitting on the front exhaust port connection for the heat exchanger

7.2 Undoing the thermostat bellows mounting screw

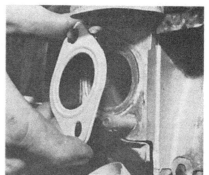

9.6a Fitting the gasket for the exhaust manifold flange on the rear of the cylinder heads

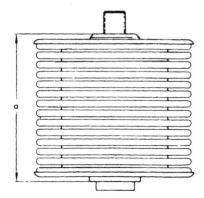

Fig. 2.4. Thermostat bellows

A = 46 mm minimum at 65 - 70º C (149 - 158º F)

9.6b Offering up the exhaust manifold

removal procedure. Make sure that when it is offered up all the joints fit true and flush before the clamps are tightened. If the nuts and clamps have to be used to force the unit into position, rather than hold it in position, stresses will be set up and something will break sooner or later. Certainly sooner than it would normally.

10 After reconnecting the control wire operate the lever to ensure that the arm moves through its full range.

7 Thermostat and controls - removal, replacement and adjustment

1 The thermostat controls flaps which restrict the air flow but do not completely obstruct it. If it should fail to operate therefore the engine will only be noticeably overheated in extreme conditions of high temperatures or hard use. The only indications of overheating are either a noticeable fall off in performance or the oil warning light indicating an exceptionally low oil pressure. It is essential to stop immediately either of these conditions appear as the engine will already have reached an undesirable state and will be seriously damaged if allowed to continue.

2 To check the operation of the flaps it is necessary to get access to the thermostat first. This is done by removing the right-hand duct plate under the cylinders. Remove the screws holding it to the heat exchanger and crankcase. The thermostat is accessible once the right-hand plate is removed. To set the flaps first remove the bolt securing the bellows to the bracket (photo). Then make sure that the bellows is screwed fully on to the operating rod. Slacken the bolt which holds the bracket to the crankcase and then push the bellows unit upwards so that the flaps are fully open. The top of the bracket loop should now just touch the top of the bellows and the bracket bolt may be tightened. Then replace the bolt securing the bellows to the

bracket (which will involve pulling the bellows down and closing the flaps if the engine is cold). If the thermostat is suspected of malfunctioning a check can be made on its length (excluding the projecting screwed bosses at each end) which should be at least 46 mm (1.8 inch) at a temperature (in water) of 65-70ºC (150-158ºF) or more. If you wish to set the thermostat so that the flaps are always open (i.e: if the bellows do not work and you have no immediate replacement) push the bellows and bracket up together into the 'flaps open' position and clamp the bracket at the raised position.

3 If the flaps themselves are suspected of jamming or being out of position on their spindles then the fan housing must first be taken off as described in Section 5. Both flap housings can be removed from the fan housing together once the eight securing screws are removed and the return spring unhooked. Examine the flaps and spindles for security and ability to stay in position. Once again, if there should be some doubt and the flaps are likely to jam shut they can be removed completely.

8 Heater exchanger controls - checking and setting

1 As previously explained the car is heated by ducting hot air from exchangers surrounding the exhaust pipes. When hot air from the exchanger is required the flap is opened so that the air pressure from the fan housing will carry it into the car. The warm air from the cylinder cooling fins has nothing to do with the heating system.

2 Should the heater efficiency drop the first thing to check is the operation of the flap control wires. These are connected to the flap operating arm on the side of the heat exchanger by means of a ferrule on the end of the wire clamped into a clevis. If the wire is broken on either side undo both. The clevis pin clamp screws are usually rusty so lubricate them well beforehand.

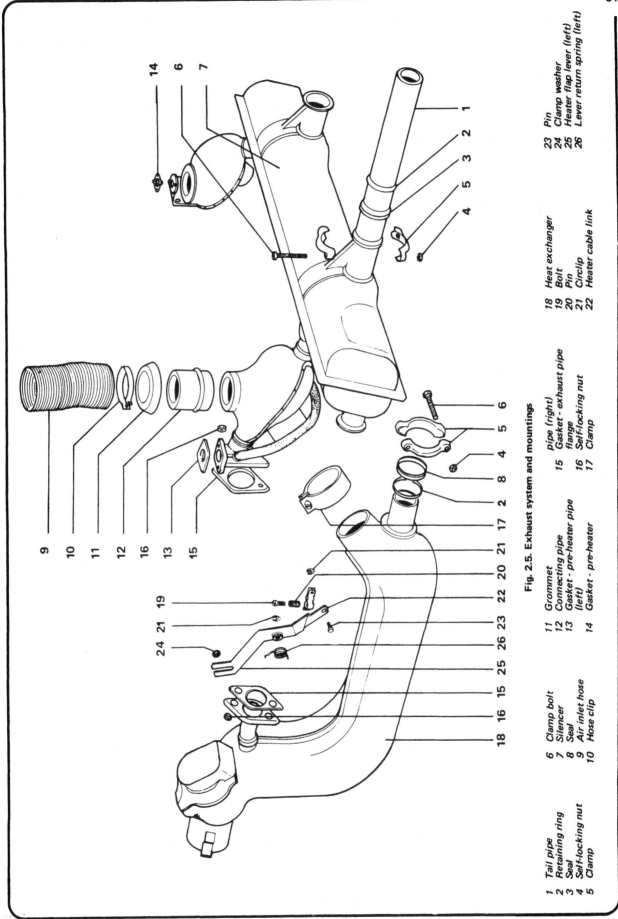

Fig. 2.5. Exhaust system and mountings

1 Tail pipe
2 Retaining ring
3 Seal
4 Self-locking nut
5 Clamp

6 Clamp bolt
7 Silencer
8 Seal
9 Air inlet hose
10 Hose clip

11 Grommet
12 Connecting pipe
13 Gasket - pre-heater pipe (left)
14 Gasket - pre-heater

15 Gasket - exhaust pipe
   pipe (right)
   flange
16 Self-locking nut
17 Clamp

18 Heat exchanger
19 Bolt
20 Pin
21 Circlip
22 Heater cable link

23 Pin
24 Clamp washer
25 Heater flap lever (left)
26 Lever return spring (left)

3 Once slackened the ends may be pulled out. Remove the plugs from the guide tubes. Inside the car remove the nut securing the right-hand operating lever, remove the friction washers and pull the lever away. Then disconnect the hooked ends of the control wires and pull them out.

4 When fitting new cables grease them first and replace them in the reverse order of removal, note that the longer of the wires goes in the lower of the two guide tubes. Replace the sealing plugs securely in the guide tubes.

5 Having clamped the cable ends onto the flap operating levers make sure that they operate through their full range.

6 Details of the control wires and flaps for the heater outlets in the rear footwell are similar in principle to the heat exchanger flaps except that the cables are joined together where they are attached to the left-hand control lever and cannot be replaced separately.

7 Access to the rear ends of the cables is by removing the rear seat and the vertical kick board in front of it. The cable end clamps can then be disconnected.

9 Exhaust system - removal, inspection and replacement

1 The Beetle exhaust and silencer is a complex unit made of heavy gauge material, which is expensive to replace. The silencer and tail pipe assembly is connected at five points on each side. These are:

a) To the exhaust pipes coming from the front of the cylinder heads through the heat exchanges (clamps).
b) To the exhaust ports on the rear of the cylinder heads (flanges).
c) To the inlet manifold pre-heater pipes (flanges).
d) To the heat exchangers (sleeve clips).
e) To the air inlet hoses from the fan housings (clips).

The exhaust manifold incorporates a small heat exchanger shrouding the upper pipes.

2 To remove the exhaust/silencer unit first remove the rear engine cover plate and the nuts, bolts and clamps which attach the assembly at the ten locations. If some of the underside nuts and bolts are badly rusted buy new ones before attempting to get the old ones off. It is quite usual for them to break or need cutting. A complete set of the gaskets should also be acquired (two exhaust flange, two inlet manifold flange, two clamp rings) before disturbing the unit.

3 Once all the connections are loosened the silencer can be drawn backwards off the studs of the cylinder head rear exhaust ports and lowered to the ground.

4 Depending on the reason for removal subsequent inspection and repair will have to be judged in the light of the seriousness of deterioration. The unit is made of heavier gauge material than more conventional exhaust systems. Thus small holes or cracks in the silencer may be patched and welded in the knowledge that the repair will last longer than on some other systems. This does not apply to the actual pipes leading into the silencer. If these are unserviceable repair is likely to be less successful. The flanges and connection to the other pipes must be examined for pitting, distortion or fractures. The mating faces of the flanges can be filed flat if necessary. The gaskets are thick enough to take up minor variations.

5 Before replacing the unit offer it up into position so that the line up of all the connection points can be made without having to strain anything. If strain is necessary to make any connection then the likelihood of a fracture developing is greatly increased. It is worthwhile taking some trouble to heat and straighten any twisted parts.

6 Replacement of the system is a reversal of the removal procedure. First put new gaskets over the studs at the rear exhaust ports (photo). Offer up the unit (photo). Put the nuts on the studs enough to prevent it falling off. The lower stud on the right-hand mounting also secures the hot air intake pipe which warms the air for the carburettor. Then assemble the lower gasket rings and clamps loosely - but sufficiently tight to prevent them becoming dislodged. Then fit the pre-heater pipe gaskets in position and replace the bolts loosely.

7 The pipe clamp and flange bolts and nuts should be progressively tightened a little at a time until fully tight. Do not overdo the tightening on any of them. Finally tighten the heat exchanger clips. After running the engine for some miles, so that it has had the opportunity to heat up and cool down a few times, recheck the connections for tightness.

10 Fault diagnosis - cooling, heating and exhaust systems

It is difficult to detect heating systems faults in a rear engined air cooled car because the tell-tale head of steam is not there to show and no temperature gauges are used. The first indications of over-heating are a falling off in power and a flickering of the oil pressure warning light. When this occurs the car must be stopped immediately.

Over-cooling is a rare experience in anything but sub-zero temperatures, even if the thermostat control was to be stuck wide open. Possible causes of overheating and heater inefficiency are tabled below.

Symptom	Reason/s	Remedy
Overheating	Slack or broken fan belt	Renew if necessary and re-adjust tension.
	Insufficient engine oil	Top up as necessary and check for leaks.
	Engine ignition timing incorrect	Reset ignition timing
	Thermostat and/or control flaps in fan housing stuck in closed position	Check operation and free as necessary.
	Oil cooler blocked	Remove, have tested and renew if necessary.
Heater ineffective	Air hoses from fan housing to heat exchanger insecure or damaged	Check hoses and secure or renew as needed.
	Air hoses from heat exchanger to car interior insecure or damaged	Check hoses and secure or renew as needed.
	Heat exchanger flaps operating control arms and/or wires jammed, broken or disconnected	Check operation of control cables and operating arms and that arms are moving the flap spindles properly.

Chapter 3 Fuel system and carburation

Contents

Air cleaner - general description	... ...	2
Air cleaner - oil bath type	... ...	4
Air cleaner - paper element type	... ...	3
Emission control equipment	... ...	12
Fault diagnosis - fuel system and carburation	... ...	13
Fuel pump - recent modifications	... ...	8
Fuel pump - cleaning filter and checking	... ...	9

Fuel tank and gauge unit	... ...	10
General description	... ...	1
Inlet manifold	... ...	11
Solex carburettor - general description	... ...	5
Solex carburettor - removal, overhaul and replacement	...	6
Solex carburettor - tests and adjustments	... ...	7

Specifications

Fuel pump:

Type	Mechanical; 'Pierburg'
Delivery rate (minimum)	400 cc/min
Pressure (maximum)	3½ pounds per square inch

Air cleaner:

Early models	Oil bath; metal body
Later models	Dry paper element; plastic body

Carburettors:

	1300 engine	1600 engine
Type	Solex 31 PICT 4	Solex 34 PICT 3 or 4 *
Venturi diameter	25.5 mm	26 mm
Main jet	130	127.5 (130) **
Air correction jet	110Z	75 (60) **
Pilot jet	100	55 (55/20) **
Auxiliary fuel jet	45	42.5
Auxiliary air jet	130	90
Injection capacity (cm^3 per stroke)	1.35 to 1.65	1.45 ± 0.15 cc
Thickness of washer under float needle valve	1.5 mm	0.5 mm
Float weight	8.5 grams	8.5 grams
Idling speed rpm	750/900	
Ignition setting		5º a tdc (7.5º b tdc)

Check the specifications for 34 PICT/4 with the local agent. The settings will vary with locality.

** *Figures given are USA PICT/3 with UK in brackets where different.*

1 General description

The fuel tank is situated in the front luggage compartment and supplies fuel, via a pipe running the length of the vehicle, to the mechanical pump mounted on the crankcase. The pump is operated by a pushrod which bears on a cam on the distributor drive shaft.

A fixed, single choke downdraught carburettor is fitted which incorporates a strangler, electrically operated, an accelerator pump of the diaphram type, thermostatically controlled, and an electromagnetic cut off valve - the latter to stop fuel entering the system when the ignition is switched off. This is because an overheated engine will continue to run after the ignition has been switched off.

The rules governing emission control vary so much that it is not possible to cover the complete subject in this manual. Details of those modifications made to fit the USA/California rules to date are included but by the time this is in print they may be altered again. Owners are advised to consult with the VW agent concerning this subject.

2 Air cleaners - general description

1 The Super Beetle (UK) will most certainly be equipped with a dry paper cartridge air cleaner housed in a plastic casing on top of the carburettor.

2 The Super and basic Beetle (USA) may have either a paper cartridge or an oil bath type of air cleaner.

3 The functions of both types are identical but should it be necessary to replace an oil bath type with a paper type then the oil filter and breather, plus the connecting hose must also be changed due to the larger cross-section of the crankcase breather.

3 Air cleaners - removal, servicing and replacement - paper element type

1 To remove and clean the paper element type air cleaner the assembly must be removed from the engine.

Pull off the smaller hoses noting which end fitted where to make assembly easier. Slacken the clips holding the inlet air hose and remove the hose. Undo the screw which holds the strap from the air cleaner to the carburettor and lift the cleaner away from the engine (photos).

2 Undo the four spring clips holding the element together and open the plastic casing (photo). Take out the element and either replace it or turn it so that the side which traps the dust is underneath and shake out the dust.

3 Under no circumstances attempt to clean the filter with fluids.

4 Replacement is the reverse of removal. Make sure all the hoses are fitted securely.

5 The warm air control flap may be checked while the filter is out. There is no method of repair; if it is not functioning correctly the unit must be replaced (photo).

4 Air cleaners - removal, servicing and replacement - oil bath type

1 To check the level of the oil in the filter bowl it is necessary only to undo the clips securing the top cover and lift it off. The oil should be in line with the mark. At the same time the sludge deposits can be ascertained by dipping a suitable probe into the oil. The oil should be no less than 4-5 mm (3/16 inch) deep above any sludge.

2 To remove the sludge the lower half of the unit should be removed from the carburettor.

3 To do this slacken the clip at the base of the cleaner and undo and remove the screw holding the strap to the carburettor mounting (photo). Then detach the hoses and lift the cleaner up and off (photo). Take care not to spill the oil and do not strain the neck of the lower half which fits on to the carburettor. This can easily be fractured with the result that oil will then leak out all over the carburettor.

4 Empty out the old oil and flush away the sludge with paraffin.

5 It will be noted that there are two flaps on the air cleaner intake. On early models, one of the flaps is held closed when the engine is not running, by means of a weight.

6 The operation of the weighted flap is as follows. At idling speed it is shut so that the crankcase emission will be more readily drawn off through the vent pipe. At higher engine speeds the air stream opens the valve and the vacuum created in the intake pipe itself draws off the crankcase emission gases.

7 The other flap is thermostatically controlled and ensures that all air drawn into the cleaner comes from round No 1 and 2 cylinders via the pre-heat hose (photo). The cylinders warm up very quickly and as soon as the air temperature through the cleaner has reached 27.5°C (81°F) the flap will start to open admitting cool air in from the other inlet. At 32.5°C (90°F) the heated air supply is completely shut off. The operation of the flap can be observed when the engine is both hot and cold. Later models were fitted with a warm air inlet flap controlled by both temperatures and inlet manifold vacuum (Fig. 3.1) As the temperature of incoming air rises so the thermostatically controlled valve in the air cleaner opens the valve and permits manifold depression thereafter to control the air inlet flap by means of a diaphragm. This means therefore that the flap position may alter even after the engine has warmed up - the cooler air coming in at large throttle openings and the warmer air at small throttle openings. This arrangement is an improvement on the earlier system.

8 In very dusty conditions the build-up of sludge will occur more quickly and may require more frequent cleaning out. The intake flaps will also tend to get caked with deposits and the whole intake unit should be thoroughly flushed in paraffin.

3.1a Undo the screw holding the air cleaner clamp ...

5 Solex carburettors - general description

The carburettor is basically a tube through which air is drawn into the engine by the action of the pistons and en route fuel is introduced into the air stream in the tube due to the fact that the air pressure is lowered when drawn through the 'tube'.

The main fuel discharge point is situated in the 'tube' - choke is the proper name for the tube to be used from now on - between two flaps - operated by tha accelerator pedal and positioned at the engine end of the choke tube. The other is the strangler - which is operated by an automatic device.

When the engine is warm and running normally the strangler is wide open and the throttle open partially or fully - the amount of fuel/air mixture being controlled according to the required speed.

When cold the strangler is closed - partially or fully and the suction therefore draws more fuel and less air, ie. a richer mixture to aid starting a cold engine.

At idling speeds the throttle flap is shut so that no air and fuel can get to the engine in the regular way. For this there are separate routes leading to small holes in the side of the choke tube, on the engine side of the throttle flap. These 'bleed' the requisite amounts of fuel and air to the engine for slow speeds only.

The fuel is held in a separate chamber alongside the choke tube and its level is governed by a float so that it is not too high or low. If too high it would pass into the choke tube without suction. If too low it would only be drawn in at a higher suction than required for proper operation.

The main jet which is simply an orifice of a particular size through which the fuel passes, is designed to let so much fuel flow at particular conditions of suction (properly called depression) in the choke tube. At idling speed the depression draws fuel from orifices below the throttle which has passed through the main jet and after that a pilot jet to reduce the quantity further.

Both main and pilot jets have air bleed jets also which let in air to assist emulsification of the eventual fuel/air mixture.

The strangler flap is controlled by an electrically operated bi-metal strip. This consists of a coiled bi-metal strip connected to the choke flap spindle. When the ignition is switched off the coiled metal strip is cold and the flap is shut. When the ignition is switched on current flows through the strip which heats up and uncoils - opening the choke flap after some minutes. If anything should go wrong with this electrical arrangement the flap will return to the closed position.

3.1b ... and lift the cleaner away from the engine

3.2 Open the plastic casing and take out the element

3.5 Check that the flap works freely

4.3a Air cleaner securing clamp screws

4.3b Disconnect the air cleaner pre-heater hose and crankcase ventilation hose

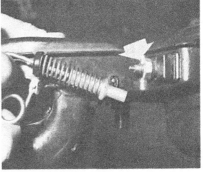

4.7 With the warm air flap control spring pulled off the thermostat unit (arrow) is accessible

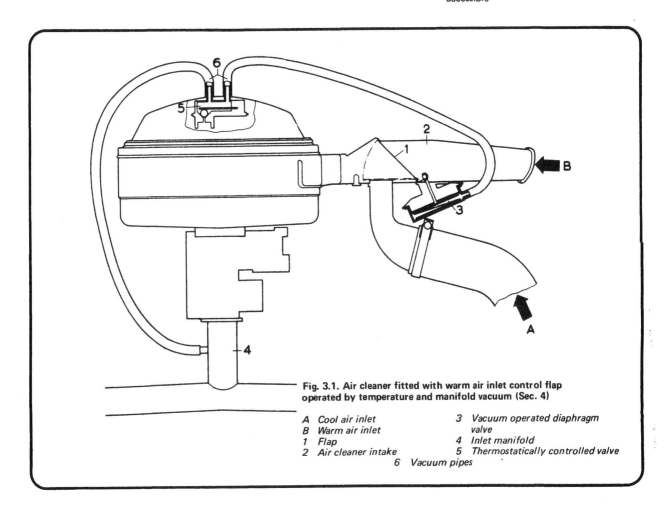

Fig. 3.1. Air cleaner fitted with warm air inlet control flap operated by temperature and manifold vacuum (Sec. 4)

A Cool air inlet
B Warm air inlet
1 Flap
2 Air cleaner intake
3 Vacuum operated diaphragm valve
4 Inlet manifold
5 Thermostatically controlled valve
6 Vacuum pipes

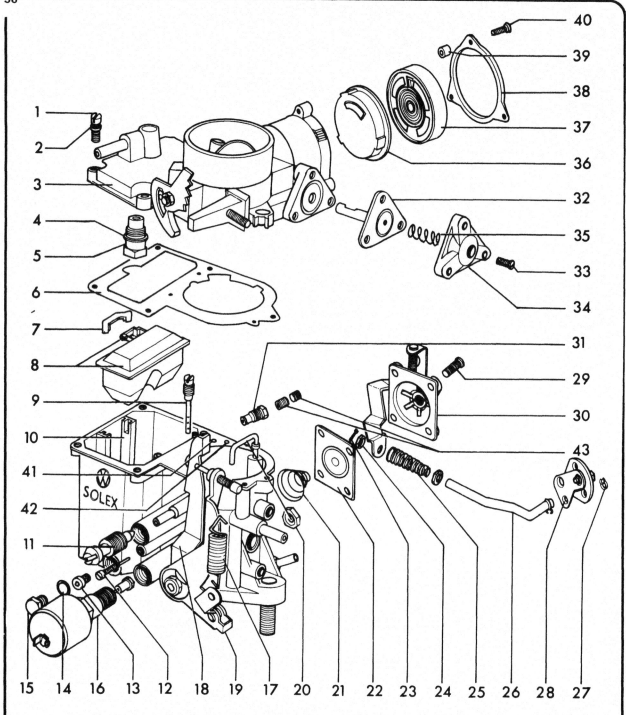

Fig. 3.2. Carburettor - Solex 31/34 PICT 3/4 - exploded view

Note 1.   The difference between 31 & 34 is in the pilot jet position angled on the 31 PICT
Note 2.   The difference between Mark 3 and Mark 4 is the addition of the thermostatically controlled accelerator pump valve. Not shown on this drawing - see Fig. 3.3.

1 Cover screw	12 Idle mixture control screw	23 Split pin	35 Spring
2 Spring washer	13 Main jet	24 Washer	36 Protection cap
3 Top cover	14 Washer	25 Spring	37 Heater coil and insert
4 Needle valve washer	15 Plug	26 Connecting link	38 Retaining ring
5 Needle valve	16 Electromagnetic cut off valve	27 Circlip	39 Spacer
6 Gasket	17 Return spring	28 Bell crank lever (adjustable)	40 Screw
7 Float pin bracket	18 Fast idle lever	29 Countersunk screw	41 Pilot air jet
8 Float and pin	19 Throttle lever	30 Pump cover	42 Auxiliary air jet
9 Air correction jet and emulsion tube	20 Injection pipe from accelerator pump	31 Pilot jet	43 Auxiliary fuel jet and plug
10 Carburettor lower housing	21 Diaphragm spring	32 Vacuum diaphragm	
11 By-pass air screw	22 Accelerator pump diaphragm	33 Countersunk screw	
		34 Diaphragm cover	

With the flap closed there are two features which partially open it immediately the engine starts. The flap spindle is offset so one side tends to turn around the spindle under the depression in the choke tube. Also there is a diaphragm valve connected to another rod attached to the flap spindle. Depression in the choke tube also operates this. If these devices did not exist no air at all would get through with the fuel. This would then flood the engine.

Finally there is another device - an accelerator pump. This is another diaphragm operated pump which is directly linked to the accelerator controls. When sudden acceleration is required the pump is operated and delivers neat fuel into the choke tube. This overcomes the time lag that would otherwise occur in waiting for the fuel to be drawn from the main jet.

On the latest version of the carburettor (PICT 31/4 or PICT 34/4 the accelerator pump has a thermostatically controlled bypass valve which allows the pump to inject more petrol on acceleration when the carburettor body is cold than it does above this temperature thus improving performance when the engine is cold. The accelerator pump linkage has also been modified) (Fig. 3.3).

The fuel in the float chamber is regulated at the correct height by a float which operates a needle valve. When the level drops the needle is lowered away from the entry orifice and fuel under pressure from the fuel pump enters. When the level rises the flow is shut off. The pump delivery potential is always greater than the maximum requirement from the carburettor.

Another device fitted is an electro-magnetic cut-off jet. This is a somewhat unhappy feature which is designed to positively stop the fuel flow when the engine is stopped. Otherwise the engine tends to run on - even with the ignition switched off - when the engine is hot.

6 Solex carburettor - removal, overhaul and replacement

1 The carburettor should not be dismantled without good reason. The old fashioned idea of having a check round should be forgotten. Any alteration in carburettor or ignition settings will change the chemical composition of the exhaust gas emission, and may cause the owner to offend against Statutory Regulations. Moreover, some of the settings need to be checked with special equipment.

However, the float chamber may be detached, the float and needle valve examined, and the jets cleaned, without upsetting any adjustments. The level of the fuel in the float chamber may also be checked and adjusted.

Clean the carburettor as far as possible before it is removed from the car and lay out a clean sheet of paper on the bench plus some containers for the bits and pieces. Keep a notebook ready to put down points to remember. Always work with clean hands and do not use fluffy rag to clean the carburettor.

2 Remove the air cleaner and then detach the accelerator cable from the throttle control lever. Undo the screw which holds the

Fig. 3.3. Modified accelerator pump linkage as fitted to carburettor with thermostatically controlled accelerator pump inlet (Sec. 5)

cable end to the link, withdraw the cable and remove the link so that it does not fall out and get lost. Pull off the wire connection clips from the automatic choke and electro-magnetic cut-off.

3 Undo the two nuts which hold the carburettor to the inlet manifold and lift the carburettor off (photo). The exterior of the carburettor should be clinically clean before dismantling proceeds.

4 The first stage of dismantling should be to remove the screws holding the top of the base. Separate the two halves carefully and remove the paper gasket taking care to keep it from being damaged. It can be re-used (photo).

5 To clean out the float chamber, remove the float pin bracket and the float can then be taken out. Do not under any circumstances strain it in such a way that the pin or bracket are bent. When the float is removed the bowl may be flushed out and sediment removed with a small brush.

6 The needle valve is screwed into the top cover and when taking it out note the washer mounted underneath it (photo). The simplest way to check this for leaks is to try blowing through it. It should not be possible to do so when the plunger is lightly pushed in. If in doubt, then renew the assembly, as a leaking valve will result in an over-rich mixture with consequent loss of performance and increased fuel consumption.

7 The accelerator pump diaphragm may be examined when the four cover securing screws and cover have been removed. Be careful not to damage the diaphragm. Renew it if there are signs of holes or cracks which may reduce its efficiency.

The accelerator pump valve and thermostat are not repairable. It should be tested as in Section 7 and, if faulty,

6.3 Lifting the carburettor from the manifold

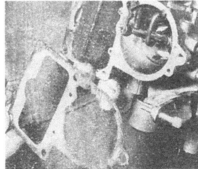

6.4 Lower half of the carburettor showing the gasket

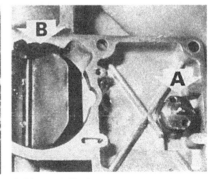

6.6 Upper half of the carburettor. Note needle valve A and strangler flap B

replaced.

8 The electric automatic strangler may be removed for cleaning but do not use petrol on the cover. If any part is suspected of malfunction the whole unit must be renewed. When refitting the bi-metal spring the looped end must be positioned so that it hooks over the end of the lever. Then the cover should be turned so that the notch lines up with the notch on the carburettor. Do not overtighten the securing screws.

9 The main jet is situated behind a hexagonal headed plug in the base of the float chamber. This can of course be removed without taking the carburettor off the car. Remove the plug and then unscrew the jet from behind it with a screwdriver. The pilot jet is fixed similarly in the body alongside the accelerator pump housing. When cleaning these jets do not use anything other than air pressure. Any poking with wire could damage the fine tolerance bores and upset the fuel mixtures. The electro-magnetic cut-off valve may be simply unscrewed from the carburettor body (photo). Do not grip the cylinder when doing so - use a suitable spanner. Never clamp the valve or carburettor body in a vice.

10 The air correction jet and emulsion tube is mounted vertically in the body of the carburettor by the side of the choke tube. This too may be unscrewed for cleaning. Blow through the passageway in the carburettor also when it is removed.

11 Before reassembly check that the float is undamaged and unpunctured. It can be checked by immersion in hot water.

12 If the throttle flap spindle should be very loose in its bearings in the main body of the carburettor then air may leak past and affect the air to fuel ratio of the mixture. In such cases the easiest remedy is a new carburettor. An alternative is to drill and fit bushes to suit but this needs expertise and time.

13 Reassembly is a reversal of the dismantling procedure but the following points should be watched carefully (photo). Do not forget the washer when replaceing the needle valve. Make sure that the gasket between body and cover is correctly positioned. When refitting the accelerator pump cover, the screws should be tightened with the diaphragm centre pushed in. This means holding the operating lever out whilst the screws are tightened. Do not bend or distort the float arm when replacing it into the float chamber. When reconnecting the accelerator cable take heed of the procedure given at the end of the next Section.

14 If a throttle valve positioner is fitted read about the details in Section 12 on emission control.

15 Do not forget to replace the air cleaner stay bracket.

7 Solex carburettor - tests and adjustments

1 It must be emphasized that if the engine is running smoothly and performance and fuel consumption are satisfactory there are no adjustments that will materially improve any of these conditions beyond the manufacturer's specifications. If the engine is not performing as it should, be sure to check the ignition system before assuming that the carburettor is the cause of the trouble.

2 Assuming all components are clean and in good condition there are only two adjustments that can be made - these being the fuel level in the float chamber and the slow running speed.

3 To check the fuel level the carburettor must be fitted to the engine. The car should be standing on a level surface. Run the engine and then switch it off and remove the fuel line from the carburettor.

4 Remove the air cleaner assembly and then take out the five screws securing the upper half of the carburettor to the lower. Put a finger over the fuel inlet pipe (to prevent the little fuel in the top cover coming out when the top is lifted) and take off the top cover and gasket.

5 The level of the fuel - with the float in position - can be measured by using a depth gauge or by placing a straight edge across the top of the float chamber and measuring down with a suitable rule. Do not measure too near the edge as capillary action up the side of the chamber could cause a false reading. If the level is incorrect it may be altered by fitting a washer of a different thickness under the needle valve which is screwed into the top cover. Washers are available in a range of thicknesses from 1/2 to 1 1/2 mm (it can be seen that the fuel level measurement has to be taken fairly accurately to be of any use in deciding whether alteration is necessary). If the level in the chamber needs raising a thinner washer should be fitted and vice versa. If you are tempted to try and alter the level by bending the bracket on the float - forget it. It cannot be done accurately enough to be of any use and more often than not the result of such attempts is either breakage or distortion. In the latter case the net result is a sticking float which gives you more problems than you had to start with.

6 While the cover is removed check the condition of the needle valve as given in Section 6:6.

7 The thermostat and valve for the accelerator pump present a difficult task to check. For the PICT 31/4 the valve should be closed at temperatures below 16°C (60.5°F) and for the PICT 34/4 at 23°C (73.5°F). Above these temperatures it should be open. The only way the author can suggest is to immerse the valve and thermostat in water at the correct temperature and by blowing through the valve ascertain that it does open at the right temperature. If it doesn't then it must be replaced.

8 Reassemble the top cover with the gasket the right way round, reconnect the fuel line and clip it and replace the air cleaner.

6.9 Removing the electro magnetic fuel cut off valve

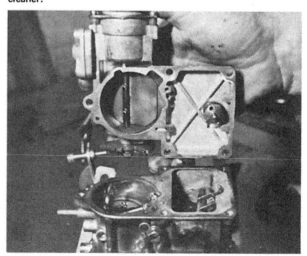

6.13 Reassembling the two halves of the carburettor

9 The next item to check is the slow running adjustment. This can be done only when the engine is warm and the strangler flap fully open.

10 Screw out the throttle stop screw (Fig. 3.5) until a gap exists between the end of the screw and the fast idle cam. Now screw it back until it just touches the cam. Now screw it in 1/4 of a turn further.

11 Leave the throttle stop screw alone from this point onwards. Screw in the volume control screw gently as far as it will go and then screw it out 3 turns. Start the engine and set the speed to 900 rpm with the bypass screw. Now turn the volume control screw in, or out, to get the highest engine speed possible by this adjustment. Now turn the screw inwards until the revs drop, by about 20 rpm. This has now set the volume control screw.

12 Finally adjust the bypass screw until the engine speed is set at 800-900 rpm.

13 If the accelerator cable connection has been disturbed then it must be reset to ensure that when the accelerator pedal is fully depressed the throttle is at maximum opening, and no further strain can be put on the throttle valve spindle.

Two people are required for this check. First disconnect the throttle lever return spring, move the lever to the fully open position and come back about 1 mm (1/32 inch). The cable should be loose in the clamp. Press the accelerator pedal to the floor and reclamp the cable. Check the operation of the throttle and the setting of the stopscrew as in paragraph 10, of this Section.

14 A recent innovation enables the amount of petrol injected by the accelerator pump to be measured but it requires special tools which are not likely to be available to the owner-driver.

The kit consists of a special pipe which may be fitted to eject the output of the pump into a measured cylinder. The amount should be 1.7 cc below 20ºC or 1.1 cc above 20ºC both critical to 0.15 cc per stroke. Adjustment is carried out by turning the screw shown in Figure 3.6. It is felt this kit is best left to the VW Agent.

15 New regulations in California, USA state there must be provision for means to close the throttle should the cable break. This has been done by fitting a flat coil spring, Fig. 3.7. It is not shown on Fig. 3.12 which is PICT 34/3.

Fig. 3.4. Thermostatically controlled fuel valve (A) fitted to SOLEX PICT 31/34/4 shown removed from the carburettor body (Sec. 7)

Fig. 3.5. Carburettor adjustment points (Sec. 7)

A Throttle stop screw on strangler cam in open position
B By-pass air screw
C Idle mixture adjustment screw (volume control screw)

Fig. 3.6. The adjusting screw which controls the amount of petrol injected by the accelerator pump (Sec. 7)

Fig. 3.7. The flat coil spring fitted to close the throttle should the cable break (Sec. 7)

8 Fuel pump - recent modifications

1   Early models of the Super and basic Beetle (USA) may have the old fuel pump with a separate cutoff valve (photo). In late 1972 the cutoff valve was incorporated in the pump.

2   Apart from the fact that there is no external cutoff valve the only way to tell the difference between the two types is by the number stamped on the stem. Old models have "VW,15", new ones "PE 20,000". (Fig. 3.8).

3   The interior is different however. This is shown in Fig. 3.9 and detailed in Section 9.

4   In 1973 with the introduction of the alternator yet another type of pump appeared which is angled so that it can fit on the casing but make room for the alternator. This is shown in Fig 3.10. The interior is the same as for the old pump but the pushrod length has been modified from 108 mm (4.2520 inches) to 100 mm (3.9370 inches). The angle of inclination of the pump is 15° to the left.

9 Fuel pump - cleaning filter and checking

1   The pump cannot be dismantled other than for the cleaning of the filter. Refer to Fig. 3.9. The screw is removed from the cover and the cover lifted from the body. It is not necessary to remove the hose unless you wish to take the pump away from the engine.

2   Carefully lift out the filter element - the sealing ring will probably come with it (photo). If it does not, then do not disturb it. Blow the sediment out of the gauge, and wash the filter in clean petrol. Make certain there are no holes (other than the mesh perforations) and replace the filter. If there is any doubt about it then get a new filter. Refit the top.

3   It is as well to check the pump delivery. Pull off the petrol hose from the carburettor, spin the engine on the starter and petrol should come out from the hose in spurts. If it does not, then either the cutoff valve, or the pump is faulty. On the old type of pump the external cutoff valve may be replaced and then all may be well, if it isn't then the pump must be replaced. If a new type pump is fitted then the complete pump must be replaced if delivery is faulty.

4   Do not allow the petrol to spray out over the engine, catch it in a container.

5   The only other check that can be done is to measure the protrusion of the pushrod. It is hardly likely that this will alter, but if the fuel pump gives continual trouble, regularly punctured diaphragms or starvation, then it is possible that the pushrod is at fault. Take off the pump and measure the protrusion of the pushrod (photos) above the distance piece. It should be 13 mm

8.1 Old type fuel pump with external cut off valve

9.2 Removing the filter from the petrol pump

9.5a Removing the fuel pump

9.5b The fuel pump actuating rod

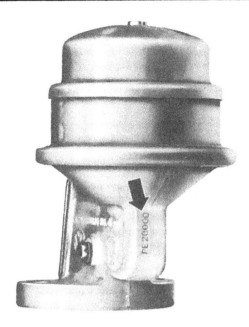

Fig. 3.8. Fuel pump with built-in cut off valve. The arrow points to the part number P.E. 20000 (Sec. 8)

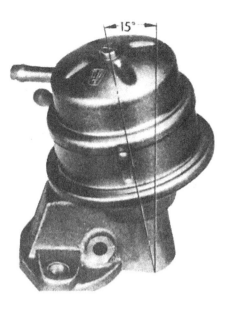

Fig. 3.10. Exterior of fuel pump as fitted to some models with alternators (Sec. 8)

Fig. 3.9. Comparison of the fuel pump with the built-in cut off valve (left) and the older pattern (right) (Sec. 8)

(0.512 inch) at maximum protrusion. Turn the engine to get full protrusion. Adjustment is by putting more or less gaskets between the flange and the distance piece - but this should not be necessary; so if you have trouble of this kind, seek expert advice. The length of the pushrod is, of course, vital so check that it is either 100 mm or 108 mm (3.937 or 4.252 inches).

6 If the pump has been removed be careful when replacing it that all mating surfaces are clean and smear a little grease on the metal ones before tightening down.

10 Fuel tank and gauge unit transmitter

1 The fuel tank is mounted in the front luggage compartment. An electrically operated sender unit controlled by floats in the tank is mounted in the top.
2 Access to the tank is obtained by first removing the fibre board trim.
3 If the fuel gauge is not working first bridge the two terminals on the tank unit. If there is a reaction on the dashboard gauge then the tank unit is faulty. Otherwise the gauge is faulty or the wires leading to it are broken.
4 If it is wished to remove the gauge unit it is now unfortunately necessary to remove the fuel tank. This is because the fresh air box which is now welded to the bulkhead gets in the way. Remove the tank as described in paragraph 7 below and having disconnected the wiring turn the sender unit anticlockwise to undo the bayonet fitting and withdraw the whole unit with its floats (photo).
5 If the floats are punctured or the contact wiper blade on the rehostat is not making contact it may be possible to rectify the trouble but do not expect to be able to buy individual parts. Improvisation will be needed otherwise the whole unit should be renewed.
6 The fuel tank is provided with twin vent pipes at each side

which lead into an activated carbon filter unit behind the ventilation duct inlet (photo). This is designed to filter out the harmful elements of evaporating fuel.
7 If the tank is to be removed for any reason the level of fuel should first be low enough to prevent any fuel leakage when the vent pipes are disconnected. If necessary it can be siphoned out from the filler neck. With the vent pipes and filler neck disconnected remove the four holding down screws. Lift the tank a little so that the flexible outlet pipe connection is accessible. This can then be pulled off and held whilst the tank is taken off. The rest of the fuel can then be drained off.

11 Inlet manifold - removal, inspection and replacement

1 The inlet manifold is in three sections. Each outer section fits inside the ends of the centre section and there is a rubber sealing boot over each connection held by hose clips. The outer sections are each twin branch leading to the twin port head.
2 It is not practicable to remove the inlet manifold either in part or in whole with the engine installed in the car.
3 When removing the inlet manifold with the engine removed from the car the fan housing will have to be taken off before the centre section can be taken out (photo). There is no way to get it out from between the fan and generator pedestal. It is secured by a lug to the crankcase.
4 The end sections are held to the cylinder heads by two nuts on studs (photo).
5 It is important that the mating faces of the flanges to the cylinder head are smooth and undistorted. Also there should be no signs of cracks or holes in the rest of the manifold. The rubber boots must be in perfect condition also (photo).
6 When replacing the manifolds always use new gaskets for the cylinder heads (photo). See that the joining surfaces are quite clean. Jointing compound must not be used.
7 Reassemble all three sections loosely at first and get the rubber boots in position over the joints (photo). Tighten down

10.4 The fuel gauge transmitter unit

10.6 The filler pipe and the pipe leading away to the charcoal filter. There is a similar pipe on the other side of the tank

11.3 Inlet manifold centre section being positioned

11.4 The manifold outer sections are held by the cylinder head studs

11.5 The sections of the inlet manifold are joined by rubber boots and clips ...

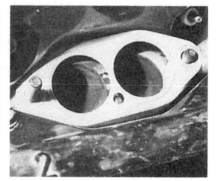
11.6 Inlet manifold gasket

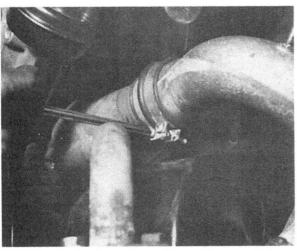

11.7 The rubber boots must be carefully positioned and not over-tightened

the end sections - taking care not to overtighten and then clamp the centre section. Finally tighten the rubber connector clips.

12 Emission control equipment

1   However carefully the metering equipment of the carburettor is designed it can only react to the different states of pressure, air speed, and temperature which occur in the inlet manifold as they occur, so there must always be a time lag. Inevitably the exactly right mixture will not arrive in the cylinders for combustion. To give good performance in the past the motto was always to "pour it in", or translated to keep the mixture on the rich side. This results in unburnt gases of a toxic nature being exhausted to the atmosphere. On the other hand if the mixture is too weak the performance suffers and the owner is dissatisfied.

The carburettor can never produce the exactly correct answer, only a close approximation to it. This is why it is essential that the ignition settings and carburettor adjustments laid down by the manufacturer should not be altered.

2   As development in this field is still continuing and the rate of official documentation must lag behind physical developments this Section can only give an indication of the moves made so far and show the primary areas and methods used to clean up emissions.

There are four main areas to deal with. These are :
a) Burning of the fuel in all engine running conditions to keep unburnt hydrocarbons to a minimum.
b) Recirculation of exhaust gas to deal with unacceptable levels of emission dependent on the efficiency of the first stage.
c) Recirculation of crankcase fumes into combustion chambers.
d) Filtration of raw petroleum vented fumes from fuel tanks.

In general items c) and d) are the simplest to deal with. All modern cars - regardless of official regulations are now fitted with devices which re-circulate crankcase fumes to the inlet manifold. On the VW there is a flexible pipe from the oil filler neck to the intake duct of the air cleaner for this purpose. The fuel tank is vented through an activated filter unit as already described.

Fuel combustion relative to power output is notoriously inefficient in the internal combustion engine and is the main cause of the noxious emissions - being as they are unused components of the fuel. The fixed choke carburettor as fitted to the VW is much more difficult to modify than the variable choke variety in terms of fuel/air mixture control throughout the full range of engine speeds and load requirements. One of the principle objectives is to weaken the mixture which is always too rich in over-run situations when the throttle is shut. This is the reason for the air bypass system which enables more air to be introduced when manifold depression is high and the throttle is closed. Coupled with these carburettor modifications are ignition timing changes which positively retard the spark to aid combustion also under these conditions. The changes have been considerable and have resulted in difficulties because of effects on performance known as 'progression' problems - better known as flat spots. This manual does not go into the detail of the modifications involved because they have not yet been fully concluded. Any owner who may not be satisfied with a car's performance should refer to a VW dealer who will be able to advise the most up to date and suitable remedies. There is a cooling coil device that cools part of the exhaust gases themselves and re-circulates them via the combustion chambers. This has a beneficial effect on the resulting exhaust gas emission. It is fitted to those models where regulations are set to certain emission levels.

On the type 1 Automatic the cooling coil and cyclone filter (Fig. 3.11 parts 2 and 3) have been replaced by an element type filter to filter out coarse impurities. The new filter can be installed in older vehicles in place of the coil and cyclone filter.

The crankcase gas recirculation and the carbon filter for the fuel tank venting have already been referred to earlier. The air bypass system in the carburettor is standard on all models and is an integral part of the carburettor.

The exhaust gas recirculation device designed to reduce emission of nitrogen oxide is fitted to stickshift models in California (USA). A portion of the exhaust gases is cooled, filtered and metered back through the combustion chambers. Fig 3.11 gives an indication of the general layout.

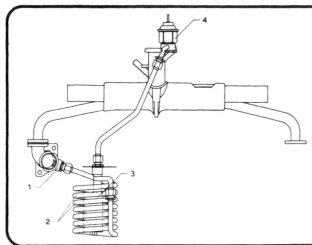

Fig. 3.11. Emission control - exhaust recirculation apparatus (Sec. 12)

1   *Left rear exhaust flange*   3   *Cyclone filter*
2   *Cooling coil*   4   *Recirculating valve*
Note: In later models 2 and 3 are replaced by an element type filter on Automatic/USA vehicles

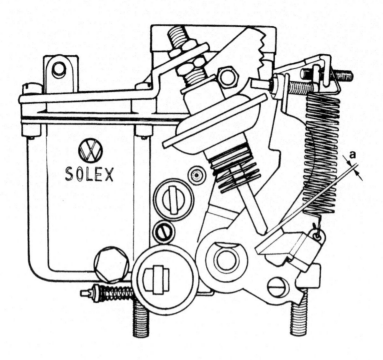

Fig. 3.12. Emission control - throttle valve return damper device (a = 1 mm) (Sec. 12)

13 Fault diagnosis - fuel system and carburation

Before acting on the fuel system it is necessary to check the ignition system first. Even though a fault may lie in the fuel system it will be difficult to trace unless the ignition is correct. The table below therefore, assumes that the ignition system is in order.

Symptom	Reason/s	Remedy
Smell of petrol when engine is stopped	Leaking fuel lines or unions Leaking fuel tank	Repair or renew as necessary. Fill fuel tank to capacity and examine carefully at seams, unions and filler pipe connections.
Smell of petrol when engine is idling	Leaking fuel line unions between pump and carburettor Overflow of fuel from float chamber due to wrong level setting or ineffective needle valve or punctured float	Check line and unions and tighten or repair. Check fuel level setting and condition of float and needle valve and renew if necessary.
Excessive fuel consumption for reasons not covered by leaks or float chamber faults	Worn jets Sticking strangler flap	Renew jets. Check correct movement of strangler flap.
Difficult starting, uneven running, lack of power, cutting out	One or more jets blocked or restricted Float chamber fuel level too low or needle valve sticking Fuel pump not delivering sufficient fuel Intake manifold gaskets leaking, or manifold fractured	Dismantle and clean out float chamber and jets. Dismantle and check fuel level and needle valve. Check pump delivery and clean or repair as required. Check tightness of mounting nuts and inspect manifold connections.

Chapter 4 Ignition system

Contents

Coil 9
Contact breaker adjustment 3
Condenser 5
Distributor - removal and replacement 4
Distributor - inspection and overhaul 6
Distributor - drive shaft 7

Examination of ignition system 2
Fault diagnosis - ignition system 10
General description 1
Ignition timing 7
Spark plugs and leads 8

Specifications

Spark plugs
Type: Temperate climate		Bosch W 145T1, Beru 135.14 or Champion L88A
Tropical climate		Bosch W 175T1, Beru 175.14
Plug thread		14 mm
Electrode gap		0.7 mm (0.028 inch)

Distributor
Type and voltage ... ...   Bosch, 12 volt
Firing order 1 4 3 2
Contact breaker points gap ... ...   0.4 mm (0.016 inch)
Dwell angle (wear limit) ... ... $42^o - 58^o$
Automatic advance ... ...   Centrifugal and vacuum

Coil
Type ... ...   Bosch, 12 volt (043905115 or 311905 115A)

Ignition timing *

Engine type and serial	Firing point setting	
1300 cc/78.3 cu in. F 0 000 001 to F2 140 820	7.5º btdc	vacuum hose off
1300 cc/78.3 cu in. AB 000 001 to AB 313 344 (double vacuum unit)	5º atdc	vacuum hose on
1300 cc/78.3 cu in. AB313 346 on	7.5º btdc	vacuum hose off speed 850 ± 50
1600 cc/96.7 cu in. B 6000 001 to B 6440 900	0º (tdc)	vacuum hose off
1600 cc/96.7 cu in. B 6000 002 to B 6440 899 (M9, double vacuum unit)	0º (tdc)	vacuum hoses on
1600 cc/96.7 cu in. AD 000 00 to 279 999 (double vacuum units)	5º atdc	vacuum hoses on
AE 000 001 to 999 999	5º atdc	vacuum hoses on
AK 000 001 on	5º atdc	vacuum hoses on
AH 000 001 on	5º atdc	vacuum hoses on
1600 cc/96.7 cu in. AD 280000 on (single vacuum units)	7.5º btdc	vacuum hose off
AK 120 009 on	7.5º btdc	vacuum hose off
AH 090 024 on	7.5º btdc	vacuum hose off

Ignition timings: These are up-to-date at the time of writing but with the continued developments going on they may alter. Check with the VW agent.

Timing marks
'V' notch in belt pulley at firing point setting at 800 — 900 rpm (stroboscope setting).

1 General description

1 A conventional 12 volt system is used employing both vacuum and mechanical advance and retard mechanisms in the distributor. The circuit diagram is shown at Fig. 4.1. The LT circuit starts with the battery under the backseat and goes, via the ignition switch on the steering column, to the coil (terminal 15), through the primary winding to terminal "1" and thence to the distributor, where it is connected to the moving arm of the distributor. When the points are closed the current flows to earth. The condenser is connected in parallel with the points.

2 The HT circuit starts at the secondary winding of the coil which is also connected to terminal "15" but leaves the coil at the centre terminal on the top, and the HT current goes, via a thick lead, to the centre of the distributor cap.

From here a spring loaded carbon brush takes the current to the rotor arm. As the rotor arm rotates the current crosses to each segment in the distributor cap in turn and thence to each plug, where a spark is produced between the centre and outside electrodes.

3 If the engine is correctly timed this will occur just as the piston is nearing TDC on the compression stroke.

All this is very elementary but it is essential to keep the principles in mind when ignition problems arise.

4 Due to different spark timing requirements under certain engine conditions (of varying speed or load) the distributor also has an automatic advance device (advancing the spark means that it comes earlier in relation to the piston position).

The spark timing is altered by two methods. One is by centrifugal force acting on bob-weights attached to the distributor cam. As these move out so the cam position is altered in relation to the distributor shaft. The second method - in addition to the first - is by vacuum from the induction manifold. Engine speed governs the centrifugal advance. Throttle opening governs the vacuum advance.

Recent developments in the field of exhaust emission control have resulted in changes in carburettor design. The traditional methods of setting up and turning the engine are somewhat changed also and it is important to understand that the settings of both carburettor and ignition timing are even more inter-dependent than they were before. Previously if one or the other was fractionally adrift no serious symptoms were apparent. This is not now the case and flat spots, poor performance and excessive fuel consumption can result if everything is not spot-on.

2 Examination of the ignition system

1 If the engine rotates but will not start then the problem resolves itself into one of four (or a combination of four) conditions:

a) There is no spark at the plugs.
b) There is a spark but not at the right time.
c) The plug sparks in vain, for there is no fuel.
d) There is no compression in the cylinder.

2 Items (c) and (d) have been dealt with in Chapters 1 and 3. Item (b) will probably be obvious because of backfiring through the carburettor or silencer because the timing arrangements have slipped causing the mixture to ignite while the valves are open.

3 The most likely cause is item (a) and this is soon tested. Remove a plug lead from the plug, bare the end of the lead by turning back the insulating cover, and hold the plug lead so that the metal end of the lead is 3 mm (1/8 inch) from the cylinder block.

Get someone to operate the starter (turn the key) and as the engine rotates there should be a nice fat blue spark between the lead and the block. If there is not there is a fault in the ignition circuit so do not go on running the battery down but get out the tools and look for the fault.

4 The most important tool is a simple voltmeter capable of measuring 12 volts. Such a meter is obtained cheaply, can be used for a very large number of jobs on the car, and will soon save its cost in garage bills. Screwdrivers and a pair of pliers, a plug spanner (get a VW special spanner), and a set of metric spanners complete the necessary tool kit.

5 To test the LT circuit first check the voltage at coil terminal "15" with the ignition switched on. No volts means a break in the wire between the coil and switch, or the switch and battery.

If the engine does not turn when the starter is operated then the battery is probably at fault so check the voltage across the terminals. It should be 12 volts. The voltage at terminal "15" should be at least 9 volts. If it is less, then there is a loose connection somewhere.

6 If the voltage at terminal "15" is satisfactory, next check the voltage at terminal "1". Before measuring this, remove the distributor cap and see whether the points are open or closed. If the points are closed the voltage at terminal "1" should be zero - because the terminal is shorted direct to earth through the points. If there is an appreciable voltage when the points are closed then there is an open circuit between terminal "1" and the contact breaker points which must be found. No voltage between terminal "1" and earth when the points are open means either a faulty coil or a faulty condenser. Disconnect the lead from terminal "1" to the distributor and try again. Zero volts (with at least 9 volts at terminal "15") indicates a faulty coil. If the coil is in order then reconnect the lead and check again. Zero voltage this time indicates a short circuit in the condenser, which must be replaced; or a short circuit in the wiring between the terminal "1" and the contact breaker points which must be cleared.

7 The LT circuit is correct so now check the contact breaker points. When open there should be a gap of 0.4 mm (0.016 inches) and the point's surfaces should be clean. The method of setting is discussed in this Chapter later on (Section 3). Make sure this setting is correct and then with the knowledge that the LT circuit is in order preceed to test the HT circuit. First of all, repeat the plug lead test as in paragraph 3. If there is still no spark then a methodical examination of the HT circuit is indicated.

8 The checking of the HT circuit is a little more difficult. Because of the high voltage (15 - 20 KV) it is not possible to use a voltmeter. Remove the HT lead from the centre of the distributor, hold it near the cylinder block and spin the engine with the starter. There should be a fat spark. No spart means either a faulty HT winding in the coil, a faulty lead, or more probably a faulty connection at terminal "4". Check the lead and the connection. If they are alright then the coil should be taken to the agent for checking and possible replacement. The agent will test the coil under load on a special appliance which involves measuring 18 KV, which the normal owner cannot do.

9 If there is a fat spark then HT is getting to the distributor and the fault is probably here. Check the seating of the centre lead in the distributor cap. Now check the small carbon bush in the cap. It is spring loaded and should make contact with the top of the rotor arm. The blade of the rotor arm should be clean and free from burns; remove any fouling with a fine file or emery paper. The segments in the cap should be equally clean. Examine the cap for 'tracking' which is usually an accumulatation of carbon dust and oil in a hair line crack, probably turned into hand carbon which will short circuit the HT and prevent functioning. Such cracks, or faulty segments, on centre bush mean a new distributor cap.

10 Finally check the plug leads. It is most unlikely that all four of them are at fault, but even one will cause hard starting and uneven running. The resistance of the lead overall should be between 5 and 10,000 ohms. Damage is nearly always obvious on the exterior.

11 Systematic checking always pays dividends. It is a good idea to check all the suggested points when the car is running well, noting the voltages at various places so that when something does go wrong the testing procedure is familiar. The author looked for an intermittent LT fault for two days only to find it was "the connection which couldn't possibly be wrong". He now practises what he preaches.

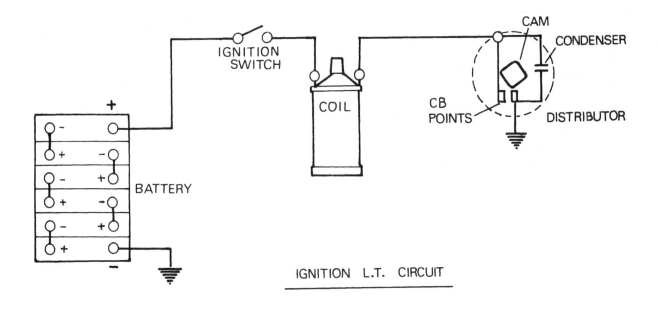

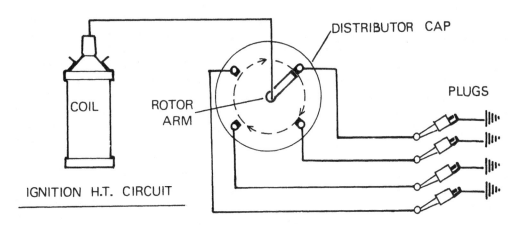

Fig. 4.1. Circuit diagram of ignition system (Sec. 2)

3 Contact breaker points - adjustment, removal and replacement

1 Volkswagen service procedures check the contact points by measuring the cam dwell with special equipment. All else being equal the correct cam dwell gives a points gap of 0.4 mm (0.016 ins). To check the gap, first remove the distributor cap by undoing the two retaining clips, and pull off the rotor arm. Remove the plastic covers (photos).

2 Push back the moving contact point against the spring just enough to see whether the surfaces of both contacts are clean and flat. If dirty, clean them with a piece of dry clean cloth. If one contact has a peak and the other a pit, it will be impossible to set them with a feeler gauge and they should be removed (as described later on) for renewal or temporary renovation until a new set can be obtained.

3 Having established that the contact faces are clean and flat turn the engine (use a spanner on the crankshaft pulley nut)

until the cam follower on the spring contact is resting on the highest point of one of the four cam lobes (photo).

4 Place a feeler gauge of the correct thickness in the points gap and if it is either tight or slack the points need adjustment. To do this slacken the screw holding the fixed point on to the mounting plate (photo). Then use the screwdriver blade in the notch to lever the fixed point plate either way as needed. It is best not to have the screw too loose when doing this. The feeler blade should slide between the two contacts, touching both but not forcing them apart.

5 When set tighten the securing screw and check the gap again to ensure the gap has not altered.

6 Replace the rotor arm and distributor cap.

7 If the points have to be removed take out the securing screw completely. Pull off the wire at the single terminal connector clip. The points assembly complete may then be lifted off the pivot post. Although it is not necessary, it is as well to understand the circuitry of the contact points, otherwist the fault tracing procedures described later are somewhat meaningless.

3.1a Remove the distributor cap ...

3.1b ... and the rotor arm ...

3.1c ... followed by the plastic cap

3.3 The distributor ready for points gap check

3.4 The feelers should just be gripped by the points

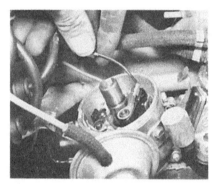
3.8 Disconnect the lead before removing the points

The fixed contact is the earth side, so it is mounted, and in contact with the distributor body itself via the base plate. The moving contact is the 'live' side and when assembled it must be insulated from earth. The current travels from the LT wire on the coil to the spring arm to the contact or condenser. The spring contact (and the wires connected to it) must be insulated from the distributor. Similarly the pivot point of the spring contact must be insulated from earth. If this is borne in mind there should be no problem. When finally assembled the two contact breaker surfaces should line up.

8 The points may be removed completely by removing the adjusting clamp screw and disconnecting the lead at the connection (photo). The whole assembly lifts out.

9 If the points are being cleaned it is best to separate the two pieces of the assembly.

10 To clean up the faces of the contacts use a very fine oil stone. Stone the two faces flat ensuring particularly that the 'peak' is completely removed. If the pit in the other contact is very deep do not try and grind it right out. The points can be adjusted once the peak is removed. Make a note to get a new set at the earliest opportunity.

11 Reassemble the two halves if separated and replace the assembly over the pivot post. Put back the securing screw but do not fully tighten it down

12 Reconnect the wires at the connector blade terminal.

13 Having re-adjusted the gap on one cam lobe it is advisable to check it on the other three also. Also check that there is not sideways play in the distribution shaft which could cause gap setting variations.

4 Distributor - removal and replacement

1 The distributor should be removed only if indications are such that it needs renewal or overhaul.

2 Take off the distributor cap and pull the LT wire which runs to the coil off the coil terminal. Detach the pipes which fit to the vacuum advance unit.

3 The distributor is held in position by a clamp which grips the lower circular part of the body. The clamp itself is held to the crankcase by a single bolt. If the bolt is removed the distributor and clamp together may be lifted out of the crankcase.

4 It must be realised that if the bolt which secures the clamp to the distributor is slackened - and the relative positions of the distributor and clamp altered - then the static ignition timing is upset.

5 The lower end of the distributor drive shaft has a driving dog with offset engagement lugs. These engage into corresponding slots in the distributor drive shaft. Being offset it ensures that the shaft cannot be inadvertently set $180°$ out of position when the distributor is replaced.

6 It is a good idea to renew the rubber 'O' ring in the annular exterior groove of the body if possible. This seal prevents oil from creeping up on the outside of the body.

7 Replacement of the distributor is a reversal of the removal procedure. See that the offset drive shaft dogs are correctly aligned otherwise they will not engage and the body will not go fully home.

5 Condenser - testing, removal and replacement

1 The condenser or capacitor as it is sometimes called, functions as a storage unit for the low tension current which flows into it when the points are closed. When the points open it discharges and sends a boost through the LT circuit to the coil. If the condenser does not function correctly the current shorts to earth across the contact points. This causes arcing and rapid deterioration of the points and also causes the spark producing

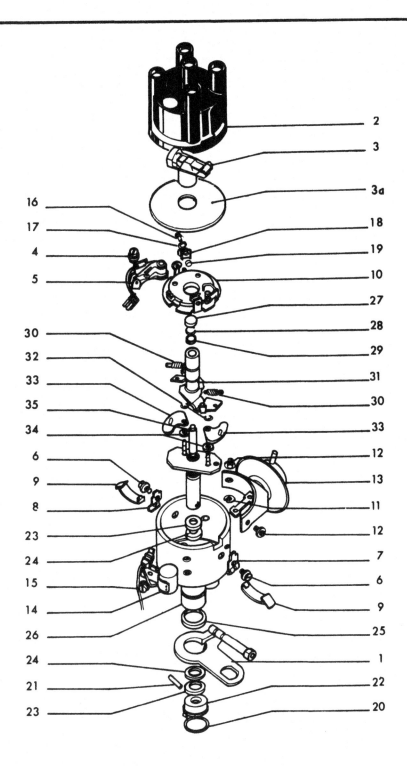

Fig. 4.2. Distributor - exploded view (Sec. 6)

1	Mounting clamp bracket	10	Contact points mounting plate	18	Retaining spring	27	Felt washer
2	Cap	11	'E' clip for pull rod	19	Ball	28	Circlip
3	Rotor	12	Screw	20	Circlip	29	Thrust ring
3a	Plastic cap.	13	Vacuum unit	21	Pin	30	Return spring
4	Contacts securing screw	14	Condenser	22	Driving dog	31	Cam
5	Contact points	15	Screw	23	Shim	32	Circlip
6	Clip screw	16	Screw	24	Fibre washer	33	Bob weights
7	Clip retainer	17	Spring washer	25	'O' sealing ring	34	Washer
8	Clip retainer			26	Distributor body	35	Driveshaft
9	Cap clip						

properties of the coil to malfunction or cease entirely. If, therefore, persistent misfiring and/or severe burning and pitting of the contact points occurs, the condenser is suspect and should be tested right away.

2   To make a simple check on the condenser remove the distributor cap and turn the engine until the contact points are closed. Then switch on the ignition and push open the points with something non-metallic. If there is a considerable spark then this confirms that the condenser is faulty. Normally there should be a very mild spark - almost invisible - across the points.

3   The condenser is mounted on the outside of the distributor and is easily removed and replaced (together with the wires and connectors) by undoing the securing screw.

6   Distributor - inspection and repair

1   If a dwell test has been done then the condition of the shaft and bushes will be known, but it is not necessary to do a dwell test specially.

2   Wear in the bushes and shaft will make it difficult to set the points accurately and affect the timing. If the shaft is worn then it is safe to assume that the bushes are also worn. The shaft may be replaced, but the bushes are not replacable, so that if there is appreciable side rock on the shaft it is best to obtain a complete replacement.

5   With the cap and plastic cover removed it is possible, with the rotor arm replaced to turn the shaft a few degrees in a clockwise direction. When released the rotor arm should return to its original position. If it does not then the centrifugal advance and retard mechanism is either very dirty or the springs have lost their tensional strength. To check this the distributor must be removed from the engine and then dismantled. Remove the distributor as in Section 4 of this Chapter.

4   To dismantle the distributor first remove the contact breaker points. Refer to Fig. 4.2.

5   The next job is to remove the driving collar from the bottom of the shaft but before doing this it is important to note which way it is fitted. See which way the driving dogs are offset in relation to the rotor arm notch in the top of the shaft. The

notch and the offset of the dogs should face the same way.

6   When the relative position is noted clamp the collar in a vice and punch out the retaining pin. The collar may then be drawn off the shaft followed by the shims which control the endfloat of the shaft in the body.

7   Carefully unhook the pullrod from the vacuum unit to the contact breaker mounting plate and after removing the screws take off the vacuum unit. Then remove the mounting plate and shaft taking note of the position of the thrust washers.

8   Carefully clean all the moving parts and reassemble the distributor in the reverse order to dismantling. Take care not to mix the springs but put them back where they came from.

9   Do not under any circumstances wash the shaft bushes in paraffin or any other solvent.

10 With the distributor reassembled hold the shaft between soft packing in a vice and once again test the centrifugal mechanism but turning the rotor and checking whether it returns to its original position, when released. If it does then the trouble was caused by dust and stickiness; if it doesn't, then the springs need renewal.

11 At this point, take the whole assembly to the agent and accept his advice. It may be possible to fit new springs but the unit should be tested. It is unlikely that this trouble will bother the more recent Beetle model for sometime yet and if it does it is suggested that a lot of time and frustration may be avoided by fitting a replacement unit right away.

7   Ignition timing and distributor drive shaft

1   In the 'Description' Section of this Chapter it was pointed out that the ignition timing and carburettor setting was a little more critical than on earlier models. It is a good idea when this method is used to get hold of someone experienced who has some idea of what the idling speed (800-900 rpm) sounds like. Provided the carburettor is set correctly to start with (Chapter 3) progressive setting changes at the distributor will achieve the desired results. If you can obtain a strobe light and a tachometer for temporary hook up you will save a lot of time. You will also be sure that the settings are spot-on first time. The main point to

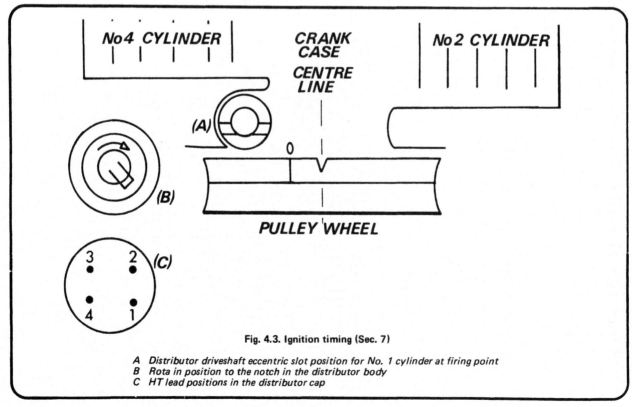

Fig. 4.3. Ignition timing (Sec. 7)

A   Distributor driveshaft eccentric slot position for No. 1 cylinder at firing point
B   Rota in position to the notch in the distributor body
C   HT lead positions in the distributor cap

remember is that having set it all up stationary and being delighted when the engine starts first time there will almost certainly be further adjustments necessary. If the pull away through the gears seems a bit 'flat' nudge the distributor more to advance (anticlockwise). If the engine fluffs a bit in the lower revolutions and then zooms away as the revs increase then back it off a little.

These tips are given here because the setting procedures given in the following paragraphs are precise - only when they have been done should you carry out any final 'sweetening'. There should be little need to alter the timing except in cases of engine overhaul or distributor overhaul.

2 If the timing has to be reset from scratch the distributor should be removed first so that the distributor drive shaft position may be verified and set as required.

3 The distributor drive shaft may be removed and installed with the engine assembled and in the car provided that the distributor, fuel pump and fuel pump intermediate flange have first been removed. (The distributor drive shaft also drives the fuel pump pushrod from a face cam incorporated on the shaft.) If the engine is being reassembled after overhaul the drive shaft should be refitted after the oil pump, lower cover plate and crankshaft pulley have been refitted.

4 To withdraw the drive shaft from the crankcase first set No.1 cylinder to firing position. This is done by setting the correct mark on the pulley wheel to the crankcase joint. The offset slot in the top of the shaft should then be parallel with and towards the pulley wheel. Remove the spacer spring. Before starting to lift the shaft out it must be understood that there are thrust washers underneath the lower end and with the engine installed in the car there are dangers of these being irretrievable moved out of position. In any case they can only be lifted out with a narrow magnet on the end of a stick (if the engine is installed). So-don't disturb the thrust washers underneath. The shaft may now be lifted up and out, rotating anticlockwise as it is lifted. The main problem is getting hold of it. If you do not have the special tool there are a variety of ways namely: jamming a piece of suitable sized wooden dowel into the centre hole; gripping the sides of the hole with a pair of long nosed expanding circlip pliers; jamming a piece of thin wooden batten into the slot.

5 If the thrust washers are removed for some reason they should be replaced by dropping them down over a suitable guide rod so that they lie flat and central in the bottom of the shaft housing bore (photo).

6 The engine should be set at the firing point for No.1 cylinder. (The firing point is either before or after tdc on the compression stroke - see Specifications for details).

7 To find the compression stroke with the distributor drive shaft removed is not easy because there are no reference points. The only sure way is to remove No.1 spark plug and turn the engine until compression is felt when the timing marks come into line. It is easy to feel the compression by placing a finger over the plug hole. If the right-hand rocker cover is removed the compression stroke can also be pinpointed when both valves are closed.

8 The distributor drive shaft should now be lowered into the crankcase with the offset slot positioned slightly anticlockwise from its final correct position as detailed in paragraph 4 (photo). When it is lowered into mesh with the crankshaft worm gear it will turn slightly clockwise to the final correct position. Replace the thrust spring (photo).

9 With the engine and distributor drive shaft set and not moved from the position as described in the preceding paragraph the distributor may be placed in position with the shaft lined up so that the eccentric dogs engage the eccentric slots. Provided the

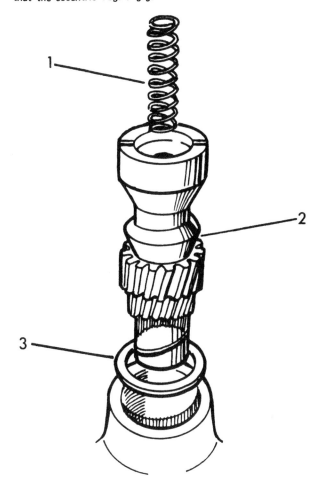

Fig. 4.4. Distributor driveshaft (Sec. 7)

1 Spacer spring   3 Thrust washer
2 Fuel pump drive cam

7.5 Fitting the distributor drive shaft washer over a suitable guide rod

7.8a Replacing the distributor drive shaft

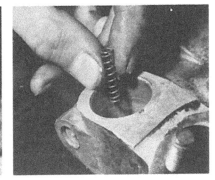
7.8b Replacing the thrust spring

clamp has been undisturbed no further adjustment is necessary after the clamp securing bolt has been replaced and tightened.

10 If the clamp ring has been slackened the body of the distributor should be turned so that the centre line of the rotor arm electrode matches up with the notch in the edge of the distributor body. This gives the near correct position. Final adjustment is made after the contact points have been checked and the gap set. With the crankshaft at the No.1 firing position the contact points should just be opening. To do this the distributor body should be first turned clockwise a fraction from the setting mark until the points are shut. The body is then turned anticlockwise until they are just open.

11 From now on the ignition timing is set with the engine running at idling speed (800-900 rpm). Check with the Specifications the type of distributor fitted (photo) and the rules as to whether the hose or hoses should be left on for timing or removed. On some distributors there are two hoses, one for advance and one for retard. Since April '73 the double hose type has been discontinued, even in the USA (except California). The basic settings of the carburettor are checked as described in Chapter 3 and the engine is started, warmed up and set to run at the correct idling speed by using the by-pass air screw on the carburettor. Then stop the engine again.

12 Connect the strobe light into No. 1 HT lead on the distributor cap. See also that the V notch in the crankshaft pulley wheel is clean and visible (paint it white if necessary). Start the engine again and shine the strobe light onto the pulley. The notch should line up with the crankcase joint. If it does not, slacken the distributor clamp and turn the body of the distributor one way or the other until it does. It is not necessary to tighten the distributor clamp each time an adjustment is made provided the distributor is held reasonably tight.

13 When an adjustment is made it is likely that the engine idling speed will alter so if it falls outside the specified limits adjust the by-pass air screw on the carburettor until it is once more correct. Then check with the stroboscope again.

14 When the mark lines up with the crankcase joint, clamp up the distributor. Reconnect the vacuum hose.

15 With the timing set stroboscopically any performance problems with the engine will be due to incorrect carburettor or valve clearance settings. In cold climatic conditions malfunction of the inlet manifold pre-heater and the air intake pre-heater systems could also cause flat spots and poor performance, particularly during acceleration.

8 Spark plugs and leads

1   It is most important that only the correct type of plug is fitted. The recommended types are given in the Specification Section. If the car is to be run at high speeds in hot climates (ambient temperature over 25ºC (77ºF) then the next plug up in the heat grade table should be used. (Bosch W175 T.I, Beru 175.14 or equivalent).

2   The VW service practice is to fit new plugs every 12,000 miles. However plugs can be cleaned and reset, but not with a knife and a brush. This method only succeeds in pushing the fouling further into the plug.

3   Plugs should be cleaned and tested on the proper machine which shot blasts the electrodes and blows all the fouling out. They are then tested under pressures similar to those they have to work under.

4   The sensible thing to do is to buy a new set of plugs at 12,000 miles, fit them, and have the old set serviced and then fit them at 24,000 miles - repeating the operation as necessary. In this way the engine will be working efficiently and the owner happy that in the event of a plug change being necessary he can

7.11 Some distributors have two vacuum connections, both of which should be on when setting the timing by stroboscope

do the job in minutes.

5   If you haven't got a replacement plug then as a *temporary* measure remove the fouling visible with a knife but be gentle, and reset the gap to 0.7 mm (0.028 inches), by bending the side electrode, **not** the centre one.

6   Under no circumstances use petrol or paraffin to clean a plug; that only washes the dirt in and makes sure that it stays in place.

7   The examination of the plug electrode is instructive. Look at the deposit and compare it with the plug diagram. If the plug has light greyish-brown deposits and is undamaged then combustion is proceeding properly.

However it may be otherwise as the chart explains, and there may be more to do than change the plug.

8   The plug leads should last the life of the car but seldom do because of neglect. They should be kept free from oil and grease, and protected from chafing or other abrasion. Examine them carefully from time to time and if there are signs of damage or wear replace them with the correct type of cable. It would be best to get this from the VW agent. Do not use ordinary cable; the resistance of the lead is critical to the suppression of radio interference. Above all do not try to repair the cable with insulation tape.

9 Ignition coil

1   The testing of the ignition coil has already been discussed in Section 2. There is one further test which is very simple. Check the insulation of the windings to earth by measuring the voltage drop between the terminals and the casing. This will indicate a fault between the windings and earth, but not unfortunately a short circuit in the windings .

2   It is rare for a coil to become faulty and for this reason the coil is generally neglected. Too often the coil is covered with oil and sludge. This can interfere with heat dissipation and lead to failure. Keep the casing clean, wipe the cap with a clean soft cloth and check that the terminals fit tightly.

3   Other than this leave well alone. The coil is the most important part of the system, the rest is only wiring and switches of various types.

For 'Fault diagnosis' see page 74

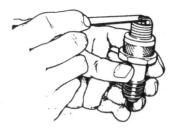

Checking plug gap with feeler gauges

Altering the plug gap. Note use of correct tool.

Spark plug maintenance

White deposits and damaged porcelain insulation indicating overheating

Broken porcelain insulation due to bent central electrode

Electrodes burnt away due to wrong heat value or chronic pre-ignition (pinking)

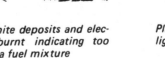

Excessive black deposits caused by over-rich mixture or wrong heat value

Mild white deposits and electrode burnt indicating too weak a fuel mixture

Plug in sound condition with light greyish brown deposits

Spark plug electrode conditions

Fig. 4.5. STANDARD PLUG CONDITIONS

10 Fault diagnosis - ignition system

Symptom	Reason/s	Remedy
1 Engine will not start from cold (fuel system is correct)	1 Dirty plugs 2 CB points incorrect 3 Fault in LT or HT circuit	1 Change plugs (Sec. 8) 2 Clean and reset (Sec. 3) 3 Check system (Sec. 2)
2 Engine overheating	1 Fan belt slipping 2 Ignition retarded 3 Check automatic advance	1 Adjust 2 Check CB points and ignition timing (Sec. 3 and 7) 3 Dismantle and clean (Sec. 6)
3 Engine runs roughly and misfires at low revolutions	1 Dirty plugs 2 CB points incorrect 3 Distributor shaft and bearings worn	1 Change plugs (Sec. 8) 2 Gap too large (Sec. 3) 3 Check wear and replace (Sec. 6) distributor
4 Engine misfires at high revolutions	1 Dirty plugs 2 CB points incorrect 3 Distributor shaft and bearings worn	1 Change plugs (Sec. 8) 2 Gap too small (Sec. 3) 3 Replace distributor (Sec. 6)
5 Engine sluggish and slow to accelerate	1 Automatic advance and retard	1 Check mechanical advance and retard (Sec. 6) 2 Check vacuum advance and retard (Sec. 7)

Chapter 5 Clutch

Contents

Clutch adjustment 10
Clutch cable - removal, adjustment and replacement ... 3
Clutch cover (spring plate and toggle type) - inspection
and repair 5
Clutch cover (diaphragm type) - inspection and repair ... 6
Clutch release mechanism - inspection and repair 8

Clutch - removal and replacement 4
Clutch pedal 9
Fault diagnosis 11
Friction plate and flywheel - inspection and overhaul ... 7
General description 1
Main points of wear 2

Specifications

Type

Early models	Plate spring and toggle, single plate dry clutch
Later and current models	Diaphragm spring, single plate dry clutch

Operating mechanism ... ... Mechanical (cable)

Pedal free-travel ... ... 10 — 20 mm (3/8 in. — 3/4 in.)

Torque wrench setting

	lb ft	kg m
Cover plate to flywheel	18	2½

1 General description

A single plate, dry clutch is fitted. The new models are all fitted with a diaphragm spring but there are a few of the earlier models with the plate spring and toggle fingers so both are described in this Chapter. Refer to Fig. 5.3 which shows the difference.

In both cases the operation of the clutch is the same: a cable from the foot pedal operates the pivot arm of the release shaft causing the shaft to rotate so that the fingers on it move the clutch release bearing.

The release bearing presses either on the centre of the diaphragm spring or the inner ends of the toggle arms. In the latter case the toggle arms pivot about their centres and the outer ends, which are connected by bolts to the pressure plate, pull the plate towards the clutch cover compressing the plate spring which is held between the clutch cover and the pressure plate. This frees the friction plate which is situated between the pressure plate and the flywheel. Since the clutch cover is bolted to the flywheel and the plate spring presses between the clutch cover and the pressure plate, the pressure plate is forced strongly towards the flywheel face and under normal running conditions clamps the friction plate firmly to the flywheel. The friction plate may move axially on the splines of the main driveshaft.

The diaphragm spring replaces the plate spring and toggle arrangement. The diaphragm spring, clutch cover and pressure plate are assembled in one piece and bolted to the flywheel, the friction plate being inserted between the clutch cover assembly and the flywheel. Pressure on the inner fingers of the diaphragm plate releases the force on the pressure plate and frees the friction plate.

In the release bearing there is a ballrace which transmits the axial motion from the static thrust ring to the rotating part of the thrust ring. It is this part together with the friction plate that give rise to trouble if the clutch is misused.

2 Main points of wear in the clutch

Generally speaking with the friction plate held between the pressure plate and the flywheel no wear occurs at all. Similarly, if there is no load on the thrust bearing no wear occurs here. It is only during the time when the pedal is depressed that wear occurs. If the pedal is fully down then the friction plate is not under load and again no wear takes place, but if the plate is allowed to transmit power while slipping then the heat generated by the friction surfaces will quickly lead to the failure of the entire mechanism.

Similarly the thrust race is designed to transmit load for a short while only. If, by using the clutch pedal as a footrest, the pedal is slightly depressed and all the free play removed then the thrust race is working all the while and wear is proportionally greater.

The only other trouble comes from a leaking oilseal which may allow oil to contaminate the friction surfaces (which will cause the clutch to slip) or grit in the clutch (which will cause scoring).

Thus, it may be seen, that the life of the clutch depends largely on the driver, so keep your foot off the pedal except when changing gear, do not slip the clutch, and put the car out of gear at traffic lights or road blocks. That is unless you like taking the engine out of the car, and buying new parts.

3 Clutch cable - removal, replacement and adjustment

1 Clutch cables rarely break and do not stretch significantly sc

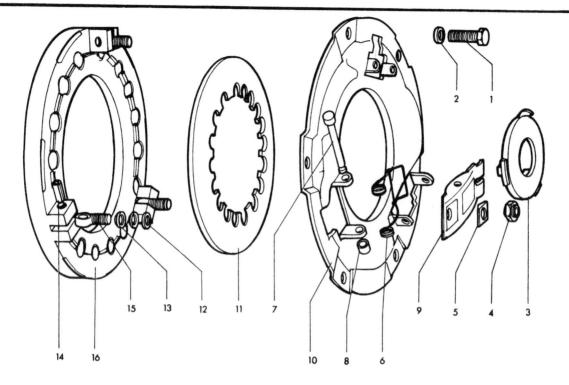

Fig. 5.1 Typical clutch unit (early type) – exploded view (Sec. 1)

1	Bolt	5	Thrust piece	9	Release lever	13	Concave washer
2	Lock washer	6	Spring	10	Clutch cover	14	Spring pin
3	Release ring	7	Clutch cover pin	11	Diaphragm spring	15	Pivot pin
4	Adjusting nut	8	Locking bush	12	Pivot pin washer	16	Pressure plate

Fig. 5.2. Clutch unit - diaphragm type (Sec. 1)

1 Clutch cover and diaphragm spring   2 Friction plate   3 Flywheel

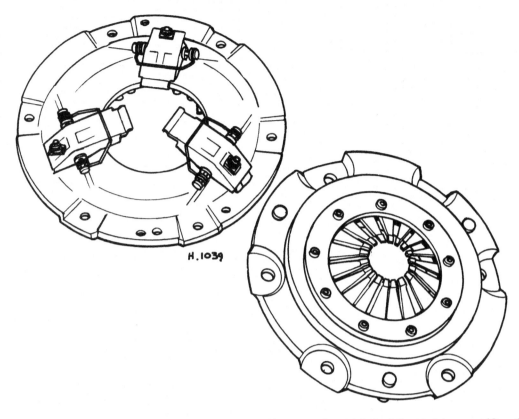

Fig. 5.3. Comparison of typical early type (left) and later version (right) of the clutch cover (Sec. 1)

if you find that the clutch is slipping and further adjustment is not possible the cause is the clutch friction plate. Do not think that the cable is at fault.

2 Disconnect the cable from the clutch operating lever and pull off the rubber sleeve from the guide tube and cable.

3 If the cable inner only is to be removed it is not necessary to disturb the outer sheath. If the outer is being taken off as well then the mounting bracket bolted to the transmission casting should be taken off. Reassembly will then be much easier.

4 Inside the car it will be necessary to detach the foot pedal cluster assembly. On right-hand drive cars this requires care and patience and the procedure is given in Chapter 9. The front end of the clutch cable is fitted with a square loop which hooks on to a bracket of the clutch pedal inside the tunnel and is drawn out with the foot pedal.

5 Having unhooked the front end of the cable it can be drawn out of the guide tube. A new cable can be fed into the tube in the same manner although it may be a bit of a fiddle to get it started as you are working partly blind. Make sure the cable is well greased and try and keep the grease off the interior trim and seats. The real difficulty comes when hooking the end on to the lever and reassembling the pedal cluster. This is covered in Chapter 9.14.

6 Once the cable has been connected properly at the front, and after the pedal cluster has been reassembled, replace the cable through the operating lever at the other end and refit the adjusting nut.

7 When adjusting the clutch, the pedal is the indicating factor. The top of the pedal should move forward - between 10-20 mm. (3/8 to ¾ inch) before firmer resistance is felt. If it moves more than this the adjuster needs screwing up to shorten the cable. If it moves less then slacken the adjuster. When the adjustment is taken up all the way and the free play is excessive then the driven plate is in need of replacement. Sometimes after replacing a cable it is found that the threaded rear end is too short to

reach the operating lever easily. This is because the other end is not properly engaged in the hook recess. With luck a bit of waggling back and forth on the clutch pedal will settle it in position.

8 Stiff or uneven operation of the clutch could be due to several factors. One check worth making before doing anything too drastic is on the cable outer cover between the rear end of the tunnel and on the transmission casing. The outer sleeve should have a bend in it and the lowest point of this bend should be between 25 - 45 mm (1 - 1¾ inches) from an imaginary straight line between the ends of the sleeve. The latitude is generous so the measurement is easy enough. Should there be a variation outside these limits (a most unusual occurrence unless the sleeve has been disconnected and wrongly refitted) adjustments can be made. Disconnect the inner cable from the clutch operating lever on the transmission casing and add or remove washers to the shoulder of the sleeve as required. (Fig. 5.4).

9 A grease nipple is incorporated in the cable outer under the rubber boot at the tunnel end. If squeaks occur a few shots from a grease gun should be given. Another clutch modification at around the same time resulted in the bend in the cable sleeve being increased to 70 mm (7.75 in). If the cable breaks on one of these types obtain the parts which will reduce the bend to the limits given in paragraph 8.

4 Clutch - removal and replacement

1 To remove the clutch it is necessary first to remove the engine from the frame (Chapter 1). The clutch withdrawal mechanism remains in the transmission casing.

2 With the engine removed clean off all oil and mud and set the engine firmly on packing on a bench.

3 When an engine is assembled in the factory the engine and clutch are balanced so it is essential to mark the position of the

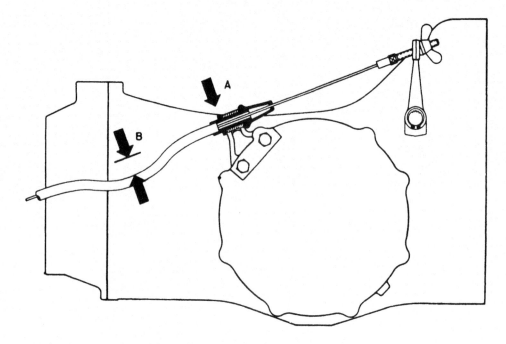

Fig. 5.4. Clutch operating cable (Sec. 3)

A   *Put washers here if necessary to alter the bend in the cable*
B   *Cable bend measurement*

clutch cover and flywheel so that they can be reassembled correctly. This can be most conveniently done with a centre punch.

4   Slacken off the securing screws a few threads at a time alternately, and diagonally, until the clutch cover can be removed from the flywheel. The friction plate will be loose between the clutch cover and the flywheel; check which way round it is and make sure it does not fall out as the clutch cover is removed, it could be damaged that way.

5   The various parts of the clutch may now be inspected and overhauled or replaced as necessary. The procedure for this is detailed in Sections 7, 8, 9 and 10.

6   Replacement is the reverse of removal. Make sure the friction plate is the right way round (photo) and that it is central to the flywheel (photo). If it is not then you will be unable to assemble the engine to the transmission. In order to make sure of this spend a little time fabricating a wooden or metal bar which will fit snugly into the flywheel, and wind insulating tape or some other medium around it until it equals the inside diameter of the friction plate boss. Assemble the plate and cover as concentrically as possible by eye and then tighten the clutch cover bolts until the friction disc is just held but can be moved. Now centralize the disc with the centralizing bar. If an old mainshaft is available this is even better.

It is worth taking a lot of trouble over this for if it is not done carefully a lot of hard words will be used when, with the engine balanced on a jack, it is finally decided that the mainshaft will not enter. If the plate is central and the shaft will still not enter turn either the shaft or the engine a fraction as the splines may not be lined up. It should slide in quite easily. If it does not then take the engine away and look for the trouble - above all do not use force - that will be expensive.

7   Remember to line up the centre punch marks on the cover with those on the flywheel. If a new cover is to be fitted look for the imbalance marks. On the flywheel this can be a 5 mm countersunk hole or a white paint mark on the outer edge. On the clutch cover it is a white paint mark on the outer edge. If only one part had an imbalance mark it doesn't matter. If both

of them have such marks then keep them 180° apart, (or as near as possible).

8   On the spring plate type make sure no securing clips are left in the cover if a new one is fitted. There are no indications on the package so ask the supplier about this.

9   The final torque of the cover to flywheel bolts should be 18lb ft. (2½ mkg). Before fitting the engine check the gearbox input seal (Chapter 6) and the release operating mechanism. (Section 8).

10   **Do not** oil or grease the input shaft (the oil may get on to the clutch lining). Dust the shaft and splines with graphite or molybdenum powder and put a little molybdenum paste on the face of the release bearing.

5   Clutch cover - inspection and overhaul (spring plate and toggle type)

1   Check the cover for cracks or distortion. If any damage is found a new cover is required.

2   A distorted or scored pressure plate may be reground. The maximum allowance for metal removal is 1 mm (0.040 inch). When new a plate is slightly dished in a concave manner.

3   The release levers must be discarded if cracked or worn, and the retaining springs should be checked for tension. They should hold the return arm firmly in place. Be careful to replace the arm in the same position.

4   The plate spring should be placed on a flat surface and the depth of the 'dish' measured. This should be not less than 9.1 mm (0.358 inch) from the top of the spring to the flat surface.

5   Now comes the difficulty. It is most unlikely that spares will be obtainable and more probable that the assembly will have to be replaced as an assembly. If a VW assembly is not obtainable it may be possible to get spares from a reputable manufacturer (eg. Borg & Beck). On the other hand, it is possible to replace the assembly with a diaphragm type unit (VW part no. 311 141 025c). This should be discussed with the agent before proceeding.

4.6a Replacing the driven plate and cover assembly (typical old pattern cover plate)

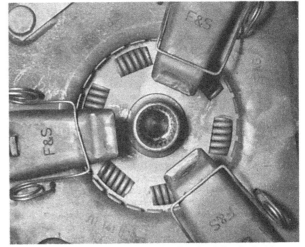

4.6b Centre the clutch plate on the flywheel (typical old pattern cover plate)

6 Clutch cover - inspection and overhaul (diaphragm type)

1 The only operation possible is a thorough inspection. It is not possible to replace parts in this unit and should faults be found the unit must be replaced with a new one.

2 The pressure plate face must be free from cracks, burns, and scoring. A concave 'dish' of 0.3 mm (0.012 inch) between the outer and inner edges, measured with a straight edge and feelers, is permissible. If in doubt take the whole unit to the dealer for an expert opinion.

3 Check the ends of the diaphragm spring which come in contact with the release bearing. Scoring up to 0.3 mm (0.012 inch) may be neglected; above this, replacement is required.

The straps between the pressure plate and cover should be checked for loose rivets and/or cracks.

4 The diaphragm spring is held in place by two wire rings and rivetted to the clutch cover. Damage or wear on the rivet heads or rings indicate a new cover should be fitted. (see Fig. 5.5).

5 Heat generated by a slipping clutch may have affected the diaphragm strength. If this is suspected then the unit should be taken to the agent for testing. The spring pressure is between 380 and 440 kilograms (837 to 970 lbs).

7 Friction plate and flywheel - inspection and overhaul

1 The friction plate should be checked for burns and grease. A black shiny surface indicates contamination. In this case a new plate is required and the source of the oil causing the contamination must be located and rectified before the unit is reassembled.

2 The thickness of the lining is critical. Wear is gauged by the depth of the rivet heads below the lining surface. If this is less than 0.6 mm (0.025 inch) then a new friction disc is required.

3 If possible the disc should be mounted between centres on a lathe and checked for 'run-out'. This should not be more than 0.5 mm (0.020 inch at 195 mm (7½ inches) diameter.

4 Do not try to reline the clutch friction plate yourself. It is appreciated that a good mechanic can do this job but as special linings are required, and special rivets, plus the fact that the special tools should be used, the job becomes an uneconomical task, and if you do make a mess of it you will have to buy a new one instead of getting a reconditioned plate.

5 The flywheel face should be free from scores and should be bright and smooth. If there is deep scoring then the flywheel must be removed and sent for machining to a specialist. It may

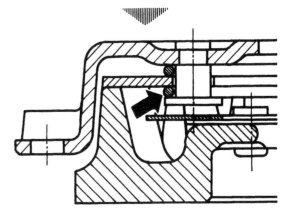

Fig. 5.5. Section through diaphragm pressure plate assembly showing rivet heads and wire rings (arrowed) which must be examined for wear (Sec. 6)

even need replacement. Although this is a costly business it is useless assembling a new friction plate to a damaged flywheel face; clutch judder and rapid wear of the friction plate will result. This is an added incentive to treat the clutch gently while driving.

8 Clutch release operating mechanism - inspection and repair

1 Clutch operation can be adversley affected if the release thrust ring and retaining springs are worn or damaged. Squeals, juddering, slipping or snatching could be caused partly or even wholly by this mechanism being worn.

2 Full examination is possible only when the engine has been removed and normally it is carried out when the clutch is in need of repair. The mechanism is contained in and attached to the transmission casing. Check first that the operating lever return spring mounted on the exterior of the shaft on the left-hand side is not broken. If it is it can be renewed without removing the engine, once the lever has been disconnected from the cable and taken off the cross shaft. However, the damage which failure of this spring may have caused has probably occurred already. If you are going to examine the clutch anyway it will be easier to renew the spring after the engine is removed.

3 The clutch release bearing operates round a sleeve which is attached to the transmission casing. There is no thrust ring fitted

in the centre of the clutch cover. The thrust bearing operates directly on to the ends of the three release levers, or on the inner ends of the diaphragm spring.

4 With the engine removed examine the release bearing and the plastic face. It should spin silently and show no signs of wear or other damage. The retaining clips at each side must be a tight fit so that the bearing does not rattle about on the mounting forks (photo).

5 Do not wash the bearing in cleaning fluid. It is sealed and although fluid may wash some grease out you cannot get any more in. If it needs renewal pull off the clips and lift it out.

6 When replacing the thrust release bearing fit the clips so that the ends point upwards (photo).

7 The cross shaft itself runs through the casing and should move freely without any sign of slackness in the bushes.

8 If it is necessary to renew the bushes the cross shaft can be taken out after first taking the operating lever and return spring off the end of the shaft. Then remove the screw which locates the bush in the casing and remove all the components. When replacing the shaft lubricate well with molybdenum grease and ensure that the two concertina type grease seals are intact and properly seated inside the casing (photos). If one should come out on the inside of the casing make sure you get it put back. This bush takes considerable forces when the clutch is operated and should not be ignored or treated lightly. (photos).

9 When fitting a new return spring first remove the operating lever by undoing the circlip and taking it off the splined shaft. Fit the new spring so that the hooked end will eventually go round the lever and hold it back. Replace the lever and hook the spring end round it (photo).

10 Re-adjust the clutch pedal play after the engine has been replaced.

9 Clutch pedal

The removal, inspection and replacement of the clutch pedal for left and right-hand drive vehicles is discussed in Chapter 9 with the brake and accelerator pedal cluster.

10 Clutch adjustment

1 Apart from checking the various parts for wear and if

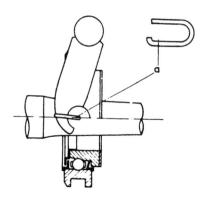

Fig. 5.6. Clutch release bearing - Cross section showing shape and location of retaining clip (a) (Sec. 8)

8.4 Clutch thrust release bearing

8.6 View of thrust bearing attachment clips

8.8a Fitting the clutch release shaft bush...

8.8b ... followed by the shaft ...

8.8c ... and the bearing sleeve and seals

8.8d Make sure the bush and seal do not come out like this on the inside

8.8e The locating screws for the bush and sleeve

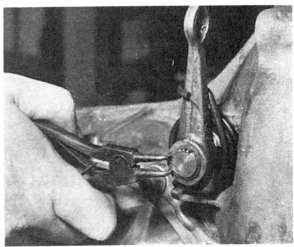

8.9 The release shaft operating lever showing circlip, splines and return spring

necessary replacing them the only adjustment required on the clutch is the amount of free-play at the clutch pedal. This is adjusted by altering the length of the clutch cable as detailed in

Section 3, para 6.

This measurement should be checked regularly to ensure that the clutch is correctly adjusted or wear will be accelerated.

11 Fault diagnosis - clutch

Symptom	Reason/s	Remedy
Judder when taking up drive	Loose engine/gearbox mountings or over flexible mountings	Check and tighten all mounting bolts and replace any 'soft' or broken mountings.
	Badly worn friction surfaces or friction plate contaminated with oil carbon deposit	Remove engine and replace clutch parts as required. Rectify any oil leakage points which may have caused contamination.
	Worn splines in the friction plate hub or on the gearbox input shaft	Renew friction plate and/or input shaft.
	Badly worn roller bearings in flywheel centre for input shaft spigot	Renew roller bearings in flywheel gland nut.
Clutch spin (failure to disengage) so that gears cannot be meshed	Clutch actuating cable clearance too great	Adjust clearance.
	Clutch friction disc sticking because of rust on lining or splines (usually apparent after standing idle for some length of time)	As temporary remedy engage top gear, apply handbrake, depress clutch and start engine. (If very badly stuck engine will not turn). When running rev up engine and slip clutch until disengagement is normally possible. Renew friction plate at earliest opportunity.
	Damaged or misaligned pressure plate assembly	Replace pressure plate assembly.
Clutch slip - (increase in engine speed does not result in increase in car speed especially on hills)	Clutch pedal free play too little or non-existent resulting in partially disengaged clutch at all times	Adjust clearance.
	Clutch friction surfaces worn out (beyond further adjustment of operating cable) or clutch surfaces oil soaked	Replace friction plate and remedy source of oil leakage.

Chapter 6 Transmission and final drive

Contents

Differential and side covers - replacement 5h	General description 1
Differential gears 8	Input shaft - assembly 5a
Differential limited slip (plate type) 9	Input shaft - oil seal removal and replacement 7
Fault diagnosis 13	Main casing - installing needle bearings and reverse
Gear carrier - fitting bearings 5d	gear 5c
Gear carrier - selector shafts and forks 5e	Pinion shaft - assembly 5b
Gear carrier - assembly to maincasing 5f	Synchromesh hubs - inspection and assembly 6
Gear shift housing - reassembly 5g	Transmission - removal and replacement 2
Gear shift linkage - removal and replacement 10	Transmission - dismantling 3
Gear shift linkage - adjustment 11	Transmission - inspection 4
Gear shift linkage - GT Beetle 12	Transmission - assembly - general notes 5

Specifications

General	Final drive and gearbox maincasing in one piece, tunnel type alloy casting
Number of gears	4 forward 1 reverse
Synchromesh	Baulk ring on all forward gears

Oil capacity of casing:

	litres	pints (US)	pints (Imperial)
Initial	3	6.3	5.3
Refill	2.5	5.3	4.4

Gear ratios:

	1300 cc 78.3 cu in. engine	1600 cc 96.7 cu in. engine
First	3.78 : 1	3.78 : 1
Second	2.06 : 1	2.06 : 1
Third	1.26 : 1	1.26 : 1
Fourth	0.93 : 1	0.93 : 1
Reverse	3.79 : 1	3.79 : 1

Final drive ratio:

1300 cc/78.3 cu in.	4.375 : 1
1600 cc/96.7 cu in.	3.875 : 1

Torque wrench settings:

	lb ft	kg m
Oil drain plugs	14	2.0
Oil filter plug	14	2.0
Transmission carrier to frame bolts	166	23.0
Spring plate bolts/nuts	72	10.0
Final drive cover nuts	22	3.0
Gear change cover nuts	11	1.5
Gear carrier to housing nuts	14	2.0
Pinion bearing retainer ring	108	22
Reverse lever guide screw	14	2.0
Selector fork screws	18	2.5
Pinion shaft round nut (ball bearings)	87	12.0
(taper roller bearings)	144	20.0

83

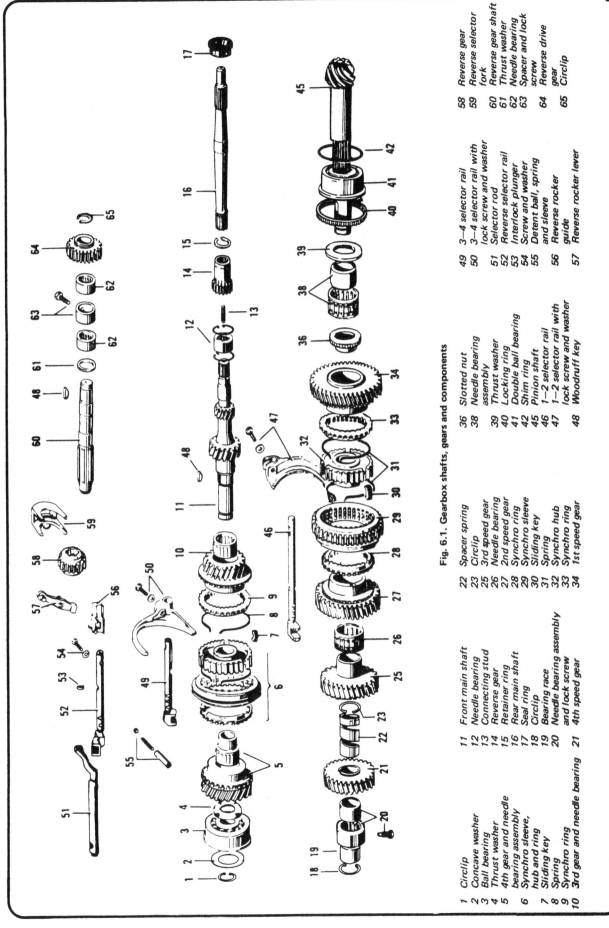

Fig. 6.1. Gearbox shafts, gears and components

1 Circlip
2 Concave washer
3 Ball bearing
4 Thrust washer
5 4th gear and needle bearing assembly
6 Synchro sleeve, hub and ring
7 Sliding key
8 Spring
9 Synchro ring
10 3rd gear and needle bearing

11 Front main shaft
12 Needle bearing
13 Connecting stud
14 Reverse gear
15 Retainer ring
16 Rear main shaft
17 Seal ring
18 Circlip
19 Bearing race
20 Needle bearing assembly and lock screw
21 4th speed gear

22 Spacer spring
23 Circlip
25 3rd speed gear
26 Needle bearing
27 2nd speed gear
28 Synchro ring
29 Synchro sleeve
30 Sliding key
31 Spring
32 Synchro hub
33 Synchro ring
34 1st speed gear

36 Slotted nut
38 Needle bearing assembly
39 Thrust washer
40 Locking ring
41 Double ball bearing
42 Shim ring
45 Pinion shaft
46 Spring
47 1–2 selector rail with lock screw and washer
48 Woodruff key

49 3–4 selector rail
50 3–4 selector rail with lock screw and washer
51 Selector rod
52 Reverse selector rail
53 Interlock plunger
54 Screw and washer
55 Detent ball, spring and sleeve
56 Reverse rocker guide
57 Reverse rocker lever

58 Reverse gear
59 Reverse selector fork
60 Reverse gear shaft
61 Thrust washer
62 Needle bearing
63 Spacer and lock screw
64 Reverse drive gear
65 Circlip

1 General description

The gearbox and final drive is a one piece composite assembly housed in a single 'tunnel' type magnesium alloy die casting. Unlike the more orthodox design of gearbox which has an input and output shaft aligned on the same axis with a lay-shaft and gears below, the VW has an input shaft and output shaft only, mounted alongside each other and each carrying a synchro hub. This is because the input and output power is at the same end of each shaft. The output shaft incorporates the pinion gear which meshes with the crown wheel.

Synchromesh is used for all four forward speeds.

The whole assembly is mounted in the 'Y' of the floor frame - called the frame fork for obvious reasons - ahead of the engine. The differential unit and final drive, part of the assembly as already mentioned, come between the engine and the transmission gears.

In order to dismantle the gearbox the differential must first be removed.

In view of the relative complexity of this complete unit, it is felt that a few words of warning should be given in order to let potential dismantlers fully realise what they may be letting themselves in for. First of all decide whether the fault you wish to repair is worth all the time and effort involved. Secondly, if the gearbox is in a very bad state then the cost of the component parts may well   exceed the cost of a new replacement unit. Thirdly, remember that a basic knowledge of gearbox construction and function is a bare necessity before tackling this one. If you are doing one for the first time do not start on a Volkswagen! Fourthly the use of a press and some method of heating gears and shafts up to 100°C (212°F) are necessary.

Finally, unless you are on good terms with the VW agent this job is best left alone. There have been a number of changes in the gear ratios, which mean that there may be more to come, so count the teeth on a gear before ordering a new one. You will need a selection of circlips and shims. Altogether you may try the patience of the storeman, and if you finally have to admit defeat and ask for a replacement box there may be some demur about accepting a collection of gear wheels; shafts and castings in a box, as an assembly.

2 Transmission - removal and replacement

1 Remove the engine as described in Chapter 1.
2 Detach the starter motor from the transmission casing if not already done.

All except GT models (double jointed driveshafts)
3 Remove the cap screws securing the driveshaft inner flanges to the transmission on each side. Tape plastic bags over the CV joints to protect them and tie the driveshafts up out of the way.
4 Remove the adjusting nut from the end of the clutch cable.
5 Lift up the back seat and remove the cover on the tunnel which is held by a single screw. Underneath will be seen a square headed screw securing the gear change rod to the gearbox lever. Cut the locking wire and undo the screw until the coupling is free (photo).
6 Undo the two nuts holding the transmission to the front mounting (photo).
7 Support the weight of the transmission, preferably on a trolley jack.
8 Remove the two large bolts at the rear which hold the transmission to the frame fork (photo).
9 Lower the transmission and draw it back and out (photo). Take care to support and balance it. If it drops heavily the casing could be damaged.

GT models (swing axle)
10 It will be necessary to undo the axle shaft outer nuts if the tube and shaft need to be separated for any reason. In any case

it is a good idea to loosen these nuts in case of unforeseen circumstances so do it now while the wheels are still on and the vehicle is on the ground. You will not be able to do it when the assembly is removed from the car. The requirements for setting about slackening these very large and very tight nuts is given in Chapter 8, Section 5.
11 Having slackened the axle shaft nuts and wheel bolts jack up the car and remove the road wheels. Support the car on stands underneath the two rear jacking points.
12 Remove one of the front seats and the rear seat and move the other front seat fully forward.
13 Take up the floor covering and the shroud over the handbrake lever.
14 Undo the locknuts and adjusting nuts on each of the handbrake cable ends and take them off.
15 Take off the circlip in the groove at one end of the handbrake lever pivot pin and drive out the pin. Move the handbrake lever rearwards a little and it may then be lifted out. Do not press the ratchet release button whilst doing this or the ratchet mechanism will fall out.
16 The two handbrake cables may now be drawn out from the transmission casing tubes.
17 From inside the car once more, remove the cover over the frame tunnel under the back seat. It is located by a single screw. Underneath the gear shift rod coupling will be seen and the rear square headed screw should be removed after cutting off the locking wire. If the gear lever is then moved the coupling will separate.
18 Next disconnect the rear hydraulic flexible brake hoses, one on each side where they connect at the bracket mounting on top of each axle tube. For details of this procedure refer to Chapter 9.
19 Next, if you have not already done so, clean off the area where the suspension plates are bolted to the outer ends of the axle tubes. Apply some penetrating oil now to the three nuts and bolts on each side to assist removal later (see Chapter 8 for details).
20 On the flange nearest the top nut and bolt which holds the axle to the spring plate will be seen a 'V' notch in the casting. Another notch, exactly in line with it, should be made with a chisel in the edge of the spring plate alongside. The bolt holes in the plate are slotted and it is most important that the axle tube is correctly positioned on replacement.
21 Now undo and remove the bolts which secure the lower ends of the shock absorbers.
22 The clutch cable locknut and adjusting nut should next be removed from the end of the cable.
23 Undo the nuts and bolts securing the axle tubes to the spring suspension plates. The axle tubes may then be moved out and down on each side (see Chapter 8).
24 All that now remains is to remove the two nuts and two bolts mounting the unit to the frame. First remove the two nuts at the front end which hold the casing onto the flexible mounting. Take off the washers also.
25 Next support the whole unit on a jack. A trolley jack and piece of stout board is the best way of doing this. The unit can then be lowered easily. If you do not have a trolley jack then the stout board may be supported on static jacks or bricks, whichever is most convenient and stable.
26 Having prepared the necessary support the two large bolts, one into each end of the rear frame tubes, should be removed with a socket spanner. They are not excessively tight.
27 The whole assembly can then be moved rearwards. Depending on how you have arranged and positioned your support will depend how the whole lot is balanced. Most likely it will try and drop at the front so be prepared for this. Lower it down carefully until it can be drawn out from under the rear of the car.

All models
28 Replacement of the assembly   is an exact reversal of the removal procedure. Note the following points. Refit the starter to the casing first. When the unit is in position the mounting

2.5 Undoing the gear shift rod coupling screw

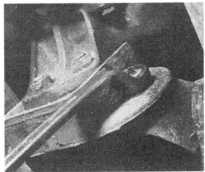

2.6 Undoing the forward mounting bolts

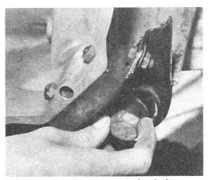

2.8 Removing the rear mounting bolts

2.9 Lowering the transmission on a trolley jack

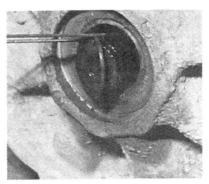

3.4 Hooking out the spacer ring

bolts at the rear should not be tightened until the nuts securing the flexible mountings have been slackened. Then tighten the two large bolts; next the two front mounting nuts and finally the four rear mounting nuts once more. This prevents distortion stresses being set up in the flexible rubber mountings.

29 On GT models, do not forget that the line up of the notches in the axle bearing housings and spring plates is important. The hydraulic system will need bleeding after connecting the brake hoses. Reconnect the handbrake cables.

30 The correct coupling of the gear shift to the shift operating rod is essential. Make sure that the point of the locking screw engages the dimple in the shaft exactly and re-lock the screw with wire. (Later models may not have locking wire; in this case the screw threads are pre-coated with thread locking compound, and a new screw should be used on reassembly). If it is found that gear selection is not quite satisfactory on completion it is in order to make minor adjustments to the position of the gear lever mounting. By slackening the two securing bolts the whole gear lever assembly can be moved a little in either a forward or rearward direction. If the assembly is moved forward engagement of 2nd and 4th gears is more positive. The same applies for the other two gears if it is moved rearwards. This adjustment is intended to centralise the gear lever in the neutral position.

31 Do not forget to refill the transmission with the correct quantity and grade of oil. This is more easily done from above before the engine is replaced.

3 Transmission - dismantling

1 *Read the homily in Section one of this Chapter again.* If you have decided to dismantle the transmission then prepare for the task sensibly.

2 Clean the casing externally until it shines. Arrange the work bench with a clean top. Drain oil from the casing and replace the plug. Have plenty of clean rag available, a paraffin bath and a number of containers for nuts and bolts. Work out where you are going to put the components after they have been cleaned. Make sure you have a notebook and pencil to put down any urgent pieces of information. Decide how you are going to keep the old gaskets, they may be needed as samples or templates. Finally take your time, there will be a lot of bits around when you have taken the box to pieces. Make sure you know where each one came from and which way up it fits. Place the box on the bench on its base, pack it so that it rests firmly and you are ready to go.

All except GT models (double jointed driveshafts)

3 Remove the sealing caps from the centres of the driving flanges by punching the blade of a screwdriver through them and levering them out.

4 Remove the circlip from round the splined shaft end. The flange can then be levered off the end of the shaft. Behind the flanges on each side will be found a spacer ring. Retrieve these spacers (photo), making a note to renew them if there is play at the flange or if they appear worn.

5 Undo the nuts holding the cover on the left-hand side and take it off. If necessary give it a few taps with a soft faced hammer to dislodge it. Do not use force. When the cover comes off the outer race of the taper roller side bearing race is moved from the side cover. Note that there are shims behind it which control the side bearing pre-load and pinion/crownwheel mesh.

6 If the casing is now turned over carefully the differential assembly can be taken out. Take care not to drop it and put it somewhere where it will not be damaged.

7 Remove the right-hand cover (if fitted) from the casing.

GT models (swing axle)

8 If not already done, remove the axle tubes and axle shafts from the transmission as described in Chapter 8, Section 6.

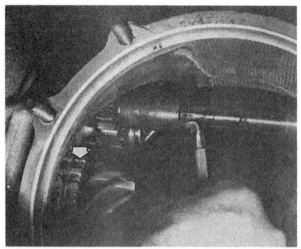

3.13 Releasing the circlip holding the reverse gear sleeve. Note the locking ring for the pinion bearing (arrowed)

3.17 Forcing out the pinion shaft with a scissor jack

9　Turn the whole unit on its side so that the left side final drive cover is upwards. (Remember, the narrow end of the casing is the front). Then undo the nuts securing the cover to the casing.

10 With a soft-faced mallet the cover plate can now be gently tapped off from the casing. Do not use any force. The side bearing may or may not come off with the cover and between the bearing inner race and the differential there is a shim. If the bearing comes away with the side cover this shim(s) will be freed so collect it and tape it to the bearing to ensure it is not lost, damaged or mixed up with the shim or shims which come off in due course from the opposite side. If the bearing remains on the differential, leave it for the time being.

11 Turn the casing over. With a suitable drift positioned against the inner race of the right hand bearing the whole of the differential assembly may now be tapped out. Take care to support it and prevent the assembly from dropping under its own weight. If it is found that it is easier to drift out the differential with the bearing left in the side cover this is in order, but remember to collect up the shims which will be released between bearing and differential and tape them to the differential straight away.

All models

12 From the front of the casing remove the three screws securing the sleeve round the input shaft (if fitted).

13 Inside the differential casing release the circlip which locates the splined collar/reverse gear to the input shaft (photo). Slide it back along the shaft and slide the collar along behind it. The rear end of the shaft may now be unscrewed from the other half. Take off the collar/gear and remove the circlip from the shaft. The shaft may now be drawn out through the oil seal. Replace this oil seal with a new one. (Note that this oil seal can be renewed with the transmission unit installed in the car. Access can be gained once the engine is removed).

14 At the front of the gearbox remove the nuts holding the gear selector lever housing and remove the housing lever.

15 Remove the nuts from the studs which secure the end casing (called the gear carrier) to the main casing and take off the braided earth strap at the same time.

16 The pinion shaft bearing is held into the casing by means of a castellated locking ring (see photo 3.13). This ring is normally undone with a special tool but careful use of a hammer and chisel can achieve the same results. First mark the position of the ring in relation to the casing so that you may re-tighten it to the same position. Then a couple of smart taps with the chisel against one of the castellations will slacken it enough to be unscrewed by hand. Be warned - if the chisel slips and chips a

gear tooth then you are in the high price repair business!

17 Once the ring is removed the whole gearbox assembly is ready to come out of the casing. This can be achieved by using a heavy copper faced mallet and striking the end of the pinion. Another way is to insert a scissor jack shallow enough to fit between the pinion and the casing opposite (photo). Pad the head of the jack against the pinion and press it out. Be sure to support the gear carrier when the gear shafts come away. As soon as it is clear, be sure to collect any shim(s) from the pinion flange.

18 The main casing has two needle roller bearings still left in it. One had the reverse gear and shaft running in it. The gear and shaft may be removed together. They may be secured by a circlip or a locating screw through the casing. Retrieve the spacer (if fitted).

19 Similarly, the other needle bearing outer race (no spacer) is secured by a screw in the casing. Once this is removed the needle roller bearing race may be drifted out. (This bearing is the one that supports the rear end of the forward half of the input shaft).

20 The large side bearings, which will be located in either the covers (GT models) or on the differential, may remain where they are unless inspection indicates that they are worn and need renewal. They can be drifted off the differential or out of the covers. If being taken out of the covers (GT models) make sure that the covers are firmly and evenly supported and drift the bearings. Do not attempt to do it the other way round or you may damage the cover and that is not the part you intend to renew.

21 So far, the dismantling process has been relatively straightforward. Now is the time to stop and reassemble if you are getting cold feet! The next step is to separate the two shafts with their clusters of gears from the gear carrier. To renew the baulk rings - which is one of the usual remedies for a less than perfect synchromesh action - this further dismantling is necessary.

22 Both gear shafts are held into their bearings by circlips. The bearings are a press fit in the carrier but not from the side. The input shaft bearing has to be taken out from the outside of the casing. The circlip retaining the shaft must therefore, be removed so that the shaft may be taken out of the bearing. This circlip is under tension from a dished thrust washer underneath and is liable to 'fly' when released from its groove. So take care and cover the end with a cloth when releasing it. The pinion shaft bearing will come out from either side after the locating bolt is removed.

23 Before moving the shafts from the carrier the selector forks must be taken off. Before any shaft is moved in relation to its

rail, mark them carefully so that they can be refitted in exactly the same place. This setting is very critical and if wrong will cause selection problems and jumping out of gear.

24 Remove the small sliding gear and fork (reverse) from the pivot on the reverse lever.

25 Next loosen the clamping bolts which hold the two other selector forks to their respective rails, The fork for 1st and 2nd gear selection on the output (pinion) shaft can be lifted away after the rail has been drawn back sufficiently far. The other fork is shrouded by the gear carrier and is not lifted out at this stage. The rail for this one should be driven back far enough to free it from the fork. Do **NOT** drive the rails out of the gear carrier. If you do a lot of extra work will be caused, probably unnecessarily, because balls and springs will be released.

26 The two shafts with their clusters of gears may now be removed from the carrier. It is a good plan to hold both together with a strong elastic band or a few turns of a self-adhesive tape. Then, when the ends of the shaft are released, they will not fall about the place. Two pairs of hands are needed. One pair should hold the carrier - with the shafts hanging down whilst the other person strikes the end of the input shaft with a soft faced mallet and supports the weight of the gear shafts as they are driven out. Do not let them drop down.

27 Once the shafts are clear of the carrier the bearings may be removed. The main (input) shaft front bearing is driven out from the inside of the carrier. This particular ball bearing is flanged on the outer race and will only come out in one direction.

28 To dismantle the input shaft first take off the thrust washer then 4th gear together with the needle bearing cage on which it runs. Remove the baulk ring. This leaves the inner race on the shaft. To get this off a press will be needed and the 'V' blocks should be suitably positioned to provide support behind the 3rd gear wheel. In this way there will be no danger of damage to the shaft or gears and the synchro hub assembly will be kept together. Make sure that all parts are supported and held whilst being pressed. 3rd gear may then be taken off together with its needle roller bearing. The 3rd gear bearing inner race need not be removed nor the key which locates the synchro hub. Keep the baulk rings with their respective gears for future reference - fix them with adhesive tape to prevent muddling.

29 The output (pinion) shaft should only be dismantled to a limited extent - which is sufficient to remove the gears, synchro hub and baulk rings. The pinion double taper roller bearing which is held by the notched locking nut should be left intact as this requires the use of more special tools to which we do not feel most owners will have ready access. The services of a press may be required in order to carry out the partial dismantling necessary to remove the baulk rings although if properly supported the shaft may be driven out of the synchro hub with a heavy soft faced mallet.

30 First remove the circlip from the end of the shaft. The inner race of the needle bearing together with 4th gear may then be driven or pressed off together. Support the gear and then press or drive out the shaft.

31 Remove the spacer spring and then take off the other circlip round the shaft.

32 Third gear, the roller bearing, 2nd gears and 1st/2nd gear synchro hub and baulk rings may then be taken off in that order.

33 The synchro hub assemblies should be handled with care to prevent them coming apart inadvertently. It is important that if the centre hub and outer sleeve are separated that they be refitted in the same relative position. Some hubs have marks etched on each part to aid reassembly, so before anything else examine them on both sides for such marks. If none can be found make some of your own with a small dab of paint to ensure reassembly in the same position. To dismantle the hubs first lift out the spring retaining clip on each side. Then carefully slide the sleeve from the hub taking care not to drop and lose the three sliding keys.

34 Do not remove the selector fork rails from the gear carrier casing unless inspection indicates that there is something wrong with the detent balls and springs.

4 Inspection of transmission components for wear

1 The degree of wear largely dictates the economics of repair or replacement with a new unit. If the crown wheel and pinion is badly worn with chipped teeth, excessive backlash then this should be replaced as a sub-assembly. The necessary jigs and fittings to assemble a differential and crown wheel assembly with correct preloading are not available to the average owner and this manual does not cover the task.

2 Having been able to obtain the use of a simple mechanical press it is possible to remove all baulk rings for examination. The grooved taper face of the ring provides the braking action on the mating face of the gear wheel cone and if the ridges are worn the braking or synchro action will be less effective. The only way to determine the condition effectively is by comparison with new parts. As the parts are relatively cheap it is considered foolish not to renew them all anyway once the gearbox is dismantled. As a guide, when a baulk ring is fitted over its cone on the gear wheel there should be a minimum gap of 0.6 mm (0.024 inch) between the baulk ring and the gear teeth. The normal gap is 1.1 mm (0.043 inch) so it is obvious that if the gap is near the lowest limit new rings should be fitted. When obtaining new baulk rings make sure that you get the Parts Store to identify and mark each one according to its appropriate gear. Modifications have taken place and although the new ones will still fit and work they are not necessarily identical to the ones you take out. So if you muddle them up you could get problems. They are also not all the same in the set - some have wider cut-outs for example. So mark the new ones you get carefully.

3 Two types of bearings are fitted - ball and needle roller. As a rule needle roller bearings wear very little, not being subject to end thrust of any sort. Check them in position and if there are signs of roughness then they should be renewed. If any bearing should feel the slightest bit rough or show any sign of drag or slackness when revolved then it should be renewed. The double taper roller bearing should be similarly checked. If there is any sign of roughness or endfloat then this is a task for a specialist. If this bearing is needing renewal the condition of the pinion gear and crownwheel must be very carefully examined. Once these need renewal then the setting of the whole box is altered and clearances and shims have to be re-calculated and changed.

4 The teeth of all gears should be examined for signs of pitted mating surfaces, chips or scoring. It must be appreciated that if one gear is damaged then its mate on the other shaft will probably be as bad and that one way or another a new pair of gears will be required.

5 The synchro hubs should be assembled for checking. It is important that there is no rock or backlash on the splines between the inner hub and outer sleeve. When the baulk rings are being renewed it is good policy to renew the three sliding keys and their locating spring rings as well. The keys fit into the cut-outs in the baulk rings and are subject to wear and the springs weaken with time.

6 One of the most critical parts of the Volkswagen gearbox is the operation of the selector forks. The two forks run in grooves in the outer sleeves of the synchro hubs and if the clearance of the forks in the grooves is excessive then there is a likelihood of certain gears jumping out. The clearance of the fork in the groove should not exceed 0.3mm (0.012 inch). Clearance in excess of the maximum could be due to wear on the fork or in the groove or both. It is best therefore first of all to take the forks along to the spares supplier and ask him to compare their thickness with new ones. If the difference in thickness is not enough to compensate for the excess gap between fork and hub groove then the hub assembly will need replacement as well. This is an expensive item but as the gap is somewhat critical there is no alternative. Much depends on the total degree of wear.

7 The selector rails on which the forks are mounted need not be removed from the casing. A certain force is needed in order that they overcome the pressure of the spring loaded ball in the groove. This can be measured with a spring balance hooked on to

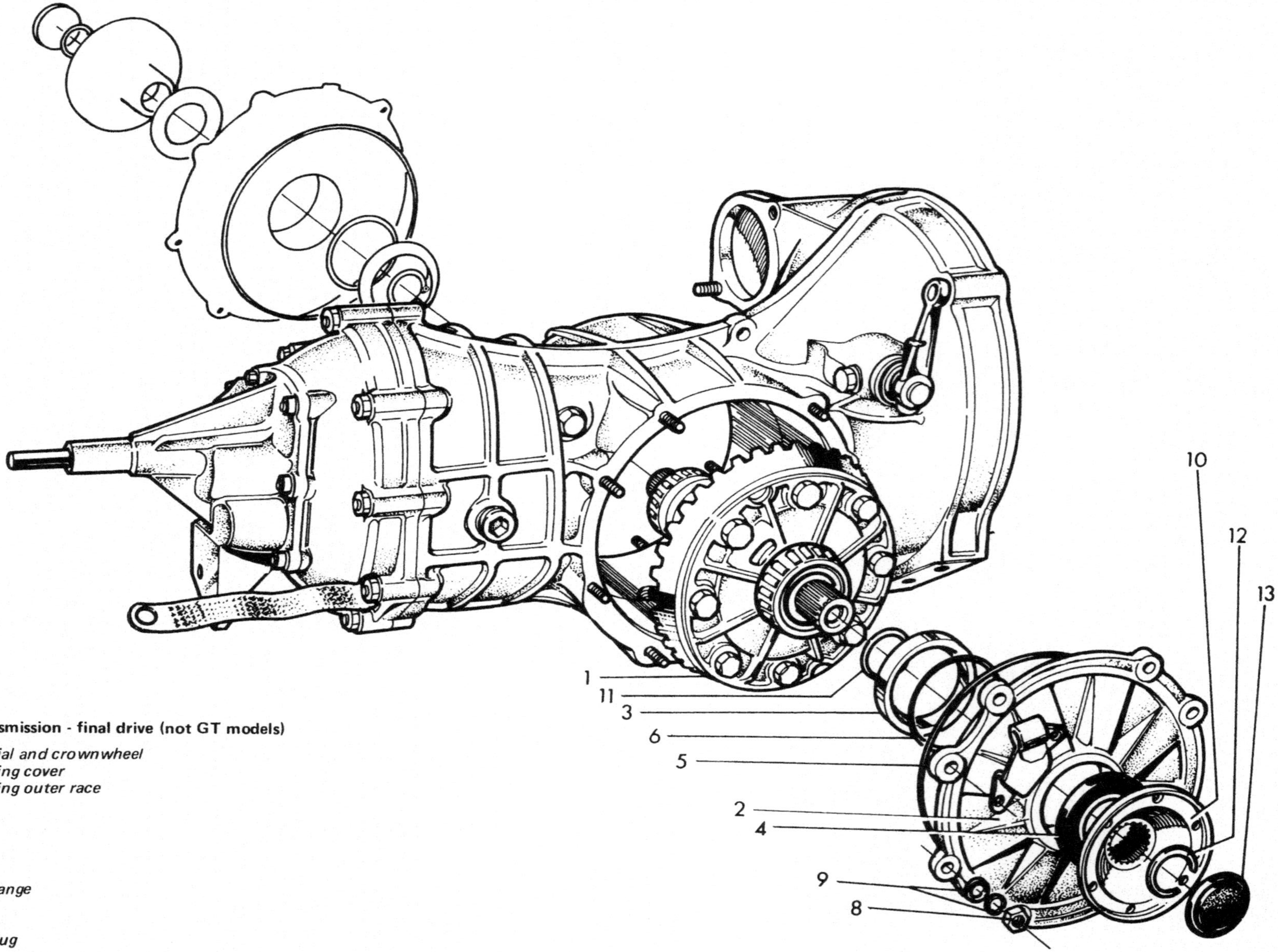

Fig. 6.2. Transmission - final drive (not GT models)

1 Differential and crownwheel
2 Side bearing cover
3 Side bearing outer race
4 Oil seal
5 'O' ring
6 Circlip
8 Nut
9 Washers
10 Driving flange
11 Spacer
12 Circlip
13 Sealing plug

the end of each selector fork. If the required pull is significantly outside the range of 15-20kgs (33-44lbs) then it is advisable to check the detent springs and balls. To do this push the selector rods right out of the casing. This will release the ball and spring but to get the springs out it is necessary to prise out the plastic plugs from the drillings opposite. Before doing this make sure you obtain some new plugs to drive in when reassembling. Check the spring free length which should be 25 mm(1 inch). If less than 22 mm they should be changed. The balls should be free from pitting and grooves and the selector rods themselves should not be a sloppy fit in the bores. The detent grooves in the rails should not be worn. When the rails are removed do not lose the interlock plungers which fit between the selector rod grooves.

9 Examine all parts of the casing for signs of cracks or damage, particularly near the bearing housings and on the mating surfaces where the gear carrier and side bearing plates join.

10 It should not normally be necessary to completely wash all the gearbox components in fluid. Wipe components on clean cloth for examination. In this way the likelihood of dry spots during the first moments of use after reassembly are minimised. The casing itself should be thoroughly washed out with paraffin and flushed afterwards with water. Do not leave the needle roller bearings in position when doing this.

5 Transmission assembly - general

Spend time in preparing plenty of clean, clear space and if your work bench is rough cover it with hardboard or paper for a good non-gritty surface. Do not start until you have all the necessary parts and gaskets assembled and make sure that all the ones you have obtained are going to fit. Gasket sets often contain items covering a variety of models so you will not need them all - this is why it helps to keep the old gaskets you take off until the job is eventually finished.

5a Input shaft - reassembly

1 First reassemble the input shaft, beginning by putting the needle roller cage for 3rd gear in position on the shaft. Then put 3rd gear with its matching synchro ring onto the roller bearings with the cone towards the front end of the shaft.

2 The 3rd/4th gear synchro hub assembly goes on next. This has to line up with the key in the shaft. Once the keyway in the centre part of the hub is lined up with the key in the shaft the hub can be driven on using a suitable piece of tube and heavy hammer. There are three very important points to note when doing this. Make sure that the hub is on the right way round -

some models have a groove in the outer sleeve 1 mm deep and this must be towards the front end of the shaft. If there is no indication then you may put the hub on either way round. Secondly, make sure that you only drive the centre part of the hub. Otherwise it will come apart and have to be reassembled. Thirdly, the slots in the baulk ring must be lined up with the keys in the hub. This is best done by someone holding the baulk ring in position with the keys whilst the hub is driven on the final amount. Be careful not to trap any fingers!

3 Next the inner race for the 4th gear needle roller bearing has to be driven on to the shaft in the same manner that the hub was driven on before it. Drive it right down to the hub. Then replace the needle roller cage followed by the baulk ring and 4th gear. The baulk ring also has three cut-outs which engage with the sliding keys in the hub.

4 Finally, place the thrust washer on the end of the shaft.

5b Pinion shaft - reassembly

1 As pointed out earlier, the pinion shaft has been dismantled only as far as the pinion bearing which has been left in position (photo). If this bearing has been renewed then the gearbox and final drive will need resetting and this is a skilled job requiring special equipment and a selection of special shims to hand from which the necessary requirements are available.

2 The first 'loose' item therefore which goes behind the pinion is the shim (if any) controlling endfloat. The endfloat is measured by a feeler gauge after the 1st gear and synchro hub have been fitted. The measurement is between the face of the gear and the thrust washer which is locked in front of the pinion taper roller bearing. The measurement range is from 0.10 - 0.25 mm (0.004 - 0.010 inches).

3 If the gap is outside this range then the shims must be altered to suit.

4 Now put 1st gear (the largest one with helically cut teeth) in position on the needle roller bearings with the cone face of the synchro pointing away from the pinion gear (photo).

5 Select the 1st gear baulk ring and place it over 1st gear and then replace the 1st and 2nd gear hub over the splines on the shaft with the selector fork groove of the outer sleeve facing towards the front end of the shaft (photo). Make sure that the three cut-outs in the synchro ring engage with the sliding keys in the hub before pushing the hub fully home. Remember that the baulk rings for 1st and 2nd gears are slightly different. That for 1st gear has narrower cut-outs than those in the 2nd gear ring.

6 Now check the 1st gear endfloat as mentioned in paragraph 2.

7 Put the 2nd gear baulk ring in position in the hub so that the slots engage with the sliding keys.

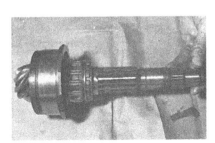

5b.1 Pinion shaft

5b.4 Fitting first gear on the pinion shaft

5b.5 Fitting 1st/2nd gear clutch hub

5b.8 Fitting 2nd gear and baulk ring

5b.9 Fitting 3rd gear and roller bearing

5b.10 Fitting 3rd gear retaining circlip

5b.12 Fitting the spacer spring, 4th gear and the bearing inner race

5b.13 Driving on the bearing race with the circlip

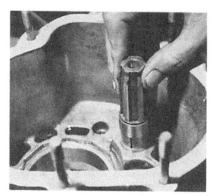

5c.2 Installing the reverse gear drive shaft

8 Replace 2nd gear with the cone towards the hub (photo).

9 Third gear, which has a large bearing boss integral with it, should now be replaced with the needle roller bearing which fits together with 3rd gear, inside 2nd gear (photo).

10 Next fit the circlip on the shaft retaining third gear in position (photo).

11 The clearance between this gear and the circlip should be 0.10 - 0.25 mm (0.004 - 0.010 inches). If the gap is outside this range then a circlip of different thickness is necessary to correct it.

12 Next fit the spacer spring, 4th gear and the inner race of the roller bearing (photo).

13 In order to drive the race and gear onto the shaft select a tube or socket of the required diameter. When the race is nearly fully on, put the circlip in position also and drive that on with it until it reaches the groove (photo).

5c Main casing - installing needle bearings and reverse gearshaft

1 Two sets of needle roller bearings are fitted at the rear end of the main casing. One set comprises two roller cages and a spacer between and in this the reverse drive shaft runs. Drive one cage into the casing with a socket on an extension or suitable drift so that it is flush with one end of the bore. The metal face of the needle cage end should face inwards. The spacer should then be inserted with its slot so lined up that it will engage with the locking bolt which is screwed in through the side of the casing. Later models have a circlip instead of a locking bolt; on such models there is no spacer.

2 If applicable, put the locking bolt in position and then drive the other needle roller bearing into the other end of the bore. Alternatively the bearings and spacer can be assembled to the shaft and put into the casing as an assembly (photo).

3 If difficulty is experienced in fitting the reverse gear shaft, heat the transmission case to 60° to 80° C (140° to 176° F) using steam or hot water, then drive the shaft in with a soft-faced hammer.

4 The gear may then be fitted to the other end and the circlip replaced (photo).

5 The other bearing supports the rear end of the input shaft front half. Fit the single needle roller cage into the bore. A circlip retains the bearing at each end.

5d Gear carrier - fitting bearings

1 The needle roller bearing for the forward end of the pinion shaft should be lined up so that the hole for the locking screw corresponds with the recess in the bearing (photo). Tap it into position and fit the locking screw.

2 The special ball bearing with the flange outer race should then be fitted into position from the outside of the carrier casing (photo).

5e Gear carrier - refitting shafts and selector forks

1 It is assumed that the selector rails are in order (see Section 4, paragraph 7) and the forks are a correct fit in the hub sleeve grooves (Section 4, paragraph 6).

2 The first task is to fit the two shafts into the gear carrier. First of all place the two assemblies together and hold them with strong elastic bands or adhesive tape (photo).

3 As an alternative the input shaft can be placed in position by itself first; whichever method is used the selector fork for 3rd/4th gear must be fitted in position on the synchro unit. It

5c.4 Fitting the gear and circlip

5d.1 Fitting the pinion shaft bearing into the gear carrier

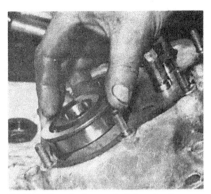

5d.2 Fitting the input shaft bearing into the gear carrier

5e.2 Tape the shaft assemblies together

5e.3 3rd, 4th gear selector fork position

5e.4 Putting the pinion shaft into the carrier

5e.5 Fitting the pinion shaft bearing after fitting the shaft

5e.6 Driving on the input shaft circlip against the concave washer

5e.7 Reverse gear selector pad and relay lever

cannot be fitted afterwards. Note that the curve of the fork shrouds the rear part of the hub (photo). When putting the shaft(s) in position the rail for the selector fork is engaged and care must be taken to see that the fork does not jam on the rail as it moves in.

4 If the pinion shaft is not put in together with the input shaft the bearing should be taken out of the casing. The shaft assembly may then be put in position (photo).

5 After that the bearing can be fitted in position round the shaft (photo).

6 With the shafts in position in the carrier the concave washer and circlip should be fitted to the end of the input shaft. Use a socket to drive the circlip against the washer and spring it into the groove (photo).

7 Next fit the selector pad and relay lever for reverse gear onto the rail (photo).

8 The fork for 1st/2nd gear may then be positioned (photo).

9 The selector forks setting is critical. If the wear between the fork and groove is outside the limit the possibility of a gear not being fully engaged and jumping out is increased. If you can get the unit set up in a Volkswagen agent's jig you would be well advised to do so.

10 Provided you have clearly marked the fork positions on the rails there need be no difficulty either although if new forks or hubs have been fitted the markings may no longer apply.

11 If you have no marks and no jig facility handy proceed as follows. Start with the forks loose on the rails. Set all three selector rails in the neutral position, which is when the cut-outs in their ends all line up, and set the synchro hub outer sleeves also in neutral with the forks in position. Then tighten the fork clamp bolts sufficiently to prevent them slipping. Now push each selector in turn so that each gear is fully engaged. The outer

5e.8 Position 1st/2nd gears selector fork

5e.13 Assemble reverse sliding gear and yoke

5f.2 Position the pinion setting shims

5f.4 Reverse sliding gear held in engagement

5f.6 Putting the gear carrier into the casing

5f.7 Replace the castellated locking ring

sleeve of the appropriate synchro hub must move fully over the dogs of the baulk ring and gear in question. In each gear selected the fork must not bind in the groove. If difficulty is experienced in engaging a gear slacken the fork clamp nut and get the synchro hub sleeve fully into mesh and then retighten the fork clamp in position. Then move the selector back to neutral and into the opposite gear position. In all three positions there must be no semblance of pressure in either direction from the fork on to the groove in which it runs. When both forward speed selector forks have been correctly set tighten the clamp bolts to 18ft lbs (2.5 mkg).

12 The sliding reverse gear and yokes can be attached to the relay lever next for setting purposes. It will tend to fall out of position because it is finally held by the reverse gear shaft in the main transmission casing.

13 To set this pinion first engage 2nd gear. Hold the pinion square and in this position it should be lined up midway between the straight cut teeth on the synchro sleeve and the helical teeth of 2nd gear on the input shaft (photo). Then move out of 2nd gear and shift into reverse. The reverse gears should mesh completely. Adjust as necessary by sliding the block along the selector rail. It is most unlikely that the relay lever pivot post is incorrect but as a check the distance from the centre of the eye to the face of the gear carrier should be 40.6 mm ± 0.4 mm (1.598 inch ± .016 inch).

5f Gear carrier - assembly to main casing

1 The main casing should be ready with bearings and reverse gear shaft installed.

2 Fit the pinion setting shims in position on the face of the flange (photo). Put a dab of grease on the shim to prevent it falling off later.

3 Place a new gasket over the studs on the casing, having made sure that the two mating surfaces are quite clean and smooth.

4 Make sure that the reverse sliding gear is not forgotten. It can be prevented from dropping out if reverse gear is engaged (photo).

5 It is best to fit the gear carrier to the casing with the casing standing upright. There are two points to watch:
a) See that the pinion shims stay put.
b) See that the splined reverse gear shaft lines up with and goes into the sliding reverse gear.

6 Provided the foregoing points are watched carefully the whole unit will drop into place quite easily and a few taps with a soft mallet will butt the mating faces together. If something 'solid' is encountered while replacing the assembly stop and look. Do not force anything. Remember the points mentioned and take care with the lining up (photo).

7 When the assembly is fully home turn the casing on its side and refit the castellated locking ring (photo). The locking ring may be tightened with careful use of a hammer and drift. Tighten it as far as the marks made prior to slackening it.

8 Replace the carrier nuts, noting that one carries the earth strap (photo). Tighten them to a torque of 14 ft lbs (2 mkg). Turn the shafts to ensure they turn freely and select all gears in turn.

9 The front section of the input shaft is now ready for installation. Oil the land in the centre which will run in the oil seal and see that the small link stud is screwed into the end of the shaft. Then carefully insert the shaft through the oil seal from the rear of the main casing.

5f.8 Replace the nuts and braided earthing strap

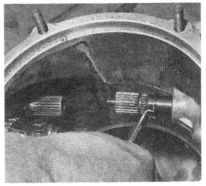

5f.10 Putting the circlip on the input shaft

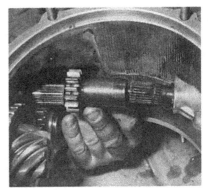

5f.11 Putting the gear sleeve onto the splines

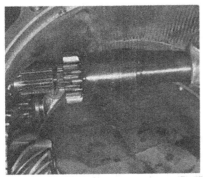

5f.12 Screw the rear extension into the input shaft

5f.13 Fit the sleeve over the input shaft extension

5g 1 Fit a new gasket on the gear shift housing

5g.4a Engage the lever in the cut outs...

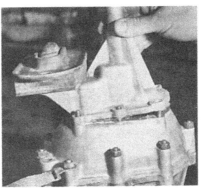

5g.4b ... and replace the housing

5h.3 Fit a new 'O' ring on the side covers

10 Once through, fit the circlip - preferably a new one - over the splines and past the groove onto the smooth part of the shaft (photo).

11 Put the reverse gear/splined sleeve onto the shaft, plain end first (photo).

12 Then screw the shaft stud into the end of the protruding input shaft (photo). Screw it in as far as it will go and then come back one spline in order to let the splined collar engage both halves of the shaft. Do not engage the sleeve with the ends of the shafts butted tight together. Move the sleeve forward so that the gears engage and then move the circlip back along the shaft so that it engages fully into the groove.

. 13 Replace the sleeve over the front of the shaft (photo).

5g Gear shift housing - reassembly

1 Clean the mating surfaces on the end of the gear carrier and shift housing and place a new gasket in position over the studs in the gear carrier (photo).

2 See that the gearbox is in neutral by checking that the cutouts in the ends of the three selector rods are lined up.

3 The gear change lever in the housing should be an easy slide fit in the housing, If it is sloppy in any way it could cause jamming or other problems of changing gear.

4 Fit the housing over the studs, at the same time moving the lever so that the end locates in the cutouts of the ends of the three selector rails (photos).

5 Replace the nuts and tighten to 11ft lbs (1.5 mkg).

5h Differential and side covers - replacement

1 Ensure that all parts are scrupulously clean.

All except GT models (double jointed driveshafts)

2 If new bearings have to be fitted (necessitating driving the old ones off the differential casing and moving the outer races from the side covers) it should be borne in mind that the new bearings will require re-shimming in order to obtain the correct bearing pre-load and pinion gear backlash. It is most unusual for the taper roller bearings to need replacement other than as part of a complete rebuild. As mentioned earlier, the setting up of the differential to the correct clearances and pre-loads - which are essential if quiet running and long life are desired - is a skilled job requiring special measuring equipment designed for this particular transmission. It is assumed therefore, that the original bearings are being refitted.

3 The right hand bearing cover is fitted first. First fit a new 'O' ring (photo). Place the cover in position making sure that the mating faces of both cover and casing are perfectly clean and free from burrs. Do not use any gaskets (on the latest models this cover plate is no longer a separate item, being cast integrally with the casing).

4 With the cover securely in position carefully lower the differential casing into the transmission housing with the crownwheel teeth facing inwards (photo).

5 Replace the left-hand cover - also fitted with a new 'O' ring (photo). No gasket should be used - the photo shows a gasket incorrectly placed.

6 Replace the spacer ring over the shaft (photo).

7 Put the driving flange onto the shaft (photo).

8 Fit the circlip over the end of the shaft and tap it into the groove using a socket of suitable diameter (photos).

9 Fit a new sealing plug (photo).

GT models (swing axle)

10 Ensure that all parts are scrupulously clean and that the shims and spacers are correct for each side of the differential casing. Remember that the shims fitted serve two functions - one is to put a pre-load on the side bearings and the other is to position the crownwheel correctly in relation to the pinion.

11 It may be argued that if new bearings are fitted then the shim requirements should be recalculated. In practice this is not necessary provided that the same crownwheel and pinion are being refitted and that no previous shim alteration has taken place in an abortive attempt to improve some earlier malfunction.

12 When fitting new bearings, support the side cover evenly and securely and arrange the bearing so that the closed side of the ball race faces the outside of the casing on assembly. The bore in the side cover must be scrupulously clean and free of any snags or burrs.

13 The new bearing can be tapped into place using a heavy mallet and a suitable article to apply the load evenly across it. Make sure that it does not tilt, particularly at the start. If it does, bring it out and start again.

14 The right hand side bearing and cover is installed first. Make sure both mating faces are perfectly clean and fit a new O-ring to the cover. No gasket is necessary. Place the cover in position (it will only fit one way) and tighten the nuts evenly to the specified torque.

15 The differential assembly goes in next. With everything perfectly clean the shims may be held in position with a dab of grease. If for some reason there has been a mix up with the shims and you do not know which should go on each side, you are in trouble because you will be unable to set the pinion/crownwheel backlash correctly. In such cases you should take the whole assembly to a Volkswagen specialist and ask him to reset it. With the proper gear it will not take too long. Do not guess!

16 If you know exactly what shims came off each side make sure they are arranged so that the thicker spacer ring is fitted first, with the chamfered side inwards and the shims after that (so that they go between the ring and the bearing).

17 With the spacer and shims in place put the differential into the casing carefully and tap it in so that the shoulder abuts fully against the inner race of the bearing in the cover already fitted.

18 Make sure the remaining shims are properly located on the crownwheel end of the differential and then fit the left hand final drive cover into position using a new O-ring as for the other one. As this cover has to fit over the differential it will be necessary to tap it down into position fully before the nuts can be replaced. It is important to note that the cover retaining nuts must not be used to pull the cover and bearing down. This could easily crack or break it. Tighten the nuts finally to the same torque as the other cover.

19 The transmission case is now completely reassembled and ready to receive the axle shafts and tubes.

6 Synchromesh hub assemblies - dismantling, inspection and reassembly

1 Unless the transmission is the victim of neglect or misuse, or has covered very high mileages, the synchro hub assemblies do not normally need replacement. Until recently they could only be replaced as complete assemblies but it should be possible to obtain the inner or outer section as required.

2 When synchro baulk rings are being renewed it is advisable to fit new blocker bars (sliding keys) and retaining springs in the hubs as this will ensure that full advantage is taken of the new, unworn cut-outs in the rings.

3 When a synchro hub is dismantled, intentionally or accidentally, there are some basic essentials to remember:
a) The splines of both parts wear into each other and provided neither is worn too far they should be kept matched if possible.
b) Where the three sliding keys fit there is a recess in the centre of the spline on the outer sleeve (photo). It is essential, for correct operation, that these be lined up.
c) Make sure that the sliding key retainer clips overlap on each side so that no key has the ends of both clips over it.

4 When examining for wear there are two important features to look at:
a) The fit of the splines. With the keys removed, the inner and outer sections of the hub should slide easily with minimum backlash or axial rock. The degree of permissible wear is difficult to describe in absolute terms. No movement at all is exceptional yet excessive 'slop' would affect operation and cause jumping out of gear. If a new part is being fitted to a worn part check the fit in each of the possible positions radially and also either way round to find the point of minimum play.
b) Selector fork grooves and selector forks should not exceed the maximum permissible clearance of 0.3 mm (0.012 inch). The wear can be on either the fork or groove so it is best to try a new fork in the existing sleeve first to see if the gap is reduced adequately. If not, then a new sleeve is needed. Too much slack between fork and groove induces jumping out of gear. Where a hub also carries gear teeth on the outer sleeve these should be in good condition - unbroken and not pitted or scored.

7 Input shaft oil seal - removal and replacement

1 Clutch contamination may be caused by failure of the oil seal that goes round the input shaft in the transmission casing. During the course of transmission overhaul it would be automatically renewed but it is possible to fit a new one with the transmission installed. The engine must be removed first.

2 With the engine removed detach the clutch release bearing from the operating forks and remove the sleeve from round the input shaft by undoing the three nuts.

5h.4 Inserting the differential assembly

5h.5 Replacing the cover. The gasket is not necessary

5h.6 Insert the spacer ring

5h.7 Replace the driving flange

5h.8a Put the circlip over the shaft

5h.8b Drive the circlip on with a socket

5h.9 Fit a new sealing plug

6.3b The indented splines in the sleeve must line up with the sliding keys

7.5 Driving the new seal into position

3 The seal surrounds the input shaft where it goes through the casing. It can be dug out with a sharp pointed instrument provided care is taken to avoid damaging the surrounding part of the transmission casing.

4 A new seal should be treated with sealing compound on the outside rim (taking care to prevent the compound getting anywhere else on the seal) and then placed in position with the inner lip of the seal facing into the transmission. Be careful not to damage the lip when passing it over the splines of the shaft and make sure it does not turn back when it reaches the part of the shaft on which it bears.

5 It should be driven into position squarely. A piece of tube is ideal for this put round the shaft (photo). If the seal tips in the early stages of being driven in take it out and start again,

otherwise it may be badly distorted and its life will be shortened considerably.

6 The seal should be driven in until the outer shoulder abuts the casing.

8 Differential gears

1 The differential gear contained in the differential casing is not normally a do-it-yourself repair job. This is because failure is extremely rare and in circumstances of extreme wear as a result of either neglect or high mileages the whole assembly would need to be renewed anyway.

2 The function of the differential is to enable the driven wheels of the vehicle to rotate at different speeds when the car is

turning and the outer wheel is obliged to travel in a wider area than the inner wheel. Each driveshaft has a bevel gear at the inner end and these are meshed constantly together with two bevel pinions. The shaft on which both pinions are mounted is fixed into the differential casing.

3 The crownwheel, which takes the drive from the gearbox, is bolted to the differential casing. When the drive rotates the differential casing, the pinion shaft is carried round with it and

the pinion gears therefore rotate the driveshaft gears.

4 If either driveshaft is slowed down, or stopped completely, the differential pinions rotate on their own shafts due to the speed difference between the driveshafts.

5 Under such circumstances the power must be transmitted through the shaft offering least resistance. In cornering this would be the outer wheel. When you have one wheel in a ditch the power always goes to that wheel!

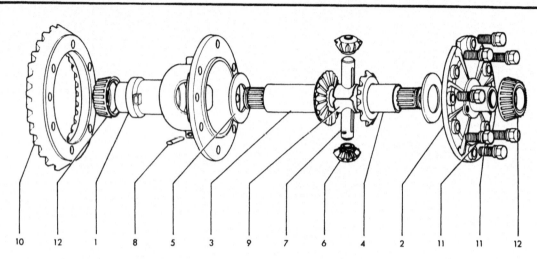

Fig. 6.3. Differential components - all models except GT

1 Differential housing
2 Differential housing cover
3 Differential side gear (long shaft)
4 Differential side gear (short shaft)
5 Thrust washer
6 Differential pinion
7 Pinion shaft
8 Shaft locking pin
9 Spacer sleeve
10 Ring gear (crownwheel)
11 Screws and spring washers
12 Side bearing inner race

Fig. 6.4. Cross-section of differential fitted to GT models

S1 Differential casing shim
S2 Differential casing shim
S3 Pinion shim

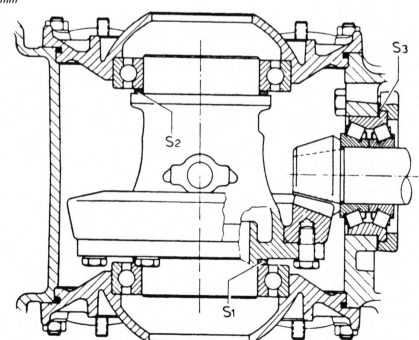

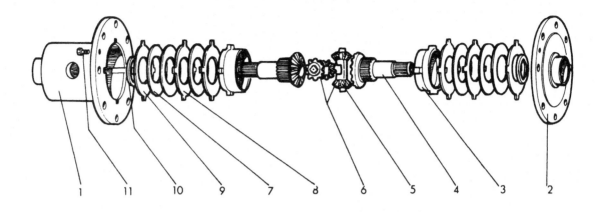

Fig. 6.5. Limited slip differential - plate type

1 Housing	4 Differential side gear	7 Inner splined plates	plates
2 Housing end plate	5 Pinion spindle	8 Outer splined plates	10 Thrust washer
3 Pressure ring	6 Differential pinions	9 Dished outer splined	11 Socket head cap screw

9 Limited slip differential (plate type)

Limited slip differential is fitted to cars where the terrain they have to cover requires both drive wheels to be able to give traction simultaneously.

Inside the differential casing there are two differential pinion shafts instead of one and these are not set in the casing direct. The casing transfers the drive to the pinion shafts by means of what is in effect a multiplate clutch. One set of plates is splined to the driveshaft gears and the others to the casing. The pinion shaft ends are sandwiched between two pressure rings which are recessed to accept them. The pressure rings are also splined to the driveshaft gears. If the driveshafts rotate at different speeds, therefore, the pressure rings ride up on the ends of the differential pinion shafts and, being forced apart exert pressure on the 'clutch' plates. This effectively locks both the driveshaft gears to the casing which then transmits the drive power equally to both.

It must be understood that there is some light pressure maintained at all times on the 'clutch' plates by inbuilt diaphragm spring plates. Also on normal road surfaces the locking mechanism will still operate on sharp turns, particularly if considerable power is used. This has a noticeable effect on handling which one has to get accustomed to.

A further point regarding vehicles fitted with limited slip differentials is that the differentials wear out more quickly. In all conditions where there is a difference between the driving wheel speeds the friction discs are working against each other to a certain extent. Thus their surfaces are subject to frictional wear.

Note also that a special oil is required for transmissions fitted with limited slip differential.

10 Gear shift mechanism and linkage - removal, inspection and replacement

1 Refer to Fig. 6.6. The shift linkage comprises a system of levers from the gear knob to the front end of the gear box.
2 To remove the system first lift the rear seat, remove the plate over the access hole in the frame fork and then remove the locking wire. Undo the square headed screw.

3 Going back to the gear lever, remove the bolts holding the gear lever bracket and take out the gear lever complete with bracket, spring and stop plate.
4 Now remove the tapping screw from the spring pin and take off the shift rod coupling.
5 There is a plate in the front apron. Remove this and if necessary the deformation element, slide the shift rod forward with a mole grip or pliers and pull it out.
6 Check all the parts for wear and replace as necessary. If the gear lever is cranked, a shift rod with a slot in the ball socket must be fitted.
7 Installation is the reverse of removal.
8 Grease the rod and slide it into the frame tunnel. Fit the guide sleeve into the front guide bracket and fit the retaining ring. Grease the guide sleeve. Install the sleeve so that the slot is at the side.
9 Push the shaft rod through the front guide until the ball socket is in the centre of the hole in the frame tunnel. Now fit the frame head plate (with gasket) and the front apron plate. Reinstall the deformation element if it was removed.
10 Install the shift rod coupling, put the spring pin in place and then tighten the tapping screw.
11 Fit the coupling to the inner shift lever, tighten the cap screw, lock it with wire and refit the cover on the frame fork.
12 Assemble the gear lever, fit the bracket, push the bellows on and fit the knob to the gear lever. Coat the bracket and socket in the shift rod with multi purpose grease.
13 Finally fit the spring and stop plate, make sure the longer raised edge is on the right and the slot with the pointed end is pointing forward. Fit the lever and securing bracket and tighten the bolts in the bracket.
14 If the gear lever or the shift rod rattle check the fit of the guide sleeve and retaining ring. If the lever rattles in the end of the shift rod fill the end of the rod with thick grease.

11 Shift linkage - adjustment

1 If the linkage has been dismantled it will be necessary to check the adjustment. During the check and adjustment the clutch should be disengaged and held disengaged.
2 Select second gear and slacken the bolts in the bracket.

3 Set the gear lever in the second gear position so that the lever is vertical in the transverse direction and at an angle of 11° to the vertical towards the rear along the centre line of the car. This applies to the straight lever, use lower part of the cranked lever.

4 With a suitable tool, eg; a screwdriver, move the stop plate under the bracket to the left until it touches the shoulder of the lever. This is shown by the arrow in Fig. 6.7. The plate must just move the gear lever. Now tighten the bracket bolts. Make sure nothing moves.

5 To check, move the knob sideways while the lever is in second gear. It should move between 15 to 20 mm (19/32 and 25/32

inch) measured at the knob. Check that all gears engage easily and check the reverse safety catch.

12 Gearchange. GT Beetle

These Beetles are fitted with a sports gear shift incorporated in a tunnel tray. The same principles exist although the mechanism is slightly extended to give a more sporty appeal. The same sports shift may be fitted to the other models as an optional extra.

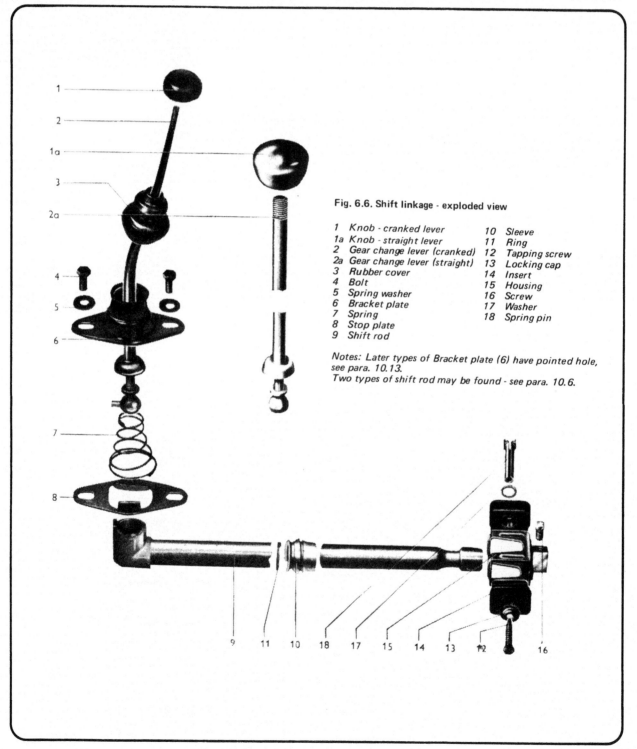

Fig. 6.6. Shift linkage - exploded view

1 Knob - cranked lever	10 Sleeve
1a Knob - straight lever	11 Ring
2 Gear change lever (cranked)	12 Tapping screw
2a Gear change lever (straight)	13 Locking cap
3 Rubber cover	14 Insert
4 Bolt	15 Housing
5 Spring washer	16 Screw
6 Bracket plate	17 Washer
7 Spring	18 Spring pin
8 Stop plate	
9 Shift rod	

Notes: Later types of Bracket plate (6) have pointed hole, see para. 10.13.
Two types of shift rod may be found - see para. 10.6.

13 Fault diagnosis - transmission and final drive

It is sometimes difficult to decide whether it is worthwhile removing and dismantling the gearbox for a fault which may be nothing more than a minor irritant. Gearboxes which howl, or where the synchromesh can be 'beaten' by a quick gear change, may continue to perform for a long time in this state. A worn gearbox usually needs a complete rebuild to eliminate noise because the various gears, if re-aligned on new bearings, will continue to howl when different wearing surfaces are presented to each other.

The decision to overhaul therefore, must be considered with regard to time and money available, relative to the degree of noise or malfunction that the driver has to suffer.

Symptom	Reason/s	Remedy
Ineffective synchromesh	Worn baulk rings or synchro hubs	Dismantle and renew.
Jumps out of one or more gears (on drive or over-run)	Weak detent springs, or worn selector forks or worn gears, or all three	Dismantle and renew.
Noisy, rough, whining and vibration	Worn bearings (initially) resulting in extended wear generally due to play and backlash	Dismantle and renew.
Noisy and difficult engagement of gear	Clutch fault	Examine clutch operation.

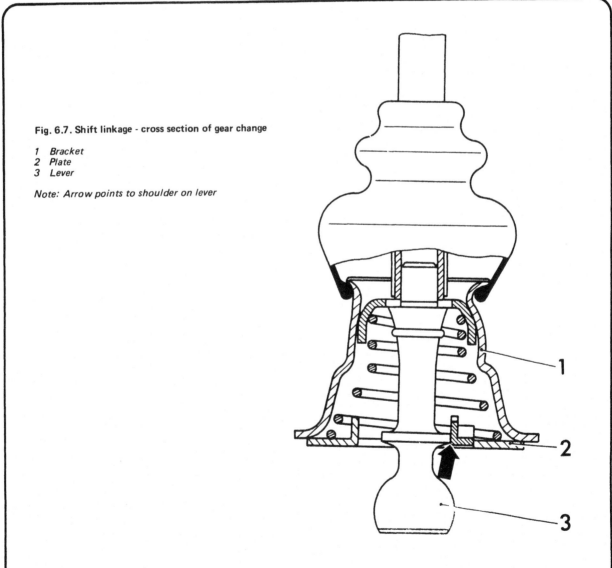

Fig. 6.7. Shift linkage - cross section of gear change

1 Bracket
2 Plate
3 Lever

Note: Arrow points to shoulder on lever

Chapter 7 Automatic stick-shift transmission

Contents

Driving technique 2
Engine differences, oil pump and torque converter plate ... 6
Engine and transmission - removal and replacement ... 4
General description 1

Maintenance and adjustments 3
Oil and vacuum tank - modifications for USA, 1973 ... 8
Recent modifications 7
Torque converter - stall speed test 5

Specifications

Gear ratios:

Low	2.25 : 1
Medium	1.26 : 1
High	0.89 : 1
Reverse	3.07 : 1

Stall speed:

1300 cc/73.8 cu in.	2000 - 2250 rpm
1600 cc/96.7 cu in.	1900 - 2100 rpm

Final drive ratio	4.375 : 1
Torque multiplication	2 : 1
Converter oil capacity (dry)	3.6 litres/7½ Imperial pints
Transmission/final drive oil capacity (dry)	3.0 litres/6¼ Imperial pints
Converter oil pressure at 4000 rpm (80° C)	38 - 52 psi (2.7 - 3.7 kg cm^2)

Torque wrench settings:

	lbs ft	kg m
Torque converter drive plate gland nut	282	39

1 General description

The automatic stick shift transmission is an optional extra. The system works as follows:

A 3-speed gearbox of conventional design, a clutch of conventional design and a torque converter are all married together. Gears are changed by a conventional gear lever. The gear lever, however, is connected to the clutch in such a way that as soon as the lever is moved longitudinally (ie; in a gear selection direction) the clutch disengages.

The torque converter operates to transmit power when the engine is turning above idling speed and so therefore acts as a moving off clutch. It also acts as a form of 'slip' between engine and gear - in other words when engine load is higher, such as when moving from rest or uphill - the engine speed can increase to impart more power even though the vehicle remains in the same gear at the same speed. This enables the gearbox to manage with only 3 forward gears. These are the same as 2nd, 3rd and top of a conventional 4 speed manual gearbox.

If the torque converter is called upon to 'slip' too much - for example when driving up a long hill in top gear, the oil will overheat. When this happens a temperature sensitive warning light on the dashboard lights up and indicates that a lower gear should be selected. Lowest gear is adequate for all normal conditions and no warning light for the low range is installed.

The operation of the clutch is pneumatic via a control valve and servo. Vacuum is drawn from the engine intake manifold and there is also a vacuum tank. The control valve is fitted on the left left rear wing. The vacuum control valve is actuated by a solenoid switch and this in turn is actuated by a special switch incorporated in the gear lever base. As soon as the gear lever is moved forwards or backwards the switch contacts close, and the solenoid operates. In addition there is a second switch. This acts as a starter inhibitor which avoids the engine being started with a gear engaged. It also prevents the clutch from engaging again during the brief period of lateral movement of the lever from one range to another through neutral.

The control valve also incorporates a device to regulate the speed with which the clutch engages. In accelerating circumstances (throttle open) the operation of the servo is quicker than would be possible with a foot pedal change. In decelerating conditions (throttle closed) the control valve controls the servo to operate less quickly. This enables the clutch to re-engage smoothly and without snatch.

Oil for the torque converter is circulated by a pump from the converter and through a reservoir tank which is mounted under the right rear mudguard. The pump is fitted on the end of the engine oil pump shaft. This oil circulation serves to cool the oil as well as maintain a constant pressure, (by means of a restriction in the return link). A relief valve is incorporated in

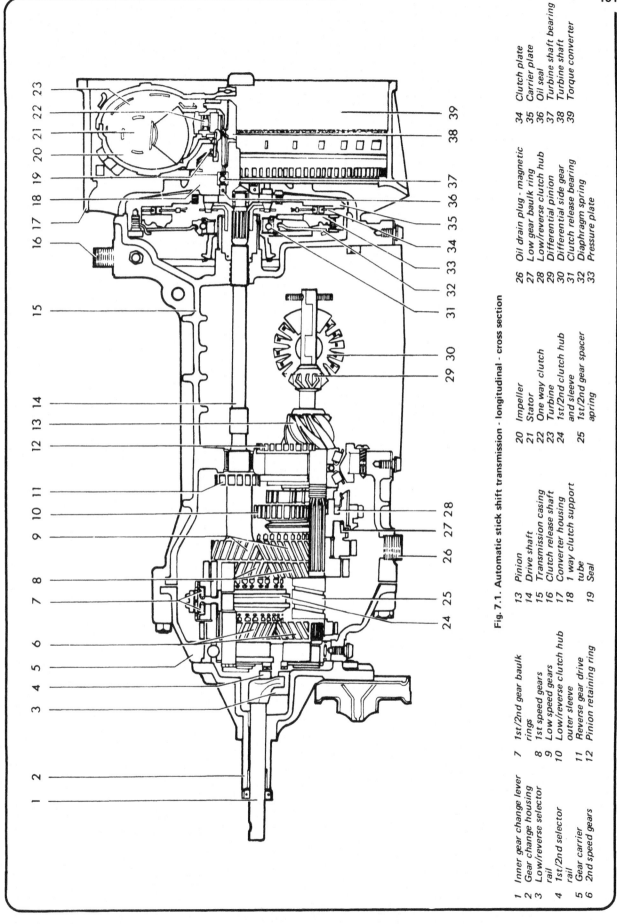

Fig. 7.1. Automatic stick shift transmission - longitudinal - cross section

1	Inner gear change lever	7	1st/2nd gear baulk rings	13	Pinion	20	Impeller
2	Gear change housing	8	1st speed gears	14	Drive shaft	21	Stator
3	Low/reverse selector rail	9	Low speed gears	15	Transmission casing	22	One way clutch
4	1st/2nd selector rail	10	Low/reverse clutch hub outer sleeve	16	Clutch release shaft	23	Turbine
5	Gear carrier	11	Reverse gear drive	17	Converter housing	24	1st/2nd clutch hub and sleeve
6	2nd speed gears	12	Pinion retaining ring	18	1 way clutch support tube	25	1st/2nd gear spacer spring
				19	Seal		

26	Oil drain plug - magnetic	34	Clutch plate
27	Low gear baulk ring	35	Carrier plate
28	Low/reverse clutch hub	36	Oil seal
29	Differential pinion	37	Turbine shaft bearing
30	Differential side gear	38	Turbine shaft
31	Clutch release bearing	39	Torque converter
32	Diaphragm spring		
33	Pressure plate		

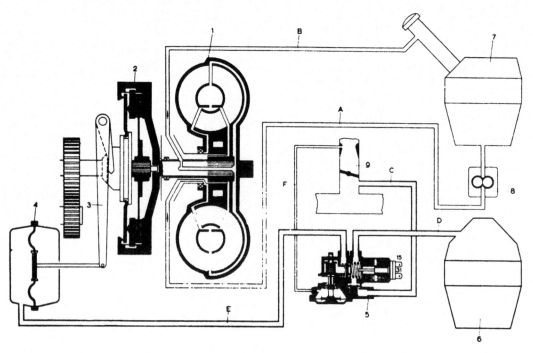

**Fig. 7.2. Schematic layout of torque converter and
auto-stick shift clutch operating systems**

1   Torque converter
2   Clutch
3   Clutch operating lever
4   Clutch servo
5   Servo control valve

6   Vacuum tank
7   Converter oil tank
8   Converter oil pump
9   Carburettor venturi
A   Oil pressure line
B   Oil return line

Vacuum lines
C   Inlet manifold to control valve
D   Tank to control valve
E   Servo to control valve
F   Control/reduction valve to venturi

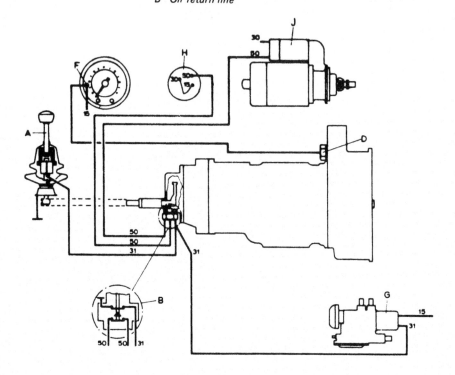

Fig. 7.3. Electrical connections for auto-stick shift

A   Shift lever and contact
B   Starter inhibitor switch and
     neutral contact

D   Temperature switch (140 –
     150º C)

F   Warning lamp
G   Control valve

H   Ignition switch
J   Starter motor solenoid

the pump to limit maximum pressure.

2 Driving techniques

1 The gear change lever looks and functions like a conventional floor change except that there are only 4 positions - 3 forward and 1 reverse. In order that the 'automatic' conventions are impressed on the driver the three forward speeds are referred to as 'L' 1 and 2, (even though they are 1st, 2nd and 3rd!). The change is through the conventional H pattern.

2 The engine can be started only in the neutral position. When the engine is cold (and the automatic choke in operation) the idling speed is higher than when warm so before engaging a gear apply brakes, otherwise the car will creep forward.

3 For normal driving it is necessary to use only the top two gears (1 and 2). This is because the torque converter applies the engine power over a wider range.

4 To engage a gear whilst stationary move the lever into position 1. As soon as the lever starts to move, the clutch will automatically disengage. It is important that the engine speed is not above idling. Let go of the gear lever and depress the accelerator. The torque converter will take up the drive and the car will move off. Speed range 0-55mph.

5 If starting on a steep slope or where tight manoeuvring is involved select 'L' for forward movement. Speed range 0-30mph approximately.

6 Once the car is under way the gear change lever can be moved when required into the most suitable driving range.

7 If excessive load is placed on the torque converter in 1 and 2 ranges the oil temperature warning light will come on indicating the need to drop to a lower gear.

8 It is not necessary to disengage from the selected gear for temporary stops in traffic, but the brakes must be applied to prevent 'creep'.

9 On the older models the handbrake must be fully on when the car is parked as there was no effective brake because the torque conventor did not connect the transmission to the engine mechanically. However in February 1973 a parking lock was introduced which will effectively overcome this problem. This is detailed fully in Section 7 of this Chapter.

10The vehicle can be tow started if the 'L' range is selected and a speed of more that 15 mph is attained. If less than that the torque converter will not 'bite'.

11The car may be towed in case of breakdown or accident with the gearchange lever in neutral.

3 Maintenance and adjustments

1 The automatic transmission fluid (ATF) level in the tank should be checked at 1000 mile or one month intervals. At the same time the converter, tank and all connection hoses should be examined for signs of leakage.

2 If the ATF level drops, yet there is no sign of external leakage, check the engine oil level.If this has risen it indicates that there is probably a leak from ATF pump to engine oil pump. This must be attended to immediately otherwise both engine and converter could be ruined.

3 Every 6000 miles check the oil level in the final drive and gearbox.

4 Every 20,000 miles change the gearbox/final drive lubricant and clean the magnetic drain plugs. Use SAE 80 or SAE 80/90.

5 Check shift clutch adjustment every 6000 miles. Indications of malfunction are slip or noisy engagement of reverse - assuming of course that the torque converter is operating correctly and engine revolutions are not too high at the time of gear engagement.

6 The clutch clearance can be checked by pulling the vacuum hose off the servo unit and then measuring the distance between the bottom of the adjuster sleeve and the upper edge of the servo mounting bracket (Fig. 7.4).

7 If this measurement is more than 4 mm, the clutch needs

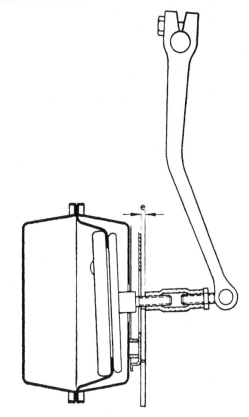

Fig. 7.4. Clutch/servo adjustment

Dimension 'e' is 4 mm maximum

adjustment.

8 To adjust the clutch, first slacken the adjuster sleeve locknut just enough to enable the adjuster to be turned. Then turn the adjuster away from the locknut until there is a gap of 6.5 mm between the two. Then move the locknut back to the end of the adjuster sleeve and tighten it once more.

9 If, as a result of adjustmant the operating lever is found to be touching the clutch housing then it indicates that the clutch plate is worn out.

10The control valve air filter will need cleaning at intervals depending on the condition in which the car is operating, 3000 miles is a suitable interval for normal conditions.

11The filter is a mushroom shaped unit fitted to the side of the control valve (Fig. 7.5). Simply unscrew it with a spanner on the hexagon shank of the mounting stud. Thoroughly flush it in petrol and if possible blow it dry completely with compressed air. It is important to avoid the possibility of any cleaning fluid being drawn into the system after it is refitted. Do not oil the filter.

12 Shift clutch engagement may need adjustment. As described earlier, the control valve governs the speed of clutch engagement. When changing to a higher gear it tends to be quick, and slower from high to low. This prevents any undue snatch. To check the clutch try changing from 2 to 1 at about 45 mph without depressing the accelerator pedal. There should be a delay of about 1 second before the drive is fully taken up. If there is any snatch then it indicates that adjustment may be necessary - all other things being equal.

13To adjust the speed of clutch engagement remove the cap from the top of the control valve to expose the head of the adjusting screw (Fig. 7.5). To decrease the speed of engagement turn the screw ¼-½ turn clockwise. To increase engagement speed turn it ¼-½ turn anticlockwise.

14After some time it may be necessary to clean, adjust or renew the switch contacts inside the gear lever which operates the shift

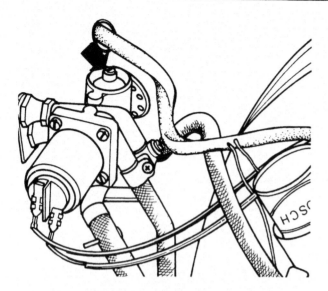

Fig. 7.5. Vacuum servo control valve mounted in engine compartment

Arrow indicates clutch engagement time regulating screw. Note perforated plate of air filter unit behind.

clutch. Raise the rubber boot round the base of the lever and slacken the locknut at the bottom of the sleeve (Fig. 7.6). Then screw the shift sleeve right off to expose the contacts when the top section of the lever comes off.

15 To set the contacts the sleeve must be screwed down until they just touch and then unscrewed ½ turn which gives a gap of 0.25 - 0.4mm (0.010 - 0.016 inch). It is important that after this setting is made the elongated hole in the sleeve runs fore and aft. It is the slight movement of the lever in this slot which pushes the contacts together prior to shifting the gear. If the slot does not lie fore and aft within the setting limits then undo the other locknut on the threaded sleeve. The whole unit can then be turned into position.

4 Engine and transmission - removal and replacement

Due to the more complex nature of the automatic transmission it is not advised that the owner tries to overhaul or repair it himself.

Removal and replacement of the assembly may be carried out. The principles of removal are the same as for a conventional model.

The following additional points should be noted as well:

1 It will be necessary to detach the torque converter oil lines. The pressure line from the pump should be raised so that oil does not run out.

2 It is necessary to detach the torque converter from the engine flex plate. If the engine is rotated each of the four screws will appear through a hole in the transmission casing. When they have been removed the engine can be separated from the transmission in the usual way.

3 When the transmission unit is being taken off, first devise a way of keeping the torque converter from falling out of the housing; a simple metal strap fixed to two of the mounting studs will do this.

4 Detach the inner ends of the double jointed axle shafts. (See Chapter 6 for details.) Cover the inner joints with plastic sheeting to keep dirt out and hang them up to the underframe with wire.

5 Disconnect the oil hose banjo unions where they join the transmission casing, pull off the two wires to the temperature switches and unclip and pull off the hose from the servo unit.

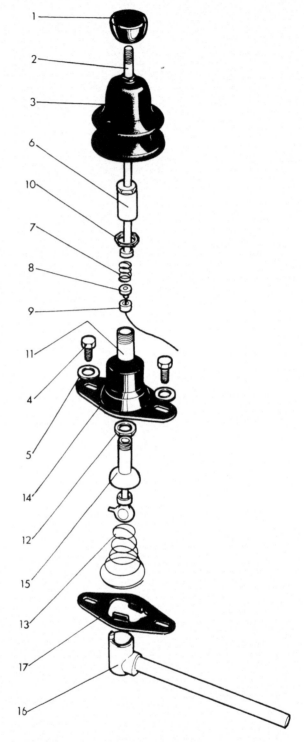

Fig. 7.6. Automatic stick shift - change lever assembly - exploded view

1 Grip	10 Locknut
2 Upper lever	11 Threaded sleeve
3 Boot	12 Lower locknut
4 Mounting bolt	13 Spring
5 Spring washer	14 Mounting plate
6 Shift sleeve	15 Lower lever
7 Spring	16 Change rod
8 Contact	17 Reverse stop plate
9 Insulating sleeve	

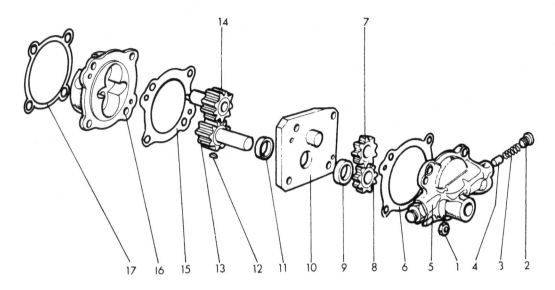

Fig. 7.7. Torque converter oil pump

1	Sealing nut	6	Gasket
2	Plug	7	Converter oil pump - upper gear
3	Spring	8	Converter oil pump - lower gear
4	Piston	9	Plate oil seal
5	Converter oil pump housing		

10	Dividing plate		upper gear and shaft
11	Plate oil seal	15	Gasket
12	Woodruff key	16	Engine oil pump housing
13	Engine oil pump - lower gear and shaft	17	Housing gasket
14	Engine oil pump -		

6 Pull the three pin plugs from the temperature selector switch on the transmission case, and also the starter inhibitor switch on the gear change housing at the front of the transmission casing.

7 Replacement is a reversal of this procedure. When restarting the engine it is important to check that the converter oil is flowing back to the tank. If not after 2 or 3 minutes then there is probably an air lock in the system. Slacken the banjo joints on the transmission to bleed air out whilst the engine is running at idling speed.

5 Torque converter - stall speed test

1 The torque converter stall speed is that speed beyond which the engine will not turn when drive is engaged and the brakes are fully on. To carry it out it is necessary to be able to know the engine rpm. This involves temporary connection of an electric tachometer.

2 It is important that the engine be in proper tune for this test and thus developing its rated power output. The converter oil level must be correct.

3 With the engine warmed up and running, range '2' selected, and all brakes firmly on, increase engine speed to maximum possible and note the revolutions per minute. This must be done quickly and not continue longer than the time to read the instruments, otherwise the converter oil will overheat seriously. If the stall speed exceeds specification (2300 rpm) it is indicative of a slipping gear clutch. If it does not reach stall speed revolutions then the power output of the engine is down.

6 Engine differences

Oil pump

The engine oil pump is elaborated to incorporate the converter fluid pump as well. Modifications to the crankshaft

pulley wheel position allow the extra length to be accommodated.

The two pumps are separated by a plate and oil seals for the common lower gear spindle are incorporated in the plate. The same 4 studs provide the mounting for both pumps.

It is important, when checking both engine and torque converter oils to ensure that a drop in the level of either does not correspond with an increase in the level of the other. Such a condition could indicate faulty seals within the pump. Damage will occur if the two oils mix.

Torque converter drive plate

In place of the flywheel a drive plate is fitted to the crankshaft by a gland nut. This nut is tightened further than that for a flywheel. The torque setting is 282 lb ft (39 kgm). A special tool locked into the holes in the plate is normally needed to tighten the nut satisfactorily. Makeshift methods are likely to distort the plate which is then rendered unserviceable.

7 Recent modifications

The introduction of a modification to the Oil and Vacuum container for USA vehicles fitted with special bumpers is discussed in Section 8.

8 Vacuum and oil container

Vehicles destined for the USA after August 1973 are fitted with modified bumpers and bumper bearers. This means that all such vehicles are fitted also with a modified Vacuum and Oil Container. Vehicles already fitted with the old type must replace the old type with a similar one as the parts are not interchangeable.

Chapter 8
Rear suspension, wheels, bearings and driveshafts

Contents

Axle shafts and tubes (GT models) - examination for wear	7
Axle shafts and tubes (GT models) - removal and replacement	6
Axle tubes (GT models) - oil seal renewal	8
Constant velocity joints - removal, inspection and replacement (not GT models)	3
Driveshafts - removal and replacement (not GT models)	2
General description	1
Oil seals and bearings (GT models) - removal and replacement	5
Rear equalizer spring (GT models) - removal and replacement	12
Rear suspension - diagonal arm - removal and replacement (not GT models)	10
Rear wheel shafts and bearings - removal and replacement (not GT models)	4
Shock absorbers - removal, testing and replacement	9
Torsion bars and spring plates - removal, spring setting and reassembly	11

Specifications

Type

All except GT Beetle	Torsion bar with trailing link and semi trailing arm. Double jointed driveshaft with two constant velocity joints
GT Beetle	Torsion bar with trailing spring plate from outer ends of torsion bar to outer ends of swing axle tube

Shock absorbers ... ... Hydraulic, telescopic

Driveshafts (double jointed type):

Length (actual)	415.5 mm	(16.35 inch)
Length (effective)	405.3 mm	(15.95 inch)

Geometry:

Rear wheel camber	negative 1° ± 40' (except GT Beetle, positive 1°)
Rear wheel toe	0° ± 15'

Suspension spring plate angle:

To May '73	20° 30' + 50'
From May '73	21° 20' + 50'

Wheels:

Super Beetle and GT Beetle (UK)	4½J x 15 with 34 mm* offset (Super Beetle)
Basic Beetle (USA)	4½J x 15
Sports Bug (USA)	5½J x 15 (styled steel) with 26 mm** offset

*41 mm with negative steering roll radius
**34 mm " " " " "

Tyres

	Size
Super and basic Beetle (USA)	155 SR 15 radial
	5.60 x 15 crossply
Super and basic Beetle (USA)	6.00 x 15 bias-ply
Sports Bug (USA)	175/70 HR 15 radial

Note: Tyre pressures depend on the make of tyre fitted.

Torque wrench settings:

								lbs ft	kg m
Wheel bolts ...	...	...	...	...	...	...	...	87 to 94	12 to 13
Socket head cap screws for drive flanges ...				...	...	...	...	25	3.5
Wheel shaft nuts (double jointed driveshafts)				...	...	...	...	253	35
Spring plate bolts (double jointed driveshafts)			...	...	...	...		80	11
Diagonal arm socket head pivot screw		...	...	...	...			87	12
Shock absorber upper and lower bolts		...	...	...	...			50	7
Rear wheel bearing cover bolts	...	...	...	...	...			43	6
Axle tube retainer nuts (swing axle)		...	...	...	...			14	2
Axle shaft nut (swing axle) ...	...	...	...	...	...			217	30
Axle tube/spring plate bolts and nuts (swing axle)			...	...				72	10

1 General description

All the models covered by this manual, except the GT Beetle, have diagonal arm torsion bar suspension with double jointed driveshafts. The GT Beetle also has torsion bar suspension, but the driveshafts (axle shafts) are jointed only at their inner ends, and run inside rigid axle tubes. Hydraulic telescopic shock absorbers (dampers) are used on all models.

This may not be easily understandable to the layman so perhaps a little more explanation is necessary. Refer to Fig. 8.1 or Fig. 8.2 as appropriate.

The engine and gearbox as a unit are fixed to the frame crosstube with bonded rubber mountings and attached to the body at the rear with a carrier frame.

On all except GT models, the driving torque is taken from the differential flanges to the wheels by short shafts having constant velocity joints at each end which provides for the angular motion of the hub in respect to the transmission casing and, since the CV joints work on splines, makes allowance for the variation in length of the driveshaft requirement.

The wheels are carried on stub axles mounted on the semi-trailing arm (diagonal arm) which is able to pivot about a bearing of 'Silentbloc' bushes mounted in the end of the diagonal arm and turning about a fitted bolt held in a bracket attached to the crosstube. This determines the radius of movement of the wheel hub in the vertical plane.

On GT models, the inner ends of the driveshafts are located in the transmission casing in spade type universal joints. Each axle shaft runs in a tube, the outer end of which is attached to the rear suspension plate. The outer end of the tube also carries the bearing. It can be seen therefore that the shaft and wheel form a rigid unit, pivoted at the inner end. This is called the swinging axle type of drive.

The axle tubes are oil filled from the transmission casing and this provides lubrication for the outer wheel bearing. Oil is retained at the outer end by a conventional seal on the shaft and at the inner end by a heavy duty flexible boot which shrouds the axle tube retainer plate. The lateral location of each axle is all carried at the inner end by the axle tube retainer plate. It can be seen that the shaft outer bearing and tube are all locked together so that the side thrust is therefore carried by the inner pivoting end of the tube. The spade end of the axle shaft in fact floats in the side gear. The side gear lateral location is by a thrust ring and circlip.

On all the models, the actual spring force is supplied by the trailing link (spring plate) and the torsion bar. The torsion bar is held firmly at its inner end being splined into a fixed bush. The outer end is splined into the spring plate which has a boss mounted in rubber bushes. The rubber bushes are held to the end of the crosstube by a cover plate. Thus if the spring plate is moved in a vertical plane about the torsion arm it will twist the torsion arm which will in turn tend to bring the spring plate back to its original position. In fact the torsion arm is stressed in such a way initially that when the spring plate is bolted to the diagonal arm there is sufficient force exerted by the torsion arm to support the weight of the car and passengers and still have sufficient power to deal with the axle movement due to unevenness in the road surface.

This suspension arrangement gives a slight variation in the camber angle of the rear wheels which assists the road holding properties.

The twin leaf spring plate shown in Fig. 8.1 has now been replaced by a single leaf of stronger design.

2 Driveshafts - removal and replacement (not GT models)

1 The vehicle should be placed over a pit or on a ramp. If it is proposed only to remove the driveshaft then there is no need to jack the wheels up.

2 The constant velocity joints are each held by six 8 m special screws. (XZN screws). To remove these a special tool is required. These are manufactured by "HAZET" which is a German firm and are obtainable through some VW agents (VW part number 990-8Lg). It is possible to remove the screws with a hexagonal allen key if it is a snug fit. We have done this many times BUT be careful. The bolts are tight (25 lb ft/3.5 mkg) and if you break the inner serrations with the key there is a long hard time ahead. Remove the bolts and lock plates (photo). Be sure that all grease and dirt has been removed before starting, wipe the joints clean again and remove the shaft bodily (photo).

3 If you are not going to replace the joints it is as well to wrap the CV joint on the shaft in a clean polythene bag.

3 Constant velocity joints - removal, inspection and replacement (not GT models)

1 If the constant velocity joint has noticeable wear it must be replaced as an assembly. It is not possible to obtain individual parts for it. If the protective boot has split, and it is suspected that dirt has entered the joint, then it is possible to dismantle the joint, clean it, and repack it with fresh grease before fitting a new boot.

2 First remove the driveshaft as described in the previous Section.

3 It is not necessary to remove the rubber boot unless it is faulty. Simply tap off the metal cover from the joint which is a press fit. Before going any further clean off the face of the joint and note any forge marks on each of the components or any other features which will enable you to ensure they all face the same way again on reassembly. If none is apparent scratch some marks of your own.

4 Remove the circlip from the end of the shaft. If the joint is now supported by vice jaws the shaft can be tapped out. Recover the concave washer from behind the joint on the shaft.

5 Flush the joint out thoroughly, let it dry and then repack it with approximately 60 grams of Castrol MS3 Grease, working it well in from both sides.

6 If the inner cage of the joint is dismantled or falls apart it must be correctly reassembled. First fit the splined hub inside the ball cage - it will only go in if two grooves are lined up (photo).

7 Then press the balls into the cage. They should be a snap fit unless the cage is worn badly (photo).

8 Place the ball and hub assembly into the outer cage so that the chamfered edge of the hub splines will be in a position against the shaft shoulder when the joint is eventually replaced on the shaft (photo). This means that it has to be the right way round in the outer cage because the outer cage goes on so that the

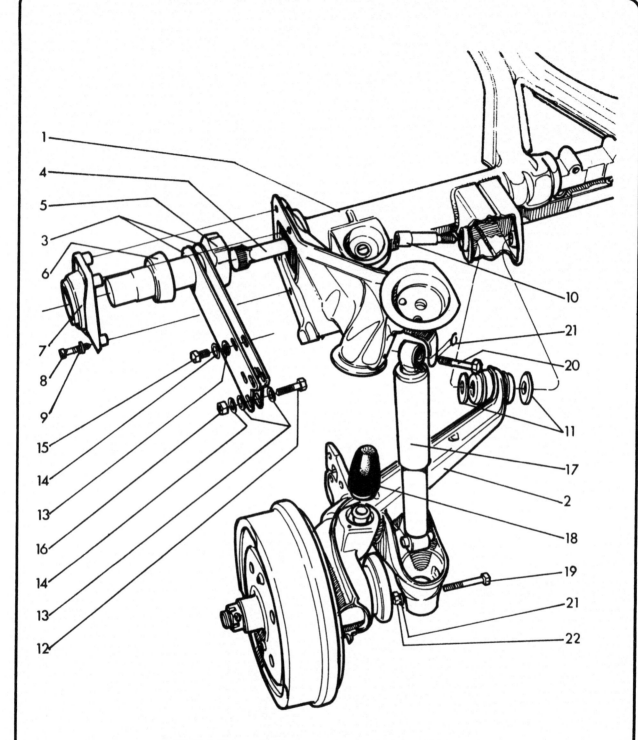

Fig. 8.1. Rear suspension details - double jointed driveshafts (Sec. 1)

1	Frame cross tube	6	Rubber bush (outer)	12	Screw	18	Bump stop
2	Diagonal arm	7	Cover plate	13	Washer	19	Screw
3	Spring plate (double leaf version	8	Screw	14	Spring washer	20	Screw
4	Torsion bar	9	Spring washer	15	Screw	21	Spring washer
5	Rubber bush (left inner)	10	Socket head screw	16	Nut	22	Nut
		11	Spacer	17	Damper		

Note: The single leaf spring plate is fitted on certain models.

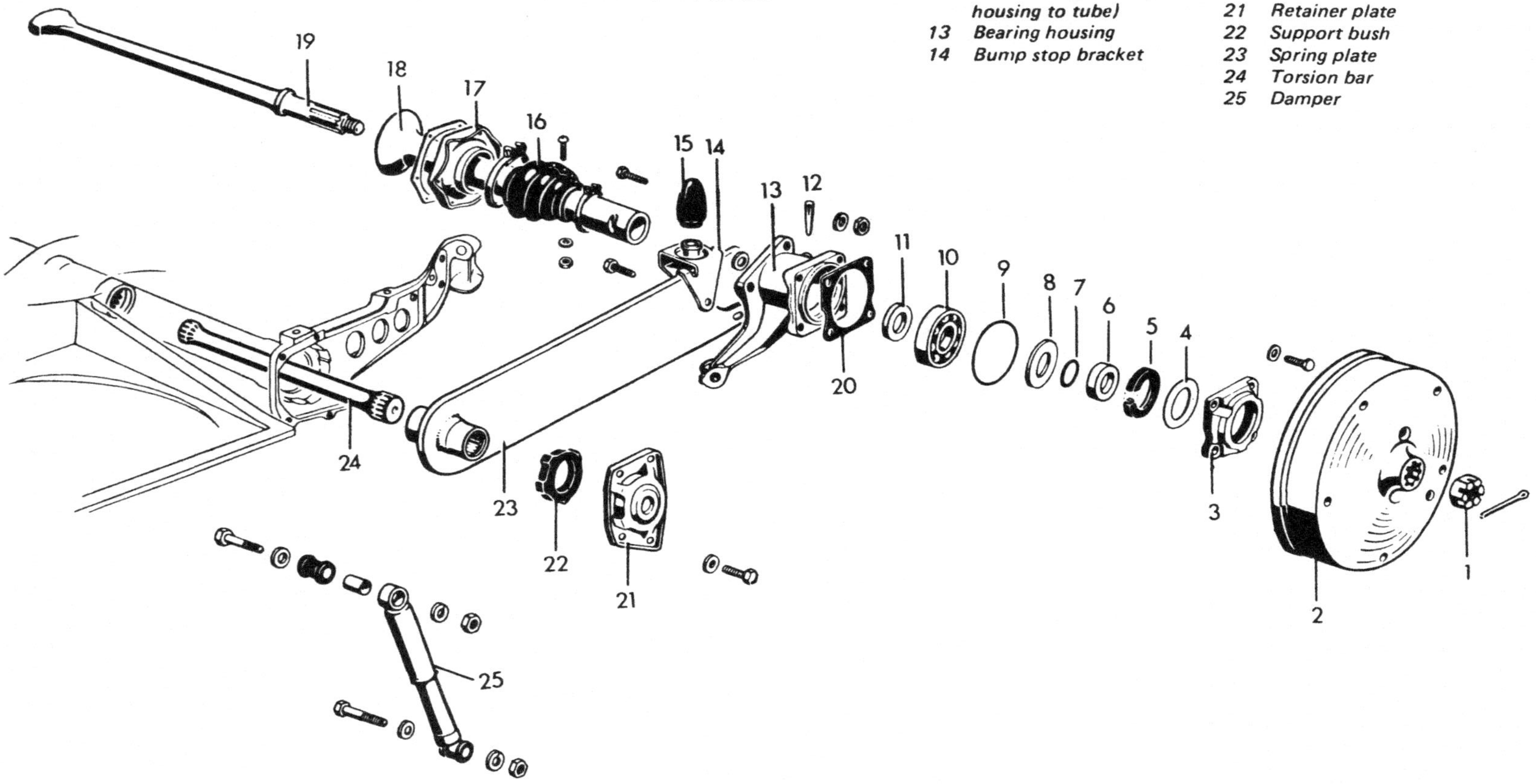

Fig. 8.2. Rear axle shaft and suspension components fitted to GT Beetle (swing axle) (Sec. 1)

1 Axle shaft nut
2 Brake drum
3 Bearing retainer
4 Oil thrower
5 Oil seal
6 Spacer (outer)
7 'O' ring
8 Shim washer
9 'O' ring
10 Bearing
11 Spacer (inner)
12 Pin (locating bearing housing to tube)
13 Bearing housing
14 Bump stop bracket
15 Bump stop
16 Gaiter
17 Axle tube retainer
18 Axle tube
19 Axle shaft
20 Gasket
21 Retainer plate
22 Support bush
23 Spring plate
24 Torsion bar
25 Damper

2.2a Undoing a drive shaft cap screw with an Allen key

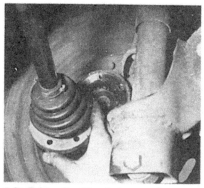

2.2b Taking the drive shaft away from the flange of the wheel shaft

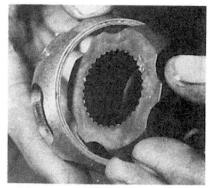

3.6 Constant velocity joint; placing hub section in cage

3.7 Fitting the balls into the cage

3.8 Fitting the hub, balls and cage into the outer section

3.9 Fitting the concave washer on the drive shaft

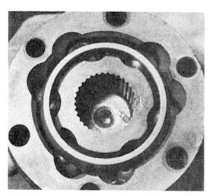

3.10 Placing the joint on the shaft

3.11a Placing the circlip over the end of the shaft

3.11b Driving the circlip home

3.12 Tapping the boot retainer plate back onto the joint

4.5a Removing the bearing retainer bolts

4.5b Taking the bearing retainer off

4.5c Removing the 'O' sealing ring

4.5d Removing the backplate and shoe assembly

4.10 Diagonal arm with the inner ball bearing in position

4.11a Packing the bearing with grease

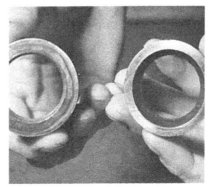

4.11b The inner spacer has a chamfered inner edge (right)

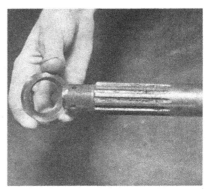

4.11c Fitting the inner spacer on the shaft

protective boot assembly can be tapped back in position on the non-shouldered side.

9 Put the concave washer back on the shaft, concave side towards the joint (photo).

10 Put the joint back on the shaft (photo).

11 Refit the circlip (photo). In order to force the joint against the concave washer sufficiently to get the circlip in the groove, support the shaft in a vice and drive the circlip down with a suit-sized socket (photo).

12 Having repacked the joint with grease tap the boot retainer plate back on to the joint. Use a screw to line up the holes in the joint and plate (photo).

---

4 Rear wheel shafts and bearings - removal and replacement (not GT models)

---

1 Refer to Fig 8.4. Remove the nave plate from the wheel, take out the split pin from the axle shaft nut and with a socket and long bar slacken the nut. This should be done before the wheel is jacked up and you may need some help as the nut is tightened to 253 ft lbs (35 kgm).

2 Remove the driveshaft as described in Section 2.

3 Slacken the wheel nuts, jack up the car and remove the wheel and axle shaft nut.

4 Draw off the brake drum.

5 Remove the four screws holding the bearing cover to the arm and then take off the cover, 'O' ring and backplate (photos).

6 Using a soft faced mallet knock the wheel shaft out and remove the inner spacer.

7 Using a tyre lever take out the inner oil seal.

8 Remove the circlip behind the oil seal and then knock out the ball bearing from the other side using a suitable drift.

9 Remove the spacer sleeve and the inner race of the roller bearing. Drift out the outer race of the roller bearing from the arm.

10 Begin reassembly by first driving in the ball race. Then refit the circlip and oil seal with the lip facing inwards (photo).

11 Pack 60 grams of suitable grease (Castrol LM) into the hub bearing and onto the lip of the seal. Put the inner spacer onto the shaft so that the chamfered edge will marry up with the radius on the shaft flange. Then drive the wheel shaft through the ball bearing until the flange just touches the inner race.

12 Fit the spacer sleeve over the wheel shaft, grease the outer race of the roller bearing and drive it into position in the housing (photos).

13 The inner race has to be fitted over the shaft next and this is best done by using a suitable length of tube. A hammer can then be used to force it in (photo).

14 If necessary fit a new seal into the bearing cover and fill the double lip of the cover with grease.

15 Fit a new 'O' ring round the bearing and install the backplate and bearing cover. Replace the bolts and tighten them to 43 lb/ft (6 kgm). Refit the outer spacer, brake drum and hub and replace the slotted shaft nuts which will be finally tightened when the wheel is replaced and the car is on the ground once more (photos)

16 The slotted wheel shaft nut has to be tightened to 253 lb ft (35.0 kgm). This needs a proper socket and an extension on the handle (photo). It should not be necessary to use a torque wrench because it will be simply a question of re-aligning the split pin holes with the castellations as before. The actual move-ment of the nut to increase the torque from, say, 150 lb ft to 253 lb ft (20 kgm to 35 kgm) is very little indeed. Always refit a new split pin and spread the split ends correctly (photo).

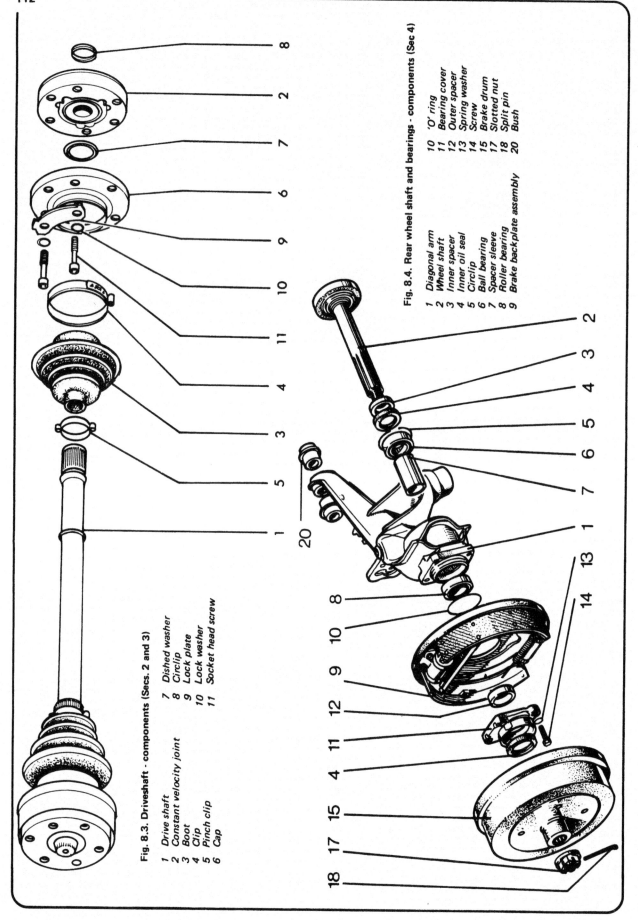

Fig. 8.3. Driveshaft - components (Secs. 2 and 3)

1 Drive shaft
2 Constant velocity joint
3 Boot
4 Clip
5 Pinch clip
6 Cap
7 Dished washer
8 Circlip
9 Lock plate
10 Lock washer
11 Socket head screw

Fig. 8.4. Rear wheel shaft and bearings - components (Sec 4)

1 Diagonal arm
2 Wheel shaft
3 Inner spacer
4 Inner oil seal
5 Circlip
6 Ball bearing
7 Spacer sleeve
8 Roller bearing
9 Brake backplate assembly
10 'O' ring
11 Bearing cover
12 Outer spacer
13 Spring washer
14 Screw
15 Brake drum
17 Slotted nut
18 Split pin
20 Bush

4.12 Fitting the spacer sleeve

4.13 Driving the roller bearing on to the shaft

4.15a Fitting the outer spacer

4.15b Replacing the wheel shaft nut

4.16a Tightening the axle shaft nut

4.16b Fitting a new axle shaft split pin

5 Oil seals and bearings (GT models) - removal and replacement

1   To renew an oil seal or bearing requires the rear axle shaft nut to be undone so before jacking the car up remove the hub caps and take out the split pin from the castellated nut on the shaft. Using a 36 mm socket spanner and a proper long handle attachment slacken the nut. It is advisable to have the handbrake on also. If the wheel still turns then some additional weight will be needed in the back of the car to prevent the wheel slipping on the ground. Slacken the road wheel bolts at the same time.

2   Jack up the car, remove the road wheel and take off the hub nut.

3   Slacken off the brake shoe adjusters as far as they will go (see Chapter 9 for details).

4   It should now be possible to draw the brake drum off the splined end of the drive shaft. If any difficulty is experienced it should be tapped with a soft mallet progressively round the edges. If this does not seem to work bolt the wheel back onto the drum again and see whether the additional grip provided enables you to pull the drum off with it. If the drum should be really tight and unmovable then it will be necessary to obtain a puller which will hook into the holes in the drum and bear on to the outer end of the axle shaft. Do not strike the drum hard around the edges or you will probably crack it.

5   Once the drum is removed the heads of four bolts which hold the bearing cover to the axle tube are revealed. This cover houses the oil seal. The brake backplate is also held by the four bolts and the whole plate assembly may be moved off the axle and hung on one side without disconnecting either the hydraulic fluid pipes or handbrake cable. The bearing cover is removed so that the 'O' ring round the bearing may be renewed at the same time as the main seal. This 'O' ring should be taken off now and if only the seal renewal is being done then adopt the method described later in this Section.

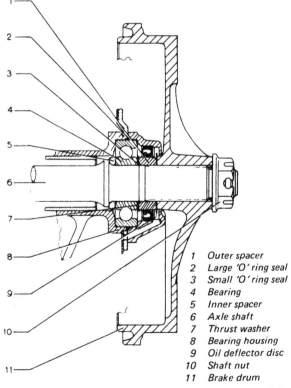

1   Outer spacer
2   Large 'O' ring seal
3   Small 'O' ring seal
4   Bearing
5   Inner spacer
6   Axle shaft
7   Thrust washer
8   Bearing housing
9   Oil deflector disc
10 Shaft nut
11 Brake drum

Fig. 8.5. Cross-section of rear bearing and hub assembly — GT models (Sec. 5)

6   To remove the bearing take off the shim next. The easiest way to remove the bearing is with a fine pronged puller which engages in between the steel balls of the bearing itself; but this is a special tool which may be difficult to obtain. It is possible to drive the shaft inwards just far enough to enable the bearing and shaft together to be pulled out of the housing just enough to get levers behind the bearing; and so remove it with a more conventional puller. There is sufficient clearance at the inner end of the shaft to permit this, but great care must be taken not to overdo it or damage will be caused to the differential pinion gears. Make sure to protect the splined and threaded end of the shaft by replacing the nut and using a block of wood as further protection. Use a heavy hammer and after each blow check by pulling the shaft outwards how far the bearing has moved in relation to it. Once there is a gap sufficient to get a lever in, stop striking the shaft. A third alternative is to lock a self-grip wrench on to the lip of the outer bearing race and then use the nose of the wrench jaws to lever against to ease the bearing out. Two wrenches - one at each side - are best for this method and the jaw teeth must be in good condition. Once the bearing is clear of the housing it is a   reasonably straightforward operation to get it right off.

7   Behind the bearing is another spacer but this need not be disturbed. If it comes out make sure it goes back the same way - with the bevelled edge inwards.

8   To replace the bearing put it over the shaft with the covered side of the ball race if any, facing outwards. It can then be drifted right into the housing.

9   Next fit the large 'O' ring from the seal kit round the outside of the bearing and up to the axle tube flange.

10 Fit the shim over the shaft followed by the smaller rubber 'O' ring.

11 Next drive out the old seal from inside the bearing cover using a suitable punch. Take care not to damage the inner surface of the flange. The new seal may then be driven into the cover with the lip of the seal facing inwards. If, when you drove out the old seal a washer (oil slinger) came out from behind it make sure that the hole which is in one edge of the bearing cover is clear and that the washer goes into the cover before the seal - which can only be fitted from the inside. Tap the seal in with a soft faced mallet or block of wood until the outer face is flush with the cover.

12 Next replace the brake backplate onto the axle tube flange (with the hydraulic cylinder uppermost). The outer spacer collar should be lubricated on its outer face and put onto the shaft.

13 Place the bearing cover in position. The cover has either a raised lug or a hole in one edge. In either case the lug or the oil drain hole goes on the bottom edge but the cover with the oil hole has a paper washer between it and the backplate. If you obtained the correct seal kit for your chassis number the paper washer will be included.

14 Replace the four cover bolts and tighten them evenly to the specified torque.

15 Replace the brake drum and refit the nut. Replace the road wheel and tighten the axle shaft nut as described in Section 4, paragraph 16.

6   Axle shafts and tubes (GT models) - removal and replacement

1   The need to renew an axle shaft is rare and can only be caused by breakage or damage to the splined and threaded outer end. If it is suspected of being badly worn on the inner spade end a check can be made but it is most unusual for such wear to take place separately from any other general wear in the transmission or final drive. Volkswagen do not recommend the removal of axle shafts unless the whole of the transmission assembly has first been removed from the vehicle. This is because in order to assess the correct clearance of the axle tube at the inner end it is considered necessary to be able to swing the tube around freely - without the restriction which results from it being in position on the car. Nevertheless it can be done; although the placing of the necessary gaskets and the constant

guard against dirt contaminating the differential make it something of a struggle. It is reasonable to say that if you have no other reason to remove engine and transmission it would be a lot of effort just to remove an axle shaft.

2   To remove an axle shaft first remove the wheel, brake drum, brake backplate assembly and bearing as described in the previous Section. Do not forget to drain out the oil first.

3   Thoroughly clean the whole area surrounding the axle tube retainer plate on the transmission casing. Clean also the axle tube itself for a distance of about six inches back from the end of the large oil retainer boot. Then slacken both boot retainer clips and draw the boot off the retainer plate and leave it a little way down the tube. This is done so that it does not get abnormally stretched and possibly ruptured during subsequent operations.

4   The next task is to detach the outer end of the axle tube which is secured to the suspension arm plate by three nuts and bolts. Clean up the bolts thoroughly and apply penetrating oil.

5   The position of the outer end of the axle tube in relation to the suspension plate can vary and it is most important that a mark is made to ensure correct re-alignment. A notch exists in the top edge of the axle tube flange so with a cold chisel make another notch exactly in line with it in the edge of the suspension plate. Be accurate.

6   Remove the bolt securing the lower end of the telescopic damper and then put a suitable support under the end of the axle and remove the three nuts and bolts. They are big, tight and probably rusty so make sure you have two spanners of the correct size available - socket or ring. It is quite likely that the spring washers for the nuts will break when the nut is undone so make a note to get some more. They are important. Note also that the front bolt of the three also secures the bump stop buffer bracket. As a result it is slightly larger than the other two.

7   With the bolts removed the axle tube outer end may be moved to the rear, clear of the suspension plate. If you have been reading this in connection with the removal of the transmission unit (Chapter 6) this is as far as you need go here now. Go back to Chapter 6 until you have removed the transmission from the car. Then come back here!

8   Moving to the inner end of the axle tube, next remove the six nuts securing the axle tube retainer plate (do not confuse these with the eight nuts surrounding them).

9   The retainer plate may now be pulled off the studs and the axle tube, together with the plate, taken right off the axle shaft. Carefully remove, intact if possible, the gaskets between the retainer plate and the transmission housing.

10 Fitted over the convex face of the axle tube location on the transmission casing is a plastic hemispherical packing piece. Carefully take this off.

11 Inside the transmission housing it will be possible to see the two eyes of a large circlip which needs contracting in order to be released. Do this with a pair of circlip pliers. The circlip and thrust ring behind it will now come out. The axle shaft, fulcrum plates and side gear can all be withdrawn also.

12 Replacement of the axle shaft and axle tube is a reversal of the removal procedure but there are one or two points which must be carefully considered.

13 When refitting the thrust ring for the side gear note the protrusion in the outer edge which engages a groove in the casing to prevent it rotating.

14 If the transmission has been completely dismantled and both axle tubes have been removed you must make sure you get them back on the correct side as they are handed. With the notch in the bearing housing upwards the shock absorber mounting lug faces forward and down.

15 It will be appreciated that the domed end of the axle tube pivots on the mating face of the transmission. The plastic packing piece in between acts as a bearing surface. The two are held together by the retainer plate. The thickness of the gaskets behind the retainer plate determines the amount of pressure it applies. Too few gaskets and it will be so tight it will move only with difficulty. Too many and it will be slack and result in endfloat of the whole axle assembly. Provided there was no evidence of excessive endfloat on dismantling and that the

plastic packing piece is in good condition there is no reason why the same gaskets should not be refitted. The theoretical clearance is 0.00 to 0.2 mm (0.000 to 0.008 inch) but as there is no satisfactory way of measuring this the only practical way is by moving the axle tube in all directions as far as possible. Friction should be felt but there should be no jamming or sticking at any point.

16 If the gaskets have been damaged, carefully separate them to see how many there are. Each is identified by having one or two holes punched in it indicating that it is either 0.1 or 0.2 mm (0.004 or 0.008 inch) thick. Make up a pack the same thickness and then add or subtract as required.

17 There is an additional rubber 'O' ring which fits in the recess in the bearing cover inside the gaskets. This should always be renewed on reassembly. Do not fit it until the gasket thicknesses have been worked out. Then fit it after the gaskets so that their edges do not get caught up on it causing possible distortion.

18 If you have some molybdenum disulphide paste available (any moly additive will be better than nothing) smear the mating faces of the axle tube and packing to aid lubrication particularly in the early stages of re-use. In any case lubricate them well with transmission oil. Tighten the retainer plate securing nuts evenly to the specified torque.

19 When reconnecting the outer end of the axle tube to the suspension plate make sure that the two marks made before removal line up exactly. Do not forget to re-fix the bump stop bracket to the front bolt. Incidentally, the bolts should be fitted with their heads inwards (to the centre of the car).

20 Do not try to replace the rubber boot until the axle tube has been re-installed. It is much easier (and less likely to cause strain) to fit when the axle is as near horizontal as possible. Make sure that the parts are perfectly clean and that the clips are serviceable and not overtightened.

21 Refill the transmission case with oil.

7 Axle shafts and tubes (GT models) - examination for wear

1 Under normal circumstances the wear on the inner spade ends of the axle shaft will be negligible and in any case should not be greater or less than the wear that will occur in the transmission unit generally.

2 To check the wear, place the end of the shaft in the side gear. First measure the gap across the end with a feeler. If it exceeds 0.20 mm (0.008 inch) then a new shaft, new gear or both will be needed to reduce it.

3 Next fit the fulcrum plates into the side gear and refit the shaft. Then measure the clearance between shaft and fulcrum plate. It should not exceed 0.25 mm (0.010 inch). It is possible to obtain oversize fulcrum plates in order to rectify any excessive clearance here. Renewal plates have grooves cut in their flat faces so you will be able to tell if this has already been done.

4 If examination shows that the gear/shaft clearances warrant buying new parts it should be remembered that the gear and shaft are grouped by size tolerance. These tolerances are colour coded and the shaft has a paint band round it. The gear has a matching colour in a recess.

5 Axle shafts should, of course, be straight and with the shaft held between centres the run-out at the bearing seat should not exceed 0.05 mm (0.002 inch). As this is not the sort of measurement that can be made accurately without precision holding and measuring equipment you should not need to worry about checking it unless you have specific reason for thinking the shaft is bent. Shafts can be straightened - cold only - so it is best to get this done at a Volkswagen agency.

6 The splines and thread on the end of the shaft should not deteriorate unless you have had the misfortune to have the shaft nut come loose for some rare reason. The best way to test the thread is with the full specified torque when the nut is re-tightened. If nothing gives then you can assume that it will serve. If the thread strips - on either nut or shaft - then you will probably need a new shaft as well as nut.

7 Axle tubes should not deteriorate. Examine the concave bearing surface at the inner end and check that the plastic packing is not breaking up. The wheel bearing housings have been known to get damaged in cases of extreme bearing wear or seizure with the result that a new bearing does not fit tightly. In such cases a new housing can be fitted to the tube but once again you are advised to have this done by a Volkswagen agent.

8 Axle tubes (GT models) - oil seal renewal

1 If an axle tube oil seal gaiter leaks oil, action must be taken without delay. Replacements are split so that they can be fitted without having to dismantle everything.

2 Drain off at leat 2 - 3 pints of the transmission oil unless you have lost so much that it will not run out when the gaiter is removed.

3 Undo the clips and cut the old gaiter off. The new split gaiter will be supplied complete with screws and clips.

4 Thoroughly clean the retainer plate and axle tube where the gaiter fits. Then coat the joining edges of the new gaiter with sealing compound and place it in position round the tube so that the joint faces towards the rear of the car. Do not put sealing compound on the ends where the circular clips go.

5 Put the small screws into position with a washer under the head and fit the nuts with a washer also. Tighten them all up evenly but do not overtighten. If the washers appear to be squeezing into the rubber the bolts are too tight.

6 Put the two clips in position and tighten them but not so much that they squeeze and distort the gaiter.

9 Shock Absorbers - removal and replacement (all models)

1 The shock absorbers (dampers) are fastened top and bottom by bolts connecting them to the suspension support frame at the top and the diagonal arm or axle tube at the bottom. The nuts at both ends are very tight so be sure the car is firmly jacked up before undoing or tightening them (photos).

2 When the shock absorber has been removed from the car fasten the piston head in a vice and move the body the full length of the stroke both ways. Equal resistance should be felt each way. Small leaks may be neglected as the damper is over-filled initially to take care of this, but large leaks or uneven movement means that the shock absorber must be scrapped and a new one fitted. Repair is not possible.

10 Rear suspension - diagonal arm - removal and replacement (not GT models)

1 Refer to Fig 8.1 and 8.6. Remove the driveshaft from the wheel shaft. Wrap the CV joint in a polythene bag. Remove the nave plate and the hub nut split pin. Slacken the slotted hub nut. Jack up the car, remove the wheel. Remove the brake drum complete with brake, hub, and backplate and hang it to one side

2 Before undoing the bolts securing the spring plates to the diagonal arm it is important to mark both the arm and plates with a chisel before moving their relative positions. The rear wheel geometry can be upset if this setting is lost (photo).

3 Unclip the brake pipes from the arm.

4 The inner end of the diagonal arm pivots on a socket head bolt (photo). Once this is undone the arm may be taken out. Note the position of the spacer washers which are both located on the outside of the pivot bush.

5 The bushes may be renewed as required. When replacing the pivot bolt it must be tightened to the correct torque of 87 lb ft (12 kgm) and peened into the arm in order to lock it in position.

6 When clamping the spring plates back to the diagonal arm the line up marks made on dismantling must correspond.

7 If extensive repairs are being made (due to damage) which call for renewal of the arm it is important to have the whole assembly checked on a VW alignment jig after assembly.

11 Torsion bars and spring plates - removal, replacement and setting

All models except GT

1 Mark the position of the diagonal arm and spring plate with a chisel. Undo the nuts and bolts holding them together.

GT models only

2 Refer to Fig. 8.2. Before any work can be carried out on the rear torsion bars and spring plates it is necessary to detach the rear axle tubes from the ends of the spring plates. To do this it will be first necessary to support the car firmly on axle stands under the rear jacking points and remove the wheels. The hand-brake cables should be slackened off at the hand lever and the spring plate marked so that it can be lined up with the axle tube on replacement. Details of the foregoing are given in the sections dealing with transmission removal and axle shaft and tube removal. The damper should be disconnected at the lower mounting. The three large mounting bolts securing the axle tube flange to the plate must then be undone and the axle tube drawn back.

All models

3 The spring plate rests on a lug in the frame casting along its lower edge and to relieve residual tension in the torsion bar it must be sprung out so that it rides over the lug. This can be done quite easily with a tyre lever.

4 At this stage the setting of the suspension can be checked. The angle of the spring plate in the unstressed position is given in the Specifications. A spirit level and a protractor will be needed to make the necessary measurements. The horizontal line of the car is taken from the bottom of the door opening in the body shell. Using a level and protractor work out how far this deviates from the true horizontal.

5 Measure the angle of the spring plate from the true horizontal in the same way, eliminating any play there may be by lifting the plate while measurement is taken.

6 Depending on which way the body deviates, the angle is added or subtracted to the plate angle to give the differences between the two. Reference to Fig. 8.7 will illustrate the examples given below:

Body deviation angle	4°
Plate deviation angle	20°
Plate/body angle (AA)	16°
Plate/body angle (BB)	24°

9.1a Rear shock absorber upper mounting bolt

9.1b Rear shock absorber lower mounting bolt

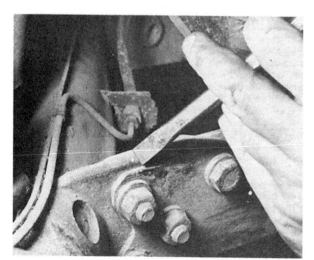

10.2 Marking the rear suspension diagonal arm

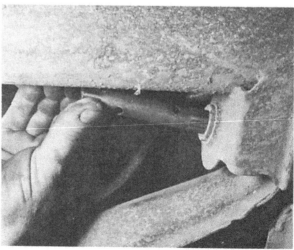

10.4 A tubular spanner inserted in the diagonal arm socket head pivot bolt

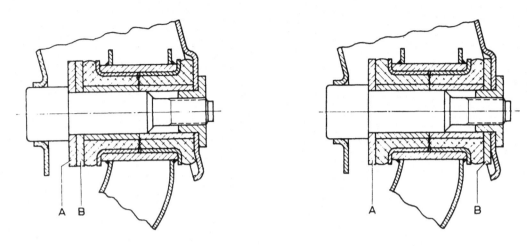

Fig. 8.6. Rear suspension diagonal arm - cross section of pivot mounting and bush (Sec. 10)

A and B Spacer washers

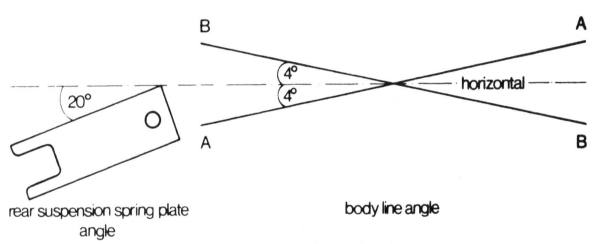

rear suspension spring plate angle

body line angle

Fig. 8.7. Rear suspension spring plate setting angle

Diagram to illustrate setting calculation. See Section 11.

If the correct body angle is 21° 20' then in situation 'AA' the plate angle needs increasing by 5° 20' and in 'BB' decreasing by 2° 40'.

7   The torsion bars are splined at each end. The inner, anchored end has 40 splines (9° per spline) and the outer end **44 splines** (8° 10' per spline) giving an alteration possibility of 50 minutes (9° - 8° 10'). In example 'AA' if the inner end of the torsion bar is rotated anticlockwise six splines and the spring plate rotated clockwise six splines on the outer end the net increase will be 5° (54° - 49°) which is as near as one can get. For situation 'BB' if the inner end is rotated clockwise three splines (27°) and the spring plate rotated anticlockwise on the outer end three splines (24° 30') the decrease is 2°30' which again is as close as one can get.

8   To withdraw the torsion bar sufficiently to rotate the splines for adjustment first remove the four screws which secure the cover clamping the rubber cushion mounting. The spring plate can now be pulled off the torsion bar and at the same time the inner end of the bar may be drawn out of the centre splined location. (Note that if one wishes to take the torsion bar right out then about five or six of the screws which hold the forward edge of the rear mudguard to the body must be removed. The mudguard can then be pulled out of the way. Torsion bars are not interchangeable side for side.)

9   Having reset the torsion bar so that the plate angle is correct make sure that the rubber mounting bushes are in good condition. Renew if in doubt. Cover with flake graphite (to prevent squeaking) and make sure the inner one is installed the proper way up. (The top edge is marked '' Oben''). Before the cover is reinstalled over the rubber bush it will be necessary to raise the plate above the stop lug on the frame casting. If this is not done now the pre-loading of the rubber bushing will be all wrong when the cover is put back. It will also be very nearly impossible to move the plate. To lift the plate put a jack under the end. If it looks as though the car is going to lift before the plate is up in position get some people to sit in the back seat for a minute or two. With the plate held in position replace the cover plate and setscrews.

10 It may be difficult to get the four plate securing screws to pick up their threads on replacement - particularly with a new bush. In such instances two longer screws will have to be obtained and used diagonally so that the plate may be drawn down enough to refit the shorter screws. (The short screws must be used finally otherwise the cover plate will not pull down far enough to stress the rubber bush properly).

11 With the cover tightened down the diagonal arm or axle tube may be reassembled to the spring plate.

12 The angle adjustment of the spring plates must be the same on both sides of the car.

13 If the spring plates have been renewed or any other work has been carried out on the rear suspension which could affect the alignment then it is important that the camber and toe settings be checked with alignment equipment. It would also be timely to mention here that if the rear suspension spring plate settings are purposely altered to give an increased or reduced ground clearance then the effects on handling under certain circumstances are, to say the least, unusual. Tyre wear is also greatly increased if the rear wheel alignment is incorrect.

12 Rear equalizer spring (GT models) - removal and replacement

1 Some later models are fitted with an additional suspension feature consisting of a lateral torsion bar (parallel to the normal one) which goes under the bottom of the luggage space behind the rear seat. It is attached at each end by a rubber bushed bracket to the body panel behind the rear wheel. It is connected to the axle tubes by levers and operating rods angled in opposite directions at each side. The effect is to progressively assist the main torsion bar under load but not to have any effect on body roll characteristics.

2 To remove the spring and its components take off the rear wheels and remove the nuts at each end of the operating rods and take out the rods and associated buffers.

3 Undo the nuts holding the supports and rubber bushes at each end of the torsion bar.

4 Remove the lever from the left hand side of the torsion bar by undoing the locknut and unscrewing the setscrew far enough to release the lever from the bar. The spring and the right hand lever can then be withdrawn together.

5 The operating rods run in guides bolted to the axle tube flange and the bushes in these may be worn. They can be prised out with a screwdriver.

6 When reinstalling remember that the right lever should point downward towards the front and the left lever downwards to the rear. The left lever is marked 'L'. Also do not overlook the hard rubber washer which goes on the torsion bar outside the levers before the inner support plates are fitted.

7 The longer of the two operating rods is fitted on the right side and the rubber clamping rings should go one each side of the lever. Fit the rods to the levers first and then put them into the guides and fit the guides to the axle tubes. This makes sure that the clamping rings are properly seated on the levers.

Chapter 9 Braking system

Contents

Brake adjustment (incl. handbrake) 2
Disc calipers, pistons and seals - inspection and renewal ... 8
Disc pads - removal, inspection and replacement 7
Fault diagnosis 16
Front drums and shoes - removal, inspection and replacement 3
General description 1
Handbrake cable and lever - removal and replacement ... 15
Hydraulic lines - inspection and renewal 12

Hydraulic system - bleeding 13
Hydraulic wheel cylinders - renewal of seals and cylinders ... 5
Pedal cluster - dismantling and reassembly 14
Rear drums and shoes - removal, inspection and replacement 4
Self adjusting brake shoes 6
Tandem master cylinder - modifications 11
Tandem master cylinder - removal, adjustment and replacement 9
Tandem master cylinder - dismantling, overhaul and reassembly 10

Specifications

Type: ... . Hydraulically operated dual circuit, tandem master cylinder (warning light optional)
Discs front Drums rear - UK GT and Super 1303S Beetles
Drums all round - UK 1303 Super Beetle; USA Super and basic Beetles, Sports Bug
Self adjusting rear drum brakes for certain countries
Handbrake operates on the rear wheels, via a cable operated linkage

Dimensions:	mm	inches	
Discs:			
Diameter	277	8.937	
Thickness	9.5 to 8.5 (min)	0.378 to 0.335	
Run-out permitted	0.2 max.	0.008	
Calipers:			
Piston diameter	40	1.575	
Friction pad thickness	10 Teves, 11.5 Girling	0.394 Teves, 0.453 Girling	
Minimum pad thickness	2	0.079	
Pad surface area (4 pads)	80 sq cm	12.4 sq ins.	72 sq cm/11 sq ins. on older models
Front drums:			
Diameter	248	9.764	
Lining width	45	1.772	
Total lining area	450 sq cm	69.7 sq ins.	
Lining thickness (new)	3.8 - 4.00	0.150 - 0.157	
Lining thickness oversize	4.3 - 4.5	0.165 - 0.177	for skimmed drums
Rear drums:			
Diameter	230 - 231.5	9.055 - 9.11	max.
Lining width	40	1.575	
Total lining area	358 sq cm	55 sq ins.	
Lining thickness (new)	3.8 - 4.0	0.150 - 0.157	
Lining thickness (oversize)	4.3 - 4.5	0.165 - 0.177	for skimmed drums
Tandem master cylinder:			
Bore	19.05	0.795	
Stroke:			
Front circuit	17.5	0.689	Up to July '73
Rear circuit	11.5	0.423	these dimensions for front discs
Wheel cylinders:			
Bore, front	23.81	0.937	only. For drums/
Bore, rear	17.46	0.687	discs both were 14 mm

Torque wrench settings:						lbs ft	kg m
Brake backplate securing screws	...	...	...	...	...	18	2.5
Brake hose and pipe unions	...	...	...	...	...	14	2
Stop light switch	...	...	...	...	...	14	2
Disc caliper securing bolts	...	...	...	...	...	29	4
Wheel cylinder to backplate screws	...	...	...	...	...	20	2.7
Caliper body screws	...	...	...	...	...	15	2.2
Wheel shaft nut (double jointed driveshafts)	...	...	...			253	35
Axle shaft nut (swing axle)	...	...	...	...	...	217	30

1 General description

The Super Beetle 1303 (UK) has drum brakes fitted to all four wheels. This also applies to the USA Super Beetle, basic Beetle and Sports Bug which have self-adjusting rear brakes to comply with saftey regulations where necessary.

The operation of the brake shoes is by hydraulic pressure. Each pair of brake shoes is operated by a single cylinder which contains two opposed pistons, one operating each shoe in the drum. This means that there is one leading shoe only in each drum. Each shoe may be adjusted nearer to the drum by a screw type tappet and notched wheel mounted on each hydraulic piston.

A master hydraulic cylinder is operated by the foot pedal and generates the pressure which passes to the four wheel cylinders. The pipe lines are rigid metal except where they link from body to moving assemblies. The master cylinder is the tandem type which maintains the hydraulic pressure to either the front or rear wheels should the other fail.

The handbrake operates on the rear wheels only and the leverage form the handle is transmitted by two cables running in tubes inside the floor frame tube.

Hydraulic fluid level is maintained in the master cylinder by a reservoir located in the front luggage compartment behind the spare wheel.

The UK Super Beetle 1303S and GT Beetle models have drums at the rear and discs at the front. The handbrake is similar to the drum braked models.

The system operates when pressure on the foot pedal moves a piston in the master cylinder (in effect-a pump). This pressurizes the hydraulic fluid in the pipe lines and forces the pistons outwards in the wheel cylinders. These in turn press the shoes against the drums. When pressure is relieved the shoes are drawn off the drums by retractor springs. The friction pads of the disc brakes are forced against the disc by hydraulic pistons also.

When the pressure is relieved the piston seals flex sufficiently to permit the piston to retract fractionally. No springs are necessary.

The master cylinder piston is fitted with a spring loaded check valve which maintains a slight residual pressure in the fluid lines but not enough to actually move pads or shoes. This ensures instantaneous movement when the brake pedal is applied.

Although this device was fitted to all types before July 1972 in that month it was decided to dispense with the residual pressure valve for vehicles fitted with drum brakes all round. This means that the master cylinders for all drum braked models are interchangeable, but that, the disc/drum type vehicles have a slightly different cylinder which may not be fitted to drum brakes models (see Section 11).

2 Brake adjustment (including handbrake)

1 It is possible to adjust the brakes without removing the wheels. Where discs are fitted the pads are self-adjusting. Remove the wheel caps and jack up each wheel in turn.

2 For the front wheels the two adjuster wheels are positioned at the bottom of the drum as you face the wheel. If the wheel is revolved they can be seen through the hole in the drum. For the rear wheels the two adjusters are at the bottom of the drum, and access is through holes in the backplate.

3 Each adjuster should be moved in the appropriate direction (see Fig. 9.1) with a screwdriver engaged in the notch until it

FRONT and REAR

Fig. 9.1. Drum brake adjusters (Sec. 2)

Arrows show direction to turn wheels to move shoes to the drum, looking at the back of the drum

can be moved no further and the wheel is locked. Then back off the adjuster one or two notches until the wheel revolves freely.

4 If any shoe(s) needs considerable adjustment (because they have been allowed to go unadjusted too long) then they will have to 'bed in' again to a different radius and this will call for further adjustment after a short interval. This is why regular brake adjustment is necessary to ensure top braking efficiency at all times. The linings will also last longer as it will ensure that the whole surface area is used evenly all the time.

5 When adjusting the rear brakes remember that when turning the wheels the drag of the transmission will be felt. Do not confuse this with binding brake shoes. The holes in the backplate through which the rear brake adjustments are made are normally covered with rubber plugs. These plugs are double - covering another hole through which the lining thickness may be seen (photo). If the plugs are missing replace them in order to keep out water and dirt.

6 Having completed adjusting one wheel it is good practice to operate the brake pedal once or twice and then adjust again. Sometimes the shoes can move fractionally off-centre during adjustment. The extra time required is well worth the trouble.

7 If a shoe still rubs against the drum a little even after being backed off more than 3 notches, leave it (provided it is only superficial). However, if the binding is quite severe then it is possible that the lining is very unevenly worn. In such instances remove the drum and have a look.

8 Once the rear brake shoes have been adjusted to the drums the handbrake may be checked. If both back wheels can be jacked off the ground together it will save some time. Pump the foot-brake two or three times (to centralise the shoes) and apply the handbrake two notches. Pull back the rubber shroud at the base of the lever and slacken the locknut on the threaded end of each cable (photo). Then tighten each cable with the adjusting nut (holding the cable with a screwdriver in the slotted end) until an equal amount of drag can be felt on each rear wheel when it is turned. Pull the handbrake on three notches. At this it should be possible only just to turn the wheels by hand.

3 Front drums and brake shoes - removal, inspection and replacement

1 The front brake drums form part of the wheel hub casting so they have to be taken off the stub axle. This involves releasing the front wheel bearings, details of which are given in Chapter

2.5 Adjusting wheel and brake lining seen through the holes in the back plate

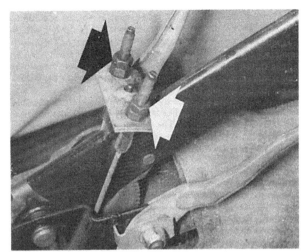

2.8 Handbrake cable adjuster and locknuts (arrowed)

Fig. 9.2. Front brake (drum removed) (Sec. 3)

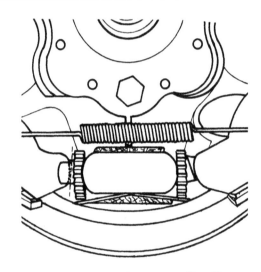

Fig. 9.3. Brake shoe adjuster screws (Sec. 3)

Make sure the angled ends are correctly related

11. Before pulling the drum off it is a good idea to back the shoe adjusters off as far as they will go.

2 In the centre of each shoe a retaining pin, held in position by a spring loaded, slotted cup washer, must first be removed. This can be done with a pair of pliers, turning the washer so that the slot aligns with the head of the pin. Washer, spring and pin can then be removed.

3 Unhook the retractor spring which connects the two shoes nearest to the notched adjuster wheels. The end of one shoe can then be lifted out of the adjuster. Both shoes can then be disengaged quite easily from the hydraulic wheel cylinder. Immediately tie a piece of string around the wheel cylinder to prevent the pistons popping out. Do not apply pressure to the brake pedal either. If the pistons come out it will be necessary to bleed the hydraulic system.

4 The shoe lining surface should be not less than 0.5 mm (0.020 inch) above the rivet heads. Anything less and new linings should be fitted. If the linings have been contaminated with oil they will not work efficiently again and should be renewed. Great care should be exercised when handling brake shoes as oily or greasy hands can contaminate them significantly. The material is extremely absorbent. It is important to isolate the cause of contamination. If not the wheel cylinder, the only other source

can be from grease flung out from the wheel bearing. (see Chapter 11, which deals with front wheel bearings). Volkswagen supply linings and rivets to fit the original shoes. If you should contemplate renewing the linings yourself it is essential to have the proper punch tools for fixing the rivets. If you do not have these the simplest thing is to ask the supplier to fix them. Provided you have cut off the old linings and rivets it takes about two minutes per lining to fix the new ones, if you have the correct tools. One of the punches is clamped in the vice and the new lining, shoe and rivet head held over it whilst the end is belled over with the other special punch. Riveting should start from the centre and work outwards diagonally. Alternatively, other sources of supply may provide exchange shoes complete with linings fitted. Whatever you do it is important that the linings are all of the same make and type. It is best to fit a complete new set and make a proper job of it, or you will have uneven braking and trouble on wet road surfaces. Never try to renew the lining on one wheel only, always in pairs, and best in complete sets. Note also that the front brake shoes are wider than the rear ones and are not interchangeable.

5 Examine the friction surfaces of the brake drums. If they are in good condition they should be bright, shiny and perfectly

smooth. If they show signs of deep scoring (due to over-worn brake linings) then they will need renewal. It may be possible to have them machined out on a lathe but if this is done it will be essential to fit oversize brake linings accordingly. This work should be carried out by a Volkswagen agent or an acknowledged brake specialist. It is a waste of time fitting new linings to work in scored drums (except when the scoring is only very light).

6 Before replacing the shoes the backplate should be thoroughly brushed off and the two adjusters removed and cleaned so that they can be freely turned. The threads may be treated with a very light touch of high melting point grease. Replace the adjusters; if the bottom one tends to fall out leave it until the shoes are refitted. Both adjusters should be screwed right in to the notched wheels. It is most important that the bottoms of the slots, which are angled, face the right way

7 Examine the hydraulic cylinder. The rubber boots should be intact and there should be no sign of fluid leakage. If there is then the cylinders must be overhauled (see Section 5).

8 Assemble the two shoes together with the heavier of the two retractor springs engaged in the two holes nearest the cut-out slots on the inner radius of the shoe. These shoe ends should then be put into place in the slots in the ends of the pistons. Next fit the other ends of the shoes into the adjusters (replace the bottom one now) so that they fit properly in the adjuster slots. Then hook the other retractor spring into the holes in the shoes.

9 Reassemble the steady pins, springs and washers, turning the washers 90° across the pin heads to secure them. If you have dismantled all the brakes together note that the steady pins are different lengths so do not get them mixed up. This is because the front linings are wider than the rear - wider linings - longer pins.

10 Centralise the shoes. (otherwise you may have difficulty replacing the drum) and then refit the drum and wheel bearing, adjusting the bearing as described in Chapter 11. If the wheel cylinders have been overhauled bleed the hydraulic system (Section 13).

11 Adjust the shoes to the drums as described in the previous Section. If new linings have been fitted further adjustment may be needed after a few hundred miles.

4 Rear drums and shoes - removal, inspection and replacement

1 Rear brake shoes tend to wear most on the front shoe at the adjuster end. If, however, brake adjustment has been neglected they will all wear more at the wheel cylinder ends of the shoes. In such cases the visual check of the brake lining material through the inspection hole could be misleading. There may be less material thickness at the other end of the shoe (Fig. 9.4).

2 To remove the brake drum involves slackening of the wheel shaft nut as described in the previous Chapter. This nut must be slackened with a proper socket and bar when the wheel is on the ground. The brake shoe adjusters should be slackened off fully.

The drums should then draw off the splined shafts without difficulty (photo).

3 Remove the steady pins, springs and washers in the same fashion as for the front brake shoes.

4 Unhook the lower of the two retractor springs and then unhook the handbrake cable from the operating lever.

5 Disengage the ends of the two shoes from the adjusters and the two shoes together with the handbrake lever and plate may be lifted out.

6 Linings should be renewed if the surface is worn to within 0.4 mm (0.020 inch) or less of the rivet heads at any point. Also, if there is any indication of oil contamination the linings must be renewed. Details for relining may be found in the Section dealing with front brakes.

7 If the shoes are to be changed remember to remove the handbrake operating lever by pulling off the clip which fixes it to the shoe.

8 When reassembling the two shoes prior to refitting, the spreader plate should engage in the two slots and the shoes with the lever attached goes to the rear with the lever notch facing the rear (photos).

9 Make sure that the adjuster wheels are free-moving and fully backed off before locating the ends of the shoes in the slots. The angled bottom of the slots should face the right way.

10 It must be emphasised that any leaks, either from the bearing or the hydraulic cylinder, should be dealt with to prevent further contamination or failure of the hydraulic system.

5 Hydraulic wheel cylinders - renewal of seals and cylinders

1 If the wheel cylinders show signs of leakage, or of pistons being seized up, then it will be necessary to dismantle them and fit new seals. The procedure for front and rear cylinders are the same although the bores of the cylinders are different requiring different diameter seals (see Fig. 9.5).

2 Remove the brake drum and the brake shoes and seal the cap of the fluid reservoir with a piece of plastic film to minimise loss of fluid from the system when the cylinder is dismantled.

3 Pull off the rubber boots from the ends of the cylinder, bringing the pistons and slotted ends with them. Behind the pistons are the seal cups and in the centre there is a spring with two 'cup expanders' which fit inside each seal and as their name implies force the seals outward into the cylinder bore under the pressure of the spring.

4 With the cylinder clear examine the bore surfaces for signs of ridging or scoring. Any residue stuck in the bore should be cleaned out with brake fluid or meths - if very stubborn a gentle rub with some No.400 wet and dry paper will clean it up. Any noticeable scores or ridges indicate that a new cylinder should be fitted. No attempt should be made to smooth them out as this will be unsuccessful.

5 To remove the cylinder undo the brake pipe union from behind the backplate. Cover the end of the pipe with the dust cap from the bleed nipple pro tem. Undo the two securing

4.2 Removing a rear brake drum

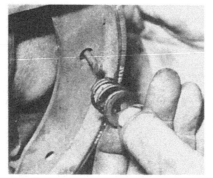
4.8a Fitting the steady pin, spring and washer during reassembly of the rear right brake shoe

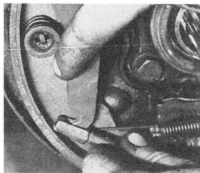
4.8b Hooking the handbrake cable to the lever on the rear right brake assembly

Fig. 9.4. Rear drum brake shoe assembly (Sec. 4)

Right hand side, this illustration is mirrored for the correct arrangement for the left rear wheel

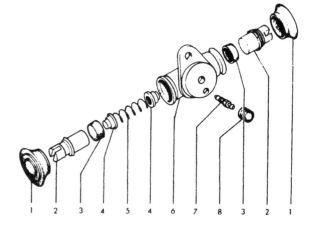

Fig. 9.5. Hydraulic wheel cylinder - components (Sec. 5)

1 Boot	5 Spring	
2 Piston	6 Cylinder	
3 Seal cup	7 Bleed valve	
4 Cup expander	8 Dust cap	

screws from the backplate and the cylinder may be lifted out. If a new cylinder is fitted the diameter of the bore must be exactly the same as the diameter of the one being replaced, otherwise the balance of the brakes will be upset.

6 With the cylinder perfectly clean lubricate the bore with brake fluid and insert the spring complete with seal cup expanders at each end.

7 Lubricate the new seals with fluid and put one in at each end of the cylinder with the lip facing inwards. Take great care not to turn the lip back whilst doing this.

8 Put a piston into the bore of the cylinder behind each seal and then fit the rubber boot over the cylinder and piston so that it

9 Absolute cleanliness of hands and parts is essential during re-assembly.

10 If a new wheel cylinder is being fitted reconnect the brake pipe union taking care not to cross the thread, kink the pipe or overtighten the union.

---

6 Self-adjusting brake shoes

1 On some models the rear brakes are self-adjusting, the adjustment being carried out as the footbrake is operated.

2 Refer to Fig. 9.6. An adjusting lever return spring pulls on the adjusting lever and moves the adjusting wheel on the connection link when the brakes are operated. The length of the connection link is thus increased and the brake shoes are automatically adjusted.

3 To adjust the footbrake when installing new linings screw the connecting link into the sleeve as far as it will go, with the adjusting wheel resting against the sleeve. Now fit the brake drum and operate the foot pedal until the lowest distance of pedal travel is experienced.

4 To adjust the handbrake first adjust the footbrake as in paragraph 3. Set the handbrake lever in the off position and tension the cable until the brake lever in the rear brake just starts to move off the stop on the secondary shoe. Watch the brake lever for movement through the inspection hole in the backplate. This job needs two people. It should only be necessary when installing new liners or cables. When the brake is correctly adjusted lock the cable with the locknut.

5 It may be that the drums will not come off easily. If so slacken off the handbrake. Now push back the brake lever past the stop on the brake shoe. This can be done with a screwdriver through the inspection hole and allows the shoes to move closer together, making the removal of the drum easier.

Fig. 9.6. Self-adjusting drum brakes (Sec. 6)

1 Wheel cylinder	6 Adjustable connecting link	
2 Brake shoe	with wheel and sleeve	
3 Upper return spring	7 Brake lever	
4 Spring, cup and pin,	8 Adjusting lever	
with wheel and sleeve	9 Return spring	
5 Lower return spring	10 Back plate	

6 The handbrake lever has a different curved section to those fitted to non-compensated systems. The bearing cover is modified to ensure sufficient clearance for the adjusting wheel. If new bearing covers are not available and for some reason an old type one must be fitted it will work well enough provided it is fitted 90° from its normal position.

---

7 Disc pads - removal, inspection and replacement

Two types of disc brake may be encountered. They are generally similar but differ in detail and the manner in which the pads are extracted. Fig. 9.7 shows the layout of the type made by Teves (ATE). Fig. 9.9 shows the layout of the type made by Girling. Both are fixed caliper types. The disc is identical for both makes of caliper.

Teves calipers

1 Remove the front wheel and support the vehicle.
2 There are two visual examinations to be made before dismantling anything. These are the thickness of the friction pad and the gap between the pad and disc.
3 Pad friction material thickness must not be less that 2 mm (3/32 inch) otherwise the pads should be renewed.
4 The residual clearance should not be more than 0.2 mm (0.008 inch) between disc and pad. This can be measured with a feeler gauge.
5 If the gap is greater it is probably due to a sticking piston. A simple remedy is given later on in this Section.
6 If the pads are to be used again mark where they came from beforehand so they may be put back in the same position. Then

drive out the retaining pins from the outside with a long nosed punch (photo). Lift off the spring retainer plate (photo).
7 Before removing the old pads it is best to force them away from the disc carefully, with a suitable flat metal lever. This will push the pistons back. Before doing this it will be necessary to remove some hydraulic fluid from the reservoir to prevent it overflowing when the pistons are pushed back. Do this with a suitable suction device such as an empty flexible plastic bottle.
8 Once the pistons are pushed back remove the pads and piston retaining plate (photo). Note that there is a cutaway portion on one side of the piston. Provided the piston is not rotated after the retaining plate is taken out there should be no cause for difficulty on replacement of the plate. For details of the correct position of the piston cut-out refer to Section 8.

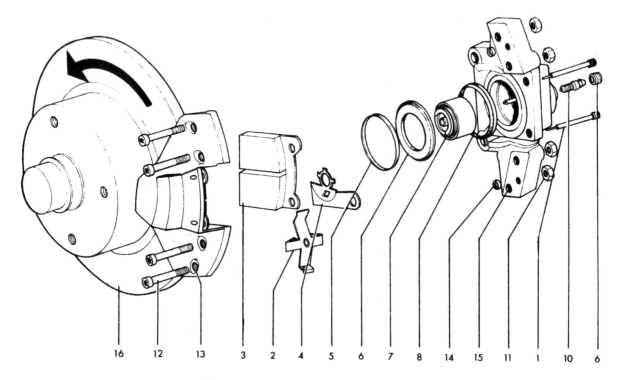

Fig. 9.7. Disc and Teves caliper - components

1 Pad retaining pin (see note)
2 Spreader spring (see note)
3 Friction pad
4 Piston retaining plate
5 Clamp ring
6 Seal
7 Piston
8 Rubber seal
9 Dust cap
10 Bleeder valve
11 Hexagon nut
12 Cheese head screw
13 Caliper outer housing
14 Seal
15 Caliper inner housing
16 Brake disc

Note: Arrow shoes forward rotation of disc. Later models have modified spreader springs and only 1 retaining pin

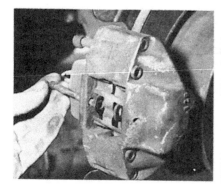

7.6a Removing the retaining pins

7.6b Removing the spring retainer plate

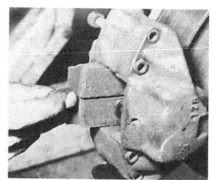

7.8 Removing a disc pad

9 Blow out the aperture in the caliper and examine the seal which should show no signs of cracking or brittleness. If it does it should be renewed (see Section 8).

10 Clean off the piston retaining plate and replace it together with new friction pads. New pad retaining spring plates are normally provided with the pads and these should be used. The spring plates have a wide and narrow side. Put the wide side upwards. When replacing the retaining pins (from the inside) do not use a punch smaller in diameter than the pin. Preferably, use no punch at all otherwise there is a possibility of shearing the shoulder off against the split clamping bush.

11 Pump the brake pedal to bring the pads up to the disc and check the level of hydraulic fluid in the reservoir.

12 If the clearance between the disc and pad is too great after brake operation then this is an indication that the inner piston rubber seal is sticking somewhat and distorting more than normally. This retracts the piston more than usual when the pressure is taken off. Movement of the piston can usually cure this. Remove a brake pad and put in a block of wood no less than 6 mm (0.236 inch) thick. Pump the brakes to force the piston further out and then force it back again. Do this a few times and the problem should disappear. If not it will be necessary to check the piston seals and caliper cylinders thoroughly as described in Section 8.

Girling calipers

13 Refer to Fig. 9.9. Remove the front wheel and support the vehicle firmly. In this operation the caliper must be removed from the steering knuckle.

14 The U-shaped retaining pin is kept in place by a locking clip; remove the clip and lever the pin out. Do not hammer on the ends of it or it will not come out at all. Remove the pad spreader spring.

15 Bend back the locking plates on the caliper mounting bolts and remove the bolts. Support the caliper so that the hydraulic hose is not strained. It is possible to tie the caliper to the upper suspension arm so that it can easily be worked on.

16 If the pads are to be refitted mark them so that they do not get mixed. The pad must go into the same place on reassembly. Ease the pad away from the piston and noise plate, turn it through 90° and draw it carefully out of the caliper. Move the noise damping plates to the centre of the caliper and remove them.

17 If one pad is worn so that the thickness of the friction lining material is less than that specified then all four pads must be replaced by new ones. The pads must always be renewed in sets of four. It is not possible to buy them singly anyway.

18 Clean out the sliding surfaces inside the caliper and blow out all rust and dirt. Inspect the piston seals by pushing the piston in a little. If the seals are swollen or hard and cracked then they must be renewed, as detailed later, while the caliper is away from the disc. Check the disc for run-out and wear as detailed later.

19 The pads must not be damaged in any way, or have cracks or oily patches. Try them in the caliper slides to make sure they move easily. When you are satisfied that all is well, install the pads as follows.

20 Fit the noise damping plates as in Fig. 9.10 and then insert the pads and turn them through 90°. Push them back so that they move the pistons in a little but watch that the brake fluid reservoir does not overflow. Be careful to fit used pads in the position you removed them from.

21 Refit the caliper to the steering knuckle. Be careful how you fit the pads round the disc; the edges of the pad are fragile and chip easily. Fit a new locking plate and tighten the caliper holding bolts to the specified torque. Bend up the tabs of the locking plate.

22 Fit a new pad spreader spring and install the U-shaped pad retaining pin. Fit the locking clip and bend the straight edge of it through 45° to stop it moving. Depress the brake pedal several times to seat the pads and then check the level of the fluid to the reservoir.

23 The calipers are symmetrical, replacement units being supplied without pads, plates and bleeder valves, and may be installed on either side. The long bleeder valve must be at the top when the calipers are fitted to the knuckle.

8 Disc caliper pistons and seals - inspection and renewal

1 Before assuming that anything is wrong which requires removal of the caliper pistons make sure that the checks in connection with renewal of the friction pads as described in Section 7 have been carried out.

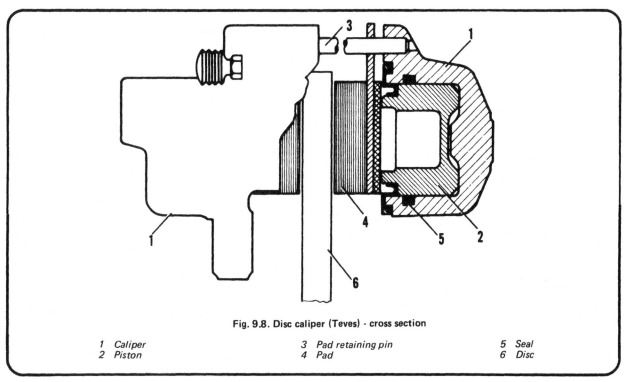

Fig. 9.8. Disc caliper (Teves) - cross section

1 Caliper	3 Pad retaining pin	5 Seal
2 Piston	4 Pad	6 Disc

8.4 Removing the caliper securing bolts

8.16 Removing the disc

9.2 Tandem master cylinder

2 Discs may deteriorate, if left unused, due to corrosion. If this happens it is best to let a VW agency repolish them with special blocks which can be inserted in place of the friction pads. Discs which are badly scored or distorted must be renewed. It is possible to have them re-machined but the economics of this against fitting new parts should be examined.

3 The run-out of the disc can be checked only with a clock gauge micrometer. With the bearing properly adjusted the run-out should not exceed 0.2 mm (0.008 inch).

Teves calipers

4 To renew a disc or repair piston seals, the caliper assembly must first be removed. It is held by two bolts from the back of the steering knuckle (photo). (If the disc only is to be removed it is not necessary to disconnect the hydraulic fluid hose. The whole assembly should be tied up onto the bodywork to prevent any strain on the hose). If the pistons are to be removed from the caliper thought must first be given as to how pressure can be applied to force them out. Only one piston can be worked on at a time as the other piston must be installed and clamped in position so as to maintain pressure to force the other out. Pressure can be applied from a foot pump if you rig up a spare hydraulic pipe union and short length of pipe to which the pump connector will fit. One piston will have to be clamped in such a way that there will still be room enough for the other to come right out. Here again a tong-like clamp may have to be made up from some 1½ x 1/8 inch (38 mm x 3.175 mm) flat steel bar if you are unable to obtain a suitable tool.

5 Mount the caliper assembly in the vice padding the jaws suitably so that the flange of the caliper will not be scored or marked. The friction pads and retaining plates should be removed (see Section 7).

6 Prise out the spring ring from the outer seal using a screwdriver. Then, with a blunt plastic or wooden tool prise out the seal itself. Do not use sharp tools for fear of scoring the piston or cylinder.

7 Using a clamp to hold one piston force the other out under pressure as described in paragraph 4. To prevent damage in case the piston should come out with force put some cloth in the caliper to prevent it striking the piston and clamp opposite.

8 With the piston out the rubber sealing ring can be taken out of its groove in the cylinder; once again use only a blunt article to get it out.

9 With methylated spirits or hydraulic fluid, clean the piston and cylinder thoroughly. If there are any signs of severe scoring or pitting then renewal will be necessary. With the cylinder this involves renewing the whole caliper unit.

10 When renewing seals the spring ring and piston retaining plate must also be renewed. The VW service kit includes all the items needed. Use them. Before reassembly it is advantageous to coat the piston and new rubber seal with VW cylinder paste specially formulated for this job. Otherwise make sure they are thoroughly lubricated with clean hydraulic fluid. On no account use anything else.

11 Fit the rubber seal in the cylinder groove and then fit the piston into the seal. Great care must be taken to avoid misaligning the seal when doing this and the piston must be kept square while it is pushed in. The cut-out portion of the piston should lie at an angle of 20° from a line across the disc diameter facing in to the centre of the disc and against the direction of forward disc rotation.

12 Fit the new outer seal and spring ring.

13 Repeat the process for the other piston.

14 Refit the caliper to the knuckle, tightening the securing bolts to 29 lb ft (4 kgm). Replace the piston retainer plates and pads as described in Section 7.

15 The disc itself may be removed after the caliper is taken off.

16 Remove the hub cap - (on the left wheel, this involves removing the 'C' washer securing the speedo cable). Undo the bearing nut clamp screw, remove the nut and pull off the disc which is an integral part of the wheel hub (photo).

17 Replace the disc in the reverse order and re-adjust the wheel bearing as detailed in Chapter 12.

18 Refit the caliper to the knuckle and tighten the two retaining bolts to the correct torque of 29 lb ft (4 kgm)

19 It is rare that the caliper housing has to be split and this should not be done unless it is obviously leaking. Renewal of the interior 'O' rings on the fluid channels may then be needed. Undo the four socket head screws to separate the two halves. Remove the two 'O' rings and fit new ones. Re-align the two halves and replace the screws. Tighten them from the centre outwards in sequence to 7 lb ft (1 kgm) and then again in sequence to a final torque of 15 lb ft (2.2 kgm).

20 When the caliper is replaced reconnect the hydraulic fluid hose and bleed the system as described in Section 13.

Girling calipers

21 The procedures for the Girling type brakes are as for the Teves type, except that the caliper must first be removed for removal of the pads.

22 If this caliper leaks, it is not possible to split it and fit new seals as with the Teves type. The unit must be renewed. If this is the case, the bleed valves must be transferred to the new unit from the old one. Make sure that the long one is at the top when the caliper is installed.

23 With the Girling type caliper, the 20° angle of the piston recess does not have to be checked; the noise damping plate may be fitted without this precaution.

24 After reconnecting the hydraulic hose remember to bleed the brakes as described in Section 13.

9 Tandem master cylinder - removal, replacement and adjustment

1 The tandem master cylinder comprises a single cylinder in which there are two pistons one behind the other. Each circuit is supplied independently with fluid. If the pressure in one circuit should fail the other is not affected. Provided the slave cylinders

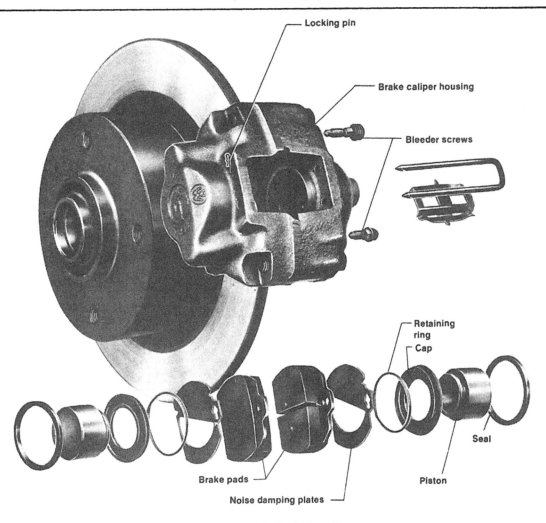

Fig. 9.9. Exploded view of Girling brake caliper components

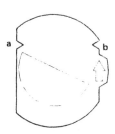

Fig. 9.10. Position of noise damping plate (Girling caliper)

Note: left-hand plate shown. Notches a and b should be at top. Arrow shows direction of rotation. Right-hand plate is mirror image of left-hand plate

and fluid lines are all in good condition and there is no air in the system then any softness or sponginess in the system will probably be due to worn seals in the master cylinder. As these are internal there will be no visible leak to indicate this.

2 To remove the cylinder assembly first jack up the car and remove the right-hand front wheel (rh drive) or left as the case may be. The cylinder is bolted to the bulkhead alongside the floor tunnel (photo).

3 Have a suitable receptacle handy to collect the contents of the fluid reservoir - if possible siphon the contents out of the reservoir itself. Otherwise pull the pipes and plugs from the top of the cylinder body and drain it into the receptacle there. Keep fluid away from paintwork.

4 Unscrew the rigid pipe unions from the body of cylinder. It is not necessary to undo the brake light switches. Just disconnect the wires.

5 The two screws in the bulkhead behind the brake pedal should now be removed to release the assembly. Take care not to drop the washers or spacers off the screws into the space below or you may have a difficult job retrieving them.

6 Replacement is a reversal of the removal procedure. Make sure that the spacers are correctly refitted. As soon as the unions have all been reconnected and the system replenished with fluid and bled, see that the unions are all perfectly leakproof.

7 It is important that the pushrod which operates the plunger from the brake pedal is correctly set. In the rest position, the ball end of the pushrod should have a 1 mm clearance before it contacts the bottom of the recess in the piston. If this clearance is absent (and the piston cannot return fully) the operation of the system is seriously affected. To adjust the length of the rod slacken the locknut and screw the rod in or out as required. This adjustment will also be affected if the pedal cluster mounting plate is moved. It is important that the pedal stop is set far enough back so that if one brake circuit fails the pedal can move far enough to operate the other circuit before it comes up against the panel.

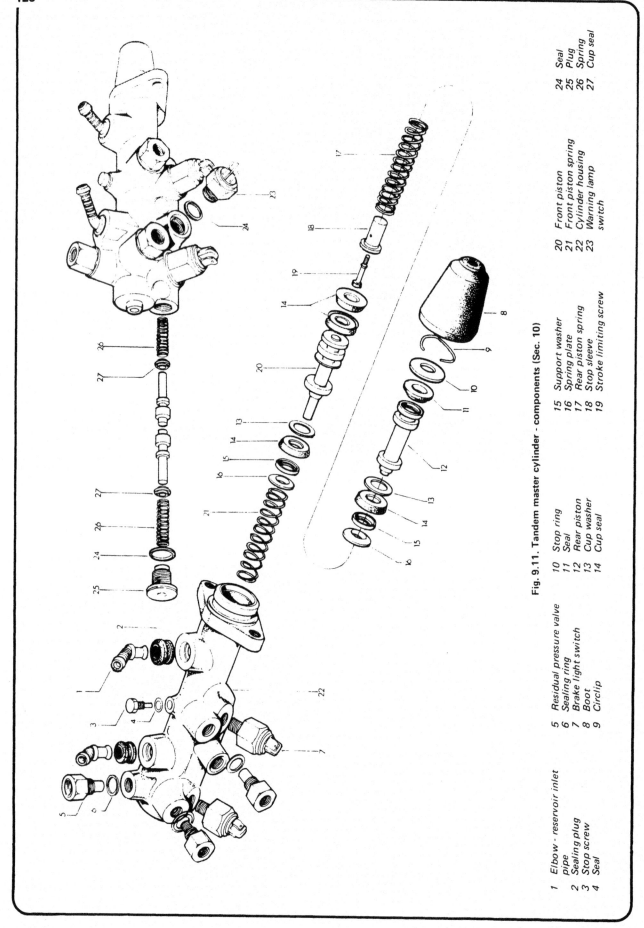

Fig. 9.11. Tandem master cylinder - components (Sec. 10)

1 Elbow - reservoir inlet
   pipe
2 Sealing plug
3 Stop screw
4 Seal

5 Residual pressure valve
6 Sealing ring
7 Brake light switch
8 Boot
9 Circlip

10 Stop ring
11 Seal
12 Rear piston
13 Cup washer
14 Cup seal

15 Support washer
16 Spring plate
17 Rear piston spring
18 Stop sleeve
19 Stroke limiting screw

20 Front piston
21 Front piston spring
22 Cylinder housing
23 Warning lamp
    switch

24 Seal
25 Plug
26 Spring
27 Cup seal

10 Tandem master cylinder - dismantling, overhaul and re-assembly

1 Thoroughly clean the exterior of the unit before starting to dismantle. Then remove the piston stop screw located between the two fluid inlet ports (Fig. 9.11).
2 Remove the boot from the rear of the cylinder and take out the internal circlip.
3 The two pistons and all their component parts may then be drawn out. Do this carefully, taking note of the order and position in which they come out.
4 All internal seals are fitted to the grooves in the pistons as indicated in Fig. 9.11. They can be pulled off and fitted without special tools but care must be taken not to overstretch them. The primary piston is fitted with three seals all the same size and shape. The front two face forward and the third to the rear. The secondary piston has two seals, both facing forwards. The front seal is the same as those on the primary piston but the rear one is the odd one out, so do not confuse it with the others.
5 When reassembling the pistons into the cylinder first place the cup washer, cup seal, support washer, spring plate and spring, in that order over the nose of the primary piston (to which the new secondary cup and rear seal should have been already fitted). Hold the cylinder vertical with the open end downwards and feed the whole assortment back in so that the loose items do not fall off the piston.
6 The secondary piston primary cup is held in location by a support washer and spring plate also. These in turn are held firm by the stop sleeve and stroke limiting screw. By undoing the stroke limiting screw inside the stop sleeve all these component parts may be released. The new seal is then easily placed in position.
7 When replacing the secondary piston it should be pushed far enough forward to enable the stop screw to be put in so that it fits behind the rear end of the primary piston. This is most important. It must not be fitted so that it engages the recessed part in the shank of the primary piston.
8 Refit the stop ring, circlip and rubber boot over the end of the cylinder.
9 Some cylinders incorporate a pressure differential warning system. This consists of a single piston held centrally in balance by the equal pressure of the two circuits. To remove the piston with its equilibrium springs the switch must first be screwed out of the body. Then the end plug can be removed and the internal components taken out.

11 Tandem master cylinder - modifications

1 Several modifications have been made to the master cylinder during the life of the models covered by this manual. Cylinders are supplied by three different makers and although they are interchangeable as an assembly the bits and pieces are not necessarily so. The three makers are 'TEVES', 'SCHAFER', 'BENDIX'.
2 The 'BENDIX' has the name marked on the casting and may be used only for vehicles with drum brakes all round. The 'BENDIX' type repair kit must be used with this cylinder; the kit is supplied in a plastic tube.
3 The 'drums all round' master cylinders after July 1972 do not have the residual pressure valve. This type of cylinder may not be used with the 'disc/drum' system. Cylinders for use with disc brakes are marked as below:

'SCHAFER'   A 4 mm diameter countersink hole, 1 to 3 mm deep on the mounting flange level with the supply line boss.
'TEVES'   Notches cut in the sides of the mounting flange.

4 In September '72 it was decided that vehicles without a dual circuit warning lamp (optional extra) would be fitted with one brake light switch instead of two, the brake light switch for the pushrod piston circuit being left off.
5 Some 'TEVES' master cylinders have a support washer and spring plate fitted separately (Fig. 9.11 pts 15 and 16), others have a combined support washer and spring plate. They are interchangeable but if a combined assembly is used to replace the spring plate then the support washer must be discarded.

12 Hydraulic lines - inspection and renewal

1 Recent research in the USA has shown that brake pipe line corrosion may be expected after only 90 days of exposure to salt spray. Such may be encountered on snow covered roads. This in effect makes a four year old car suspect with regard to this problem. A copper-alloy used in marine work called 'Kunifer 10' is being used to make replacement tubes but is not yet fitted to new vehicles. It may be worth asking about it if renewal of pipes becomes necessary. Inspect the pipe lines in the Autumn and the Spring as a routine task, especially if the vehicle is used on an area where the roads are regularly salted.

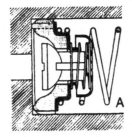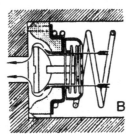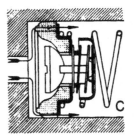

Fig. 9.12. Tandem master cylinder - function of residual pressure valve (Sec. 10)

A At rest. Main valve seated on end of cylinder under main spring pressure and inner valve seated in centre of main seal under secondary spring pressure
B Braking. Secondary valve opens under pressure of fluid which passes into system
C Brakes released. Main valve opens under fluid back pressure until main spring overcomes pressure - keeping some pressure in system. Secondary valve stays seated.

Note: A residual pressure valve is incorporated in each fluid outlet on the master cylinder.

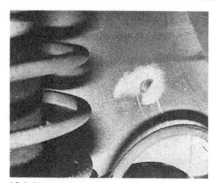

12.3 The brake hose has been rubbing against the body. The mounting bracket, lower right, was bent to keep the hose away from the body

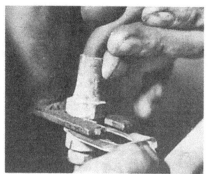

12.5 Flexible hose mounting bracket and clip

13.4 The bleed nipple on the front drum is by the tip of the fitters finger

2 Trace the routes of all the rigid pipes and wash or brush away accumulated dirt. If the pipes are obviously covered with some sort of underseal compound do not disturb it. Examine for signs of kinks or dents which could have been caused by flying stones. Any instances of this mean that the pipe section should be renewed but before actually taking it out read the rest of this Section. Any unprotected sections of pipe which show signs of corrosion or pitting on the outer surfaces must also be considered for renewal.

3 Flexible hoses, running to each of the front wheels and from the underbody to each rear wheel should show no signs of external signs of chafing or cracking. Move them about and see if surface cracks appear. Also if they feel stiff and inflexible or are twisted they are nearing the end of their useful life. If in any doubt renew the hoses. Make sure also that they are not rubbing against the bodywork (photo).

4 Before attempting to remove any pipe for renewal it is important to be sure that you have a replacement source of supply within reach if you do not wish to be kept off the road for too long. Pipes are often damaged on removal. If a Volkswagen agency is near, you may be reasonably sure that the correct pipes and unions are available. If not, check first that your local garage has the necessary equipment for making up the pipes and has the correct metric thread pipe unions available. The same goes for flexible hoses.

5 Where the couplings from rigid to flexible pipes are made there are support brackets and the flexible pipe is held in place by a 'U' clip which engages in a groove in the union (photo). The male union screws into it. Before getting the spanners on, soak the unions in penetrating fluid as there is always some rust or corrosion binding the threads. Whilst this is soaking in, place a piece of plastic film under the fluid reservoir cap to minimise loss of fluid from the disconnected pipes. Hold the hexagon on the flexible pipe coupling whilst the union on the rigid pipe is undone. Then pull out the clip to release both pipes from the bracket. For flexible hose removal this procedure will be needed at both ends. For a rigid pipe the other end will only involve unscrewing the union from a cylinder or connector. When you are renewing a flexible hose, take care not to damage the unions of the pipes that connect into it. If a union is particularly stubborn be prepared to renew the rigid pipe as well. This is quite often the case if you are forced to use open ended spanners. It may be worth spending a little money on a special pipe union spanner which is like a ring spanner with a piece cut out to enable it to go round the tube (photo).

6 If you are having the new pipe made up, take the old one along to check that the unions and pipe flaring at the ends are identical.

7 Replacement of the hoses or pipes is a reversal of the removal procedure. Precautions and care are needed to make sure that the unions are correctly lined up to prevent cross threading. This may mean bending the pipe a little where a rigid pipe goes into a fixture. Such bending must not, under any circumstances, be too acute, otherwise the pipe will kink and weaken.

8 When fitting flexible hoses take care not to twist them. This can happen when the unions are finally tightened unless a spanner is used to hold the end of the flexible hose and prevent twisting.

9 After removal or slackening of a brake pipe union the hydraulic system must be bled.

13 Hydraulic brake system - bleeding

1 The purpose of the process known as bleeding the brakes is to remove air bubbles from the hydraulic system. Air is compressible - hydraulic fluid is not. Bleeding should be necessary only after work on the hydraulic system has allowed air into the system. If it is found necessary to bleed brakes frequently then there is something wrong and the whole system should be checkedd through to find where the air is getting into the system. Cars left unused for a long time may also require brake bleeding before full efficiency is restored.

2 Normally, if work has been carried out at the extremities of the system - eg at wheel cylinders or adjacent pipes, then it should only be necessary to bleed that particular section. Work on the master cylinder, however would call for all four wheels to be bled.

3 Before starting, make sure you have an adequate supply of the proper fluid, a clean receptacle and a tube which will fit over the bleed nipple securely and which is conveniently long enough. A useful device is the tube which is fitted with a non-return valve. This avoids the necessity of keeping the other end of the tube submerged in liquid whilst bleeding is in progress.

14.1 Foot pedal cluster; pushrod to master cylinder arrowed

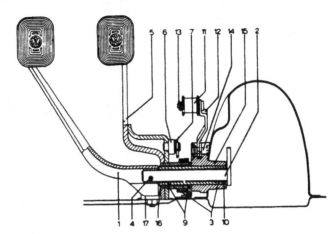

Fig. 9.13. Brake and clutch pedal cluster LHD - cross section view (Sec. 14)

1	Clutch pedal	5	Brake pedal	10	Mounting tube	14	Accelerator pedal lever pin
2	Pedal shaft	6	Master cylinder pushrod	11	Accelerator pedal roller	15	Mounting bracket
3	Bush	7	Pushrod lock plate	12	Accelerator connecting lever	16	Circlip
4	Locating pin	9	Bush	13	Clip	17	Stop plate

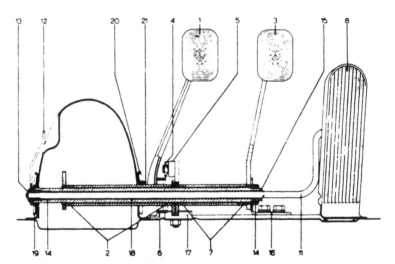

Fig. 9.14 Brake and clutch pedal cluster RHD - cross section view (Sec. 14)

1	Clutch pedal	6	Brake pedal return spring	12	Accelerator connecting lever	17	Stop plate
2	Bush			13	Circlip	18	Cross shaft
3	Brake pedal	7	Bush	14	Bush	19	Mounting bracket
4	Pushrod lock plate	8	Accelerator pedal	15	Washer	20	Cover plate
5	Master cylinder pushrod	11	Accelerator pedal shaft	16	Mounting bracket	21	Cover plate guide

As from March '72 the brake fluid reservoir is fitted with a filter to ensure dirt does not get into the lines. This filter must be removed while bleeding the brakes and replaced before adding more fluid to the system.

4 Clean off the bleed nipple (or pull off the protective cap). Put about 1 inch (2.5 cm) depth of fluid in the receptacle. Connect the pipe to the nipple and put the other end in a jar and undo the nipple about half a turn - no more is necessary (photo).

5 A second person is needed to operate the brake pedal at your instruction. The pedal should be depressed smartly one full stroke to the floor and allowed to return slowly. This should be repeated until no more bubbles emerge from the tube in the jar. Smart operation of the pedal ensures that the air is forced along the pipe rather than by-passed. Keep a watch on the level of fluid in the reservoir. If it gets too low it will let air into the master cylinder and then you will have to bleed all four wheels.

6 Once all the air is expelled, the best moment to tighten the bleed nipple is during the return stroke of the pedal.

7 Repeat the procedure for each wheel as necessary. Do not put fluid bled out of the system back in. Always use fresh.

At one time it was thought that leaving brake fluid that has come out of the bleed nipples to stand overnight would de-aerate it. This is not, in fact, true. The proper place for old brake fluid is in the waste disposal bin

14 Brake and clutch pedal cluster - dismantling and reassembly

1 The brake and clutch pedals are mounted on a common shaft which in turn is supported by two brackets (photo). One of these brackets (on rh drive cars) is fitted to the right of the brake pedal and is held to the floor by two bolts. The other is bolted to the left-hand side of the floor tunnel. The shaft is hollow allowing the accelerator rod to pass through it. At the left-hand end of the pivot shaft a bracket links to the accelerator cable. The clutch cable hooks onto a lug which is part of the pedal

inside the tunnel. This Section explains how to deal with all three items on the cluster.

2   Remove the carpet from the left-hand toe panel and pull out the panel.

3   Remove the two bolts holding the cover on the side of the tunnel. These two screws hold the bracket supporting the left end of the cross shaft as well so some movement will be noticed.

4   If only the accelerator cable is being renewed the split pin can be removed from the clevis pin, the cable eye released and the cable drawn out. If the cross shaft is being taken out then remove the lever from the accelerator rod by taking off the circlip.

5   At the other end of the shaft remove the clevis pin securing the brake master cylinder pushrod to the pedal. It is held in position by a circlip.

6   Then remove the large circlip on the end of the main cross shaft next to the mounting bracket. The two mounting bracket bolts can then be undone. When these bolts are being undone take precautions to ensure that the clutch pedal remains in an upright position - it does not matter about the brake pedal which can fall back to the floor. This will ensure that the clutch cable does not get unhooked inside the tunnel. There is a separate plate also behind the pedals which has upturned lugs acting as pedal stops. Do not disturb this although it will need adjustment on reassembly.

7   Unclip the accelerator rod from the back of the accelerator pedal, remove the link and draw the brake pedal and accelerator rod out of the tube together with the brake pedal return spring. Note the position of the intermediate washers.

8   If you wish to draw out the clutch pedal and cable detach the other end of the cable from the clutch operating lever on the transmission casing.

9   Now draw out the clutch pedal and shaft together, keeping the pedal as upright as possible so that the cable may be drawn out with it.

10 A new clutch cable must be fed into the tube through the aperture in the tunnel. All that is needed is patience to guide the end into the tube.

11 Reassembly is a reversal of the dismantling procedure. The setting of the pedal stop plate requires some care, bearing in mind that the clutch pedal free play adjustment is affected and also the setting of the master cylinder pushrod. When replacing the clutch pedal the end of the cable has to be hooked on first and then the pedal manoeuvred into position without letting the end of the cable come loose or get snagged on the hook in the wrong position. It is best to get a second person to hold the other end of the cable and keep tension on it whilst the pedal is being positioned. If the cable appears to be too short after positioning, it is probably because the hook has slewed round. Waggle the pedal back and forth a few times - still with the other end of the cable being held, and it will probably straighten out. If it does not go back to square one.

12 Before finally tightening the mounting bracket bolts check that at the end of the return movement the rubber faces of both pedals are vertical. If they are not the stop plate has slotted holes to allow their adjustment to the vertical.

13 Finally check the master cylinder pushrod clearance (as described in Section 9 of this Chapter) and then check and if necessary, adjust the free play of the clutch pedal (as described in Chapter 5).

---

15 Handbrake cables and lever - removal and replacement

1   Slacken off the locknuts at the lever end of both handbrake cables and remove them together with the adjusting nuts.

2   Remove the rear brake drums and unhook the cable from the operating lever on the shoe.

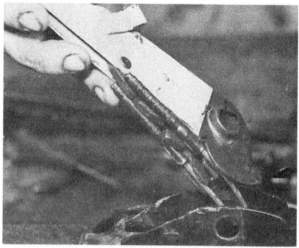
15.8 Handbrake lever lifted out to install cables

3   Undo the bolt which holds the outer sleeve clip to the brake backplate where the cable passes through. Disengage the clip from behind the washer and spring on the cable and draw the cable out from the backplate. Then pull the cables out of the tube from the other direction.

4   Before fitting a new cable make sure that at the brake end the spring and washer are properly fitted between the eye of the cable and the outer sleeve.

5   It is necessary to remove the handbrake lever before the threaded ends of the cable can be reconnected to it. Remove one of the circlips from the end of the lever pivot pin and withdraw the pin. Keep the hands well clear of the ratchet button and then move the whole lever assembly forward so that it disengages from the floor plate. If the ratchet button is inadvertently pressed the ratchet will fall down. It must be put back before replacing the lever.

6   Put the cable through the backplate and then work the sleeve clamp through the hole in the backplate so that the spring and washer are on the inside of the slotted bracket of the clamp. Replace the bolt into the back of the backplate and tighten it. Then hook the cable onto the lever.

7   Feed the threaded end of the cable into the tubes in the frame fork and finally see that the outer sleeve fits into position in the end of the tube. The threaded ends should appear inside the car under the handbrake lever mounting position. It may be necessary to hook them up with a piece of wire.

8   Making sure that they are not crossed, insert the cables into the two eyes in the base of the lever and then put the lever in position checking that the rear section engages properly in the floor section (photo). Once again be careful not to press the ratchet release button. Replace the pivot pin and circlip and screw on the adjuster and locknuts.

9   Adjust the handbrake as described in Section 2.

10 The introduction of the three point mounting for the seats in August '72 made it necessary to move the handbrake lever 60 mm (2.3/8 inches) to the rear. The cable was shortened to suit. Care should be taken not to mix the two sets of dimensions.

11 Also in August '72 a modified handbrake lever ratchet was fitted. The old type has a machined hole in the centre. The new one is solid. The new ratchet has three teeth less at the bottom and two more at the top. There is a slot in the back of the handbrake lever for the new type ratchet. The old type and new type levers can be installed only with the correct type of ratchet. The ratchets are not interchangeable.

16 Fault diagnosis - braking system

Before diagnosing faults in the brake system check that any irregularities are not caused by:

1 Uneven and incorrect tyre pressures   3 Wear in the steering mechanism   5 Misalignment of the body frame
2 Incorrect 'mix' of radial and cross-ply tyres   4 Defects in the suspension and dampers

Symptom	Reason/s	Remedy
Pedal travels a long way before the brakes operate	Brake shoes set too far from the drums	Adjust the brake shoes to the drums. (This applies equally where disc brakes are fitted but only the rear drums need adjustment).
Stopping ability poor, even though pedal pressure is firm	Linings and/or drums badly worn or scored	Dismantle, inspect and renew as required.
	One or more wheel hydraulic cylinders seized resulting in some brake shoes not pressing against the drums (or pads against discs)	Dismantle and inspect wheel cylinders. Renew as necessary.
	Brake linings contaminated with oil	Renew linings and repair source of oil contamination.
	Wrong type of linings fitted	Verify type of material which is correct for the car and fit it.
	Brake shoes wrongly assembled	Check for correct assembly.
	One of the dual hydraulic circuits is leaking resulting in only front or only rear brakes in operation	Examine hydraulic system for signs of leaks.
Car veers to one side when the brakes are applied	Brake linings on one side are contaminated with oil	Renew linings and stop oil leak.
	Hydraulic wheel cylinder(s) on one side partially or fully seized	Inspect wheel cylinders for correct operation and renew as necessary.
	A mixture of lining materials fitted between sides	Standardise on types of linings fitted.
	Unequal wear between sides caused by partially seized wheel cylinders	Check wheel cylinders and renew linings and drums as required.
Pedal feels spongy when the brakes are applied	Air is present in the hydraulic system	Bleed the hydraulic system and check for any signs of leakage.
Pedal feels springy when the brakes are applied	Brake linings not bedded into the drums (after fitting new ones)	Allow time for new linings to bed in after which it will certainly be necessary to adjust the shoes to the drums as pedal travel will have increased.
	Master cylinder or brake backplate mounting bolts loose	Retighten mounting bolts.
	Severe wear in brake drums causing distortion when brakes are applied	Renew drums and linings.
Pedal travels right down with little or no resistance and brakes are virtually non-operative. (See note at end)	Leak in both hydraulic system circuits resulting in lack of pressure for operating wheel cylinders	Examine the whole of the hydraulic system and locate and repair leaks. Test after repairing each and every leak source.
	If no signs of leakage are apparent all the master cylinder internal seals are failing to sustain pressure	Overhaul master cylinder.
Binding, juddering, overheating	One or a combination of causes given in the foregoing sections	Complete and systematic inspection of the whole braking system.

Note: Due to the safety feature of dual hydraulic circuits the possibility of both circuits failing simultaneously is very remote indeed.

Chapter 10
Electrical system I: charging and starting systems

Contents

Alternator and dynamo - routine maintenance 6
Alternator - removal, replacement and overhaul 14
Alternator - testing - 11
Battery - charging 5
Battery - maintenance and inspection 3
Battery - removal and replacement 2
Dynamo - current output and reverse current tests 10
Dynamo - no load regulated voltage test 8
Dynamo - no load unregulated voltage test 9

Dynamo - removal, dismantling and replacement 13
Dynamo - testing while still in the car 7
Electrolyte replenishment 4
Fault diagnosis 17
General description 1
Regulator - removal and replacement 12
Starter motor - dismantling and reassembly 16
Starter motor - testing, removal and replacement 15

Specifications

Battery:

Type	12 volt
Capacity	36 amp/hours
Earth	Negative

Generator:

Type	Bosch/VW generator or Bosch alternator
Maximum current	30 amps (dynamo); 50 amps (alternator)
Mean regulating voltage	14 volts
Nominal output speed	2000 rpm
Cut in speed (dynamo)	1450 rpm
Commutator minimum diameter (dynamo)	32.8 mm (1.12 inch)
Segment insulation undercut (dynamo)	0.5 mm (0.020 inch)
Brush length	Must be greater than length of holder

Regulator:

Type	Bosch or VW - matched to generator

Starter motor:

Type	Bosch or VW - pre-engaged
Nominal power	7 hp or 12 volts

Torque wrench settings:	lb ft	kg m
Generator pulley nut	43	6.0
Fan nut	43	6.0

1 General description

A 12 volt 36 amp hour battery is fitted under the rear seat. The system has a negative earth. The generator on all the early models (both USA and European) is a DC dynamo with an output of 30 amps. This has recently been replaced by a special alternator which is mounted and driven in exactly the same way and gives a rectified DC current of 50 amps, the rectification being by diodes carried in the end casing of the alternator.

For the dynamo, voltage control and cutout devices are fitted, but for the alternator a voltage control only, is necessary.

The starter motor is mounted on the transmission casing, the drive pinion being engaged in the flywheel teeth by a solenoid which completes this action before the current is switched to the starter motor, and prevents excessive wear of the starter ring teeth.

The pinion is driven through a one way roller clutch which

ensures that there is no danger from overrun.

2 Battery - removal and replacement

1 The battery is fixed under the rear seat which must first be lifted up and out.

2 There is a protective plastic cover over the top of the battery. On models with computer diagnosis there is a small lead to a connection for sensing the battery electrolyte level. Detach this.

3 Unclamp the battery terminals (earth [or negative] terminal first) and lift the battery out vertically to prevent electrolyte spillage.

4 When replacing the battery connect the earth lead last, see that both terminals and terminal clamps are clean and free from corrosion or deposits of any sort. Smear them with petroleum jelly (not grease) before connection. Never replace the rear seat without the battery cover in position. The springs of the seat can

short circuit the terminals and start a fire.

5 The alternator must **not** be run while the battery is disconnected.

3 Battery - maintenance and inspection

1 Normal weekly battery maintenance consists of checking the electrolyte level of each cell to ensure that the separators are covered by ¼ inch (7 mm) of electrolyte. If the level has fallen, top up the battery using distilled water only. Do not overfill. If a battery is overfilled or any electrolyte spilled, immediately wipe away the excess as electrolyte attacks and corrodes any metal it comes into contact with very rapidly.

2 As well as keeping the terminals clean and covered with petroleum jelly, the top of the battery, and especially the top of the cells, should be kept clean and dry. This helps prevent corrosion and ensures that the battery does not become partially discharged by leakage through dampness and dirt.

3 Once every three months, remove the battery and inspect the battery tray and battery leads for corrosion (white fluffy deposits on the metal which are brittle to touch). If any corrosion is found, clean off the deposits with ammonia and paint over the clean metal with an anti-rust/anti-acid paint.

4 At the same time inspect the battery case for cracks. If a crack is found, clean and plug it with one of the proprietary compounds marketed for this purpose. If leakage through the crack has been excessive then it will be necessary to refill the appropriate cell with fresh electrolyte as detailed later. Cracks are frequently caused in the top of battery cases by pouring in distilled water in the middle of winter after, instead of **before** a run. This gives the water no chance to mix with the electrolyte and so the former freezes and splits the battery case.

5 If topping-up the battery becomes excessive and the case has been inspected for cracks that could cause leakage, but none are found, the battery is being over-charged and the regulator will have to be checked.

6 With the battery on the bench at the three monthly interval check, measure its specific gravity with a hydrometer to determine the state of charge and condition of the electrolyte. There should be very little variation between the different cells and if a variation in excess of 0.025 is present it will be due to either:

a) Loss of electrolyte from the battery at some time caused by spillage or a leak, resulting in a drop in the specific gravity of the electrolyte when the deficiency was replaced with distilled water instead of fresh electrolyte.

b) An internal short circuit caused by buckling of the plates or a similar malady pointing to the likelihood of total battery failure in the near future.

7 The correct readings for the electrolyte specific gravity at various states of charge and conditions are:

	Temperate	Tropical
Fully charged	1.285	1.23
Half charged	1.20	1.14
Discharged	1.12	1.08

4 Electrolyte replenishment

1 If the battery is in a fully charged state and one of the cells maintains a specific gravity reading which is 0.025 or more lower than the others, and a check of each cell has been made with a voltage meter to check for short circuits (a four to seven second test should give a steady reading of between 1.2 to 1.8 volts), then it is likely that electrolyte has been lost from the cell with the low reading at some time.

2 Top up the cell with a solution of 1 part sulphuric acid to 2.5 parts of water. If the cell is already fully topped up draw some electrolyte out of it with a pipette.

3 When mixing the sulphuric acid and water **never add water to sulphuric acid** - always pour the acid slowly onto

the water in a glass container. **If water is added to sulphuric acid it will explode.**

4 Continue to top-up the cell with the freshly made electrolyte and then re-charge the battery and check the hydrometer readings.

5 Battery - charging

1 In winter time when heavy demand is placed upon the battery, such as when starting from cold, and much electrical equipment is continually in use, it is a good idea occasionally to have the battery fully charged from an external source at the rate of 3.5 to 4 amps.

2 Continue to charge the battery at this rate until no further rise in specific gravity is noted over a four hour period.

3 Alternatively, a trickle charger, charging at the rate of l.5 amps, can be safely used overnight.

4 Specially rapid 'boost' charges which are claimed to restore the power of the battery in 1 to 2 hours are most dangerous as they can cause serious damage to the battery plates through overheating.

5 While charging the battery note that the temperature of the electrolyte should never exceed 100^OF (37.8^OC).

6 Make sure that your charging set and battery are set to the same voltage.

6 Alternator and dynamo - routine maintenance

1 Check the fanbelt tension regularly. (see Chapter 2).

2 There is no maintenence possible on the bearings. These are sealed and cannot be lubricated.

3 The bushes on the dynamo may be inspected if the cover at the fanbelt end is loosened and moved back. They should protrude from their holders at the upper end. If they do not they require renewal. It is not possible to inspect the slip ring bushes on the alternator without dismantling the alternator.

4 The commutator of the generator may be inspected through the same aperature. It should be clean, smooth and have no burn marks.

5 It is strongly recommended that the electrical circuit should be tested every 10,000 miles. The best way to do this is through the VW diagnostic service which will very quickly tell whether anything is at fault, however there are other tests which are discussed in this Chapter. The main thing is not to wait until the red warning light will not go out at the proper time. That is when things become difficult.

7 Dynamo - testing while still in the car

A series of tests are described which can be done while the generator is in the car. However meters are required to measure up to 40v DC and 50 amperes. If you are one of the wise ones who has fitted an ammeter to show charge and discharge, then the test ammeter will not be required. An ammeter is a simple fitting and quite inexpensive (compared with the cost of a new battery). The meter comes in kit form with instructions and really tells you what is happening - as opposed to the red light, which only tells you when the charge ceases. Circuit diagrams are given for all tests.

8 Dynamo - no load regulated voltage test

1 Disconnect the lead from terminal "B+" on the regulator (situated under the rear seat cushion at the left) and make sure the end cannot touch any nearby part and short to earth.

2 Connect the positive lead from the voltmeter to terminal "B+" on the regulator and the negative lead to earth.

3 Start the engine and increase speed slowly to a fast tickover. The voltmeter should rise to a reading of 13-14 volts and stay

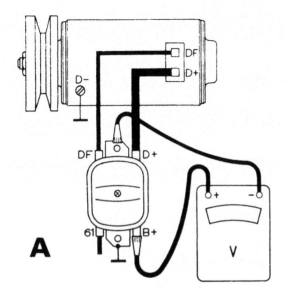

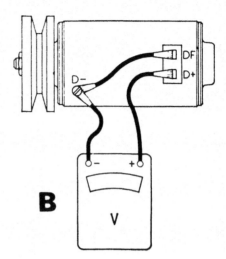

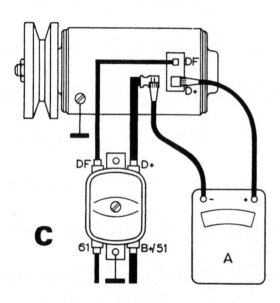

Fig. 10.1. Dynamo and regulator tests

A   Voltmeter connection for generator no load regulated
    voltage test
B   Voltmeter connected for generator no load unregulated
    voltage test
C   Ammeter connected for current output and reverse
    current test

there. If there is no reading the fault is most likely in the dynamo. If the reading is incorrect then the regulator is most probably at fault. Nevertheless both could be faulty in either case.

9 Dynamo - no load unregulated voltage test

1   This check will tell you if the dynamo is at fault and must be done quickly or you could damage an otherwise sound dynamo.
2   Disconnect the leads from terminals "DF" and "D+" on the dynamo. Connect the "DF" and "D—" terminals together.
3   Connect the voltmeter "+" terminal to the "D+" terminal on the dynamo and the voltmeter negative terminal to the "D—" terminal.
4   Start the engine. At a fast tickover - say 1500 dynamo rpm the voltage should be approximately 12 volts. At twice this speed the voltage should increase to 36 volts. Check quickly and switch off within a few seconds. If the voltage is nil, or low, then the dynamo is faulty.

10 Dynamo - current output test and reverse current test

1   The two previous tests have confirmed the presence or lack of voltage. This does not confirm the presence or lack of amps which are needed to charge the battery (even though the warning light may go out). For the current output check you will need an ammeter - with a range of 50 amps negative and positive. (If you have fitted an ammeter as an extra into the charging circuit already, this, of course, performs the function of this test and in fact tells you at all times whether the dynamo is doing its job properly).

2   Disconnect the "D+" cable from the dynamo and connect an ammeter in circuit. Under no circumstances run the engine with the "D+" connection out of circuit or the dynamo field windings will be damaged,

3   Start the engine. At low speed the ammeter should show a discharge although at very low idling speed it should move to zero when the regulator cutout functions. At high engine speed

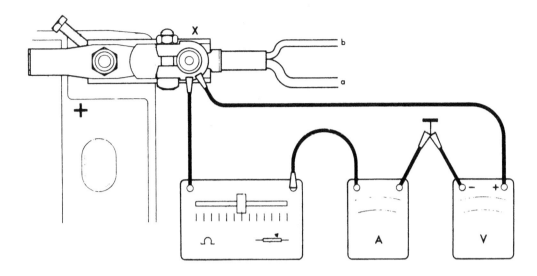

Fig. 10.2. Alternator circuit test

(x)   Battery switch   (a)   To starter   (b)   To lighting switch

the ammeter should show a positive reading. Try this with some lights switched on to ensure that it maintains a positive charge rate.

4 It the ammeter continues to show a discharge even at low idling speed it means that the cut-out is not functioning and current is flowing back from the battery to the dynamo.

5 If the cutout is not functioning the regulator unit must be changed.

11 Alternator - testing

1 This is a more difficult business. In addition to the meters (0-20 vdc and 0-60 amps) a battery cutout switch attachment and an adjustable load is required. Also the tests must be done in 30 seconds. If the test does not show that the alternator is giving 50 amps and 14 volts at 2000 rpm, then all that

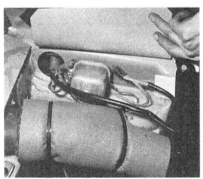

12.1 The regulator is hidden under a flap under the left of the rear seat

13.2a Removing the cover from the the dynamo

13.2b Pulling the spring up to get the brush from the holder

13.2c Undo the brush terminal tag screw

13.4 Brush and spring in position

15.2 Starter motor, top bolt. Arrow to terminal for main cable connection

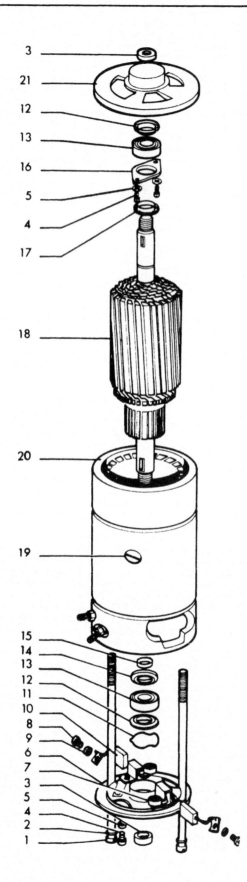

Fig. 10.3. Dynamo components

1 Through bolt
2 Lock washer
3 Spacer ring
4 Screw
5 Lock washer
6 Commutator end plate
7 Brush spring
8 Screw
9 Lock washer
10 Carbon brush
11 Lock washer
12 Splash shield
13 Ball bearing
14 Splash shield
15 Thrust washer
16 Retaining plate
17 Splash shield
18 Armature
19 Pole shoe screw
20 Field coil
21 Fan end plate

can be done is to replace the voltage regulator, and failing that have the alternator professionally serviced.

2   In view of the above it is suggested that a permanent ammeter in the charging circuit is most desirable which will tell at all times what the alternator is doing.

12 Regulator - removal and replacement

1 The regulator is under the rear seat on the left. (photo).

2 In the dynamo regulator two units are contained in the same case, the voltage regulator and the cutout. As an alternator provides its own current cutout in the shape of diodes the alternator regulator box is a different shape and the connections are different. Later models may be equipped with an alternator with integral voltage regulator - see Section 14.

3 Before doing anything disconnect the battery.

4 Look at the terminal connections very carefully and make a diagram for easy replacement. If they do not go back correctly then the generator will be damaged.

5 Remove the connections. Unscrew the regulator from its securing pad and remove it.

6 There is nothing the owner driver can do to repair or adjust it so if it is faulty it must be exchanged.

7 Replacement is the reversal. Make sure you get those connections in the right places.

13 Dynamo - removal, dismantling and replacement

1 The dynamo is removed in the manner described for the fan in Chapter 2. Before deciding to take it out completely make sure that the renewal of the brushes and cleaning the commutator are not the sole things to be done because these can be dealt with without removing the dynamo.

2 If the brushes need renewing remove the end cover. Hook up the ends of the springs which press them into the holders. Then pull the brushes out. Then undo the screw which connects the leads (photos).

3 Whilst the brushes are removed the commutator can be cleaned with a piece of clean cloth soaked in petrol. If the

commutator is very scored, changing the carbon brushes may improve things temporarily but the improvement in dynamo output is likly to be small and short lived.

4 When fitting new brushes make sure that they are of the correct type and fit snugly in the holders and slide freely. Brushes which are too loose will clatter about and soon wear out. Those which are tight will probably stick and eventually lose contact with the commutator as they wear away (photo).

5 If any of the brush retaining springs are broken or the commutator is scored the dynamo must be removed for the repairs to be made.

6 To dismantle the dynamo is not a procedure we recommend principally because there is very little the normal do-it-yourself man can do to repair it anyway. If the bearings have failed (a very rare occurrence) then the armature will need reconditioning. Skimming the commutator must be done in a lathe. Should the insulation of the armature or field coils have broken down then they will need renewal.

7 Having removed the dynamo and taken off the fan, therefore, we recommend it be replaced with an exchange unit or overhauled by a specialist firm dealing with auto electrics. Make sure when taking it to the repair firm that the regulator goes with it as their tests after rebuild will cover the complete unit.

8 Replacement of the dynamo is described in Chapter 2. Check that the spacer collars behind both the fan and pulley hubs are in position, otherwise when the nuts are tightened they will jam against the end frames.

---

14 Alternator - removal, replacement and overhaul

1 Removal from the pedestal and separation from the fan is described in Chapter 2.

2 The alterator for the Beetle has been specially designed to fit in the same space (very nearly) as the dynamo for it also carries the fan on the shaft. To house the diodes it has been necessary to enlarge the end casing but of course the body had to be the same diameter as that of the dynamo.

3 If the pulley nut is removed it is possible to take out the through bolts and separate the castings to look at the slip rings and brushes. Brush and holder assemblies are not separable.

4 A smell of burnt carbon means a short circuit in the winding somewhere. There is nothing that can be done about that.

5 Although, using a suitable heat sink (a pair of long nosed pliers) the diodes may be unsoldered and checked for correct operation (it should pass current in only one direction) the job is difficult and unless you are an auto-electrician the replacement of diodes is not easy. Furthermore, it requires a press and special arbors.

6 The author's advice is to take the alternator to a reputable Auto-Electrical firm or VW Agent and either part-exchange it or get it repaired with a warranty. The generator is such an important part of the car that it is essential to have it in 'apple pie' order.

7 Later models may be fitted with an alternator with an integral voltage regulator, or such an alternator may be supplied when renewing an older type.

8 When an alternator with built-in regulator is to be fitted to a vehicle previously equipped with an alternator with separate regulator, the following modifications must be made to the wiring:

(a) Disconnect the battery earth terminal, then remove the voltage regulator from under the rear seat, Leave the wires and connector in position

(b) In the engine compartment, detach the red (D+) wire from the alternator multi-pin connector. Cut off and discard the green (DF) and brown (D-) wires and the connector

(c) Connect the red (D+) wire to D+ on the alternator

(d) Connect the red/white (B+) and the diagnostic wires to B+ on the alternator

---

15 Starter motor - testing, removal and replacement

1 On the Volkswagen the starter is an inaccessible article and short of checking that the mounting bolts are tight and the electrical connections properly made to the solenoid, there is nothing else to be done except take it out if it malfunctions. If the starter fails to kick at all ascertain that current is being fed from the starter switch to the solenoid. This can be done by connecting a suitably long lead to test each of the terminals on the solenoid in turn. Connecting the other end via a voltmeter or bulb to earth. When connected to the smaller terminal (the lead from the ignition switch), there should be an indication on the bulb or voltmeter when the starter switch is operated. If there is not then check the other end of the wire at the starter switch terminal in the same way. If there is no voltage then the fault is not with the starter. Then connect the lead to the larger terminal on the solenoid. If there is no voltage when the starter switch is operated the solenoid is defective. If there is voltage and the starter does not turn the starter is defective. flange. To remove it the nut on the other end must be undone and access to this is between the fan housing and the bulkhead in the engine compartment. The nut on the lower stud is accessible under the car.

2 The starter is held by a bolt at the top, and a stud and nut at the bottom. The bolt head is not hexagonal (photo); it is circular with a flat which engages in a recess in the starter mounting.

3 From underneath the car, pull off the small lead at the connection and then undo the nut securing the large cable. All this must be done mainly by feel. Do not confuse the two large terminal nuts on the solenoid. The lower one connects the strap between solenoid and starter.

4 Remove the lower nut and the starter can be lifted out.

5 Replacement is a reversal of the removal procedure. Before fitting, grease the end of the pinion shaft. It runs in a plain bush in the engine crankcase casting.

---

16 Starter motor - dismantling and reassembly

1 The first stage of dismantling is to remove the end cover plate so as to get access to the brushes. If these do not protrude above the tops of their holders renewal is necessary, which calls for further dismantling.

2 Undo the nut connecting the strap between the solenoid and the starter and then the two screws holding the solenoid to the end frame (photos).

3 The solenoid can now be unhooked from the operating lever inside the end frame (photo).

4 If the solenoid only is faulty this is as far as it is necessary to go. A new solenoid unit can be fitted now.

5 Remove the two screws holding the end cover cap (photo).

6 Slide out the 'U' clip and remove the shims from the end of the shaft. These shims control the endfloat (photos).

7 Remove the two through bolts from the end cover and the end cover may then be taken off giving access to the commutator brushes (photos).

8 Hook up the springs holding the carbon brushes in the holders and push them to one side so that the pressure is relieved. The yoke complete with the brush holder mounting plate may then be drawn off the armature. Watch out for the washers on the end of the shaft (photo).

9 To renew the brushes, two may be detached by simply removing the screws whilst the other two need to be cut off and new ones soldered to the braided leads. Leave sufficient length to solder the new ones onto easily.

10 To remove the end frame from the drive end of the shaft first push back the stop ring with a suitable tube so that the jump ring underneath can be released from its groove. The end cover assembly complete with pinion may then be drawn off.

16.2a Remove the connecting strap terminal nut

16.2b Remove the solenoid retaining screws

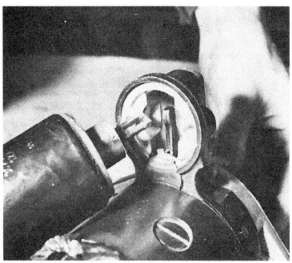

16.3 Unhook the solenoid from the operating lever

16.5 Remove the end cap cover screws

16.6a Remove the U clip from the end of the shaft ...

16.6b ... and the shim washers

16.7a Remove the through bolts ...

16.7b ... and take off the end cover

Fig. 10.4. Starter motor
components

1	Nut	16	End plate
2	Lock washer	17	Spring
3	Screw	18	Brush holder
4	Rubber seal	19	Grommet
5	Disc	20	Housing
6	Solenoid switch	21	Insulating washer
7	Stop ring	22	Thrust washer
8	Circlip	23	Pin
9	Screw	24	Nut
10	Washer	25	Lock washer
11	End cap	26	Operating lever
12	'C' washer	27	Mounting bracket
13	Shim	28	Drive pinion
14	Sealing ring	29	Armature
15	Housing screw		

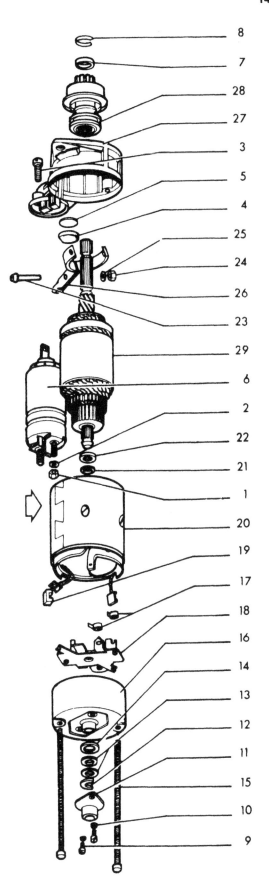

16.8 Lift the yoke and brush holder assembly from the armature

16.11 When refitting the yoke make sure the tongue and cut out fit together

11 The pinion drive should turn one-way only inside the clutch easily. If it does not the whole unit needs renewing. The pinion teeth should not be badly worn or chipped. The yoke of the pinion operating lever should be a good fit in the groove of the pinion sleeve.

12 Reassembly is a reversal of the dismantling procedure. Thoroughly grease the moving parts of the pinion operating lever first. When replacing the yoke engage the cut-out and tongue correctly (photo).

13 The carbon brushes should all be held up in their holders and this can be achieved if the springs are jammed against the sides of the brushes. The armature has two washers on the end and these must be fitted so that the thrust washer goes on first and the insulating washer after that.

14 When the pinion stop ring is refitted stake it into position over the jump ring after the latter has been fitted in its groove.

15 When refitting the solenoid ensure the plunger hooked end is securely placed over the operating lever.

16 The screw heads and joint faces of the commutator end cover, the solenoid and end frame should all be treated with sealing compound to keep water out. Use the Volkswagen product specially prepared for this if possible. It is important that it is not applied too thickly, otherwise clearance distances may be upset. If, after reassembly, the endfloat of the shaft exceeds 0.012 inch (0.4724 mm) it should be reduced by adding shim washers under the 'U' retaining clip on the end of the armature shaft under the small cover.

17 Because the pinion end bearing (bush) is located in the crankcase casting, it is not possible to rotate the starter under load or at speed when not fitted to the engine. The customary bench tests are therefore not applicable to this starter.

17 Fault diagnosis - charging and starting systems

Symptom	Reason/s	Remedy
Ignition warning light does **not** come on when the ignition is switched on	a) Battery discharged b) Battery defective c) Bulb defective d) Loose connections or e) Cables chafed and broken f) Battery terminals dirty g) Ignition switch defective h) Voltage regulator defective j) Exciter winding in alternator defective k) Brushes on commutator or slip ring not making contact	Charge battery New battery Change bulb Check and rectify Check and rectify Clean Install new switch Change regulator Change alternator Fit new brushes
Ignition warning light stays on when ignition is switched off	a) Voltage regulator contact points stuck (dynamo) b) Exciter diode short circuit (alternator)	Fit new regulator Take alternator for repair
Ignition warning light will not go out when engine is running, or only goes out at high speeds	a) Fan belt slack b) Regulator faulty c) Exciter diode faulty (alternator) d) Commutator dirty (dynamo) e) Loose cable connections or short circuit	Adjust tension Replace regulator Replace alternator Clean commutator Check circuit and repair
Starter will not turn engine. (Switch on lights during this test)	a) No lights. Loose cables, flat battery b) Lights bright but dim when starter operated Loose connections or battery run down c) Lights bright. Starter operates when Terminals 30 and 50 are connected means cable 50 to starter switch or starter switch faulty d) Lights bright solenoid switch operates. Move battery cable from terminal 30 to connector strip terminal. Starter now operates — solenoid switch faulty e) Stick shift only. Corroded starter cutout switch	Check battery and connections Clean battery terminals and check starter connections Check battery Find open circuit and repair Replace starter switch Replace solenoid switch Overhaul or replace starter cutout switch
Connect battery cable direct to connector strip terminal. Starter still does not operate	a) Worn or sticking brushes b) Weak brush springs c) Field or armature winding faulty d) Commutator dirty, worn or burned	Clean or replace Replace springs Replace starter Clean commutator - if necessary replace with new armature
Starter turns engine slowly (or not at all)	a) Flat battery b) Loose or dirty connections c) Brushes sticking or worn d) Commutator defective e) Starter windings damaged	Recharge battery Clean and tighten Service brush gear Service commutator Replace starter
Starter engages but turns engine in jerks	a) Drive pinion defective b) Flywheel teeth damaged	Replace drive pinion Overhaul complete engine
Drive pinion does not release	a) Drive pinion sticking on armature shaft b) Solenoid switch faulty	Remove and service. Replace if necessary Replace switch

Chapter 11 Electrical system II: lighting system, facia board and electrical accessories

Contents

Computer diagnosis 19	Radios - guide lines for fitting 24
Direction indicators - fault diagnosis 18	Rear lamp clusters and license plate light 4
Facia board - removal and replacement 15	Safety belt warning system (USA vehicles) 20
Fog lamps - guide notes for fitting 23	Speedometer cable - removal and replacement 17
Front parking lights and turn signals 3	Speedometer head - removal and replacement 16
Fuses and relays 14	Steering column - steering lock and ignition switch 13
General description 1	Steering column - turn signal and wiper/washer switch ... 12
Headlamps 2	Stop lamps - fault diagnosis 10
Heated rear window 22	Windscreen wipers - removal and replacement 6
Horn 11	Windscreen washer 9
Ignition key warning system (USA vehicles) 21	Windscreen wiper motor - overhaul 7
Interior light 5	Windscreen wiper mechanism - overhaul 8

Specifications

Lamps:

Headlamp	Twin filament 45/40W
(halogen)	Halogen 4 60/55W
Parking light	Tubular 4W
Turn signal	Ball 21W
Brake/tail light	Twin filament 21/5
License plate light	Ball 10W
Interior light	Festoon 10W
Reversing light	Ball 21W

For sealed beam units

Headlight	6012 (US)
Turn signal/front parking light	SL 12V 21/5W

For United States

Headlight	6014 (US) sealed beam unit
Side marker light	HL12V 4W

Fuses:

Two layouts are given but these change from time-to-time. Fuse layouts are given in the operators handbook or can be obtained from the VW agent.

Fuse No.	UK	USA
1	Parking lights front and right rear Rear number plate	Parking and side marker lights left. Tail light left
2	Parking light left rear	Parking and side marker lights right Tail light right
3	Headlamp main beam left	Low beam left
4	Headlamp main beam right	Low beam right
5	Low beam left Main beam warning light	High beam left
6	Low beam right	High beam right High beam indicator light
7	Spare	License plate light
8	Emergency flasher system	Emergency flasher system

9	Headlamp flasher/interior light	Interior light
10	Brake lights/horn	Windscreen wipers/rear window Fresh air fan
11	Windscreen wiper	Horn, stop lights, control valve and ATF warning light
12	Gauges and warning lights	Fuel gauge, turn signals and warning lights

1 General description

The electrical equipment of the various models covered by this manual varies considerably. The basic fittings, lamps, turn signals, horn, wipers and, washers are standard. The remainder is either to satisy local regulations (seat belt and ignition key warning circuit for USA) or to suit the owner (radio, fog and spot lamps). This Chapter describes the basic equipment and offers suggestions concerning the optional extras. There are VW optional extras which it would seem wise to fit if the owner needs them. Items from other sources should be fitted in the same way as the VW products.

The models with a dynamo will only take a limited amount of extra electrical loading and it is essential to work out an electrical loading table if such current consuming additions as rear window heaters are installed.

The models with an alternator have an extra 20 amperes to play with and can safely afford most extras. All the same, extra current in the wiring can cause overheating and even set fire to the car, so do not just add bits and pieces indiscriminately. There are stringent regulations about house wiring but so far thank goodness red tape has not clogged up the auto-electrical system; however, insurance companies will quite rightly quibble if a fire has been caused by an overloaded cable, and a skilled assessor will soon trace the reason from a burnt out wreck. Extras are a very good thing but be sure they are fitted sensibly.

The facia board of the Super Beetle has a new look. The old spartan VW has given way to a padded atractive layout designed to accommodate a radio. It is bolted to the body structure (previously it was welded) and is no longer accessible from the luggage compartment.

This Chapter also includes the switches, fuses, relays and the method of replacing the speedometer.

2 Headlamps

1   To remove the headlamp unit from the car unscrew the lowest screw (photo) which secures the rim. Lift up the lower edge of the rim to unhook the top edge and the assembly may be removed (photo).
2 To remove the bulb undo the bulb holder from the back of the reflector by turning it anticlockwise and pull the bulb and connection apart. (photo). When fitting a new bulb do not handle the bulb with the fingers, use a duster or the bulb will be marked. Make sure the lugs and the notches line up.
3 The beam adjusting screws (photo) move the assembly to direct the light beam. Dependant upon the locality, the statutory regulations differ as to where the beam should point. Again, left and right-hand drive models differ. These facts may be obtained through the local authorities.

Once you know the rules select a level space about fifteen feet (five metres) from a vertical wall, and place the car on it. Mark a line on the wall equal to the height of the centre of the lamps, and a vertical line to correspond with the centre line of the car. This will now give a reference on which the requirement of the regulations may be inscribed. Cover one headlamp and switch on the lights. The beam may now be trained by moving the adjusting screws. It the main beam is correct then the 'dip' beam will be also. Uncover the other lamp and cover the one which has been adjusted. Repeat the procedure.

It is not generally realized that bulbs have a limited efficient life. They continue to give light long after the efficient level has been reached. It is worth having them tested, or if you do not want to do that replace them at least annually.
4 Water does penetrate the headlamp sometimes. There is a drain plug in the housing. Make sure this works or there will be rust and damage.
5 The reflector is held into the rim with spring clips. If it is necessary to replace the glass and reflector make sure the glass is the right way up, and fit a new sealing ring.
6 The USA Super and basic Beetle and Sports Bug range are equipped with sealed beam units. Remove the rim by undoing the bottom screw. There are three screws which hold the sealed beam unit into the retaining ring, remove these but be careful as they may be rusty. Take the sealed beam unit out of the support ring and pull the cable connector away. Before fitting a new unit clean all the joints and replace the rubber gasket if necessary. Be certain that the three glass lugs engage in the support ring, insert the screw for the trim ring and engage the thread. Now fit the edge of the trim ring over the top log and tighten the screw.

3 Front turn signal lamps/parking lamps

1 The turn signal is located on the front wing. Remove the screws and lift off the unit (photo). Take care when replacing the cover that the cover seats firmly in the seal or the unit will soon corrode.

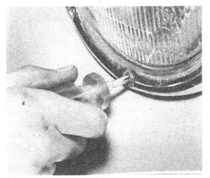
2.1a Removing the headlamp retaining screw

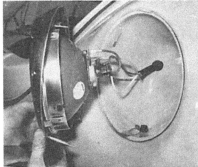
2.1b Lift the assembly and pull it away from the car

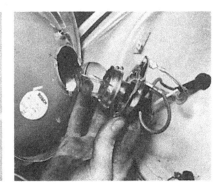
2.2 The bulb holder may be turned and withdrawn

2.3 The beam training screw (there is a similar one on the other side

3.1 Remove the holding scree and lift up the cover

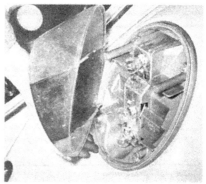

4.1 The rear lamp cluster

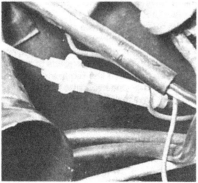

4.2 The fuse for the reversing light (a white plastic tube) is in the engine compartment

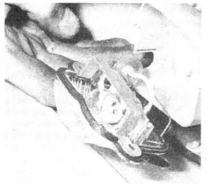

4.3 Removing the license plate lamp

5.1 Removing the interior light

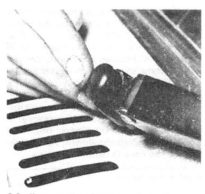

6.3a Remove the plastic cap from the wiper spindle ...

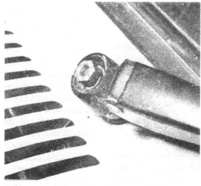

6.3b ... and the nut and draw off the wiper arm

6.3c Remove the spacer ...

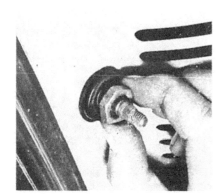

6.3d ... and undo the securing nut

6.4 Remove the cover plate ...

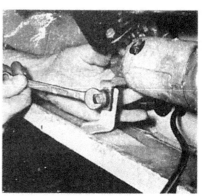

6.5a ... undo the clamp nut ...

4 Rear light cluster and licence plate light

1 All the rearward facing lights have been gathered together, except the licence plate light. Remove the fixing screws and ease out the plastic cover. (photo).

2 The bulbs may be replaced as necessary, but again do not handle them with bare fingers. The fuse for the reversing light is in a white plastic tube in the engine compartment. (photo).

3 The licence plate light may be serviced by taking out two screws (photo).

5 Interior light

1 This may be prised out of the roof using gentle pressure. Take care not to mark the head lining. The festoon bulb may be replaced and the unit pressed into the head lining (photo).

6 Windscreen wipers - removal from car

1 On the curved screen models the wiper blades are marked "R" and "L". Check these marks before proceeding further.

2 Disconnect the battery.

3 Remove the plastic covers from the wiper shafts (photo) and the hexagon nuts underneath. (photo). The wiper blades may now be drawn off the splines and set aside. Remove the spacers (photo) and then the thin nut (photo). The spindles are now free from the body.

4 Open the lid of the luggage compartment. Remove the hard board lining and undo the screws holding the cover of the fresh air box and take it off (photo).

5 Undo the nut of the clamp (photo) and the whole wiper assembly may be lifted away (photo). Take off the plastic cover.

6 The leads go through a grommet to the dashboard. (photo) The grommet may be eased out of the bulkhead.

7 There is a small cover over the lower part of the steering column inside the car. Remove the two securing screws and access may then be had to the wiring. The wiper cable will be seen coming through the bulkhead. Trace it to the column and a multipin plug will be found. Disconnect this (photo). This may be eased through the hole in the bulkhead and the wiper assembly may now be taken from the car.

8 Replacement is the reverse procedure. When lining up the wiper shafts make sure they are not jammed or too tight. Be careful also to fit the blades back on the right side, they are of different lengths. The hose to the jet and the cables to the motor must be routed so that they do not foul the linkage.

7 Wiper motor - dismantling and reassembly

1 Other than for the renewal of brushes dismantling is not an economical proposition.

2 To renew the brushes remove the motor from the car as described in Section 6. Take the lock washer and spring washer off the drive shaft and remove the connection rod. Unscrew the nut on the motor shaft, undo the securing nut and take the motor out of the frame.

3 Remove the armature end cover. The brushes are held in tension against the commutator with a spring. Unhook this and swing the brushes outwards.

4 Renewal is by replacing the complete brush plate assembly.

5 A wiring diagram is given. It is for consideration however if the car can be off the road for a little while (it is illegal to drive it with no wiper mechanism) whether it would not be better to get an experienced auto-electrician to fit the new brush gear. If it isn't right and it does not bed down properly the wiper motor will interfere with the radio.

8 Windscreen wiper mechanism and spindle bearings

1 While the wiper mechanism is out of the car check all the joints and bearings for wear and lubrication. It all works away in the dark and will have had no maintenance since it was installed. The spindle bearing may be worn, which could cause the wiper to jam, and certainly overload the motor. If they are worn then replace the bushes, and fit new seals. A little molybdenum grease should be smeared on the shaft.

9 Windscreen washer

1 The washer header tank is fitted in the front luggage compartment (photo). It is pressurized by the spare wheel which has a special connection (photo). The liquid is fed through a valve operated by the switch on the steering column to a jet mounted on the body in front of the screen.

2 The spare wheel should be inflated to 42 psi. The valve cuts off the supply of air to the washer tank when the pressure in the wheel drops to 28 psi.

3 It is a good idea to add a glass cleaning solution to the water when charging the tank. As well as improving the washing facilities it will act as an antifreeze in the winter. Otherwise use methylated spirits (3 water to 1 meths) if there is frost about. It is unlikely that the tank will freeze but the jets will and they are difficult to thaw out.

4 If the jet is blocked clean it with a fine wire. If that does not work then detach the tube, remove the jet and replace it with a

6.5b ... and lift the motor and mechanism clear

6.6 The leads go through the bulkhead in a rubber grommet

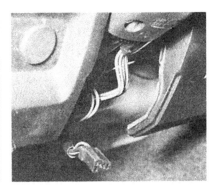
6.7 The multi-pin plug for the wiper cable

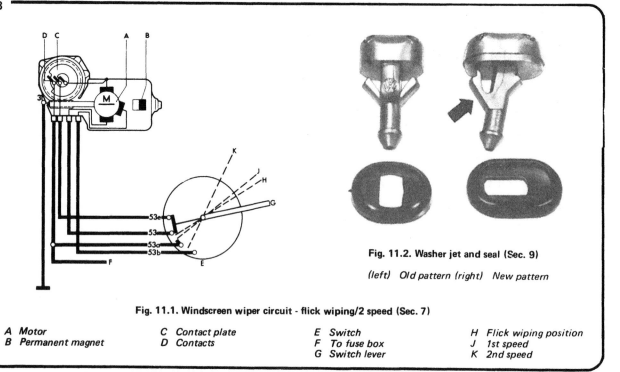

Fig. 11.2. Washer jet and seal (Sec. 9)

(left) Old pattern (right) New pattern

Fig. 11.1. Windscreen wiper circuit - flick wiping/2 speed (Sec. 7)

A Motor	C Contact plate	E Switch	H Flick wiping position
B Permanent magnet	D Contacts	F To fuse box	J 1st speed
		G Switch lever	K 2nd speed

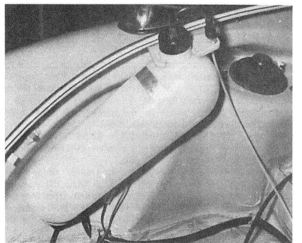

9.1a The washer tank in the front luggage compartment

9.1b The control valve on the spare wheel

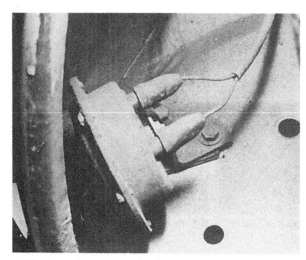

11.1 Position of the horn under the left front wing

11.2 Prise the cover off the spigots to get at the horn connections

new one.

5 The jet is held in a plastic insert by projections from below. Later models have only one projection. The two types are interchangeable. If the jet is disconnected from the hose be sure the reconnection is made firmly for the pressure is 42 psi and will soon wet the contents of the luggage compartment if it comes adrift.

The method of getting at the control valve is discussed in the section on the steering column switch.

10 Stop lamp - fault diagnosis

1 The stop lamps are operated by either one or two hydraulic switches mounted on the brake master cylinder (see Chapter 9).
2 If, after checking that the bulbs, fuse and connections are in order, the brake lights still do not work (with the ignition switched on) pull off the leads from each hydraulic switch and touch them together. If the stop lamps now light the switch is at fault and should be renewed. The brakes must be bled afterwards (see Chapter 9).
3 If the stop lights still do not work when bridging the terminals of the switch then the fault lies in the wiring circuit. First check that voltage is coming to the switch terminal and carry on from there, tracing back to the connections with the aid of the wiring diagram.

11 Horn

1 The single horn is mounted behind the left front wing (photo).
2 If the horn should fail to work after checking the fuse check that the horn ring is operating the contact in the centre of the steering wheel (photo). This can be seen after the steering wheel hub has been levered out. The three screws will release the ring. A contact spring is fitted in the turn signal switch to carry the horn earth wire. It must be remembered that when the ignition is switched on the current flows first to the horn and the circuit is made when the horn ring switch is earthed.
3 The terminals on the horn itself should be perfectly clean and the insulation in good condition.
4 If the horn has to be removed check it once again with an independent supply before condemning it. There is a central adjusting nut in the back of the horn which may possibly give advantageous results if rotated in one direction or the other. It is not normally adjustble and if wrongly set can damage an otherwise good horn. It is important to emphasise therefore that any 'fiddling' with this is a positively last resort, having checked the complete circuit first.
5 The horn is removed by undoing the mounting bolt which secures it to the bracket.
6 When refitting the horn it is important to make sure that it does not contact the surrounding bodywork in any way. If it does it will not function properly.

12 Steering column - turn signal and wiper switch

1 Refer to Fig. 11.3. Disconnect the battery (Chapter 10).
2 The horn pad may be levered off the plugs and set aside.
3 The steering wheel may be removed by removing the securing nut and pulling the wheel away. Disconnect the horn lead.
4 The various pieces of the switch may now be removed in turn. Be careful with the circlip, it may fly off, if not held firmly when removing. Remove the contact plate and the felt ring.
5 To remove the turn signal and wiper switches together press the connection tabs together against the switch housing with a piece of wood. The guide channels may then be taken from the wiper switch. When reassembling be careful not to crush the cables with the wiper switch.
6 The windscreen washer valve may be seen below this and removed if necessary. Do not disconnect the hoses unless absolutely necessary. If you do then the clip must not be replaced. A special piece of 'double hose' should be obtained

from the dealer and fitted over the washer hose. The washer hose should then be pushed up hard to the enlarged section of the washer valve pipe and the 'double hose' then pushed over this enlarged section. Use a drop of water as lubricant, but nothing else.

13 Steering column - steering lock and ignition switch

1 Refer to Fig. 11.3. The ignition/starter switch is connected to the harness by a multi-pin plug.
2 It may be removed after the turn signal and wiper switches have been removed.
3 The lock is fastened to the switch by a small grub screw. Once this is removed the lock and switch may be separated.

14 Fuses and relays

1 This is one heading on which this manual cannot be specific. The fuse box connections vary according to the amount of electrical equipment to be safeguarded. Two typical layouts are given in the specification, but they may not suit your Beetle.
2 The fuse layout is given in the Instruction Manual supplied with the car.
3 The fuse box is situated centrally under the facia board, (photo) and if the plastic cap is removed the fuses may be removed and replaced. It is suggested that in the peace and quiet of your garage you remove each fuse in turn and check that it does control the stated circuit. Keep a box of spare fuses with the list of fuses in the glove pocket.
4 If a fuse blows it is important to discover why. It may have been due to a momentary overload, water in the circuit, or just old age; it could also be due to a chafed wire making a short circuit with the bodywork. The more you can trace the wiring, especially at the bulkheads, in quiet conditions the better so that you know where to look if there is trouble. Never replace a fuse with one of a higher current rating - that is the way to start a fire.
5 In the author's experience fuses always blow in the heavy rain or heavy traffic. There seems to be some natural law about this. Make certain you know which is the fuse for the horn. Removing that one stops the horn blowing when the horn circuit has a fault and saves you pulling wires off in a panic.
6 If the fuse box is removed (photos), by undoing the retaining screws it can be lowered down and turned to get at the relays. These are small boxes plugged in to the top of the fuse box. On the model photographed the black box "VW 111953227A" is the turn signal/emergency light relay. The other one "SWF R 200958" is the combi relay which in conjunction with the switch allows the headlamps to be switched from high beam to low beam, or flashed.
7 On more complicated wiring/accessory systems there may be up to three more relays plugged in. If the vehicle is fitted with intermittent screen wiping as an optional extra there will be a relay for that. Fog lights, also an optional extra, have their own relay, and in the USA Super and basic Beetle there is a relay for the ignition key and seat belt warning devices.
8 The intermittent screen wiping relay (111955531) can cause a problem if there is a heated rear window. It may be that if the heated rear window element is switched off the windscreen wiper will start to operate. Change the relay (don't ask why!) for a newer one and the problem will be solved.

15 Facia board - removal

1 The facia board is a completely new design. It is bolted to the body and is not accessible from the luggage compartment. A lot of thought has gone into the design and provision has been made for a radio. Blanked spaces are provided for extra switches to be installed, and a clock if wished. The glove box is contoured to match the remainder. It is well padded and apparently stuck in

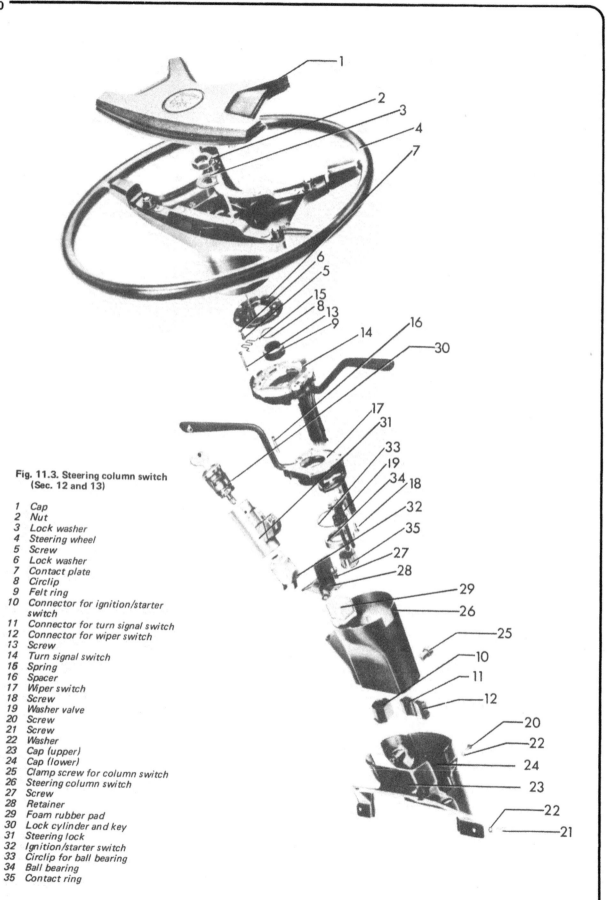

Fig. 11.3. Steering column switch
(Sec. 12 and 13)

1 Cap
2 Nut
3 Lock washer
4 Steering wheel
5 Screw
6 Lock washer
7 Contact plate
8 Circlip
9 Felt ring
10 Connector for ignition/starter switch
11 Connector for turn signal switch
12 Connector for wiper switch
13 Screw
14 Turn signal switch
15 Spring
16 Spacer
17 Wiper switch
18 Screw
19 Washer valve
20 Screw
21 Screw
22 Washer
23 Cap (upper)
24 Cap (lower)
25 Clamp screw for column switch
26 Steering column switch
27 Screw
28 Retainer
29 Foam rubber pad
30 Lock cylinder and key
31 Steering lock
32 Ignition/starter switch
33 Circlip for ball bearing
34 Ball bearing
35 Contact ring

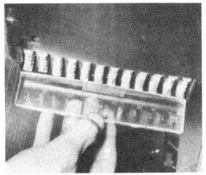

14.3 The fuse box under the centre of the dashboard. The plastic cap has been removed

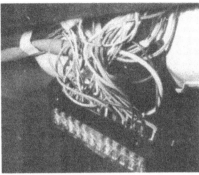

14.5a Remove the two screws holding the fuse box and lower it down. Be careful not to damage the cables

14.5b By turning the fuse box the relays become accessible

15.5a Removing the strip hiding facia insert screws

15.5b Removing the button hiding facia insert screw

15.5c Removing the facia insert screws

15.5d The inset may now be removed and the switches taken out of the insert

15.6 A switch showing the cable mechanism

16.3 Take the speedometer out to the front when the drive connection is disconnected

place with glue for no screw heads are visible.

2   The facia board may be removed entirely, or more sensibly piecemeal since the switches and instruments are grouped in or adjacent to well planned inserts which may be removed without disturbing the remainder of the board.

3   To remove the entire board, first disconnect the battery. Then remove the steering wheel and column switch. Remove the speedometer drive from the back of the speedo.

At the extreme ends of the board where it abuts the door pillar on each side are two small caps, one at the top and one at the bottom. Prise these off and screw heads are visible. Remove the panel support above the fuse box, and lift the panel slightly to unhook it. It may now be drawn away. However, it is still connected to the car by a large number of wires. The method of disconnecting this is discussed later. Only when all of the wires are free from the board may it be removed.

4   Replacement of the board is the reverse of removal, make sure

it is firmly hooked on and that the air duct is fitted securely over the outlet adapter.

5   It is unlikely that the owner will wish to remove the entire board, but that the insert (photo) will be sufficient. To remove this prise out the small strips (photo) and the small buttons under the speedometer (photo) and fixing screws will be found. Remove these and the inset complete with contents may be withdrawn. (photo).

6   It will be seen that by depressing the clip the switches may be pushed out of the insert (photo). The space terminals are pushed on. Always label a wire before removing it. Switches are not repairable, only replaceable. It will be seen that there are spaces for extra switches. The blanks may be removed and switches installed if required for the heated rear window and fog lights.

8   The removal of the insert also permits servicing action to the warning lamps for the seat belt system and brake system.

9   To remove the clock simply pull it forward. It is held in place

by a rubber boot. There is sufficient extra wiring to allow it to come clear so that access can be had to the terminals.

16 Speedometer head - removal and replacement

1 The speedometer head also carries the fuel gauge.
2 To remove the speedometer head first remove the insert as described in the previous Section.
3 The speedo-cable retaining ring may now be reached through the insert space. Unscrew this and the speedometer head may be withdrawn to the front (photo). It is held in a rubber boot.
4 There are at least five bulbs pushed into the back of the speedometer head (photo) for the warning lights, oil pressure, generator charging, turn signals, high beam, plus possibly warning lights for the temperature of the automatic transmission fluid and parking lights. If you pull them all out and disconnect the fuel gauge the speedometer head may be taken away. You may also spend an hour trying to reassemble them as we did. Mark the leads with numbers and write the numbers on the case by the side of the bulb holder. You can reassemble them in one minute flat that way.
5 The fuel gauge may be removed and checked separately, if possible against a gauge which is known to be correct. If it is faulty it must be replaced with a new one.
6 When reassembling the head refit the bulbs and connections, push the speedo-cable forward and reconnect it and then feed the cable back through the bulkhead as the speedometer head is pressed into place. (photo).

17 Speedometer cable - removal and replacement

1 The speedometer drive is from the left front wheel hub. The axle is hollow to permit the drive cable to go through it, and the cable is driven by a square hole in the bearing dust cover, and secured either by a circlip or a split pin. The drive may be separated after the dust cover has been removed.
2 The routing of the cable is most important. On left-hand drive vehicles there should be a protective cap on the slotted nut of the drive arm to prevent damage to the speedometer drive on full left lock. When installing the cable make sure there are no unnecessary bends. The cable must be routed on the vehicle centreline side of the steering gear.
3 There is a mark on the cable about 22 inches (56 cm) from the square drive (road wheel) end of the cable. This should be level with the drop arm. The cable should pass through a grommet in a plate on the suspension strut (except torsion bar suspension models).
4 The cable must not be squeezed. Do not grease the cable at the speedometer head end or grease may penetrate into the head and cause the speedo to stick.

18 Direction indicators - fault diagnosis and rectification

1 One of the most usual causes of failure is due simply to bad connections to earth. This can occur at the bulb holders (usual) or the terminal connections. If, therefore, the flashers can be heard but do not light - or only operate slowly - check all the bulbs, holders and screws for signs of whitish corrosion deposits (which may have been caused by seepage of water past the lamp housing seals). Check also the appropriate fuse.
2 First check that the flasher relay itself is not faulty. The simplest way to do this is by substitution with a new one. The relay is located on the fuse rack behind the dash panel.
3 If the fault is in the switch itself the steering wheel must be removed (Chapter 11) so that the switch may be removed. This combined switch, if faulty, must be renewed as a unit.

19 Computer diagnosis

Volkswagen has developed a maintenance check system linked into a recording and measuring apparatus.

The main purpose of the system is to reduce the human error, primarily one of omission, in the check list for their 6000 mile service.

A standard print-out sheet to cover all models lists 88 separate checks. 65 of these checks apply to all models.

It must be emphasised that the scheme is purely a diagnosis and that apart from enduring that the tyre pressures are correct to start with (so that headlamp alignment may be measured correctly) the diagnosis service man does not do any rectification work.

All models from August 1971 onwards (1972 model year) are fitted with a central multipin socket which is wired to all the necessary points for the computer which is plugged into it. (photo).

The model of car is first determined together with any of the standard options fitted. Since the introduction of the plug-in socket every car carries a sticker in the engine compartment showing its computer diagnosis code number. This number corresponds with a plastic card measuring about 12 x 6 inches (30 x 15 cms) which is punched full of holes corresponding to the specifications for that particular car. This card is fed into the computer. From then on everything measured on the vehicle is compared with the norm on the punch card. The print-out indicates + (OK) or - (not OK) for those operations where the checking is done automatically.

The technician has a hand set connected to the computer and a window in this hand set shows each check requirement. At the time of writing only 24 of the 88 items are checked automatically. The rest are checked by the technician and where all is well he presses a button on the hand set marked '+'. If not

16.4 The speedometer view from the back

16.6 The drive connector and the wiring stays behind

19.1 The computor diagnosis plug in the engine compartment

applicable there is another button and if unsatisfactory a third button marked "-". When any of these are pressed the mark is noted on the print-out sheet and the window in the hand set moves forward to the next item for checking.

The items which are measured by the equipment automatically are the steering geometry, ignition and charging systems and cylinder compression. Lights and battery condition are checked automatically only on those models fitted with the connection socket.

The steering geometry is checked by photo electric beams and mirrors as the steering wheel is turned through 180°,90° each side of the straight ahead position. This is done within a 20 second period and measures toe and camber and prints out the answer in degrees and minutes. The ignition and charging systems are measured for the resistances of the various circuits. It is important that all connections are clean and that cable sizes are standard.

The cylinder compression is measured by calculating the load on the starter motor when the engine is turned over, the state of the battery and the temperature of the engine oil is measured and taken into account for this check.

There is no doubt that the system is quick, accurate and calculated to tell the unhappy customer all the awful things wrong with his vehicle in the shortest possible time. However, it is gratifying to be able to record that like all computer systems it is dependent on the information it is given and in this case the information is based on the experience and conscientiousness of the technician in control.

As far as the car owner is concerned there are a few words of warning to be given. The diagnosis can only be carried out accurately (as far as the automatic side of it is concerned) when the vehicle being processed conforms exactly to the types and options of the computer card which sets the standard. Addition and modifications in the electrical system can upset the measured resistances. Damage to the wiring system, or unusual resistances caused by faulty connection, corrosion or deteriorated insulation can also affect readings. It is perhaps for this reason that the automatic diagnosis is as yet not very extensive, depending as it does on electrical measurement within the vehicle circuitry.

To sum up therefore, it can be seen that the computer diagnosis system had the following positive advantages as part of any routine maintenance programme.

1 A complete check list which follows a logical sequence in the shortest possible time - thus saving time and money.

2 A great reduction in the possibility of human error by omission.

3 A printed record of the decision made on each and every check by the diagnosis technician.

4 Provided the record is kept regularly the car's value is maintained at a much higher lever than otherwise.

But the system is still only as good as the personnel using it.

20 Safety belt warning system

1 To satisfy legal requirements in the USA a warning system is fitted, both by buzzer and light signal. When the engine is started and a gear engaged the buzzer sounds and the light remains on until both driver and passenger have fitted their safety belts correctly; then, and only then does the alarm switch off.

2 The warning lamp is built into the facia board. There are electrical connections in the seat belt locks bolted to the centre tunnel which are operated by the belt tongues.

3 Contact strips are fitted to the passenger seat, a switch is fitted to the left-hand side of the gear housing and a starter cutout switch is installed. A wiring diagram is included

4 The testing of this system is somewhat complicated and eventually finishes up by replacing one or several parts and in view of the strictness of the law it is recommended that if the system becomes faulty the repair should be left to the VW agent who has the proper test equipment and can replace the defective parts correctly.

Fig. 11.4. Bulb holder and warning light - safety belt warning circuit (Sec. 20)

1 Window

2 Bulb 12v/1.2 watts
3 Case

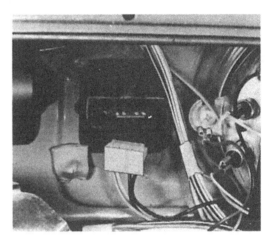

Fig. 11.5. Bulb holder and warning light - rear view - safety belt warning circuit (Sec. 20)

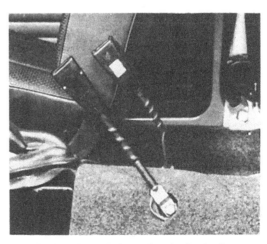

Fig. 11.6. Safety belt warning circuit - Locks

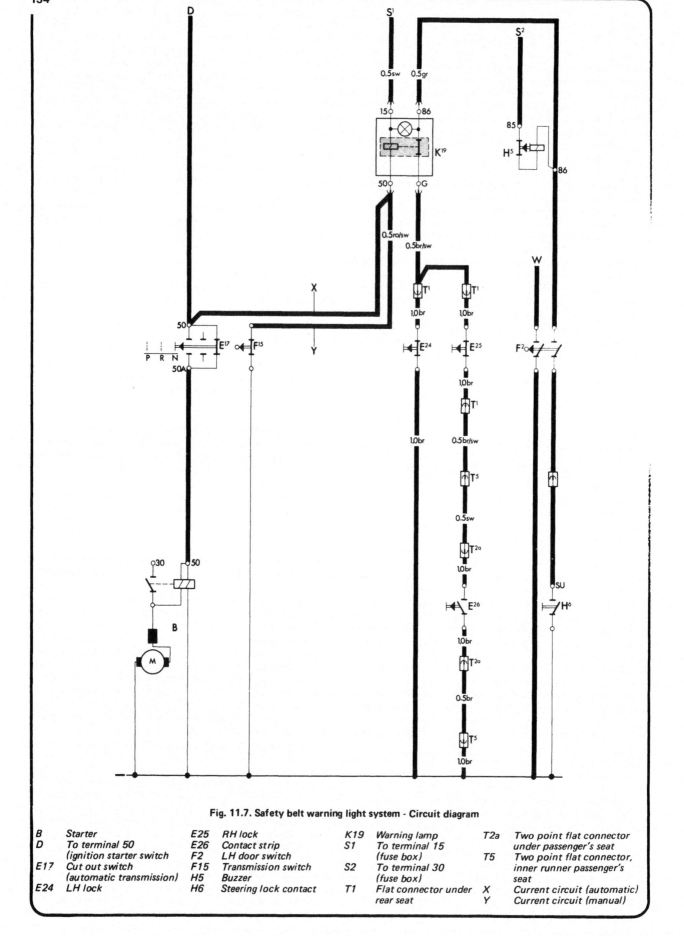

Fig. 11.7. Safety belt warning light system - Circuit diagram

B	Starter	E25	RH lock	K19	Warning lamp	T2a	Two point flat connector
D	To terminal 50	E26	Contact strip	S1	To terminal 15		under passenger's seat
	(ignition starter switch	F2	LH door switch		(fuse box)	T5	Two point flat connector,
E17	Cut out switch	F15	Transmission switch	S2	To terminal 30		inner runner passenger's
	(automatic transmission)	H5	Buzzer		(fuse box)		seat
E24	LH lock	H6	Steering lock contact	T1	Flat connector under	X	Current circuit (automatic)
					rear seat	Y	Current circuit (manual)

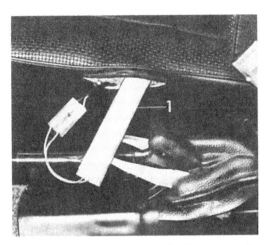

Fig. 11.8 Safety belt warning circuit - Contact strip for
passenger's seat

1   *Contact strip connected to the supply system*

Fig. 11.9. Safety belt warning circuit - contact strip for
passenger's seat

2   *Flexible harness*

21 Ignition key warning device

1 Fitted to all vehicles in the USA and many others a buzzer
alarm is provided to give a warning when the key remains in the
ignition/ starter switch on the lock cylinder as the driver leaves
the vehicle. The alarm sounds when the door is opened; the door
contact switch has two pairs of contacts, one for the interior
light and the other for the alarm system.
2 In the starter/ignition switch a contact is closed when the key
is inserted. Refer to Fig. 11.10 which gives a circuit diagram
for the system.
3 The buzzer is installed on the console on the fuse box.
4 Defective parts cannot be repaired but must be replaced.

22 Heated rear windows - installation guide lines

1 There are many versions of this accessory but undoubtedly
the best one for the Beetle is the VW version.
2 This includes a switch tailored to fit on the facia board, a
relay and a rear window with a built in heater element.
3 The heated rear window comes as an optional extra or can be
bought and fitted by the owner. For wiring details refer to the
wiring charts.

23 Fog lights - installation guide lines

Provision is made for fitting fog light switches for both front
and rear fog lights, and for relays to operate the front lamps.
These may be obtained through VW agents. For wiring details
refer to the wiring charts.

24 Radio sets - installation guide lines

1 Several types of radio sets are available from the VW agent
specially designed to fit the Beetle. There are many others too
from other sources, all of which supply their own fitting
instructions.
2 A retractable aerial is available from VW to fit the aperature
on the left of the screen.
3 The main problem is suppression. Condensers are fitted to the

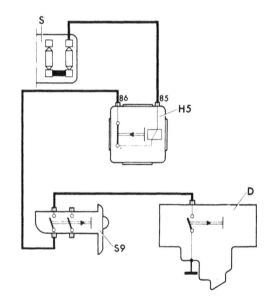

Fig. 11.10. Ignition key warning circuit (Sec. 21)

S	Fuse box	S9	Door contact switch
H5	Buzzer		(door sheet)
		D	Steering lock contact (no key)

wiper motor, ignition coil and voltage regulator. It is advisable to
consult the VW agent or the Auto-Radio specialist before fitting
the radio. The set should have a separate fuse. When the set is
installed it may be necessary to tune the set and aerial together
with the aerial trimmer to give optimum performance.
4 Whichever set is installed it is obvious that there will be
problems and advice should be sought as to how best to overcome them.

Key for Wiring Diagram: UK Super Beetles (1303/1303S) with dynamo - from August 1972

Key:

A — Battery
B — Starter
C — Generator
C1 — Regulator
D — Ignition/starter switch
E — Windscreen wiper switch
E1 — Lighting switch
E2 — Turn signal switch (switch for dimmer and headlight flasher)
E3 — Emergency flasher switch
E9 — Fan switch
E15 — Heated rear window switch
F — Brake light switch
F1 — Oil pressure switch
F2 — Door contact switch left
F3 — Door contact switch right
F4 — Reversing light switch
G — Fuel gauge sender unit
G1 — Fuel gauge
H — Horn button
H1 — Horn
J — Relay for headlight dimmer and flasher
J2 — Turn signal - emergency flasher relay
J6 — Fuel gauge vibrator
J9 — Relay for heated rear window
K1 — High beam warning lamp
K2 — Generator charging warning lamp
K3 — Oil pressure warning lamp
K5 — Turn signal warning lamp
K6 — Emergency flasher warning lamp

K7 — Dual circuit brake warning lamp
K10 — Heated rear window warning lamp
L1 — Twin-filament bulb, left headlight
L2 — Twin-filament bulb, right headlight
L10 — Instrument panel light
M1 — Parking light, left
M2 — Tail/brake light, right
M3 — Parking light, right
M4 — Tail/brake light, left
M5 — Turn signal, front, left
M6 — Turn signal, rear, left
M7 — Turn signal, front, right
M8 — Turn signal, rear, right
M16 — Reversing light, left
M17 — Reversing light, right
N — Ignition coil
N1 — Automatic choke
N3 — Electro-magnetic cut-off valve
O — Distributor
P — Spark plug connector
Q — Spark plug
S1 — Fuses in fuse box
to
S12
S13 — Separate fuse for reversing lights (8A)
S14 — Separate fuse for rear window (8A)
T — Cable adaptor on right behind engine compartment lining
T1 — Cable connector, single
  a - under rear seat
  b - near fuse box

  c - behind engine compartment lining
  d - in front luggage compartment on right
  e - in front luggage compartment on left
T2 — Cable connector 2 pin
  a - on engine compartment lid
  b - modified to 8 pin connector behind instrument panel
  c - modified to 8 pin connector behind instrument panel modified to: single connector near fuse box
T3 — Cable connector, 3 pin
  a - in front luggage compartment on left
  b - behind engine compartment lining on right
T4 — Cable connector, 4 pin behind engine compartment lining on left
T6 — Cable connector, 8 pin behind instrument panel
T20 — Central socket
V — Wiper motor
V2 — Fan motor
W — Interior light
X — License plate light
Z1 — Heated rear window
1 — Earth strap from battery to frame
2 — Earth strap from transmission to frame
4 — Earth wire on steering column coupling
10 — Earthing point, instrument panel
11 — Earthing point, speedometer
15 — Earthing point in front luggage compartment, on left
16 — Earthing point in front luggage compartment, on right

Test network: The small circles containing numbers are connections in the test network which are wired to the central plug (T20). Numbers within circles relate to the terminals in the central plug.

Colour code:

BK Black	RD Red	YW Yellow	BL Blue	GY Grey	PUR Purple
BR Brown	OR Orange	GN Green	VT Violet	WH White	

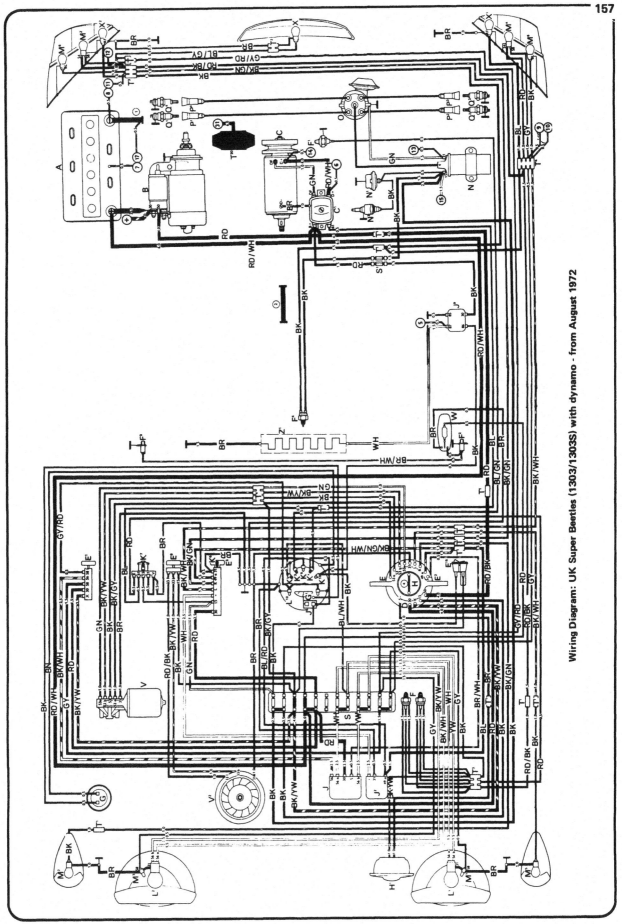

Wiring Diagram: UK Super Beetles (1303/1303S) with dynamo - from August 1972

Key for UK Super Beetles (1303/1303S): Accessory wiring diagram - from August 1972

It contains: The fog lights, rear fog light, connections for gasoline heater, wiper intermittent operation, automatic transmission, trailer bracket.

Key:

B	Starter	S10	Fuses in fuse box
D	Ignition/starter switch	S11	Fuses in fuse box
E1	Lighting switch	S16	Separate fuse for heater (16A)
E16	Heater switch	S20	Separate fuse for rear fog light (8A)
E17	Starter inhibitor switch	S22	Separate fuse for items in trailer
E21	Selector lever contact	T	Cable adaptor on right behind
E22	Wiper switch for intermittent operation		engine compartment lining
E23	Fog and rear fog light switch	T1	Cable connector, single
J5	Fog light relay		a - behind instrument panel
J11	Intermittent wiper relay		b - under rear seat
J20	Trailer turn signal warning light relay		c - on tunnel, right
K11	Heater warning lamp		d - in front luggage compartment on left
K17	Fog and rear fog light warning lamp		e - in front luggage compartment on right
K18	Trailer warning lamp		f - in engine compartment on left
L20	Rear fog light		g - behind engine compartment lining on left
L22	Fog light, left		h - behind engine compartment lining on right
L23	Fog light, right	T2	Cable connector, 2 pin
M2	Tail/brake light, right		in engine compartment lid
M4	Tail/brake light, left	T3	Cable connector, 3 pin
M6	Turn signal, rear, left		behind engine compartment lining on right
M8	Turn signal, rear, right	T4	Cable connector, 4 pin
N7	Control valve		behind engine compartment lining on left
S7	Fuses in fuse box	U	Trailer socket
S8	Fuses in fuse box	V	Wiper motor
S9	Fuses in fuse box	X	License plate light

Colour code:

BK	Black	OR	Orange	BL	Blue	WH	White
BR	Brown	YW	Yellow	VT	Violet	PUR	Purple
RD	Red	GN	Green	GY	Grey		

UK Super Beetles (1303/1303S): Accessory wiring diagram - from August 1972

Key for Wiring Diagram: 1303 from August 1974

Designation		in current track				
A	Battery	5	N^3	Electro-magnetic cut-off valve	52	
B	Starter	6, 7	O	Distributor	48, 49, 50	
C	Alternator	1, 2	P	Plug connector	49, 50	
C^1	Regulator	1, 2	Q	Spark plugs	49, 50	
D	Ignition/starter switch	7, 11, 12	S^1		11, 17, 19,	
E	Windscreen wiper switch	13, 14	to	Fuses in fuse box	22, 25, 27,	
E^1	Lighting switch	18, 20, 22	S^{12}		30, 37, 38	
E^2	Turn signal switch	41	S^{21}	Separate fuse for reversing lights (8 amp)	45	
E^3	Emergency light switch	38, 39, 43	S^{22}	Separate fuse for rear window (8 amp)	8	
E^4	Headlight dimmer and flasher switch	16	T	Cable connector		
E^9	Fresh air fan switch	15	a	— under rear seat		
E^{15}	Heated rear window switch	9	b	— behind engine compartment damping		
F	Brake light switch	30, 31, 32	T^1	Flat connector, single on tunnel		
F^1	Oil pressure switch	35	a	— behind dash		
F^2	Door contact switch left	28	b	— under rear seat		
F^3	Door contact switch right	27	c	— behind engine compartment damping		
F^4	Switch for reversing lights	45	d	— in front luggage compartment on right		
F^9	Handbrake warning lamp switch	33	e	— in front luggage compartment on left		
G	Fuel gauge sender unit	37				
G^1	Fuel gauge	37	T^2	Flat connector, 2-pin		
H	Horn button	29	T^3	Flat connector, 3-pin		
H^1	Horn	29	a	— in luggage compartment on left		
J	Headlight dimmer and flasher relay	16, 17, 18	b	— behind engine compartment damping on right		
J^2	Turn signal — Emergency light relay	38	c	— 3-pin connector in engine compartment		
J^6	Voltage stabilizer	37	T^4	Flat connector, 4-pin		
J^9	Heated rear window relay	8, 9	a	— behind engine compartment damping on left		
K^1	High beam warning lamp	18	b	— connector 4-pin, under rear seat		
K^2	Generator warning lamp	34	T^8	Connector 8-pin, behind dash		
K^3	Oil pressure warning lamp	35	T^{20}	Central socket	47	
K^5	Turn signal warning lamp	36	V	Wiper motor	12, 13, 14	
K^6	Emergency light warning lamp	44	V^2	Fan motor	15	
K^7	Dual circuit brake system and handbrake warning lamp	31, 32, 33	W	Interior light	27	
K^{10}	Heated rear window warning lamp	10	X	Number plate light	23	
L^1	Headlight bulb, left	17	Z^1	Heated rear window	8	
L^2	Headlight bulb, right	19	1	Earthing strap from battery to frame	5	
L^3	Instrument light	20, 21	2	Earthing strap from transmission to frame	4	
M^1	Parking light bulb, left	25	10	Earthing point, instrument panel		
M^2	Tail light bulb, right	24	11	Earthing point, speedometer		
M^2	Brake light bulb, right	32	15	Earthing point, front luggage compartment left		
M^3	Parking light bulb, right	26	16	Earthing point, front luggage compartment right		
M^4	Tail light bulb, left	22				
M^4	Brake light bulb, left	30				
M^5	Turn signal front, left	39				
M^6	Turn signal rear, left	40				
M^7	Turn signal front, right	43				
M^8	Turn signal rear, right	42				
M^{16}	Reversing light bulb, left	46				
M^{17}	Reversing light bulb, right	47				
N	Ignition coil	49, 50				
N^1	Automatic choke	51				

Colour code:

BK	Black
BR	Brown
RD	Red
OR	Orange
YW	Yellow
GN	Green
BL	Blue
VT	Violet
GY	Grey
WH	White
PUR	Purple

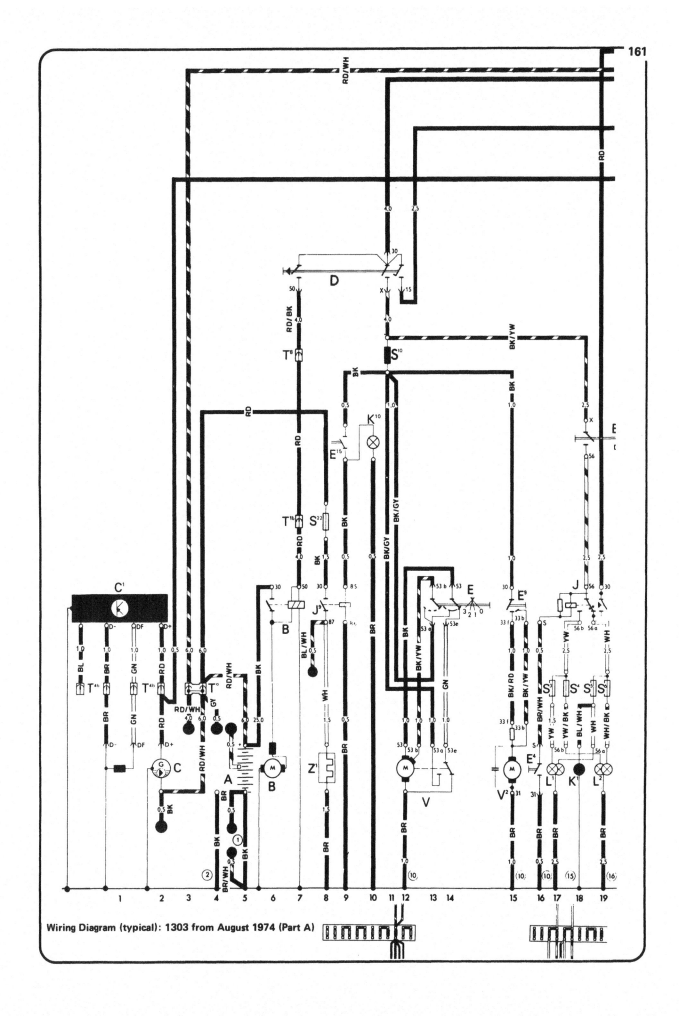

Wiring Diagram (typical): 1303 from August 1974 (Part A)

Wiring Diagram (typical): 1303 from August 1974 (Part B)

Wiring Diagram (typical): 1303 from August 1974 (Part C)

Key for Wiring Diagram: USA Basic Beetle from August 1969 to August 1971

Key:

A	Battery	M4	Tail and brake light, left
B	Starter	M5	Turn signal and parking light, front, left
C	Generator	M6	Turn signal, rear, left
C1	Regulator	M7	Turn signal and parking light, front, right
D	Ignition/starter switch	M8	Turn signal, rear, right
E	Windshield wiper switch	M11	Side marker light, front
E1	Light switch	N	Ignition coil
E2	Turn signal and headlight dimmer switch	N1	Automatic choke
E3	Emergency flasher switch	N3	Electro-magnetic pilot jet
F	Brake light switch with warning switch	O	Ignition distributor
F1	Oil pressure switch	P1	Spark plug connector, No. 1 cylinder
F2	Door contact switch, left with contact for buzzer H5	P2	Spark plug connector, No. 2 cylinder
		P3	Spark plug connector, No. 3 cylinder
F3	Door contact switch, right	P4	Spark plug connector, No. 4 cylinder
F4	Back-up light switch	Q1	Spark plug, No. 1 cylinder
G	Fuel gauge sending unit	Q2	Spark plug, No. 2 cylinder
G1	Fuel gauge	Q3	Spark plug, No. 3 cylinder
H	Horn button	Q4	Spark plug, No. 4 cylinder
H1	Horn	R	Radio connection
H5	Ignition key warning buzzer	S	Fuse box
J	Dimmer relay	S1	Back-up light fuse
J2	Emergency flasher relay	T	Cable adapter
J6	Vibrator for fuel gauge	T1	Cable connector, single
K1	High beam warning light	T2	Cable connector, double
K2	Generator charging warning light	T3	Cable connector, triple
K3	Oil pressure warning light	T4	Cable connector (four connections)
K5	Turn signal warning light	V	Windshield wiper motor
K6	Emergency flasher warning light	W	Interior light
K7	Dual circuit brake system warning light	X	License plate light
L1	Sealed beam unit, left headlight	X1	Back-up light, left
L2	Sealed beam unit, right headlight	X2	Back-up light, right
L10	Instrument panel light	1	Battery to frame ground strap
M2	Tail and brake light, right	2	Transmission to frame ground strap

Colour code:

BK	Black	OR	Orange	BL	Blue	WH	White
BR	Brown	YW	Yellow	VT	Violet	PUR	Purple
RD	Red	GN	Green	GY	Grey		

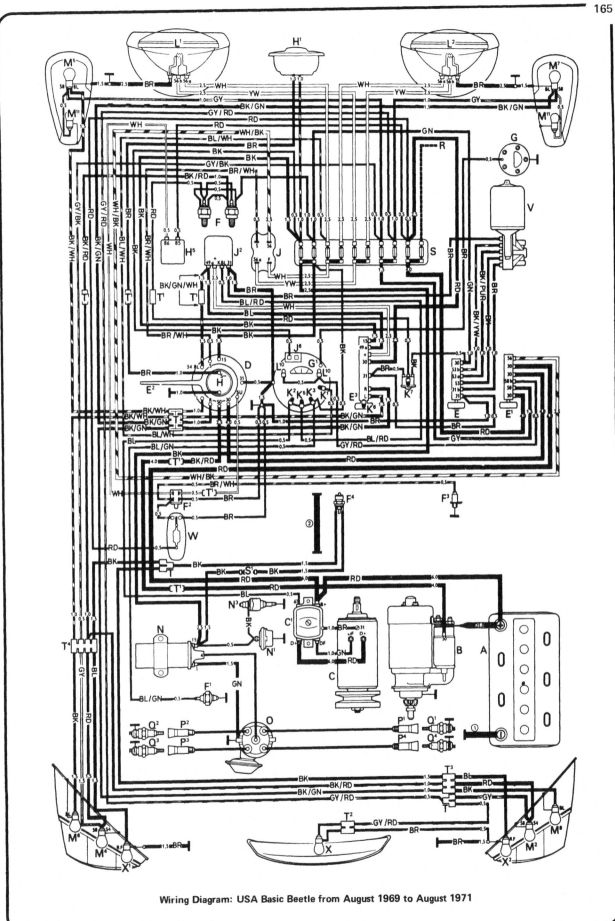

Wiring Diagram: USA Basic Beetle from August 1969 to August 1971

Key for Wiring Diagram: USA Basic Beetle from August 1971 to August 1972

Key:

A Battery
B Starter
C Generator
C1 Regulator
D Ignition/starter switch
E Windshield wiper switch
E1 Light switch
E2 Turn signal and headlight dimmer switch
E3 Emergency flasher switch
E9 Fan motor switch (Sedan 113 only)
E15 Rear window defogger switch (Sedan 113 only)
F Brake light and dual circuit warning light switch
F1 Oil pressure switch
F2 Door contact and buzzer alarm switch, left
F3 Door contact switch, right
F4 Back-up light switch
G Fuel gauge sending unit
G1 Fuel gauge
G4 Ignition timing sensor
H Horn button
H1 Horn
H5 Ignition key warning buzzer
J Dimmer relay
J2 Emergency flasher relay
J6 Fuel gauge vibrator

J9 Rear window defogger relay (Sedan 113 only)
K1 High beam warning light
K2 Generator charging warning light
K3 Oil pressure warning light
K5 Turn signal warning light
K6 Emergency flasher warning light
K7 Dual circuit brake warning light
K10 Rear window defogger warning light (Sedan 113 only)
L1 Sealed beam unit, left head light
L2 Sealed beam unit, right head light
L10 Instrument panel light
M1 Parking light, left
M2 Tail/brake light, right
M4 Tail/brake light, left
M5 Turn signal warning light
M6 Turn signal, rear, left
M7 Turn signal and parking light front right
M8 Turn signal, rear, right
M11 Side marker light, front
N Ignition coil
N1 Automatic choke
N3 Electro-magnetic pilot jet
O Distributor
P1 Spark plug connector, No. 1 cylinder
P2 Spark plug connector, No. 2 cylinder

P3 Spark plug connector, No. 3 cylinder
P4 Spark plug connector, No. 4 cylinder
Q1 Spark plug, No. 1 cylinder
Q2 Spark plug, No. 2 cylinder
Q3 Spark plug, No. 3 cylinder
Q4 Spark plug, No. 4 cylinder
S Fuse box
S1 Fuses for rear window defogger, back-up light (8 amp)
T Cable adapter
T1 Cable connector, single
T2 Cable connector, double
T3 Cable connector, triple
T4 Cable connector (four connections)
T5 Cable connector (five connections)
T20 Test network, central plug
V Windshield wiper motor
V2 Fan motor (Sedan 113 only)
W Interior light
X License plate light
X1 Back-up light, left
X2 Back-up light, right
Z1 Rear window defogger heating element (Sedan 113 only)
1 Ground strap from battery to frame
2 Ground strap from transmission to frame
4 Ground cable on steering coupling

Colour code:

BK Black
BR Brown
RD Red
OR Orange
YW Yellow
GN Green
BL Blue
VT Violet
GY Grey
WH White
PUR Purple

Test network:
The small circles containing numbers are connections in the test network which are wired to the central plug (T20). Numbers within circles relate to the terminals in the central plug.

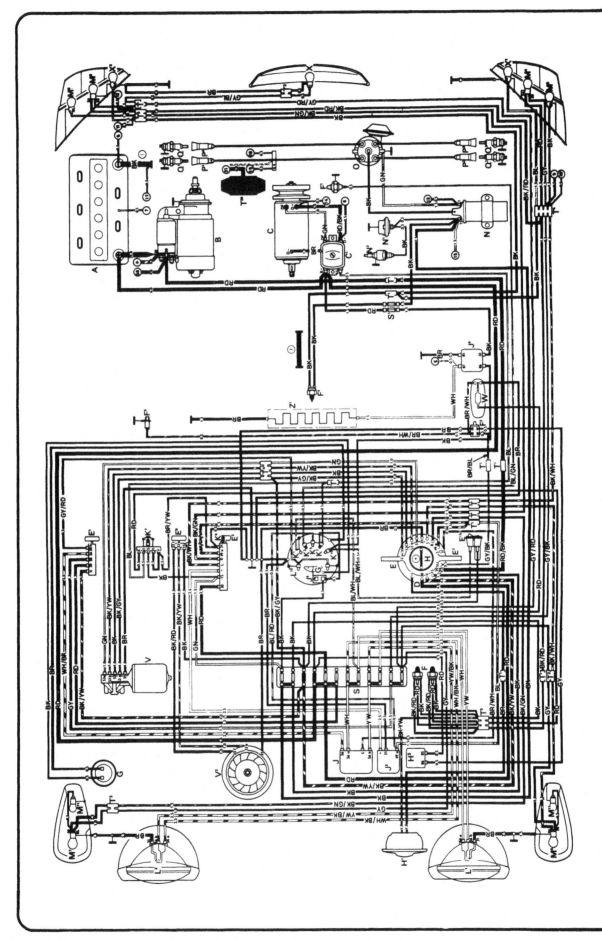

Wiring Diagram: USA Basic Beetle from August 1971 to August 1972

Key for Wiring Diagram: USA Basic Beetle from August 1972 onwards

Key:

A	Battery	K1	High beam warning light	P3	Spark plug connector, No. 3 cylinder	
B	Starter	K2	Generator charging warning light	P4	Spark plug connector, No. 4 cylinder	
C	Generator	K3	Oil pressure warning light	Q1	Spark plug No. 1 cylinder	
C1	Regulator	K5	Turn signal warning light	Q2	Spark plug No. 2 cylinder	
D	Ignition/starter switch	K6	Emergency flasher warning light	Q3	Spark plug No. 3 cylinder	
E	Windshield wiper switch	K7	Dual circuit brake warning light	Q4	Spark plug No. 4 cylinder	
E1	Light switch	L1	Sealed beam unit, left headlight	S	Fuse box	
E2	Turn signal and headlight dimmer switch	L2	Sealed beam unit, right headlight	S1	Fuses for rear window defogger back-up light (8 amp)	
E3	Emergency flasher switch	L10	Instrument panel light	T	Cable adapter	
F	Brake Light and dual circuit warning light switch	M1	Parking light, left	T1	Cable connector, single	
F1	Oil pressure switch	M2	Tail/brake light, right	T2	Cable connector, double	
F2	Door contact and buzzer alarm switch, left	M4	Tail/brake light, left	T3	Cable connector, triple	
F3	Door contact switch, right	M5	Turn signal and parking light front left	T4	Cable connector (four connections)	
F4	Back-up light switch	M6	Turn signal, rear, left	T5	Cable connector (five connections)	
G	Fuel gauge	M7	Turn signal and parking light front right	T20	Test network, central plug	
G1	Fuel gauge sending unit	M8	Turn signal, rear, right	V	Windshield wiper motor	
G4	Ignition timing sensor	M11	Side marker light, front	W	Interior light	
H	Horn button	N	Ignition coil	X	License plate light	
H1	Horn	N1	Automatic choke	X1	Back-up light, left	
H5	Ignition key warning buzzer	N3	Electro-magnetic pilot jet	X2	Back-up light, right	
J	Dimmer relay	O	Distributor	1	Ground strap from battery to frame	
J2	Emergency flasher relay	P1	Spark plug connector, No. 1 cylinder	2	Ground strap from transmission to frame	
J6	Fuel gauge vibrator	P2	Spark plug connector, No. 2 cylinder	4	Ground cable on steering coupling	

Colour code:

BK	Black	RD	Red	BL	Blue
BR	Brown	OR	Orange	VT	Violet
		YW	Yellow	GY	Grey
		GN	Green	WH	White
				PUR	Purple

Test network:
The small circles containing numbers are connections in the test network which are wired to the central plug (T20). Numbers within circles relate to the terminals in the central plug.

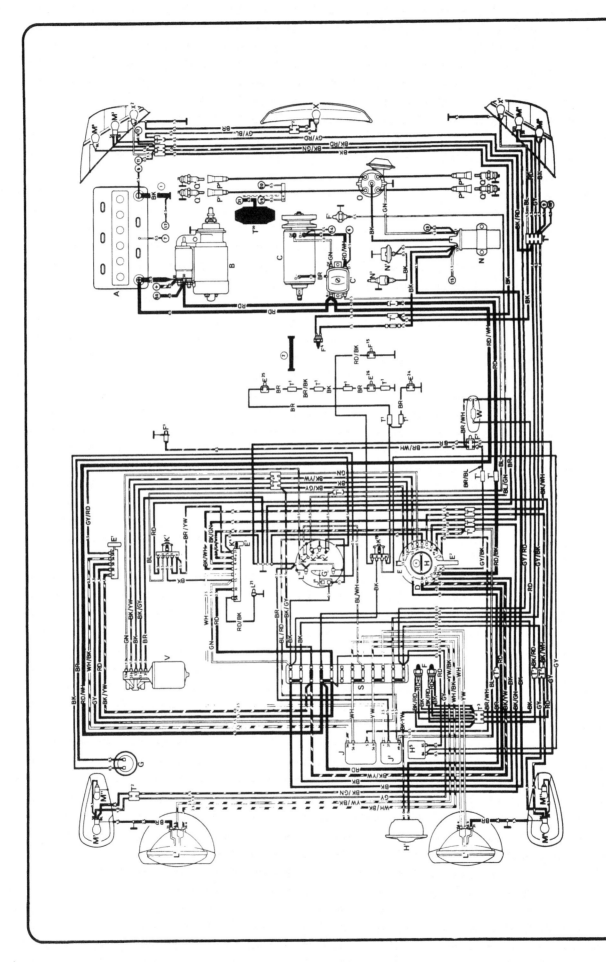

Wiring Diagram: USA Basic Beetle from August 1972 onwards

Key for Wiring Diagram: USA Super Beetle from August 1972 to August 1973

Key:

A	Battery
B	Starter
C	Generator
C1	Regulator
D	Ignition/starter switch
E	Windshield wiper switch
E1	Light switch
E2	Turn signal and headlight dimmer switch
E3	Emergency flasher switch
E9	Fan motor switch (Sedan 113 only)
E15	Rear window defogger switch (Sedan 113 only)
E24	Safety belt lock left
E25	Safety belt lock right
E26	Contact strip in passenger seat
F	Brake light and dual circuit warning light switch
F1	Oil pressure switch
F2	Door contact and buzzer alarm switch, left
F3	Door contact switch, right
F4	Back-up light switch
F15	Transmission switch for safety belt warning system (manual transmission)
G	Fuel gauge sending unit
G1	Fuel gauge
G4	Ignition timing sensor
H	Horn button
H1	Horn
H5	Ignition key warning buzzer
J	Dimmer relay
J2	Emergency flasher relay
J6	Fuel gauge vibrator
J9	Rear window defogger relay (Sedan 113 only)
K1	High beam warning light
K2	Generator charging warning light
K3	Oil pressure warning light
K5	Turn signal warning light
K6	Emergency flasher warning light
K7	Dual circuit brake warning light
K10	Rear window defogger warning light (Sedan 113 only)
K19	Safety belt warning system light
L1	Sealed beam unit, left headlight
L2	Sealed beam unit, right headlight
L10	Instrument panel light
L21	Light for heater lever illumination
M1	Parking light, left
M2	Tail/brake light, right
M4	Tail/brake light, left
M5	Turn signal, rear, left
M6	Turn signal and parking light front left
M7	Turn signal and parking light front right
M8	Turn signal, rear, right
M11	Side marker light, front
N	Ignition coil
N1	Automatic choke
N3	Electro-magnetic pilot jet
O	Distributor
P1	Spark plug connector, No. 1 cylinder
P2	Spark plug connector, No. 2 cylinder
P3	Spark plug connector, No. 3 cylinder
P4	Spark plug connector, No. 4 cylinder
Q1	Spark plug No. 1 cylinder
Q2	Spark plug No. 2 cylinder
Q3	Spark plug No. 3 cylinder
Q4	Spark plug No. 4 cylinder
S	Fuse box
S1	Fuses for rear window defogger back-up light (8 amp)
T	Cable adapter
T1	Cable connector, single
T2	Cable connector, double
T3	Cable connector, triple
T4	Cable connector, (four connections)
T5	Cable connector (five connections)
T20	Test network, central plug
V	Windshield wiper motor
V2	Fan motor (Sedan 113 only)
W	Interior light
X	License plate light
X1	Back-up light, left
X2	Back-up light, right
Z1	Rear window defogger heating element (Sedan 113 only)
1	Ground strap from battery to frame
2	Ground strap from transmission to frame
4	Ground cable on steering coupling

Colour code:

BK	Black	RD	Red
BR	Brown	OR	Orange
YW	Yellow	BL	Blue
GN	Green	VT	Violet
GY	Grey	PUR	Purple
WH	White		

Test network:
The small circles containing numbers are connections in the test network which are wired to the central plug (T20). Numbers within circles relate to the terminals in the central plug.

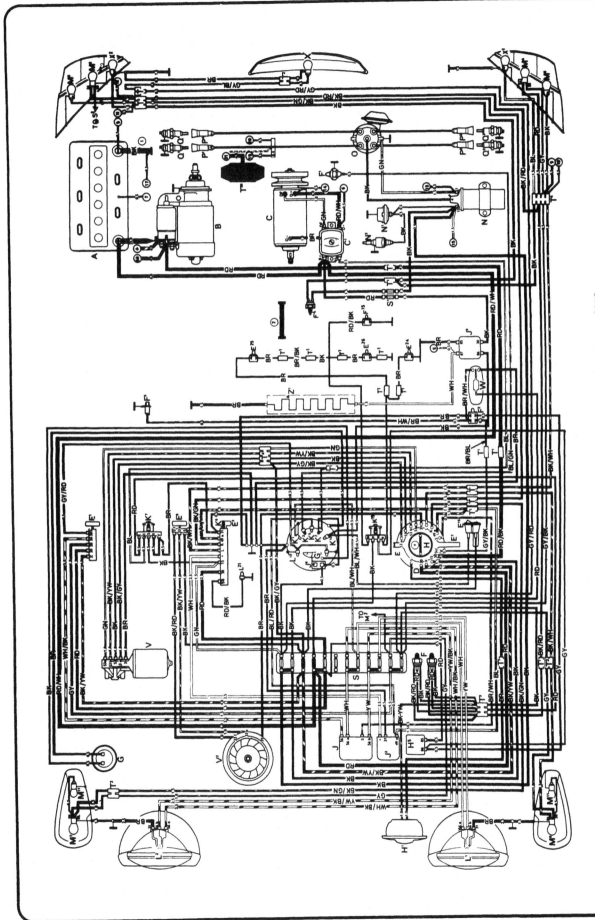

Key for Wiring Diagram: USA Super Beetle from August 1973 onwards

Key:

A	Battery
B	Starter
C	Alternator
C1	Regulator
D	Ignition/starter switch
E	Windshield wiper switch
E1	Light switch
E2	Turn signal and headlight dimmer switch
E3	Emergency flasher switch
E9	Fan motor switch (Sedan 113 only)
E15	Rear window defogger switch (Sedan 113 only)
E24	Safety belt lock - left
E25	Safety belt lock - right
E31	Contact strip in drivers seat
E32	Contact strip in passengers seat
F	Brake light and dual circuit warning light switch
F1	Oil pressure switch
F2	Door contact and buzzer alarm switch, left
F3	Door contact switch, right
F4	Back-up light switch
F9	Parking brake control light switch
G	Fuel gauge sending unit
G1	Fuel gauge
G4	Ignition timing sensor
H	Horn button
H1	Horn
J	Dimmer relay
J2	Emergency flasher relay
J6	Fuel gauge vibrator
J9	Rear window defogger relay (Sedan 113 only)
J34	Safety belt warning relay
K1	High beam warning light
K2	Generator charging warning light
K3	Oil pressure warning light
K5	Turn signal warning light
K6	Emergency flasher warning light
K7	Dual circuit brake warning light
K10	Rear window defogger warning light (Sedan 113 only)
L1	Sealed beam unit, left headlight
L2	Sealed beam unit, right headlight
L10	Instrument panel light
L21	Light for heater lever illumination
M2	Tail/brake light, right
M4	Tail/brake light, left
M5	Turn signal and parking light front left
M6	Turn signal, rear, left
M7	Turn signal and parking light front right
M8	Turn signal, rear, right
M11	Side marker light, front
N	Ignition coil
N1	Automatic choke
N3	Electro-magnetic pilot jet
O	Distributor
P1	Spark plug connector, No. 1 cylinder
P2	Spark plug connector, No. 2 cylinder
P3	Spark plug connector, No. 3 cylinder
P4	Spark plug connector, No. 4 cylinder
Q1	Spark plug, No. 1 cylinder
Q2	Spark plug, No. 2 cylinder
Q3	Spark plug, No. 3 cylinder
Q4	Spark plug, No. 4 cylinder
S	Fuse box
S1	Fuses for rear window defogger back-up light (8 amp)
T	Cable adapter
T1	Cable connector, single
T2	Cable connector, double
T3	Cable connector, triple
T4	Cable connector (four connections)
T5	Cable connector (five connections)
T20	Test network, central plug
V	Windshield wiper motor
V2	Fan motor (Sedan 113 only)
W	Interior light
X	License plate light
X1	Back-up light, left
X2	Back-up light, right
Z1	Rear window defogger heating element (Sedan 113 only)
1	Ground strap from battery to frame
2	Ground strap from transmission to frame
4	Ground cable on steering coupling

Colour code:

BK	Black		
BR	Brown		
RD	Red		
OR	Orange		
YW	Yellow		
GN	Green		
BL	Blue		
VT	Violet		
GY	Grey		
WH	White		
PUR	Purple		

Test network:
The small circles containing numbers are connections in the test network which are wired to the central plug (T20). Numbers within circles relate to the terminals in the central plug.

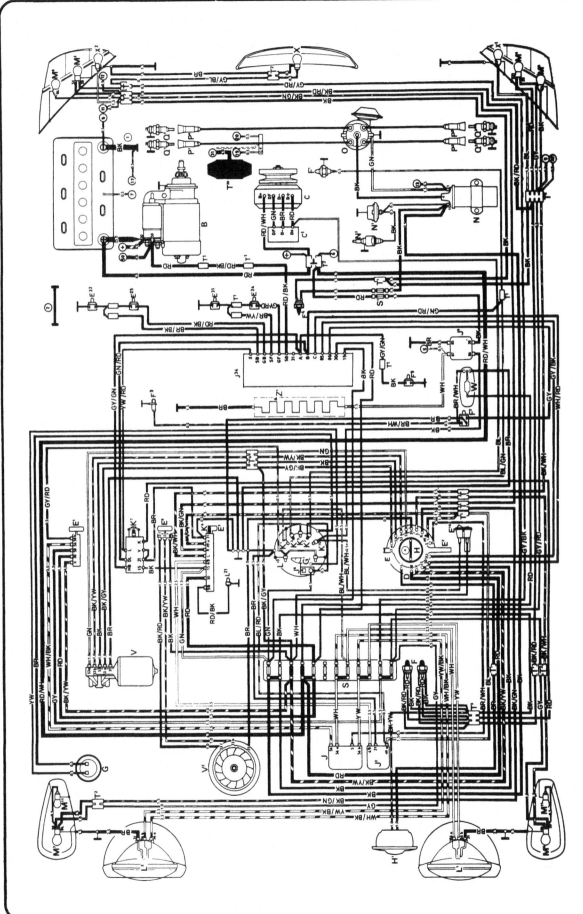

Wiring Diagram: USA Super Beetle from August 1973 onwards

Chapter 12 Steering
mechanism, front suspension and wheels

Contents

To make reference more simple the USA basic Beetle and UK GT Beetle are referred to as "Torsion Bar" and the remainder of the models (Super Beetles and Sports Bug) as "MacPherson Strut"

Care and maintenance of tyres 28	Steering gear - overhaul 17
Fault diagnosis 29	Steering gear - removal and replacement (MacPherson strut) 16
Front suspension - general description 1	Steering gear - removal and replacement (torsion bar) ... 18
Front suspension ball joint - inspection, removal and replacement (MacPherson strut) 3	Steering damper - removal, checking and replacement (MacPherson) 23
Front suspension ball joints - inspection, removal and replacement (torsion bar) 4	Steering damper - removal, checking and replacement (torsion bar) 24
Front axle - removal and replacement (torsion bar) ... 7	Steering geometry 26
MacPherson strut - removal and replacement 9	Steering wheel and column - removal and replacement (MacPherson strut) 19
MacPherson strut - overhaul 10	Steering wheel and column - removal and replacement (torsion bar) 20
Modification for negative steering roll radius (MacPherson strut) 14	Tie-rods and joints - removal and replacement (MacPherson) 21
Shock absorbers - removal and replacement (torsion bar) ... 8	Tie-rods and joints - removal and replacement (torsion bar) 22
Stabilizer bar - removal and replacement (MacPherson strut) 11	Torsion arms - removal and replacement 5
Stabilizer bar - removal and replacement (torsion bar) ... 12	Torsion bars - removal and replacement 6
Steering gear - adjustments 25	Track control arms and bushes - removal and replacement (MacPherson) 13
Steering gear - general description 15	Wheel balancing 27
	Wheel bearings - removal and replacement 2

Specifications

Front suspension:
Super Beetle and Sports Bug

Type	Independent suspension struts with built in shock absorbers, the wheel stub axle mounted on a steering knuckle. Stabilizer bar between the frame head and the steering knuckles	
Track:	**UK**	**USA**
Drum brakes	1375 mm (54.1 inches)	1387 mm (54.6 inches)
Disc brakes	1379 mm (54.3 inches)	
Turning circle	9,000 mm (354 inches)	9,600 mm (378 inches)
Coil springs:		
No. of coils	10.5	
Effective coils	9	
Wire diameter	10.45 mm (0.41 inch)	
Mean coil diameter	110 mm (4.331 inch)	
Suspension strut ball joint clearance:		
New	1.00 mm (0.039 inch)	
Maximum	2.5 mm (0.098 inch)	

Note: The modification to give negative steering roll radius does not change the wheel alignment specifications.

Front suspension:
USA basic Beetle and UK GT Beetle

Type	Twin laminated leaf tension bar each with a trailing arm to the steering knuckle. Stabilizer bar clamped to each steering knuckle

Torsion bars:
    Number of leaves   10
    Length   ...   .   954 mm (37.56 inches)
    Fitting angle:
        top   ...   .   44º (± 30')
        bottom   ...   .   35º 30' (± 30')

Steering knuckles:
    Upper ball joint main vertical play   ...   .   2.00 mm (0.079 inch)
    Lower ball joint main vertical play   ...   .   1.00 mm (0.040 inch)

Steering (all models)

Type ...   .   Worm and roller

Geometry:	MacPherson strut	Torsion bar
Toe-in ...	30' ± 15'	30' ± 15'
Toe-in (pressed 10 kg) ...	10' ± 15'	5' ± 15'
Camber ...	1º (+ 20' or −40')	30' positive ± 20'
Castor angle ...	2º ± 35'	3º 20' ± 1º

Steering gear ratio ...   .   17 : 8

Overall steering ratio   ...   .   16 : 5

Steering wheel turns (lock-to-lock) 2¾

Wheels and tyres (all models)

Wheels:	UK Super & GT Beetles	USA Super & basic Beetles	USA Sports Bug & optional on other models
Standard fitting ...	4½J x 15	4½J x 15	5½J x 15
Tyres:			
Standard fitting ...	5.60 x 15 crossply or 155SR x 15 radial	6.00 – 15 bias-ply	175/70 HR – 15 radial

Note: The Super Beetle & Sports Bug with positive steering radius roll have 34 mm offset
The Super Beetle & Sports Bug with negative steering radius roll have 41 mm offset

Torque wrench settings: (MacPherson strut)	lb ft	kg m
Strut upper bearing nut ...	51 to 61	7 to 8.5
Steering knuckle and ball joint to strut bolts ...	29	4.0
Front wheel bearing clamp nut screw (max) ...	7 to 10	1.0 to 1.3
Strut to body nuts ...	14	2
Frame head to body bolts ...	25	3.5
Track control arm to frame head nut ...	29	4.0
Track control arm to ball joint nut ...	29	4.0
Stabilizer to track control arm nut ...	22	3.0
Stabilizer clip to frame head bolt ...	14	2.0
Steering gear to body bolts ...	29	4.0
Drop arm to steering gear nut ...	72	10.0
Steering tie-rod joint nuts ...	22	3.0
Steering damper to frame head bolt ...	43	6.0
Steering damper to drop arm bolt ...	29 to 32	4.0 to 4.5

Torque wrench settings: (torsion bar)	lb ft	kg m
Front damper bolt on side plate ...	24	3.4
Front damper nut on side plate ...	14	2.0
Front damper nut on lower torsion arm ...	24	3.4
Steering ball joint nuts M12 ...	38	6.0
Steering ball joint nuts M10 ...	33	4.5
Steering ball joint nuts with split pin ...	22	3.0
Wheel bearing inner nut ...	29	4.0
Wheel bearing lock nut ...	50	7.0
Wheel bearing clamp nut socket screw ...	9	1.3 (max)
Steering damper nut on tie-rod ...	18	2.5
Steering damper screw on axle tube ...	31	4.4
Torsion bar setscrew and locknut ...	33	4.5

1 Front suspension - general description

All the models described in this book have the Macpherson type strut independent front wheel suspension except the USA basic Beetle and the UK GT Beetle which both have torsion bar suspension with trailing links.

Later models of the Super Beetle and Sports Bug have modified Macpherson struts and radius arms to give a negative steering roll radius.

All models are fitted with hydraulic, telescopic, shock absorbers and with stabilzer bars.

Figs. 12.1 and 12.2 show the layouts and the text is so grouped to deal as far as possible with the same aspect of both types in turn.

Briefly, the independent strut suspension consists of a spring and shock absorber mounted concentrically with the top end fixed into the wheel arch and the lower end into the steering ball joint (knuckle). A simple radius arm pivoted on the frame head is fastened to the steering knuckle so that a triangular frame consisting of the frame head, radius arm and suspension strut supports the car on the wheel. (See Fig. 12.3 and 12.4).

The torsion bar type of suspension has two torsion bars mounted one vertically above the other fixed to the frame head and held rigid in the centre. Torsion arms (trailing links) carry the steering knuckle (with wheel) between them so that the linkage is almost a parallelogram.

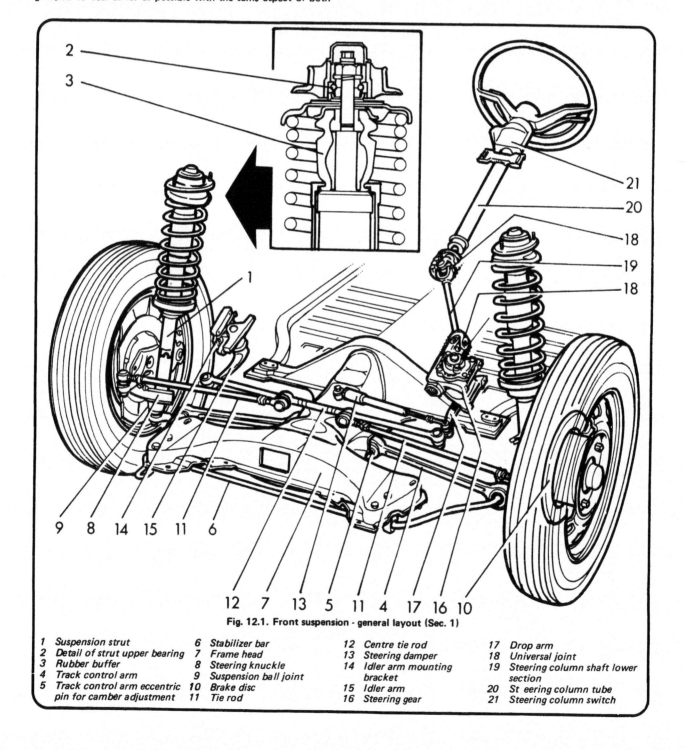

Fig. 12.1. Front suspension - general layout (Sec. 1)

1 Suspension strut	6 Stabilizer bar	12 Centre tie rod	17 Drop arm
2 Detail of strut upper bearing	7 Frame head	13 Steering damper	18 Universal joint
3 Rubber buffer	8 Steering knuckle	14 Idler arm mounting	19 Steering column shaft lower
4 Track control arm	9 Suspension ball joint	bracket	section
5 Track control arm eccentric	10 Brake disc	15 Idler arm	20 St eering column tube
pin for camber adjustment	11 Tie rod	16 Steering gear	21 Steering column switch

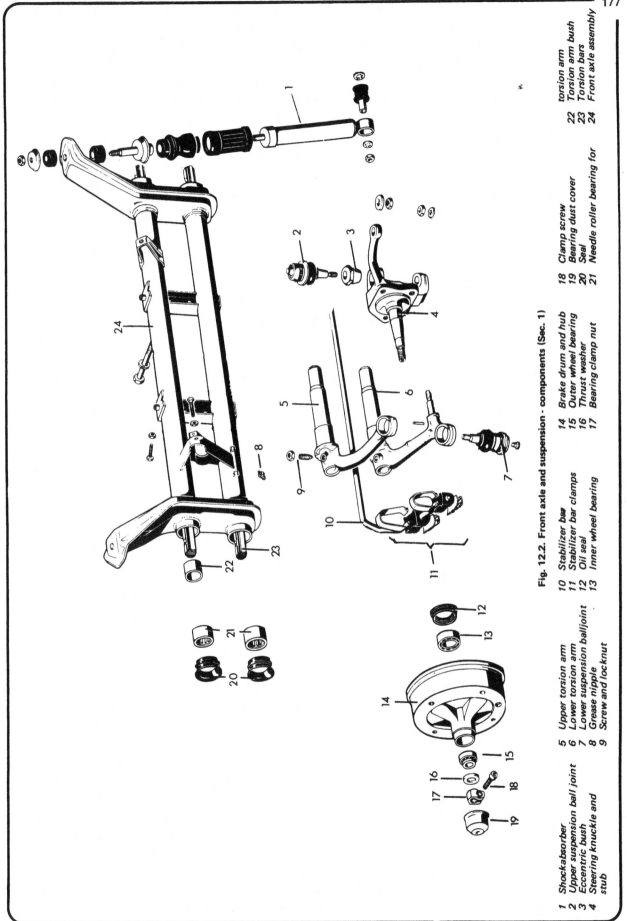

Fig. 12.2. Front axle and suspension - components (Sec. 1)

1 Shockabsorber
2 Upper suspension ball joint
3 Eccentric bush
4 Steering knuckle and stub

5 Upper torsion arm
6 Lower torsion arm
7 Lower suspension balljoint
8 Grease nipple
9 Screw and locknut

10 Stabilizer bar
11 Stabilizer bar clamps
12 Oil seal
13 Inner wheel bearing

14 Brake drum and hub
15 Outer wheel bearing
16 Thrust washer
17 Bearing clamp nut

18 Clamp screw
19 Bearing dust cover
20 Seal
21 Needle roller bearing for

22 Torsion arm bush
23 Torsion bars
24 Front axle assembly
torsion arm

178

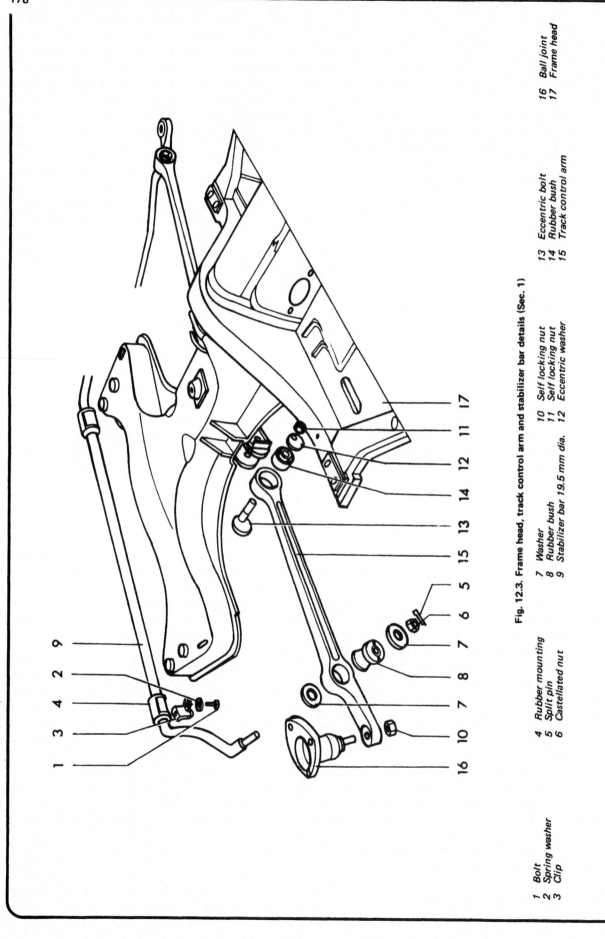

Fig. 12.3. Frame head, track control arm and stabilizer bar details (Sec. 1)

1 Bolt	4 Rubber mounting	7 Washer	10 Self locking nut	13 Eccentric bolt	16 Ball joint
2 Spring washer	5 Split pin	8 Rubber bush	11 Self locking nut	14 Rubber bush	17 Frame head
3 Clip	6 Castellated nut	9 Stabilizer bar 19.5 mm dia.	12 Eccentric washer	15 Track control arm	

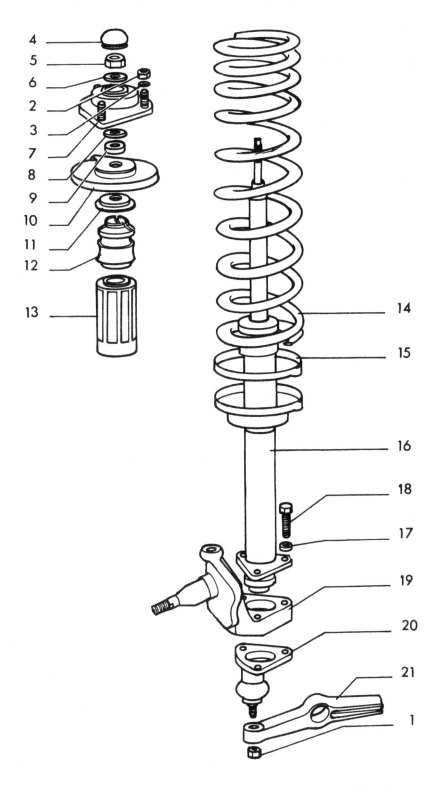

Fig. 12.4. Front suspension strut (positive steering roll radius) - details (Sec. 1)

1 Self-locking nut	7 Strut bearing	13 Protective sleeve	19 Steering knuckle
2 Self-locking nut	8 Small washer	14 Coil spring	20 Ball joint
3 Spring washer	9 Spacer	15 Damping ring	21 Track control arm
4 Cap	10 Spring cap	16 Damper	
5 Self-locking nut	11 Large washer	17 Lockwasher	
6 Washer	12 Rubber buffer	18 Bolt	

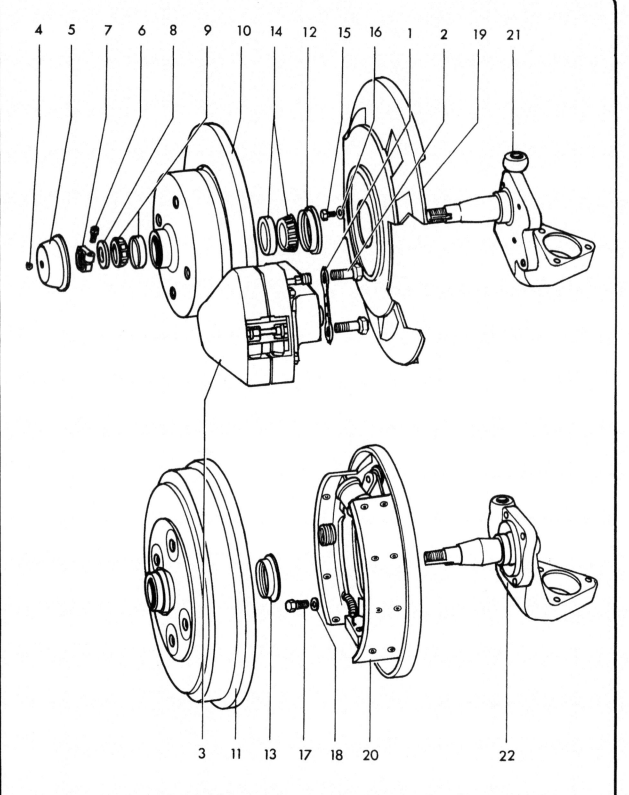

Fig. 12.5. Front wheel hub bearing details (positive steering roll radius)
drum or disc brakes (See Sec. 12.2)

1 Lock plate	7 Bearing adjusting nut	13 Seal for drum	18 Washer
2 Caliper mounting bolts	8 Thrust washer	14 Taper roller bearing 50 mm	19 Backplate
3 Caliper	9 Taper roller bearing 40 mm	15 Backplate bolt	20 Brake shoe
4 Circlip for speedo cable	10 Brake disc	16 Spring washer	21 Stub axle assembly
5 Hub cap	11 Brake drum	17 Bolt	22 Stub axle assembly
6 Clamp screw	12 Seal for disc		

2 Front wheel bearings - removal, replacement and adjustment (all models)

1 The front wheel hubs each run on two taper roller bearings. Adjustment is effected by a clamp nut which is locked into position by a socket head cap screw incorporated into it.

2 The left-hand front hub has a left-hand thread. The axle is hollow to permit the speedometer drive cable to go through it. This cable is driven by a square hole in the bearing dust cover. Jack up the wheel and remove the securing bolts and wheel.

3 To remove the bearing dust cover, first take out the split pin or circlip securing the speedometer cable and tap the dust cover from side to side until it comes free.

4 Undo the socket head cap screw and undo the wheel bearing clamp nut.

5 If the thrust washer is now taken off, the complete drum may be removed. There will be the outer races of each bearing left in the hub and the inner race of the inner bearing left on the axle. These should be drifted out of the hub from the inside if the bearings are to be renewed. If the same bearings are being replaced, they may be left in position and merely flushed out. The race on the shaft should be drifted off also. Note that if the races are renewed then the oil seal on the inner part of the hub will be renewed as well.

6 Refitting new bearings means that the outer races will first have to be driven into the hub and the new oil seal fitted on the inside. Coat the bearings and the space between them in the hub with liberal quantities of 'Castrol LM Grease' and place the hub back on the shaft. Fit the outer bearing followed by the thrust washer and screw on the clamp nut (photos).

7 To adjust the bearing endfloat correctly the nut should be tightened up firmly to make sure the bearings are properly located, spinning the wheel at the same time to ensure the bearings are not overtightened. Then the nut should be backed off until the axial play is between 0.03 – 0.12 mm (0.001 – 0.005 inch) at the spindle. This seems quite a lot and can result in some quite noticeable rock at the outer rim of the wheel. It is nevertheless correct although the axial play should be kept to the screw (photo).

8 Replace the hub cover and re-secure the speedometer drive cable where appropriate.

3 Front suspension ball joint (MacPherson strut suspension) - removal and replacement (Super Beetles and Sports Bug)

1 At the bottom of the suspension strut a single ball joint carries the main load and steering movement of the front wheel. It is secured to the track control arm on a taper pin and to the base of the strut and steering knuckle by three screws.

2 The joint has a spring loaded nylon shell for the ball and when new the spring can be compressed 1 mm before the shell touches the joint casing inside. As the shell wears the spring holds it onto the ball. The gap between the shell increases accordingly and must not exceed 2.5 mm.

3 To check the clearance the bottom of the strut and the track control arm must be forced apart. If the wheel is raised they must be forced together. Theoretically this latter movement may be achieved by putting a jack under the ball pin nut when the wheel is off the ground. In practise the wheel lifts also. The solution is to make up a lever which will rest on the top flange of the steering knuckle at the base of the strut and can hook under the track control arm (see Fig 12.6). The play can then be ascertained.

Fig. 12.6. Sketch of lever arrangement for checking clearance of lower suspension ball joints (Sec. 3)

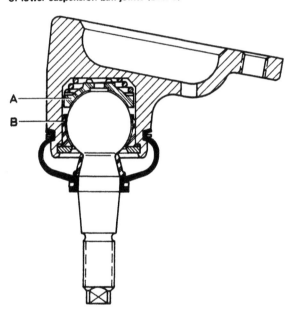

Fig. 12.7. Suspension strut ball joint - cross section (Sec. 3)

A Upper plastic shell - spring loaded
B Lower plastic shell

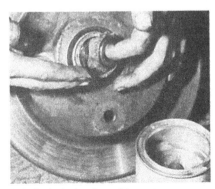

2.6a Pack the bearing with grease ...

2.6b ... replace the thrust washer

2.7 Tighten the clamp screw to 8 ibs ft (1 mkg)

4   To renew a joint, jack the car up and remove the wheel. Undo the nut on the joint pin. Drive the pin out of its seat in the end of the track control arm. The arm can be forced down to release it. Undo the three bolts that secure the joint to the strut and take the joint off.

5   Replacement is a straightforward reversal of this procedure. Fit new lock plates and tighten the screws and nut to the correct torque.

4 Suspension ball joints (torsion bar suspension) - removal, inspection and replacement (USA basic Beetle and UK GT Beetle)

With the exception of the correct setting of the camber adjusting bush on the upper joint pin there are no adjustments or lubrication requirements. When the joints are worn beyond specification limits they must be renewed.

2   To check the vertical play first turn the front wheels to one side and find a jack that will fit under the lower torsion arm at the ball joint end. If ground clearance is too little jack the car up and rest the wheel on a block. If the jack under the torsion arm is now raised any play in the joint should be apparent. It is difficult to measure accurately unless you have a caliper gauge which can be placed across the head of the joint pin and the bottom of the torsion arm.

3   The upper joint is a little more difficult but in general practice if the lower joint is within tolerance limits the upper one will be also. If the lower one is not then it is easier to check the top one when the steering knuckle has been removed. In any case the joints should normally be renewed in pairs on each side.

4   In order to renew the ball joints they have first to be removed from the knuckle by unscrewing the taper pin nuts and pressing them out of the knuckle eyes with a claw clamp. To do this, first remove the hub and brake backplate assemblies and disconnect the upper damper mounting. It must be emphasised here that these ball joints pins are usually a very tight taper fit. If you do not have a proper clamp you might succeed by striking the side of the eye with a hammer to spring it loose. If this does not succeed do not risk bending anything by excessive use of striking force. Also the two torsion arms will have a tendency to force the two joints towards each other so before they can be taken out of the knuckle the two torsion arms must be spread apart. One way to do this is by using a scissor jack between them.

5   Finally the ball joints have to be pressed out of the torsion arms and to do this the torsion arms must be removed from the torsion bars. The renewal of the torsion bars is explained in the next Section.

6   With the torsion bars removed we strongly recommend that you take them to the Volkswagen agent when the new parts are to be ordered and get him to fit them. Without the proper press tools it is easy to make a real nonsense of this job. If they are not properly fitted the whole safety and steering properties of the car are in jeopardy.

7   With new ball joints fitted the torsion arms are replaced and the knuckle refitted in the reverse order of removal. The top ball joint is fitted with an eccentric bush which controls the camber angle setting. This bush has a positioning notch in the edge which should be set to face directly forward. The nuts (new ones always) should be tightened to the specified torque (38 lb ft/6 mkg).

5 Torsion arm - removal and replacement (USA basic Beetle and UK GT Beetle)

1   If indications show that a torsion arm is distorted or worn then it must be renewed.

2   First remove the wheel hub assembly and on earlier models take out the link pins and link nut. If a lower torsion arm is being removed the stabiliser bar must also be taken off (see Section 12).

3   Loosen the lock nuts on the ends of the torsion arm securing pins and then screw the pins right out. The torsion arm can then

be pulled out of the axle tube. The torsion arm tube is positioned in two bearings - an inner bush and outer needle roller. If either of these is seriously worn causing radial movement of the torsion arm they should be renewed by a specialist with the correct tools. If you have already carried the dismantling of the front axle a considerable way it may be simplest to disconnect the brakes and steering gear as well and detach the whole assembly from the car. This can be done by removing the four securing screws from the centre section (see Section 7 for complete procedure).

4   Replacement is a reversal of the removal procedure.

6 Torsion bars (front) - removal and replacement (USA basic Beetle and UK GT Beetle)

1   One would normally only need to remove a torsion bar if it broke and this is a rare occurrence.

2   First remove the hub and steering knuckle and torsion arm from one end of the torsion bar concerned. Then detach the steering knuckle from the torsion arm on the opposite side but do not remove the other arm from the torsion bar.

3   In the centre of the torsion bar tube slacken the locating pin locknut and remove the pin. The bar and the attached torsion arm may then be drawn out.

4   The torsion bar is composed of a number of leaves. Make sure that any replacement is of the correct type.

5   When refitting a torsion bar make sure first it is liberally coated with grease and position it so that the recesses for the locating pins will line up. Fix the centre pin and locknut and then reassemble the torsion arm and steering assemblies in the reverse order of dismantling.

7 Front axle assembly (torsion bar suspension) - removal complete (USA basic Beetle and UK GT Beetle)

1   In certain circumstances, such as damage, which has caused the axle tubes to be bent or where the complete assembly is in need of thorough overhaul and checking, it may be advantageous to remove it as an assembly and dismantle it afterwards. The sequence of operations to be followed and details of the procedure for each stage can be found in the appropriate Sections.

2   Detach the flexible fuel hose under the fuel tank and plug or clip it.

3   Jack up the car and remove the wheel.

4   Detach the horn cable from the steering column and uncouple the flange of the steering column where it joins the steering box.

5   Unclip the split pin or circlip from the end of the speedometer cable in the left front wheel bearing dust cap. Pull the cable out.

6   Undo the hydraulic brake fluid lines at the unions where the brackets on the axle tube are fitted.

7   Undo the steering damper mounting bolt at the axle end and then undo the two track rod ends on the long track rod. Take off the track rod and damper together.

8   Remove the two body securing screws on the upper side of the top axle tube.

9   Support the axle securely and remove the four setscrews holding the assembly to the frame head.

10 The complete unit can now be lowered and taken out.

8 Front shock absorbers (torsion bar suspension) - removal and replacement (USA basic Beetle and UK GT Beetle)

1   The removal of the front damper is a little tricky because the upper mounting is through a horizontal plate.

2   The buffer stud at the top may be detached from the main piston rod of the damper.

3   Jack up the car and remove the wheel.

4   The steering tie rod on the same side should also be detached from the steering knuckle or it will be severely strained by the

downward force exerted by the torsion bars when the damper is released.

5 The top hexagon nut of the damper should now be undone. If the whole rod turns, the hexagon on the buffer stud must be held with a 42 mm, thin open ended spanner. If difficulty is experienced the alternative is to unscrew the piston rod from the buffer stud now. This will make it easier to detach the damper from the bracket.

6 Remove the nut securing the lower end ot the torsion arm and take the damper off.

7 If the upper mounting buffers and damper rings are damaged they should be renewed. The stud can be unscrewed from the piston rod to release the buffer.

8 The lower bush is a tight press fit. If this needs renewal use the new one and a piece of tube to press out the old one between the jaws of a vice.

9 When refitting the damper make sure that the buffer stud is screwed back tightly on to the piston rod and that the damper rings are fitted one each side of the mounting plate with the shoulders against the plate.

9 Front suspension strut (MacPherson strut type) - removal and replacement (Super Beetles and Sports Bug)

1 A defective spring or damper means that the whole front suspension must be removed from the car. At this point review the spare situation and the facilities available and decide whether renewal or repair is the most economical process to adopt.

2 To remove the unit first take off the brake assembly. It is not necessary to disconnect the hydraulic line. With drum brakes, the backplate and shoes can all be taken off as an assembly once the drum/hub has been removed. With discs, remove the caliper and hang it up with wire nearby. Then remove the disc/hub unit.

3 Remove the three bolts securing the lower end of the strut to the steering knuckle and track control arm (photo).

4 Remove the three nuts holding the top of the strut assembly to the wing valance in the luggage compartment (photo).

5 The steering knuckle can be separated from the bottom of the strut and swung away on the end of the steering tie-rod.

6 The strut assembly is then drawn down to disengage it from the wing valance and lifted away from the car (photos).

9.3 Undoing the lower strut securing bolts

9.4 Undoing the upper strut securing nuts

9.6a Taking the strut away

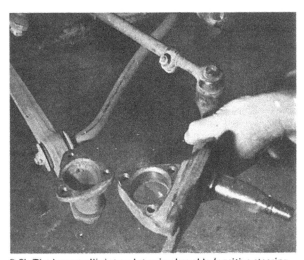
9.6b The lower balljoint and steering knuckle (positive steering roll radius)

10 Front suspension strut (MacPherson strut type) - dismantling and reassembly (Super Beetles and Sports Bug)

1 If either the spring or damper needs renewal check first whether it would be best to renew the whole assembly. The damper cannot be repaired.

2 To separate the spring and damper it is essential to obtain a proper and suitable spring compressor to hold the spring in compression whilst the securing nut on the top stud of the damper is released. It is dangerous to attempt to release the spring without proper retainers.

3 Once the spring seat is released the damper can be checked, held in its installed position. The damping action should be felt throughout its stroke in both directions. Any very slight leaks which are visible on the outer casing need not give cause for concern provided that the damping action continues to be satisfactory.

4 Coil springs come in three versions each with a colour code. Make sure a new spring fitted has the same colour code as the one removed. The close coils of the spring go at the top.

5 When reassembling make sure that the upper strut bearing is in good condition. Tighten the upper strut retaining nut to the correct torque holding the damper rod end with a suitable spanner.

11 Front stabilizer bar (MacPherson strut type) - removal and replacement (Super Beetles and Sports Bug)

1 The stabilizer bar is clamped to the front of the frame head and the ends are fixed into the track control arm at each side. All mounting points are in renewable rubber bushes.

2 The stabilizer bar has two functions. It acts as an anti-roll bar but more importantly it provides fore and aft location of the front suspension struts taking the loading of the braking torque.

3 To remove the bar, first remove the clips holding the rubber mounting to the frame head. Then remove the split pins from the retaining nuts on the track control arms and take off the nuts and large washers. The stabilizer bar is then taken out.

4 If the stabilizer bar bush in the track control arm is worn it is possible to renew it in place provided a suitable draw bolt and tube can be made up to pull the old one out and draw the new one in. If the inner track control arm bush is in need of renewal as well it would be simpler to do it after removing the track control arm as described in the next Section. In any case check the details mentioned in the next Section.

5 When replacing the stabilizer bar it is particularly important that the nuts holding the ends into the track control arms are tightened to the specified torque. They should then be tightened further as necessary in order to be able to replace the split pins.

12 Front stabilizer bar (torsion bar suspension) - removal and replacement (USA basic Beetle and UK GT Beetle)

1 The stabilizer bar is fixed to the lower torsion arms on each side of the car and is clamped in position. The bar is held by special clamps secured by sliding clips. Lift up the lug on the end of the clip and slide it off the ends of the clamp which goes round metal securing plate.

2 When refitting the clamps and clips note that the tapered slot end goes towards the wheel and that the lugs which bend down on the clips point towards the centre of the car when being installed.

13 Track control arms and bushes (MacPherson strut suspension) - removal and replacement (Super Beetles and Sports Bug)

1 The track control arm and bushes control the main aspects of the steering geometry so if they are damaged or worn they must be attended to.

2 The inner pivot pin of the track control arm is eccentric and fitted with eccentric washers to provide adjustment in the setting of the wheel camber angle (photo). Any disturbance therefore, will require checking and re-aligning of the steering geometry after reassembly. It is helpful to mark the position of the eccentric pin before removal so that it will be as near as possible accurate until such time as the geometry can be checked properly.

3 To remove the control arm, jack up the car and remove the wheel. Remove the stabilizer bar and disconnect the strut ball joint pin from the end of the control arm.

4 Mark the position of the eccentric washers at the inner end. Undo the self-locking nut and washer and drive out the pin. The arm may then be taken off.

5 Bushes should be pressed or drawn in and out. A tool may be made up from a bolt, washers and a piece of pipe of suitable diameter to draw them in and out. However, as you will most likely be obtaining the new parts at a VW agency it would be easier to ask them to fit them into the arm for you.

6 Two points must be noted when fitting the bushes. The inner pivot bush has a recess which must be on the arm centre line and facing the wheel end. The stabilizer bar bush has two lugs which must be horizontal and face the rear of the car.

7 The track control arm is refitted to the car in the reverse order. The inner pivot pin nut should be tightened to the correct torque when the car is standing on the wheels. This will normally be done when the camber angle is being set.

13.2 Inner end of the track control arm showing eccentric pin and washer (positive steering roll radius)

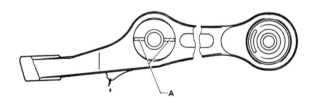

Fig. 12.8. Track control arm - detail of bushes (Sec. 13)

A   Rubber lugs on stabilizer bar bush facing rearwards. Note position of slot in pivot bush

14 Modification to the MacPherson strut front suspension to give negative steering roll radius (Super Beetles and Sports Bug)

1 In August 1973 a modification to the suspension was introduced to give negative steering roll radius. Refer to Figure 12.9. Illustration "A" shows the pre 1973 angle with (1), 'the steering roll radius', as the distance between the vertical centreline of the wheel and centreline of the MacPherson strut measured along the surface on which the wheel rests. It will be noted that the centreline of the steering knuckle is coincident with that of the strut.

2 Illustration "B" shows the new layout. The strut has been shortened and the flange connection between the strut and steering knuckle replaced with a clip. The centreline of the effective control on the radius of swing of the steering knuckle now passes through the top anchorage of the strut and the centre of the steering knuckle, intersecting the ground plane outside the centreline of the wheel. This gives a 'negative' steering roll radius

3 In order to preserve the steering geometry the track control arm has been modified. In place of the forged control arm a fabricated sheet metal arm is fitted. The control arm pivot on the frame head is located 20 mm higher up with the result that the camber angle and wheel alignments are not changed.

4 The steering ball joint is pressed into the control arm, stud upwards and located with a fixing bolt.

5 Obviously the two assemblies are not interchangeable.

6 The effect on the steering is to give improved stability during uneven braking conditions, even that of a burst front tyre. In conventional steering with positive steering roll radius any uneven braking force and drag on the front wheels is amplified and the driver has to apply strong corrective action to the steering wheel. With negative radius the uneven force is cancelled, (the road wheel tries to turn the other way) and the greater the force the better the correction and straight line stability.

7 On the rear engined Beetle little difference is felt on the steering wheel during normal driving. On full lock the steering is lighter but when reversing on full lock the wheel requires more effort. This is the only small disadvantage of the system and a very tiny price to pay for the additional safety benefits of the system.

8 Removal and reassembly of the system is much as for the old system. The tool used to check wear of the steering ball joint is the same but the upper edge is used. The tolerance is the same, 2.5 mm (0.10 ins).

9 The steering ball joint may be pressed out of the radius arm in a mandrel press. Press in a new joint from the deeper side.

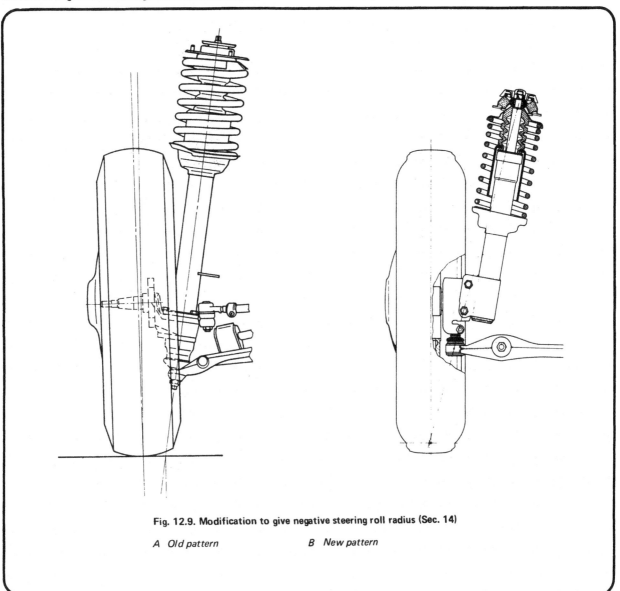

Fig. 12.9. Modification to give negative steering roll radius (Sec. 14)

A Old pattern   B New pattern

15 Steering gear - general description

All models use a worm and roller type steering box. The layout of the box and steering arms is however different. The models fitted with Macpherson strut suspension have one design of box plus a steering layout incorporating an idler. The torsion bar suspension models have a single track rod running from the drop arm to the steering knuckle of each front wheel. The systems are illustrated in Figs. 12.12 and 12.13.

Plastic mouldings are incorporated in the steering column and the steering wheel mounting. This is a mixed blessing for although it will help to reduce injury in a head on crash it is also imperative that the column be dismantled and the plastic mouldings checked if even the slightest knock is experienced. If the moulding is cracked and subsequently fractures when the car is travelling at speed the front wheels will cease to answer to the steering wheel (Figs. 12.10 and 12.11).

Both types of steering are fitted with a hydraulic telescopic damper.

On the older types of Super Beetle it may be possible to adjust the steering box through a hole in the luggage compartment, but on the later models (certainly the one we took to pieces) this hole was filled with a welded plug and coated with a mastic substance which would seem to indicate that adjustment this way is not now favoured.

16 Steering gear - removal and replacement (Super Beetles and Sports Bug)

1 The steering gear is mounted on the sidemember of the body frame and may be removed from underneath the car. It is connected to the lower section of the steering column by a splined coupling at the universal joint.
2 First of all the steering damper and tie-rod ends must be detached from the drop arm. For the tie-rod this will require a suitable claw extractor. There are lugs on the drop arm to enable the extractor claws to grip.
3 Undo the bolt and nut on the universal joint attachment to the splined worm shaft and take the bolt right out.
4 Remove the three bolts holding the gear to the sidemember. They are accessible under the wheel arch alongside the suspension strut.
5 The steering gear may now be pulled off the universal joint and taken down and out from underneath.
6 Replacement is a reversal of the removal procedure. When fitting the splined worm spindle into the universal joint see that the recess in the splined section matches up with the bolt hole in the joint. If it does not the clamp bolt will not go through. Install a new self-locking nut onto the clamp bolt and tighten it to the correct torque of 18 lb ft (2.5 kgm).

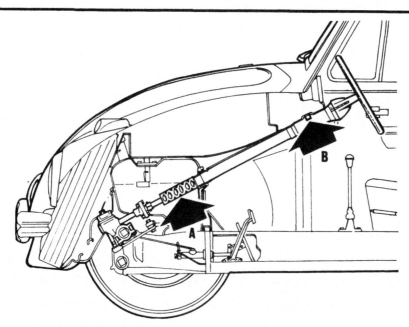

Fig. 12.10. Collapsible steering column (torsion bar suspension)

A   Lattice work safety element   B   Upper mounting bracket with shear type fittings

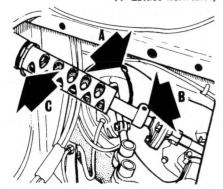

Fig. 12.11. Collapsible steering column (torsion bar suspension)
Detail of column mounting (tank removed)

A   Horn cable connection
B   Column clamp screw
C   Column tube support ring

187

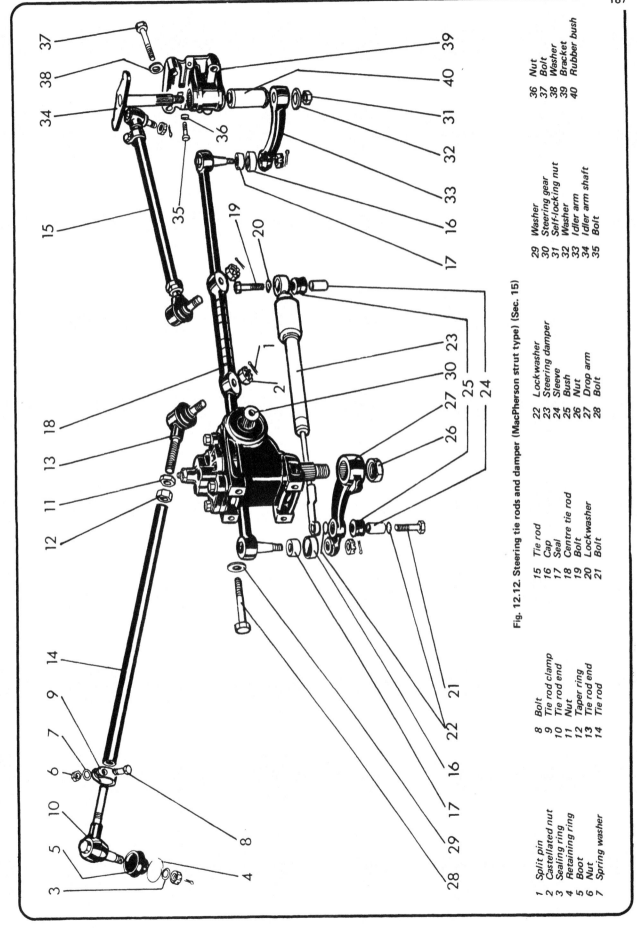

Fig. 12.12. Steering tie rods and damper (MacPherson strut type) (Sec. 15)

1 Split pin
2 Castellated nut
3 Sealing ring
4 Retaining ring
5 Boot
6 Nut
7 Spring washer

8 Bolt
9 Tie rod clamp
10 Tie rod end
11 Nut
12 Taper ring
13 Tie rod end
14 Tie rod

15 Tie rod
16 Cap
17 Seal
18 Centre tie rod
19 Bolt
20 Lockwasher
21 Bolt

22 Lockwasher
23 Steering damper
24 Sleeve
25 Bush
26 Nut
27 Drop arm
28 Bolt

29 Washer
30 Steering gear
31 Self-locking nut
32 Washer
33 Idler arm
34 Idler arm shaft
35 Bolt

36 Nut
37 Bolt
38 Washer
39 Bracket
40 Rubber bush

188

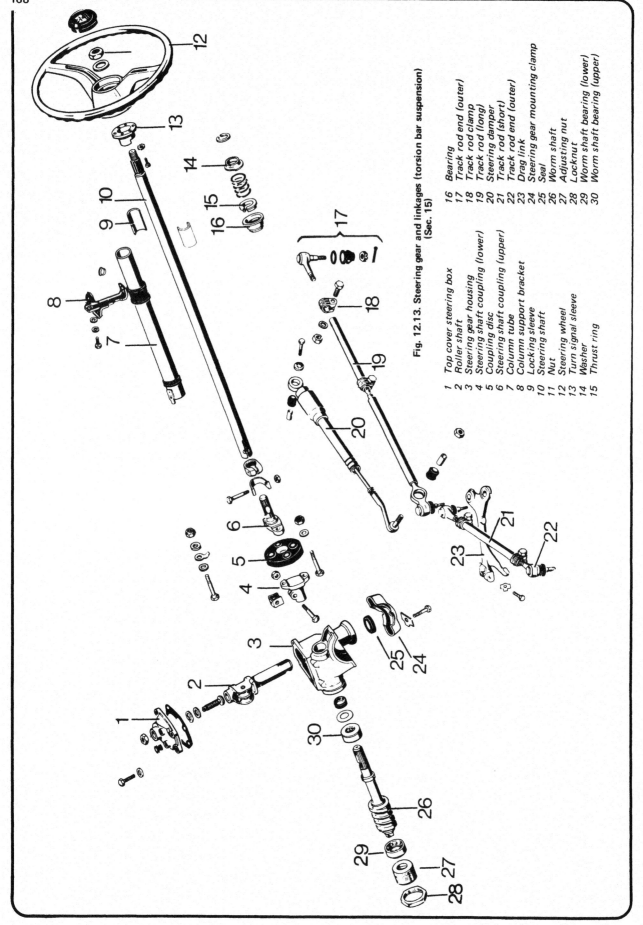

Fig. 12.13. Steering gear and linkages (torsion bar suspension) (Sec. 15)

1 Top cover steering box
2 Roller shaft
3 Steering gear housing
4 Steering shaft coupling (lower)
5 Coupling disc
6 Steering shaft coupling (upper)
7 Column tube
8 Column support bracket
9 Locking sleeve
10 Steering shaft
11 Nut
12 Steering wheel
13 Turn signal sleeve
14 Washer
15 Thrust ring
16 Bearing
17 Track rod end (outer)
18 Track rod clamp
19 Track rod (long)
20 Steering damper
21 Track rod (short)
22 Track rod end (outer)
23 Drag link
24 Steering gear mounting clamp
25 Seal
26 Worm shaft
27 Adjusting nut
28 Locknut
29 Worm shaft bearing (lower)
30 Worm shaft bearing (upper)

17 Steering gear - dismantling and overhaul (all models)

1 The decision to dismantle and rebuild a steering gear assembly will depend to a large extent on the availability of parts. It is inevitable that if adjustments fail to rectify play adequately then most of the interior components will need renewal. The steering gear with its hour glass worm and roller is subject to some very critical settings and requires shims and setting jigs which only a Volkswagen agency is likely to have. We do not therefore, recommend that the do-it-yourself owner attempts this job. The time and cost expended to do the job properly cannot justify any saving over the purchase of a replacement unit.

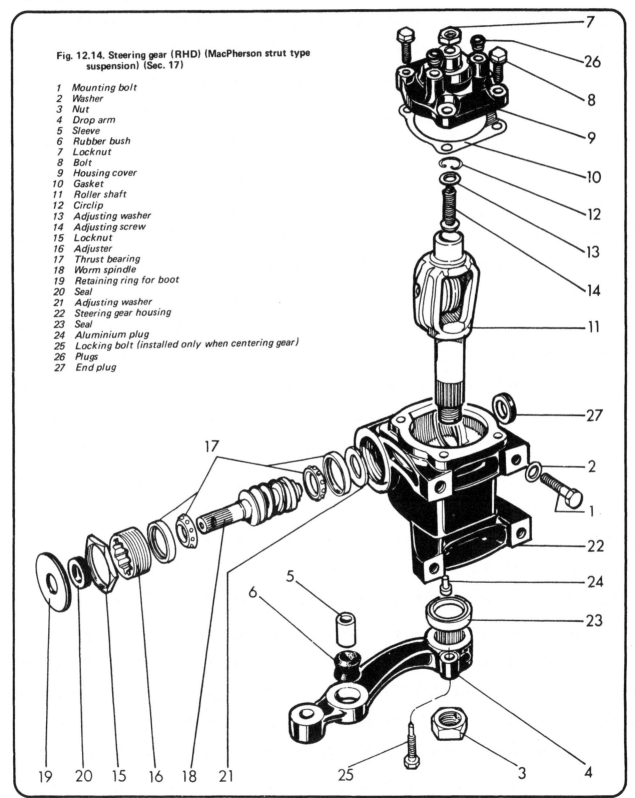

Fig. 12.14. Steering gear (RHD) (MacPherson strut type suspension) (Sec. 17)

1   Mounting bolt
2   Washer
3   Nut
4   Drop arm
5   Sleeve
6   Rubber bush
7   Locknut
8   Bolt
9   Housing cover
10 Gasket
11 Roller shaft
12 Circlip
13 Adjusting washer
14 Adjusting screw
15 Locknut
16 Adjuster
17 Thrust bearing
18 Worm spindle
19 Retaining ring for boot
20 Seal
21 Adjusting washer
22 Steering gear housing
23 Seal
24 Aluminium plug
25 Locking bolt (installed only when centering gear)
26 Plugs
27 End plug

18 Steering gear - removal and replacement - (USA basic Beetle; UK GT Beetle)

1 The steering gear is mounted on the upper axle tube and held by a clamp. It is connected to the steering column by a flanged coupling.

2 The simplest way to disconnect the gear form the track rods is to pull the drop arm off the shaft with the tie-rods still attached. This can be done after undoing the drop arm clamping screw and turning the wheels to a position where the arm can be drawn away.

3 Moving to the coupling flange undo the clip holding the horn wire and then remove the two nuts and bolts from the flange.

4 Before undoing the two bolts which clamp the steering box to the upper axle tube it is important to make sure that you know the correct position to refit it. There is a cutout in the clamp plate which locates over a welded stud on the tube.

5 Once the correct positioning of the box on the tube is assured undo the clamp bolts and take it off.

6 When replacing the clamp make sure that it is fitted the right way round. There will be two numbers on it, "13" and "14", next to the two cutouts. No."13" is the one for Beetles and the arrow should point forward with the cutout on the left.

7 Always use new lock plates on the clamp bolts and bend the tabs down over the hexagon flats. It is also recommended that new self locking nuts are used for the column coupling flange.

8 The steering geometry should be checked for alignment after replacing the steering gear.

19 Steering wheel and column - removal and replacement (Super Beetles and Sports Bug).

1 The steering shaft is in two parts linked by two universal joints. The lower section which joins on the steering gear runs at an angle to the main column so that in case of end thrust (as in a collision) the assembly will collapse rather than be pushed up inside the passenger compartment. The column tube surrounds the upper section of shaft.

2 To remove the steering wheel prise the centre cap out of the wheel. Undo the screw holding the horn switch earth wire.

3 Put the wheel in position with the spokes horizontal and then undo the centre clamping nut and washer.

4 Pull the wheel off the splined end of the shaft.

5 If the column and shaft are being removed next remove the fuel tank from the front luggage compartment as described in Chapter 3. Underneath the lower section of steering shaft is accessible (photo).

6 Undo the clamp bolt on the upper universal joint. Take the bolt out.

7 Disconnect all wires from the steering column switch where they join behind the instrument panel and then pull them all through into the passenger compartment.

8 Remove the bolts securing the column tube to the instrument panel and lift the assembly out from inside the passenger compartment.

9 The column shaft and tube may be separated after the column switch has been removed from the column.

10 The lower shaft together with the universal joints may be removed after the lower universal joint bolt has been removed from the steering gear end. If it is intended to remove the lower shaft and universal joints only, the upper column need only be unfixed on the mounting bracket bolts. This will enable it to be lifted just far enough to disengage the upper steering shaft from the universal joint.

11 Replacement of all components is a straightforward reversal of these procedures. Make sure the splined connections to the universal joints are made so that the locking bolt will engage in the cut-out.

12 It is important that the steering wheel spokes are set horizontal when the steering gear is in the central position. The steering gear is central when the hole in the drop arm lug is directly in line with the countersunk depression in the aluminium plug in the bottom of the steering gear casing. Use a drill of suitable diameter to put through the hole and engage in the depression to line them up.

20 Steering wheel and column - removal and replacement (US basic Beetle; UK GT Beetle)

1 Disconnect the battery earth wire.

2 Remove the petrol tank (Chapter 3, Section 10)

3 Remove the earthing cable from the steering column coupling (photo) unlock the nut on the clip holding column, and remove the screws which clamps the column into the coupling upper half. Bend up the tabs on the column tube support and remove the ring.

4 Prise off the centre cover from the steering wheel and disconnect the horn switch wire. Remove the nut and washer form the centre of the wheel and pull off the wheel and horn ring. Remove the circlip from the steering column. Set the ignition key to the "Drive" position.

5 Remove the screws holding the column tube and the switch clamping screw (three socket head cap screws).

6 Hang the switch mechanism away from the column so that the cables are not strained.

19.5 Steering column lower shaft section (tank removed)

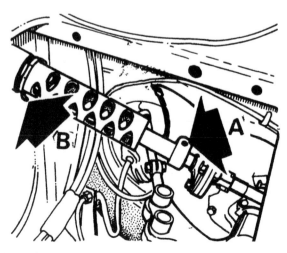

20.3 "A" steering column clip "B" support and support ring

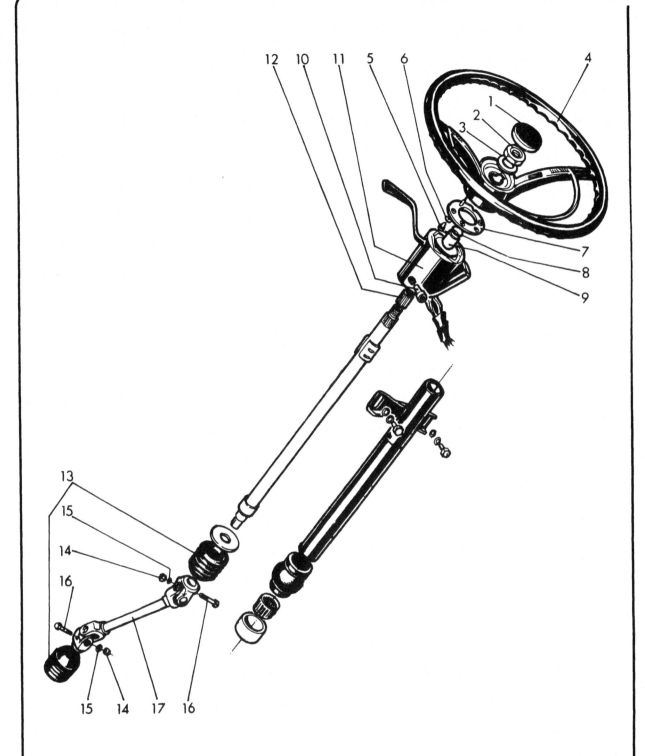

Fig. 12.15. Steering column details (MacPherson strut type suspension) (Sec. 19)

1	Cap	6	Lockwasher	11	Column switch	16	Bolt
2	Nut	7	Cancelling ring	12	Contact ring	17	Universal joint shaft
3	Lockwasher	8	Circlip	13	Boot		
4	Steering wheel	9	Spacer	14	Self-locking nut		
5	Screw	10	Socket head screw	15	Spring washer		

7 The column may now be pulled upwards with the tube.

8 Check the mounting plate for the column tube is secure. The closed sides of the slides must face forwards.

9 Installation is a reversal of removal. Push the column tube into the rubber bush in the partition. Now slide the column into the tube and attach it to the coupling.

10 Refit the steering column switches and partly tighten the clamping screws.

11 Now fit the contact ring in the column switch ball bearing from underneath and fit the circlip.

12 Now set the steering gear in the central position, refit the clamp screw in the steering wheel clip and tighten it. Use a new locking plate.

13 Reconnect the earth cable at the base of the steering column

14 Refit the support ring for the steering column, and install the steering wheel. Make sure the turn signal lever is in the central position. Tighten the centre nut to 5 kgm (36 lb ft). The spokes of the steering wheel should be horizontal.

15 There should be a gap of 2 to 3 mm (1/16 to 1/8 inch) between the steering wheel hub and the switch. Adjust the position of the switch accordingly and tighten the securing screws.

16 Refit the petrol tank and connect the pipes and cables.

21 Steering tie-rods and joints - removal and replacement (Super Beetles and Sports bug)

1 The steering gear transmits the motion of the steering wheel to the road wheels via three tie-rods. The end of the drop arm is connected to one end of a central tie-rod the other end of which is supported by an idler arm on the opposite side. From this tie-rod two other tie-rods run to the steering knuckle of each wheel. Each end of the tie-rods has a swivel ball joint which allows the variety of angles to be adopted by the wheels during movement of steering and suspension. If the track rods are bent, or of the incorrect length, or if the swivel joints are worn, the wheels will take up an incorrect position of alignment, or, in the case of worn joints, be able to move independently of the steering gear. Both these conditions result in inaccurate steering and control.

2 Each ball joint is attached to the steering knuckle at the outer end, or centre tie-rod at the inner end by a tapered pin through a tapered hole and secured by a hexagon nut. The joints are screwed on to the tie-rods with a left and right-hand thread on each rod.

3 The ball joints on the outer tie-rod ends are held in position to the tie-rods by a clamp round the split end of the tie-rods. The joints on the inner ends of these rods are clamped by sleeves with a hexagonal nut and a tapered inner sleeve. The two joints at each end of the central tie-rod are in fact rubber bushed pins and if either of these becomes worn the whole tie-rod is renewed.

4 The main problem normally is removing the joint pin from the steering knuckle or from the centre tie-rod. First remove the split pin and castellated nut. The joint pin may be a very tight fit. If you have no proper extractor hold a hammer to one side of the eye and strike opposite with another. This usually succeeds.

5 Once the joint pin has been extracted from its location the position of the joint should be carefully noted in relation to the tie-rod before it is unclamped and screwed off. This will ensure that the replacement is positioned as accurately as possible. However it must be emphasised that the front wheel alignment must be checked after any renewal of tie-rod joints.

6 When obtaining new joints be careful to note whether or not there is a left or right-hand thread. Also note that the joints at the outer ends of the tie-rods are not interchangeable with those from other Beetles. This model requires a large range of movement. The proper type can be identified by either a bump or depression on the ball retaining plug.

7 Screw the new track rod end on to the rod but do not lock it tight yet.

8 If a track rod is bent it must be replaced with a new one.

Attempts to straighten track rods can only weaken the metal and may result in fracture with disastrous results on the road.

9 It is most important that the rubber seals on the track rod joints are intact and capable of retaining grease. On sealed joints any grease which escapes or which is contaminated needs special attention. It is possible to fit new seals and have them repacked but more often than not it is too late by the time the fault is seen in which case the joint must be renewed.

10 When the track rods are fitted with the ends replace the taper pins into their respective eyes and refit and tighten the hexagon nuts to the correct torque. Replace the split pins after lining up the holes.

11 It is important to see that both ball joints are correctly aligned on the rod so push both of them either fully forward or backwards. Then tighten the nut or pinch bolt and bend over the lock tab.

12 It is important to have the wheel alignment checked properly at the earliest opportunity.

22 Steering tie-rods and joints - removal and replacement (USA basic Beetle; UK GT Beetle)

1 From the drop arm (or steering arm) on the steering gear the movement is transmitted to each wheel by a track rod. The inner and outer ends each have a swivel ball joint which allows the variety of angles to be adopted by the wheels during movement of steering and suspension. If the track rods are bent, or of the incorrect length, or if the swivel joints are worn, the wheels will take up an incorrect position of alignment or, in the case of worn joints, be able to move independently of the steering gear. Both these conditions result in inaccurate steering and control.

2 Each ball joint is attached to the steering knuckle at the outer end, or drop arm at the inner end by a tapered pin through a tapered hole and secured by a hexagon nut. The joints are screwed on to the tie-rods with a left and right-hand thread on each rod.

3 Jack up the car and remove the wheel(s). Remove the split pin from the hexagon nut and take off the nut. The joint pin may be a very tight fit. If you have no proper extractor hold a hammer to one side of the eye and strike opposite with another. This normally succeeds.

4 One track rod has the steering damper fitted into it so this must be detached from it if the whole rod is to be removed. If only the outer ball joints are being renewed it is, of course, unnecessary to detach the joints from the drop arm.

5 The ball joints are screwed into the rod and held by one of two methods - both of which may be used on the same vehicle. The ends of the tie-rods are split and these are clamped to the threaded end of the ball joint. The difference is in the method of clamping. One uses a simple U clamp and pinch bolt. The other method uses a sleeve with a tapered inner face and a hexagon outer face. This taper is forced up to the matching tapered end of the tie-rod by a second hexagon nut. Between the two there is a double tab washer. Whichever type is used slacken it off but before screwing out the joint take careful note of its position (by counting the number of visible threads). This will help to ensure that the toe-in setting is disturbed as little as possible when it is replaced.

6 When obtaining a new joint make quire sure that the correct handed thread is obtained.

7 Screw the new track rod end on to the rod but do not lock it tight yet.

8 If the steering damper has been detached at one end take the opportunity to check it as described in the next Section.

9 If a track rod is bent it must be replaced with a new one. Attempts to straighten it can only weaken the metal and may result in fracture with disastrous results on the road. If the rubber bush for the steering damper in the long rod is in poor condition take the opportunity to renew it.

10 It is most important that the rubber seals on the track rod joints are intact and capable of retaining grease. On early models fitted with grease nipples this problem is not so critical because

grease may be added easily. On later sealed joints, any grease which escapes or which is contaminated needs special attention. It is possible to fit new seals and have them repacked but more often then not it is too late by the time the fault is seen in which case the joint must be renewed.

11 When the track rods are fitted with the ends replace the taper pins into their respective eyes and refit and tighten the hexagon nuts to the correct torque (see Specifications – depending on type of thread fitted). Replace the split pins for earlier types after lining up the holes.

12 It is important to see that both ball joints are correctly aligned on the rod so push both of them either fully forward or backwards. Then tighten the nut or pinch bolt and bend over the lock tabs.

13 It is important to have the wheel alignment checked properly at the earliest opportunity.

14 The tie-rod ends for the suspension strut type of steering are different from those of the torsion bar type and care must be taken not to mix the two types. Those for the suspension strut have either a small depression or a small boss on the centre of the boss on the face opposite to the stud.

23 Steering damper - removal checking and replacement (Super Beetles and Sports Bug)

1 The steering damper is a double acting piston which serves to smooth out vibration and shocks through the steering. One end is fixed to the centre of the frame head and the other to the drop arm. Each fixing bolt is rubber bushed.

2 If the bushes are worn allowing play the damper should be removed and new bushes fitted. New bushes comprise a rubber buffer with a steel central sleeve. Old ones can be cut or driven out and new ones pressed in between the jaws of a vice.

3 The bolts securing the ends of the damper are accessible from underneath for the tie-rod connection and from the luggage compartment for the frame head attachment. For the latter lift out the spare wheel and prise out the small circular cover plate in the floor of the compartment.

4 If the damper is leaking fluid badly and there is inadequate damping action in either direction it should be renewed. To test the action of the damper push and pull the piston throughout its full travel. There should be no roughness or variations in resistance anywhere along the travel of the piston. Note that the dampers fitted to right-hand drive vehicles are different from those fitted to left-hand drive.

5 Replace the damper (with the cylinder end mounted on the frame head) by fitting the securing bolts and nuts and tightening them to the specified torques.

24 Steering damper - removal checking and replacement (USA basic Beetle; UK GT Beetle)

1 The steering damper is a double acting piston which serves to smooth out vibration and shocks through the steering. One end is attached to a bracket on the top axle tube in a rubber bush. The other is fixed similarly to the longer of the two track rods.

2 If the bushes are worn allowing play the damper and tie rod should be removed and new bushes fitted. New bushes comprise a rubber buffer with a steel central sleeve. They can be cut or driven out and new ones pressed in between the jaws of a vice.

3 Remove the two securing bolts which will necessitate jacking up the car and removing the front wheels.

4 To test the action of the damper push and pull the piston throughout its full travel. There should be no roughness or variations in resistance anywhere along the travel of the piston. If there is it should be renewed. Note that the damper is different between vehicles with right and left-hand drive.

5 Replace the damper (with the piston end inwards) by fitting the securing bolts and nuts and tightening them to the specified torques.

25 Steering gear adjustments (all models)

1 Wear in the steering mechanism is a most serious problem and should be treated in this light. It is usually in the linkages and joints but if when all of these are satisfactorily dealt with there still remains more than 25 mm (1 inch) of free movement at the rim of the steering wheel then the steering box is out of adjustment. Although two of the three adjustments may be done with some difficulty on the Super Beetles and Sports Bug whilst the box is still in the car the third adjustment, between the worm and roller is not now possible for the hole which existed in the front compartment has now been welded up and sealed.

It follows therefore that for satisfactory maintenance this most vital part of the car must be removed from the car. Now comes the snag. Unless the jigs and fixtures necessary to test it are available the only way to test the adjustment is to put the box back in the car and try it. The backlash should be reduced to 25 mm (1 inch) but there must be **no** tight spots.

If the excessive play is in the box then something must be worn and common sense demands that whatever is worn should be rectified. The owner is therefore strongly advised to take the faulty box to the VW agent for testing, adjustment or replacement.

26 Steering Geometry (all models)

If the steering geometry of your car is wrong then the car will be unpleasant to drive, make odd noises, and will wear out tyres at an alarming rate. The latest figures available are given in the Specification. If the owner has the necessary equipment and knows how to do these adjustments no comment is required. If he does not then the right place to get these adjustments done is at the VW agency. A special protractor is required to check camber, it is fitted with a spirit level. Similarly toe-in requires special trammels and a good deal of know-how.

Always have the steering geometry checked if the front wheels have been in an accident, no matter how slight.

27 Wheel balancing (all models)

1 It is most unlikely that a wheel fitted with a new tyre will be in correct balance. It is possible to check the static balance yourself. Jack up the wheel and make sure it spins freely. Mark the lowest point with a chalk mark on the tyre and then spin the wheel four or five times, allowing it to come to rest each time. If the chalk mark comes to the bottom each time then the wheel is definitely out of balance.

2 It is not however possible to check dynamic balance. This will make itself known either as 'flutter','tramp', or'shimmy' all of which cause the steering to vibrate at certain speeds.

3 The only way to correct this is by balancing the wheel, tyre, and hub together. It is done by adding lead weights of the right size at the correct place on the wheel rim. The old method made it necessary to take the wheel off to do the job but more modern equipment will do the job with the wheel in situ.

4 All four wheels should be checked. Although out of balance will not normally affect the car if only the rear wheels are incorrectly balanced it does mean that they cannot be changed to the front.

5 It is recommended that wheels should be balanced whenever new tyres are fitted. It is also a good thing to note how many balance weights are fitted for they have been known to fly off.

28 Care and maintenance of tyres

1 If the tyre is run underinflated the edges of the tread will wear rapidly.

2 If the steering geometry is wrong then the edges of the tyres will wear unevenly.

3 In each of the above cases the tyre will become dangerous while a good 50% of the tread is unworn. The tyre companies and the garages will benefit but the owner will be paying twice as much as he should. Always check pressure, and study the treads of the tyres at least weekly.

Do not mix **Radials** with **Crossply**. It is extremely dangerous to run with **Radials** on the front and **Crossply** on the rear for the front will skid first. Even if you get home safely the **law** will be very abrupt if you are caught. If you have an accident the insurance company will be difficult, and rightly so.

Do not run with **Radial** and a **Crossply** on the same axle (front or rear). The Specification offers both VW recommendations. Radials are more expensive and tend to give a rougher ride below 50 mph. They do, however, last longer and hold the road more firmly.

Finally, if you have driven over broken glass, or sharp flints it pays to examine the tyres carefully and remove any pieces lodged in the tread. It is also a very good idea to take a tyre off and look inside to see that the case is not fractured if the car has hit the kerb or an obstruction at speed. If the tyre is damaged it will fail sooner or later, and maybe cause an accident.

29 Fault diagnosis - front suspension, wheels and steering

Before diagnosing faults in the mechanics of the suspension and steering itself, check that any irregularities are not caused by:

1 Binding brakes
2 Incorrect 'mix' of radial and crossply tyres
3 Incorrect tyre pressures
4 Misalignment of the bodyframe and suspension due to accident damage

Symptom	Reason/s	Remedy
Steering wheel can be moved considerably before any sign of movement of the wheels is apparent	Wear in the steering linkage, gear and column coupling	Check movement in all joints, and steering gear and adjust, overhaul and renew as required.
Vehicle difficult to steer in a consistent straight line - wandering	As above	As above.
	Wheel alignment incorrect (indicated by excessive or uneven tyre wear)	Check wheel alignment.
	Front wheel hub bearings loose or worn	Adjust or renew as necessary.
	Worn suspension ball joints	Renew as necessary.
Steering stiff and heavy	Incorrect wheel alignment (indicated by excessive or uneven tyre wear)	Check wheel alignment.
	Excessive wear or seizure in one or more of the joints in the steering linkage or suspension	Repair as necessary.
	Excessive wear in the steering gear unit	Adjust if possible, or renew.
Wheel wobble and vibration	Road wheels out of balance	Balance wheels.
	Road wheels buckled	Check for damage.
	Wheel alignment incorrect	Check wheel alignment.
	Wear in the steering linkage or suspension	Check and renew as necessary.
	Ineffective steering damper	Check and renew as necessary.
Excessive pitching and rolling on corners during braking	Defective dampers and/or broken springs	Check and renew as necessary.

Chapter 13 Bodywork and underframe

Contents

Bumpers (front) including spring type - removal and
replacement 9
Bumpers (rear) including spring type - removal and
replacement 10
Door latch mechanism - removal and replacement 17
Door latch mechanism - striker plate adjustment 18
Doors - rattles 13
Doors - removal and replacement 12
Doors - trim panels - removal and replacement 14
Engine compartment cover - removal and replacement ... 20
Engine compartment cover latch - adjustment 22
Front wings - removal and replacement 6
General description 1
Luggage compartment cover - removal and replacement ... 21

Luggage compartment cover latch and cable release -
adjustment 23
Maintenance - bodywork and underframe 2
Maintenance - upholstery and carpets 3
Major bodywork damage - repairs 4
Minor body damage - repair 5
Mirror (rear view) and radio aerial - provision for fitting ... 19
Quarterlight - removal and replacement 16
Rear wings - removal and replacement 7
Seats - removal repair and conversion to reclining type ... 25
Sill panels - removal and replacement 8
Ventilation (fresh air) - adjustment 24
Window regulator mechanism & window - removal and
replacement 15
Windscreen and fixed glass - removal and replacement ... 11

1 General description

The bodywork of the Volkswagen is noted for its simplicity, rigidity and corrosion free properties.

It consists basically of a flat floor pan stiffened down the centre with a fabricated sheet steel tube. At the front is a 'frame head' to which the front suspension track control arms and stabilizer bar are attached. At the rear of the floor pan is a 'frame fork' into which the engine/transmission assembly is bolted. Just forward of the frame fork is a lateral tube to which the rear suspension spring plate supports are fitted at the outer ends. The frame tunnel is closed in underneath and carries inside it the necessary guide tubes for brake cables, heater cables, clutch cable, accelerator cable and gearchange connecting rods.

The bodywork is a unit fabricated from steel panels welded together with the exception of sill panels, wings, doors and engine and luggage compartment lids. The unit is bolted to the floor frame. The doors, wings, lids and sill panels are bolted to the body and are readily detachable.

The whole frame body assembly is remarkable for its lack of 'nooks and crannies' where water/dirt can collect and is notable for being almost airtight (it is virtually impossible to slam the doors shut with the windows closed due to the air pressure build up inside).

2 Maintenance — bodywork and underframe

1 The general condition of a car's bodywork is the thing that significantly affects its value. Maintenance is easy but needs to be regular. Neglect, particularly after minor damage, can lead quickly to further deterioration and costly repair bills. It is important also to keep watch on those parts of the car not immediately visible, for instance the underside, inside all the wheel arches and the lower part of the engine compartment.

2 The basic maintenance routine for the bodywork is washing — preferably with a lot of water, from a hose. This will remove all the loose solids which may have stuck to the car. It is important to flush these off in such a way as to prevent grit from scratching the finish. The wheel arches and underframe need washing in the same way to remove any accumulated mud which will retain moisture and tend to encourage rust. Paradoxically enough, the best time to clean the underframe and wheel arches is in wet weather when the mud is thoroughly wet and soft. In very wet weather the underframe is usually cleaned of large accumulations automatically and this is a good time for inspection.

3 Periodically, it is a good idea to have the whole of the underframe of the car steam cleaned, engine compartment included, so that a thorough inspection can be carried out to see what minor repairs and renovations are necessary. Steam cleaning is available at many garages and is necessary for removal of the accumulation of oily grime which sometimes is allowed to become thick in certain areas. If steam cleaning facilities are not available, there are one or two excellent grease solvents available which can be brush applied. The dirt can then be simply hosed off.

4 After washing paintwork wipe off with a chamois leather to give an unspotted clear finish. A coat of clear protective wax polish will give added protection against chemical pollutants in

the air. If the paintwork sheen has dulled or oxidised, use a cleaner/polisher combination to restore the brilliance of the shine. This requires a little effort, but such dulling is usually caused because regular washing has been neglected. Always check that the door and ventilator opening drain holes and pipes are completely clear so that water can be drained out. Bright work should be treated in the same way as paintwork. Windscreens and windows can be kept clear of the smeary film which often appears, by adding a little ammonia to the water. If they are scratched, a good rub with a proprietary metal polish will often clear them. Never use any form of wax or other body or chromium polish on glass.

3 Maintenance — upholstery and carpets

1 Mats and carpets should be brushed or vacuum cleaned regularly to keep them free of grit. If they are badly stained remove them from the car for scrubbing or sponging and make quite sure they are dry before refitting. Seats and interior trim panels can be kept clean by a wipe over with a damp cloth. If they do become stained (which can be more apparent on light coloured upholstery) use a little liquid detergent and a soft nail brush to scour the grime out of the grain of the material. Do not forget to keep the head lining clean in the same way as the upholstery. When using liquid cleaners inside the car do not over-wet the surfaces being cleaned. Excessive damp could get into the seams and padded interior causing stains, offensive odours or even rot. If the inside of the car gets wet accidentally it is worthwhile taking some trouble to dry it out properly, particularly where carpets are involved. *Do not leave oil or electric heaters inside the car for this purpose.*

4 Minor body damage — repair

The photographic sequences on pages 199, 200 and 201 illustrate the operations detailed in the following sub-sections.

Repair of minor scratches in the car's bodywork
If the scratch is very superficial, and does not penetrate to the metal of the bodywork, repair is very simple. Lightly rub the area of the scratch with a paintwork renovator, or a very fine cutting paste, to remove loose paint from the scratch and to clear the surrounding bodywork of wax polish. Rinse the area with clean water.

Apply touch-up paint to the scratch using a fine paint brush; continue to apply thin layers of paint until the surface of the paint in the scratch is level with the surrounding paintwork. Allow the new paint at lease two weeks to harden; then blend it into the surrounding paintwork by rubbing the scratch area with a paintwork renovator or a very fine futting paste. Finally, apply wax polish.

Where the scratch has penetrated right through to the metal of the bodywork, causing the metal to rust, a different repair technique is required. Remove any loose rust from the bottom of the scratch with a penknife, then apply rust inhibiting paint to prevent the formation of rust in the future. Using a rubber or nylon applicator fill the scratch with bodystopper paste. If required, this paste can be mixed with cellulose thinners to provide a very thin paste which is ideal for filling narrow scratches. Before the stopper-paste in the scratch hardens, wrap a piece of smooth cotton rag around the top of a finger. Dip the finger in cellulose thinners and then quickly sweep it across the surface of the stopper-paste in the scratch; this will ensure

that the surface of the stopper-paste is slightly hollowed. The scratch can now be painted over as described earlier in this Section.

Repair of dents in the car's bodywork
When deep denting of the car's bodywork has taken place, the first task is to pull the dent out, until the affected bodywork almost attains its original shape. There is little point in trying to restore the original shape completely, as the metal in the damaged area will have stretched on impact and cannot be reshaped fully to its original contour. It is better to bring the level of the dent up to a point which is about 1/8 in (3 mm) below the level of the surrounding bodywork. In cases where the dent is very shallow anyway, it is not worth trying to pull it out at all. If the underside of the dent is accessible, it can be hammered out gently from behind, using a mallet with a wooden or plastic head. Whilst doing this, hold a suitable block of wood firmly against the outside of the panel to absorb the impact from the hammer blows and thus prevent a large area of the bodywork from being 'belled-out'.

Should the dent be in a section of the bodywork which has double skin or some other factor making it inaccessible from behind, a different technique is called for. Drill several small holes through the metal inside the area — particularly in the deeper section. Then screw long self-tapping screws into the holes just sufficiently for them to gain a good purchase in the metal. Now the dent can be pulled out by pulling on the protruding heads of the screws with a pair of pliers.

The next stage of the repair is the removal of the paint from the damaged area, and from an inch or so of the surrounding 'sound' bodywork. This is accomplished most easily by using a wire brush or abrasive pad on a power drill, although it can be done just as effectively by hand using sheets of abrasive paper. To complete the preparation for filling, score the surface of the bare metal with a screwdriver or the tang of a file, or alternatively, drill small holes in the affected area. This will provide a really good 'key' for the filler paste.

To complete the repair see the Section on filling and respraying.

Repair of rust holes or gashes in the car's bodywork
Remove all paint from the affected area and from an inch or so of the surrounding 'sound' bodywork, using an abrasive pad or a wire brush on a power drill. If these are not available a few sheets of abrasive paper will do the job just as effectively. With the paint removed you will be able to gauge the severity of the corrosion and therefore decide whether to renew the whole panel (if this is possible) or to repair the affected area. New body panels are not as expensive as most people think and it is often quicker and more satisfactory to fit a new panel than to attempt to repair large areas of corrosion.

Remove all fittings from the affected area except those which will act as a guide to the original shape of the damaged bodywork (eg headlamp shells etc). Then, using tin snips or a hacksaw blade, remove all loose metal and any other metal badly affected by corrosion. Hammer the edges of the hole inwards in order to create a slight depression for the filler paste.

Wire brush the affected area to remove the powdery rust from the surface of the remaining metal. Paint the affected area with rust inhibiting paint; if the back of the rusted area is accessible treat this also.

Before filling can take place it will be necessary to block the hole in some way. This can be achieved by the use of zinc gauze or aluminium tape.

Zinc gauze is probably the best material to use for a large hole. Cut a piece to the approximate size and shape of the hole to be filled, then position it in the hole so that its edges are below the level of the surrounding bodywork. It can be retained in position by several blobs of filler paste around its periphery.

Aluminium tape should be used for small or very narrow holes. Pull a piece off the roll and trim it to the approximate

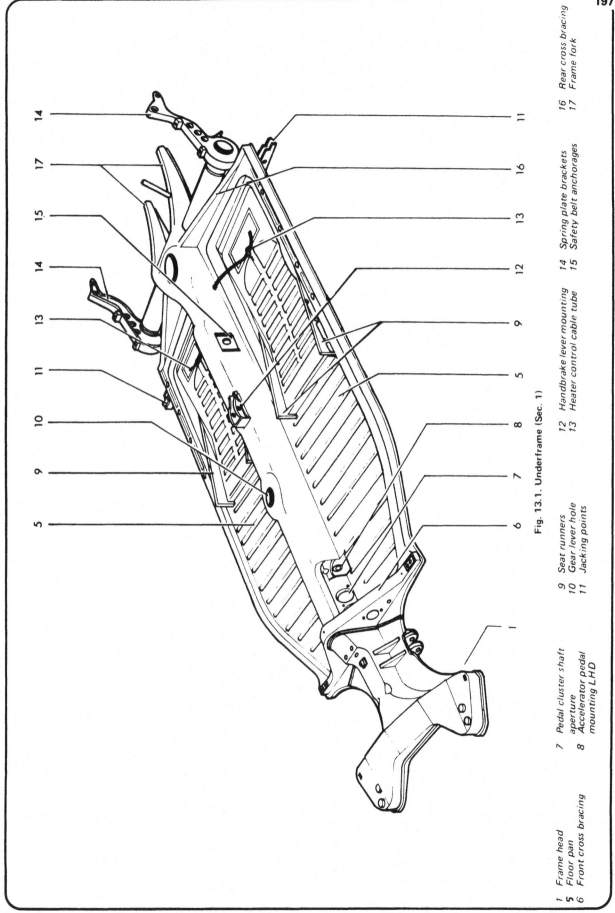

Fig. 13.1. Underframe (Sec. 1)

1	Frame head	7	Pedal cluster shaft aperture	12	Handbrake lever mounting	16	Rear cross bracing
5	Floor pan	8	Accelerator pedal mounting LHD	13	Heater control cable tube	17	Frame fork
6	Front cross bracing	9	Seat runners	14	Spring plate brackets		
		10	Gear lever hole	15	Safety belt anchorages		
		11	Jacking points				

size and shape required, then pull off the backing paper (if used) and stick the tape over the hole; it can be overlapped if the thickness of one piece is insufficient. Burnish down the edges of the tape with the handle of a screwdriver or similar, to ensure that the tape is securely attached to the metal underneath.

Polyurethane foam is best used where the hole is situated in a section of bodywork of complex shape, backed by a small box section (eg; where the sill panel meets the rear wheel arch - most cars). The unusual mixing procedure for this foam is as follows: Put equal amounts of fluid from each of the two cans provided in the kit, into one container. Stir until the mixture begins to thicken, then quickly pour this mixture into the hole, and hold a piece of cardboard over the larger apertures. Almost immediately the polyurethane will begin to expand, gushing out of any small holes left unblocked. When the foam hardens it can be cut back to just below the level of the surrounding bodywork with a hacksaw blade.

Bodywork repairs – filling and respraying

Before using this Section, see the Sections on dent, deep scratch, rust holes and gash repairs.

Many types of bodyfiller are available, but generally speaking those proprietary kits which contain a tin of filler paste and a tube of resin hardener are best for this type of repair. A wide, flexible plastic or nylon applicator will be found invaluable for imparting a smooth and well contoured finish to the surface of the filler.

Mix up a little filler on a clean piece of card or board — measure the hardener carefully (follow the maker's instructions on the pack) otherwise the filler will set too rapidly or too slowly.

Using the applicator apply the filler paste to the prepared area; draw the applicator across the surface of the filler to achieve the correct contour and to level the filler surface. As soon as a contour that approximates to the correct one is achieved, stop working the paste — if you carry on too long the paste will become sticky and begin to 'pick up' on the applicator. Continue to add thin layers of filler paste at twenty-minute intervals until the level of the filler is just proud of the surrounding bodywork.

Once the filler has hardened, excess can be removed using a metal plane or file. From then on, progressively finer grades of abrasive paper should be used, starting with a 40 grade production paper and finishing with 400 grade wet-and-dry paper. Always wrap the abrasive paper around a flat rubber, cork or wooden block — otherwise the surface of the filler will not be completely flat. During the smoothing of the filler surface the wet-and-dry paper should be periodically rinsed in water. This will ensure that a very smooth finish is imparted to the filler at the final stage.

At this stage the 'dent' should be surrounded by a ring of bare metal, which in turn should be encircled by the finely 'feathered' edge of the good paintwork. Rinse the repair area with clean water, until all of the dust produced by the rubbing-down operation has gone.

Spray the whole repair area with a light coat of primer — this will show up any imperfections in the surface of the filler paste or bodystopper, and once more smooth the surface with abrasive paper. If bodystopper is used, it can be mixed with cellulose thinners to form a really thin paste which is ideal for filling small holes. Repeat this spray and repair procedure until you are satisfied that the surface of the filler, and the feathered edge of the paintwork are perfect. Clean the repair area with clean water and allow to dry fully.

The repair area is now ready for final spraying. Paint spraying must be carried out in a warm, dry, windless and dust free atmosphere. This condition can be created artificially if you have access to a large indoor working area, but if you are forced to work in the open, you will have to pick your day very carefully. If you are working indoors, dousing the floor in the work area with water will help settle the dust which would otherwise be in the atmosphere. If the repair area is confined to one body panel, mask off the surrounding panels; this will help to minimise the effects of a slight mis-match in paint colours. Bodywork fittings (eg chrome strips, door handles etc) will also need to be masked off. Use genuine masking tape and several thicknesses of newspaper for the masking operations.

Before commencing to spray, agitate the aerosol can thoroughly, then spray a test area (an old tin, or similar) until the technique is mastered. Cover the repair area with a thick coat of primer; the thickness should be built up using several thin layers of paint rather than one thick one. Using 400 grade wet-and-dry paper, rub down the surface of the primer until it is really smooth. While doing this, the work area should be thoroughly doused with water, and the wet-and-dry paper periodically rinsed in water. Allow to dry before spraying on more paint.

Spray on the top coat, again building up the thickness by using several thin layers of paint. Start spraying in the centre of the repair area and then, using a circular motion, work outwards until the whole repair area and about 2 inches of the surrounding original paintwork is covered. Remove all masking material 10 to 15 minutes after spraying on the final coat of paint.

Allow the new paint at least two weeks to harden, then using a paintwork renovator or a very fine cutting paste, blend the edges of the paint into the existing paintwork. Finally, apply wax polish.

---

5 Major bodywork damage - repair

1 Volkswagen owners are fortunate in that what would be relatively severe damage in some cars is not so for them. This is where wings or sills are badly damaged beyond economical repair. Being bolted on they can be removed and a new unit fitted by the owner (see subsequent Sections).
2 Where serious damage has occurred or large areas need renewal due to neglect it means certainly that completely new sections or panels will need welding in and this is best left to professionals. If the damage is due to impact it will also be necessary to check the alignment of the body structure. In such instances the services of a Volkswagen agent with specialist checking jigs are essential. If a body is left misaligned it is first of all dangerous as the car will not handle properly - and secondly, uneven stresses will be imposed on the steering, engine and transmission, causing abnormal wear or complete failure. Tyre wear will also be excessive.

---

6 Front wings - removal and replacement

1 Jack up the car and remove the headlamp and direction indicator lamp housing.
2 Pull the wires and grommets out of the holes where they pass through the wing.
3 Remove the nut and bolt holding the wing to the sill panel and subsequently the bolts holding the wing to the bodywork. It is more than likely that these bolts are difficult to move. If this is so clean the heads and surrounds thoroughly and use plenty of penetrating fluid to ease the threads. If resort to cutting is necessary - with either saw or chisel - take care not to damage or bend the bodywork. One of the safest ways if you have a power drill and stone is to grind the heads off stubborn bolts.
4 When clear, lift off the wing and beading strip.
5 It is a good idea to fit a new beading strip when putting the wing back. If the wing is a new one do any necessary paint spraying before fitting.
6 Use new bolts and treat them with grease or some anti-seize compound before fitting. There should be a new rubber washer on the bolt between the wing and sill panel.
7 The headlamp must be realigned after replacement. Make sure all the wires and grommets are properly replaced to avoid chafing or strain which could lead to failure.

Preparation for filling
Typical example of rust damage to a body panel. Before starting ensure that you have all of the materials required to hand. The first task is to ...

... remove body fittings from the affected area, except those which can act as a guide to the original shape of the damaged bodywork - the headlamp shell in this case.

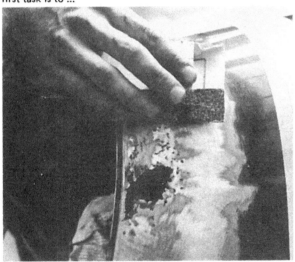

Remove all paint from the rusted area and from an inch or so of the adjoining 'sound' bodywork - use coarse abrasive paper or a power drill fitted with a wire brush or abrasive pad. Gently hammer in the edges of the hole to provide a hollow for the filler.

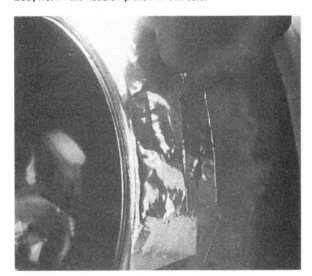

Before filling, the larger holes must be blocked off. Adhesive aluminium tape is one method; cut the tape to the required shape and size, peel off the backing strip (where used), position the tape over the hole and burnish to ensure adhesion.

Alternatively, zinc gauze can be used. Cut a piece of the gauze to the required shape and size; position it in the hole below the level of the surrounding bodywork; then ...

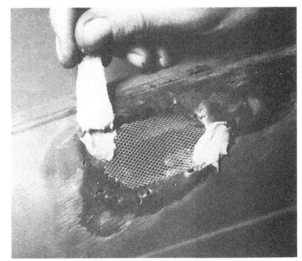

... secure in position by placing a few blobs of filler paste around its periphery. Alternatively, pop rivets or self-tapping screws can be used. Preparation for filling is now complete.

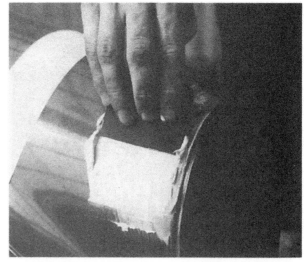

Filling and shaping
Mix filler and hardener according to manufacturer's instructions -
avoid using too much hardener otherwise the filler will harden
before you have a chance to work it.

Apply the filler to the affected area with a flexible applicator -
this will ensure a smooth finish. Apply thin layers of filler at 20
minute intervals, until the surface of the filler is just 'proud' of
the surrounding bodywork. Then ...

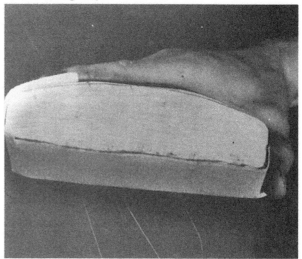

... remove excess filler and start shaping with a Surform plane or
a dreadnought file. Once an approximate contour has been
obtained and the surface is relatively smooth, start using ...

... abrasive paper. The paper should be wrapped around a flat
wood, cork or rubber block - this will ensure that it imparts a
smooth surface to the filler.

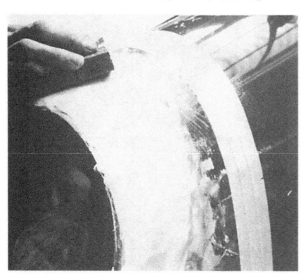

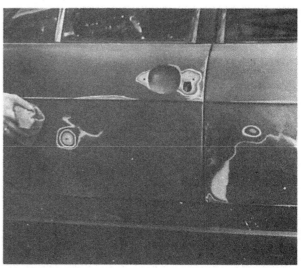

40 grit production paper is best to start with, then use progressively finer abrasive paper, finishing with 400 grade 'wet-and-dry'.
When using 'wet-and-dry' paper, periodically rinse it in water
ensuring also, that the work area is kept wet continuously.

Rubbing-down is complete when the surface of the filler is
really smooth and flat, and the edges of the surrounding paintwork are finely 'feathered'. Wash the area thoroughly with clean
water and allow to dry before commencing re-spray.

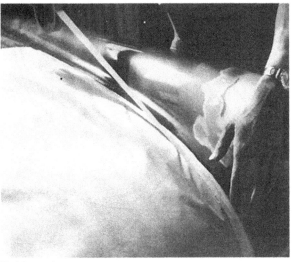

Masking and spraying
Firstly, mask off all adjoining panels and the fittings in the spray area. Ensure that the area to be sprayed is completely free of dust. Practice using an aerosol on a piece of waste metal sheet until the technique is mastered.

Spray the affected area with primer - apply several thin coats rather than one thick one. Start spraying in the centre of the repair area and then work outwards using a circular motion - in this way the paint will be evenly distributed.

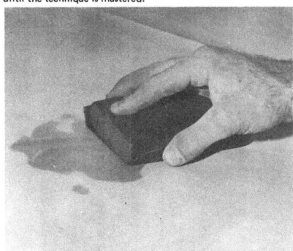

When the primer has dried inspect its surface for imperfections. Holes can be filled with filler paste or body-stopper, and lumps can be sanded smooth. Apply a further coat of primer, then 'flat' its surface with 400 grade 'wet-and-dry' paper.

Spray on the top coat, again building up the thickness with several thin coats of paint. Overspray onto the surrounding original paintwork to a depth of about five inches, applying a very thin coat at the outer edges.

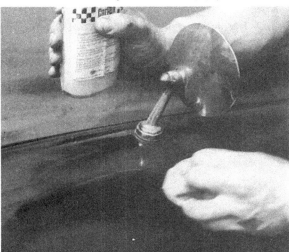

Allow the new paint two weeks, at least, to harden fully, then blend it into the surrounding original paintwork with a paint restorative compound or very fine cutting paste. Use wax polish to finish off.

The finished job should look like this. Remember, the quality of the completed work is directly proportional to the amount of time and effort expended at each stage of the preparation.

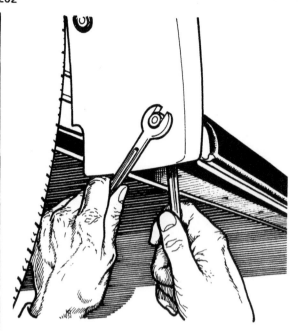

Fig. 13.2. Removing the bolt connecting the front wing to door sill (Sec. 6)

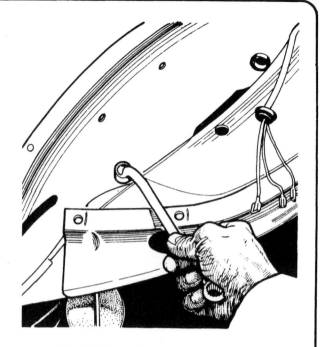

Fig. 13.3. Removing rear wing bolts (Sec. 7)

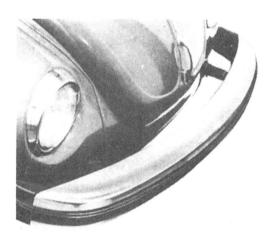

Fig. 13.4. Front bumper with spring buffers (USA) (Sec. 9)

Fig. 13.5. Rear bumper with spring buffers (USA) (Sec. 10)

Fig. 13.6. Bumper removed showing attachment of buffer (Sec. 9)

Fig. 13.7. Attachment of front bumper buffer to frame (Sec. 9)

7 Rear wings - removal and replacement

1 The principle of removing and replacing the rear wings is exactly the same as that for the front wings as described in the previous Section except that the rear bumper and bumper brackets should be removed first. Do not forget to remove the bolt securing the wing to the sill panel.

2 On replacement fit new beading and rubber washer between wing and sill as required.

8 Sill panels - removal and replacement

1 The sill panel is bolted to the body and to the wings at the front and rear. Once all the bolts have been removed - bearing in mind the precautions for stubborn bolts as mentioned in the Section on front wing removal - the sill can be lifted off.

2 When fitting a new sill panel make sure the washers fit correctly over the slots and when tightening the bolts tighten up the ones to the bodywork before the ones to the wings.

9 Front bumpers

1 With the reshaping of the body (Super Beetles and Sports Bug) has come a revised type of bumper. On European and early USA models the bumper is fixed rigidly to the frame but is reinforced. It may be removed with the brackets complete, or it may be taken off the brackets depending on the reason for dismantling. If the brackets have been distorted they should not be re-bent cold, but heated, reformed correctly and normalized. This is a blacksmith's job and if it isn't done properly the bumper will be askew and it may not be possible to get the bolts into position.

2 Models currently sold in the USA have bumpers mounted on spring type buffers. This allows a 60 mm (2.36 inches) travel and is designed to prevent serious damage in collisions of up to 5 mph. (Parking damage). Removal and replacement is straightforward enough if no damage has occurred, but if the mounting has been distorted then the car should be taken to the VW agent for dimension checking. (See Figs. 13.4 and 13.7).

10 Rear bumpers

The rear bumpers now extend to protect the exhaust tail pipes and are much stronger. The same modifications have been done to the rear bumpers as described in Section 9 for the front bumpers. The buffer type for the USA offers protection to 5 kph (3 mph) and is designed to minimise damage when parking. (See Fig. 13.5).

11 Windscreen and fixed glass - removal and replacement

1 The windscreens on the Super Beetles and Sports Bug are curved, or as the pamphlet says "panoramic". The USA basic Beetle and UK GT Beetle have flat screens. The method of replacement is the same, although the curved glass is a little more daunting. The weather strip is fastened in a plated tube on the top centre of the screen.

It is important to know which type of glass is being fitted. Toughened safety glass is expensive but will stand a certain amount of pressure, but any other kind will crack and splinter if handled roughly. The job can be done quite easily but if you are apprehensive - the fitting charge may be less than cost of the second screen and the doctor's bill.

2 After taking off the windscreen wiper arms, loosen the rubber sealing strip on the inside of the car where it fits over the edge of the window frame. Use a piece of wood for this. Anything sharp may rip the rubber weatherstrip. The screen can

be pushed out, weatherstrip attached, if pressure is applied at the top corners. Two people are needed on this to prevent the glass falling out. Push evenly and protect your hands to avoid accidents. Remove the finisher strip from the weatherstrip.

3 When fitting a screen first make sure that the window frame edges are even and smooth. Examine the edges of the screen to see that it is ground smooth and no chips or cracks are visible. Any such cracks could be the start of a much bigger one. The rubber weatherstrip should be perfectly clean. No traces of sealing compound should remain on rubber, glass or metal. If the sealing strip is old, brittle or hard, it is advisable to fit a new one even though they are not cheap.

4 Fit the weatherstrip to the screen first so that the joint comes midway along the top edge.

5 Next fit the decorative moulding into the weatherstrip. This is done by first feeding fine cord into the slot (use a piece of thin tubing as a guide and time saver) and leave the ends overlapping long enough to be able to grip later. The two halves of the moulding are then put in place and the cord drawn out so that the edge of the strip locks them into place.

6 Apply suitable sealing compound to the weatherstrip where it will seat onto the metal window frame and also onto the outside faces of the frame at the lower corners.

7 Fit a piece of really strong thin cord into the frame channel of the weatherstrip as already described and then offer up the screen to the aperture. A second person is essential for this.

8 When you are sure that the screen is centrally positioned, pull the cord out so that the lip of the weatherstrip is drawn over the inner edge of the frame flange. One of the most frequent difficulties in this job is that the cord breaks. This is often because of sharp or uneven edges on the frame flange so a little extra time in preparation will pay off.

9 The same methods apply to the rear window and the fixed windows in the side. The important thing to remember is to go gently and not to force the glass. . Even if it does go in there will be a residual strain which will cause the glass to crack when you next go over a bump.

12 Doors - removal and replacement

1 The door hinges are welded to the door and the assembly is fastened to the car with countersunk crosshead type screws. They were tightened with an impact type screwdriver so unless you have an impact screwdriver of the right size do not try to undo them. If the heads are damaged then the screws will have to be drilled out - which is expensive.

2 If the door is to be replaced after repair then the best answer is to knock out the hinge pins with a punch but the sill panel must be removed to get at the lower hinge. However the problems of alignment will be overcome this way.

3 If the hinge screws must come out remove the plastic plug (photo) and undo the screws with an impact screwdriver (or get someone else to do it).

4 Most reasonable garages will undo the screws for a fee, and do them up again. Once they are loose tighten them with an ordinary crosshead screwdriver - which will be good enough to get you home.

5 When refitting a new door it will make things much easier if a second person holds the door while the hinge screws are inserted. Tighten one screw in each hinge sufficiently to hold the door whilst it is set centrally and flush in the door opening.

6 The operation is made more simple if the latch striker plate is removed while the fitting is being done.

13 Door rattles - tracing and rectification

Door rattles are due either to loose hinges, worn or maladjusted catches, or loose components inside the door. Loose hinges can be detected by opening the door and trying to lift it. Any play will be felt. Worn or badly adjusted catches can be found by pushing and pulling on the outside handle when the

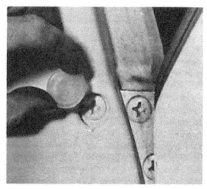

12.3a Nylon plug covering the door hinge screw

12.3b Door check strap rivet

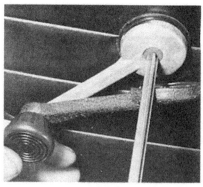

14.1a Prise off the plastic cover and remove the screw from the centre of the winder handle

14.1b Remove the recess plate from the inner door handle lever ...

14.1c and remove the screw

14.2a Take out the screws holding the door pull ...

14.2b ... and the trim may be lifted away as the clips are eased out of the door

14.3a Do not forget the tension spring on the winder handle ...

14.3b ... or the rubbing washer

15.2 Undo the screws holding the window support to the winding mechanism

15.3 Removing the glass

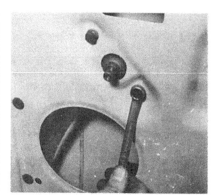

15.4a The bolts holding the winder handle mechanism

door is closed, Once again any play will be felt. To check the window mechanism open the door and shake it with the window first open and then closed. Loose components will rattle when the window is open and the rattle usually ceases when the window is closed tightly.

14 Door trim panels - removal and replacement

1 First remove the window winder and door latch lever. The winder handle has a plastic cover which should be prized off at the spindle end. A crosshead screw is then accessible and should be removed (photo). The recessed finger plate behind the inner door handle lever can be prized out also with a screwdriver (photo). The crosshead screw behind it can then be removed to release the assembly (photo).
2 The door of the Super Beetle is modified and the arm rest is bolted to the frame. Remove these screws (photo). Now use a wooden or plastic strip to go between the panel and the door and ease out the retaining clips. Be careful not to tear them from the trim panel. The trim panel may now be lifted from the door. (photo).
3 Replacement is the reverse of removal. Remember to fit the tension spring behind the trim panel over the window regulator spindle (photo) and the rubbing washer behind the window handle. (photo)

15 Window regulator mechanism and window - removal and replacement

1 Remove the door trim (Section 14) and the plastic sheet. If care is used the plastic sheet will come away in one piece and can be used again, otherwise it is a rather tedious job cutting out another one.
2 Lower the window and undo the screws holding the window frame to the winding mechanism (photo).
3 Undo the screws holding the winder to the door, ease the winder forwards and the glass may be drawn out downwards. (photo).
4 Now undo the screws holding the winding handle mechanism to the door (photo) and the winder mechanism may be eased out downwards (photo). A photograph of the winder mechanism held against the door is given. Note the plastic bushes.
5 It is not possible to repair the winder mechanism. Do not grease the drive spiral, a little light oil is all that is required. If there are tight spots it may be possible to straighten the tube. Should this not cure the trouble a new mechanism is required.
6 The refitting is quite a struggle. We are sure the winder goes in, in seconds, at Wolfsburg; but it doesn't when you are on your knees apparantly praying to the door. Get someone with

patience to help you. Fit the winder in through the slot with the front location (winder hub) in first. Wriggle the winder mechanism until you can pick up all the securing bolts thread holes but do not put the bolts in yet. This is where a second pair of hands helps a lot. Insert the glass behind the winder from the bottom and ease it gently into the door channels.
7 Holding the glass in position fit the screws which hold the glass carrier (the plated piece) to the winder. Fasten the winder to the bottom of the door and replace the winder fixing screws (3) and then the two bolts which hold the nut.
8 Tighten all the screws gently and try the mechanism. It may be necessary to slacken the screws holding the window to the winder and reposition them a little.
9 Above all do not rush the job or force things.
10 Replace the plastic sheet and the trim (Section 14).

16 Quarterlight - removal and replacement

1 If only the glass is being renewed the top pivot pin must be drilled out (photo). The glass may then be lifted up and out.
2 When fitting a new glass the upper pin should be properly rivetted and hard material used, otherwise the car security is jeopardised.
3 If the lower pivot is giving trouble it will be necessary to remove the main window and lifter and take out the whole main frame channel to get to it. This involves removing all the weatherstrips and undoing the securing bolts at the rear edge of the door frame. The channel strip is then taken out complete with the window dividing strip.

17 Door latch mechanism - removal and replacement

1 Remove the door trim (Section 14).
2 The latch mechanism is divided into three sections:
a) The inside handle.
b) The locking mechanism worked from inside the car.
c) The latch proper and the outside handle.
3 The inside handle may be removed by undoing two bolts (photo).
   The remote control rod with its packing may then be removed (photo).
4 The inside lock mechanism may now be disconnected (photo).
5 Ease the sealing strip away from the door (photo) and remove the screws holding the lock, and the handle. (photo). The lock handle may now be taken off the door. (photo).
6 The lock is quite complicated and if it does not work properly then it should be replaced (photo) by a new one.
7 Reassembly is straightforward. Refit the inside (remote

15.4b Remove the winder mechanism

15.4c The mechanism ready for refitting

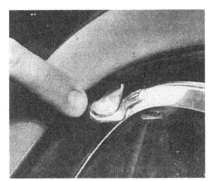
16.1 Quarterlight upper pivot

17.3a Remove the bolts holding the inner handle ...

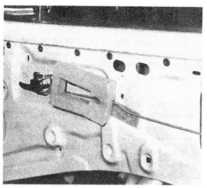

17.3b ... and take it away with the remote control lever

17.4 Unclip the inside lock control

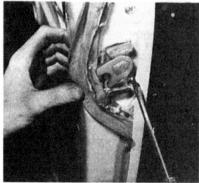

17.5a Undo the screw holding the lock in the door edge ...

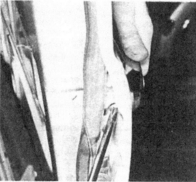

17.5b ... and the one holding the handle

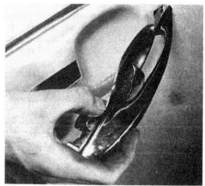

17.5c The handle may now be removed

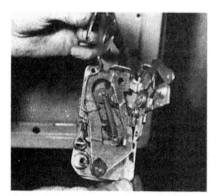

17.6 and the lock removed from inside

19.2 The removable disc for an extra mirror

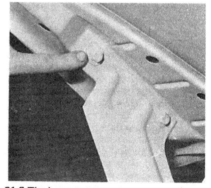

21.2 The luggage compartment mounting screws

23.2 The lock plunger may be screwed in or out to adjust the luggage compartment lid

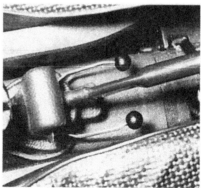

24.1 The levers for the heater controls

control) handle. The lock should be in the locked position. Do not forget the foam rubber packing. Fit the lock to the door, make sure it works from inside, and finally refit the interior locking pin. Replace the trim.

18 Door latch striker plates - adjustment and renewal

1 Rattles in doors are usually due to an incorrect striker plate position.
2 First check that the door fits the aperture properly by seeing that the gaps are more or less equal all round and that it fits flush with the side panel of the bodywork. There should be no rubbing and all the weatherstrip should show signs of equal compression.
3 Then make sure that the latch on the door is working properly.
4 If the door will shut and latch only when slammed it means that the rubber wedge at the top of the striker plate is too far out thus preventing the corresponding wedge on the door from moving right in. If the door can be rattled in and out when latched the wedge on the striker plate is too far in. To remedy either of these conditions slacken the striker plate fixing screws and move the upper end in or out as required.
5 If adjustment still fails to prevent any looseness when the door is shut then it is in order to put some packing between the wedge and the bracket, to which it is held by two screws.

19 Fitting an extra rear view mirror or radio aerial

1 VW make vehicles for many countries so a thoughtful designer has made provision for a rear view mirror fixing on either side of the vehicle.
2 A small disc is fitted into the door on the opposite side to the provided mirror and this may be removed to fit an extra mirror. (photo).
3 It is obviously best to get the extra mirror from VW, as it fits the hole. It may be necessary to open the hole a little with a round file and to cut a small slot for the fixing tab, and bend it in.
4 File off the triangular tab on the mirror locknut, screw the nut onto the mirror arm about two turns, make sure the flat sides of the lugs are towards the mirror. Fit the mirror arm and nut through the panel and turn it until the locknut contacts the bent-in tab. Pull the mirror towards you and screw the arm into the nut, tighten the nut and at the same time adjust the mirror.
5 In the same photo will be seen the existing hole for the radio aerial. Remove the plug and fit the aerial according to the instructions provided with it.

20 Engine compartment cover - removal and replacement

1 The lid is held by two conventional hinges and is kept open by a strong spring.
2 Mark the position of the hinge and brackets as clearly as possible and slacken off all the hinge and bracket bolts. Remove the spring by squeezing the two 'L' shaped ends out of their holes. If you have doubts about the spring flying off and causing an accident leave it where it is and undo the bolts, using the cover to hold and eventually ease the spring tension.
3 If the cover is being removed in order to remove the engine fan housing the hinge brackets must be taken off as well.
4 When replacing the cover the spring can be fitted after the lid has been attached provided you are able to get sufficient leverage on to it. If not, replace the brackets and then hook the spring into position and use the cover once again to take up the tension whilst the hinge bolts are replaced.
5 Do not first attach the hinge brackets to the cover. It is much easier to fit the brackets to the body and then fit the cover to the brackets.

6 It is important to position the lid so that when closed it is central in the aperture. For this reason the bracket holes are slotted to allow adjustment.

21 Luggage compartment cover - removal and replacement

1 Mark the position of the hinge plates on the cover and then slacken mounting bolts and remove one from each side.
2 Remove the other hinge bolts with assistance from another person and lift the cover off (photo).
3 Replacement is a reversal or the removal procedure. Fit the hinge bolts loosely to start with so that the cover can be positioned correctly in the slotted holes.

22 Engine compartment cover latch - adjustment

1 Before adjusting the latch the cover must be correctly set on its hinges so that it fits centrally in the aperture. If the cover is distorted or out of position no adjustment of the latch can rectify it.
2 The adjustment is confined to the striker plate fitted to the body. The hook on the latch should centralise in the notch and the plate should be raised or lowered to ensure adequate engagement. Slacken the two striker plate mounting screws and move the plate as required.

23 Luggage compartment cover latch and release cable - adjustment

1 Before any adjustment is made see that the cover fits centrally over the aperture. If it has been buckled the latch can be adjusted only a limited amount to compensate for it.
2 To centralise the lock bolt (on the cover) to the aperture in the latch, the latch must be removed after first slackening the latch securing screws. To adjust the engagement of the lock bolt into the latch plate the lock bolt can be lengthened or shortened in its mounting. (photo). The bolt should engage when firm pressure is applied to the bottom of the cover. If the cover needs slamming the bolt should be screwed out a little. If the cover rattles, move the bolt in.
3 The latch has a fail safe arrangement in the design so that if the cable breaks the latch will release rather than lock the cover.
4 To gain access to the cable end the latch mounting screws should be removed and the cover plate eased down from the lower half. The clamping screw is undone and the cable drawn out of the bracket. It can than be drawn out from inside the car.
5 When fitting a new cable into the bracket push the bracket back against the spring tension before tightening the screw.

24 Fresh air ventilation

1 In addition to the two heater controls on the floor, one each side of the handbrake lever (photo), there are two rotary knobs on the facia panel. These control flaps which permit outside air to enter through the slots on the top edge of the facia panel. The air enters through the grille just forward of the windscreen. On some models exported to hot countries the air stream is boosted by an electric blower fan. Otherwise the air enters under the pressure caused by the car's movement.
2 Each control knob adjusts the air inlet independently on the driver's and passenger's side.
3 The fresh air inlet is quite independent of the heating system.
4 So that the car may be properly ventilated even when all the windows are shut and the heater/fresh air inlets are in operation special outlet slots are incorporated in the bodywork behind the rear side window glasses. This ensures that stale air is exhausted and keeps interior condensation to a minimum under certain conditions of humidity.

Fig. 13.8. Kit for converting three point seats to reclining seats (Sec. 25)

1   Cross bar   2   Segment   3   Tension spring

Fig. 13.9. Adjust lever and knob (Sec. 25)

4   Lever
5   Knob
6   Clip

25.7a Fit the lever in the existing hole (arrowed) and rivet it in place

25.7b Fit the bracket inside the seat frame and the segment outside (arrowed)

5   Access to the cables is from inside the luggage compartment. When the compartment lining is removed the air intake duct is removed by undoing the self-tapping screws.
6   The air control flaps are controlled by nylon racks fitted to the cables which move the pinions on the valve spindles.

25 Seats - removal, repair and conversion to reclining type

1   The type I is now fitted with 3 point seats (as fitted to VW types 3 and 4).
2   These can be had as a fixed seat with integral head support, or as a reclining seat variable in steps of 35°.
3   To remove the three point front seat push the seat back to the last but one position. Take the covers off the runners then insert a screwdriver into the bracket from the front and push the locking plate down. Now pull the longitudinal position adjusting lever on the frame tunnel and slide the seat out to the rear.
4   Before installing the seat check the friction pads and spring clips. If the clips are not pressed into the upper friction pads the seat will rattle.
5   Insert the seat into the runners at the rear first and then into the front bracket. The positional lever on the frame tunnel should be pulled to the rear. Refit the covers to the runners.
6   It is possible to convert a normal three point seat to a reclining seat. A special kit should be obtained from the VW agency. (Fig. 13.8 and 13.9).
7   Remove the backrest retaining bolts (10 mm) and remove the backrest. Fit the lever in the existing hole in the seat frame and rivet it on (photo). Fit the bracket in the seat frame on the inner side of the seat and the segment in line with it on the outer side and fasten the segment with a bolt. (photo).
8   Refit the backrest and bolt it into position, attach the trim, and fit the knob with the clip and spring. (photo).
9   The three point seats are liable to sag causing creases on the seat surface, which is not only unsightly but also uncomfortable. This may be easily remedied. Remove the seat from the vehicle and lay it upside down on a clean surface so that the springs are visible. It will be seen that there are round helical springs and flat springs. These are connected with wire clips. Remove the rear three and shorten them about ¾ inch (20 mm). Refit them. Join the flat springs together with clips made out of welding wire. (photo).
    Remove the seat cover, smooth out the wadding and insert sufficient extra to fill the seat.

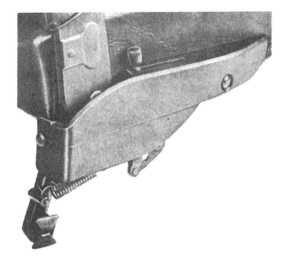

25.8 Replace the trim; fit the knob with hook spring and clip

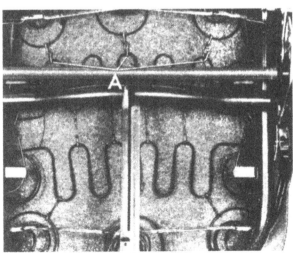

25.9a Shorten the clips (A) about ¾ inch

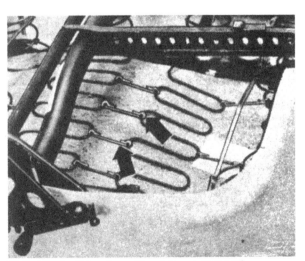

25.9b Join the flat springs with welding wire (arrows)

Conversion factors

Length (distance)

Inches (in)	X	25.4	=	Millimetres (mm)	X	0.0394	= Inches (in)
Feet (ft)	X	0.305	=	Metres (m)	X	3.281	= Feet (ft)
Miles	X	1.609	=	Kilometres (km)	X	0.621	= Miles

Volume (capacity)

Cubic inches (cu in; in³)	X	16.387	=	Cubic centimetres (cc; cm³)	X	0.061	= Cubic inches (cu in; in³)
Imperial pints (Imp pt)	X	0.568	=	Litres (l)	X	1.76	= Imperial pints (Imp pt)
Imperial quarts (Imp qt)	X	1.137	=	Litres (l)	X	0.88	= Imperial quarts (Imp qt)
Imperial quarts (Imp qt)	X	1.201	=	US quarts (US qt)	X	0.833	= Imperial quarts (Imp qt)
US quarts (US qt)	X	0.946	=	Litres (l)	X	1.057	= US quarts (US qt)
Imperial gallons (Imp gal)	X	4.546	=	Litres (l)	X	0.22	= Imperial gallons (Imp gal)
Imperial gallons (Imp gal)	X	1.201	=	US gallons (US gal)	X	0.833	= Imperial gallons (Imp gal)
US gallons (US gal)	X	3.785	=	Litres (l)	X	0.264	= US gallons (US gal)

Mass (weight)

Ounces (oz)	X	28.35	=	Grams (g)	X	0.035	= Ounces (oz)
Pounds (lb)	X	0.454	=	Kilograms (kg)	X	2.205	= Pounds (lb)

Force

Ounces-force (ozf; oz)	X	0.278	=	Newtons (N)	X	3.6	= Ounces-force (ozf; oz)
Pounds-force (lbf; lb)	X	4.448	=	Newtons (N)	X	0.225	= Pounds-force (lbf; lb)
Newtons (N)	X	0.1	=	Kilograms-force (kgf; kg)	X	9.81	= Newtons (N)

Pressure

Pounds-force per square inch (psi; lbf/in²; lb/in²)	X	0.070	=	Kilograms-force per square centimetre (kgf/cm²; kg/cm²)	X	14.223	= Pounds-force per square inch (psi; lbf/in²; lb/in²)
Pounds-force per square inch (psi; lbf/in²; lb/in²)	X	0.068	=	Atmospheres (atm)	X	14.696	= Pounds-force per square inch (psi; lbf/in²; lb/in²)
Pounds-force per square inch (psi; lbf/in²; lb/in²)	X	0.069	=	Bars	X	14.5	= Pounds-force per square inch (psi; lbf/in²; lb/in²)
Pounds-force per square inch (psi; lbf/in²; lb/in²)	X	6.895	=	Kilopascals (kPa)	X	0.145	= Pounds-force per square inch (psi; lbf/in²; lb/in²)
Kilopascals (kPa)	X	0.01	=	Kilograms-force per square centimetre (kgf/cm²; kg/cm²)	X	98.1	= Kilopascals (kPa)
Millibar (mbar)	X	100	=	Pascals (Pa)	X	0.01	= Millibar (mbar)
Millibar (mbar)	X	0.0145	=	Pounds-force per square inch (psi; lbf/in²; lb/in²)	X	68.947	= Millibar (mbar)
Millibar (mbar)	X	0.75	=	Millimetres of mercury (mmHg)	X	1.333	= Millibar (mbar)
Millibar (mbar)	X	0.401	=	Inches of water (inH₂O)	X	2.491	= Millibar (mbar)
Millimetres of mercury (mmHg)	X	0.535	=	Inches of water (inH₂O)	X	1.868	= Millimetres of mercury (mmHg)
Inches of water (inH₂O)	X	0.036	=	Pounds-force per square inch (psi; lbf/in²; lb/in²)	X	27.68	= Inches of water (inH₂O)

Torque (moment of force)

Pounds-force inches (lbf in; lb in)	X	1.152	=	Kilograms-force centimetre (kgf cm; kg cm)	X	0.868	= Pounds-force inches (lbf in; lb in)
Pounds-force inches (lbf in; lb in)	X	0.113	=	Newton metres (Nm)	X	8.85	= Pounds-force inches (lbf in; lb in)
Pounds-force inches (lbf in; lb in)	X	0.083	=	Pounds-force feet (lbf ft; lb ft)	X	12	= Pounds-force inches (lbf in; lb in)
Pounds-force feet (lbf ft; lb ft)	X	0.138	=	Kilograms-force metres (kgf m; kg m)	X	7.233	= Pounds-force feet (lbf ft; lb ft)
Pounds-force feet (lbf ft; lb ft)	X	1.356	=	Newton metres (Nm)	X	0.738	= Pounds-force feet (lbf ft; lb ft)
Newton metres (Nm)	X	0.102	=	Kilograms-force metres (kgf m; kg m)	X	9.804	= Newton metres (Nm)

Power

Horsepower (hp)	X	745.7	=	Watts (W)	X	0.0013	= Horsepower (hp)

Velocity (speed)

Miles per hour (miles/hr; mph)	X	1.609	=	Kilometres per hour (km/hr; kph)	X	0.621	= Miles per hour (miles/hr; mph)

Fuel consumption*

Miles per gallon, Imperial (mpg)	X	0.354	=	Kilometres per litre (km/l)	X	2.825	= Miles per gallon, Imperial (mpg)
Miles per gallon, US (mpg)	X	0.425	=	Kilometres per litre (km/l)	X	2.352	= Miles per gallon, US (mpg)

Temperature

Degrees Fahrenheit = (°C x 1.8) + 32   Degrees Celsius (Degrees Centigrade; °C) = (°F - 32) x 0.56

*It is common practice to convert from miles per gallon (mpg) to litres/100 kilometres (l/100km), where mpg (Imperial) x l/100 km = 282 and mpg (US) x l/100 km = 235

Use of English

As this book has been written in England, it uses the appropriate English component names, phrases, and spelling. Some of these differ from those used in America. Normally, these cause no difficulty, but to make sure, a glossary is printed below. In ordering spare parts remember the parts list may use some of these words:

English	American	English	American
Accelerator	Gas pedal	Locks	Latches
Aerial	Antenna	Methylated spirit	Denatured alcohol
Anti-roll bar	Stabiliser or sway bar	Motorway	Freeway, turnpike etc
Big-end bearing	Rod bearing	Number plate	License plate
Bonnet (engine cover)	Hood	Paraffin	Kerosene
Boot (luggage compartment)	Trunk	Petrol	Gasoline (gas)
Bulkhead	Firewall	Petrol tank	Gas tank
Bush	Bushing	'Pinking'	'Pinging'
Cam follower or tappet	Valve lifter or tappet	Prise (force apart)	Pry
Carburettor	Carburetor	Propeller shaft	Driveshaft
Catch	Latch	Quarterlight	Quarter window
Choke/venturi	Barrel	Retread	Recap
Circlip	Snap-ring	Reverse	Back-up
Clearance	Lash	Rocker cover	Valve cover
Crownwheel	Ring gear (of differential)	Saloon	Sedan
Damper	Shock absorber, shock	Seized	Frozen
Disc (brake)	Rotor/disk	Sidelight	Parking light
Distance piece	Spacer	Silencer	Muffler
Drop arm	Pitman arm	Sill panel (beneath doors)	Rocker panel
Drop head coupe	Convertible	Small end, little end	Piston pin or wrist pin
Dynamo	Generator (DC)	Spanner	Wrench
Earth (electrical)	Ground	Split cotter (for valve spring cap)	Lock (for valve spring retainer)
Engineer's blue	Prussian blue	Split pin	Cotter pin
Estate car	Station wagon	Steering arm	Spindle arm
Exhaust manifold	Header	Sump	Oil pan
Fault finding/diagnosis	Troubleshooting	Swarf	Metal chips or debris
Float chamber	Float bowl	Tab washer	Tang or lock
Free-play	Lash	Tappet	Valve lifter
Freewheel	Coast	Thrust bearing	Throw-out bearing
Gearbox	Transmission	Top gear	High
Gearchange	Shift	Torch	Flashlight
Grub screw	Setscrew, Allen screw	Trackrod (of steering)	Tie-rod (or connecting rod)
Gudgeon pin	Piston pin or wrist pin	Trailing shoe (of brake)	Secondary shoe
Halfshaft	Axleshaft	Transmission	Whole drive line
Handbrake	Parking brake	Tyre	Tire
Hood	Soft top	Van	Panel wagon/van
Hot spot	Heat riser	Vice	Vise
Indicator	Turn signal	Wheel nut	Lug nut
Interior light	Dome lamp	Windscreen	Windshield
Layshaft (of gearbox)	Countershaft	Wing/mudguard	Fender
Leading shoe (of brake)	Primary shoe		

Index

A

Air cleaners
description — 53
Air cleaners (oil bath type)
servicing — 54
Air cleaners (paper element type)
servicing — 54
Alternator
overhaul — 139
removal and replacement — 139
routine maintenance — 135
testing — 137
Automatic shift stick transmission
adjusments — 103
description — 100
driving techniques — 103
engine differences — 105
maintenance — 103
oil pump — 105
recent modifications (USA) — 105
removal and replacement — 104
specifications — 100
torque converter drive plate — 105
torque converter — stall speed test — 105
torque wrench settings — 100

B

Battery
charging — 135
electrolyte replenishment — 135
maintenance — 135
removal and replacement — 134
Bodywork
description — 195
engine compartment cover — 207
engine compartment cover latch — 207
fitting an extra rear view mirror — 207
fitting a radio aerial — 207
fresh air ventilation — 207
front wings — 197
luggage compartment cover — 207
luggage compartment cover latch — 207
maintenance — 195
major repairs — 201
minor repairs — 196
rear wings — 203
sill panels — 203
Braking system
adjustment — 120
bleeding — 130
description — 120
disc caliper pistons and seals — 125
disc pads — 123
fault diagnosis — 133
front drums and brake shoes — 120
handbrake adjustment — 120
handbrake cables and lever — 132
hydraulic lines — 129
hydraulic wheel cylinders — 122
pedal cluster — 131
rear drums and shoes — 122
self-adjusting brake shoes — 123
specifications — 119

tandem master cylinder — 126, 129
torque wrench settings — 120
Bumpers — 203

C

Camshaft
reassembly — 30
Camshaft
removal and renovation — 25
replacement — 30
Carburation
description — 53
fault diagnosis — 64
specifications — 53
Carburettor (Solex)
description — 54
overhaul — 57
tests and adjustments — 58
Clutch
adjustment — 80
cable — 75
cover (diaphragm type) — 79
cover (spring plate and toggle type) — 78
description — 75
fault diagnosis — 81
flywheel — 79
friction plate — 79
pedal — 80, 131
release operating mechanism — 79
removal and replacement — 77
specifications — 75
torque wrench setting - 75
wear — 75
Computer diagnosis — 152
Condenser — 68
Connecting rods
reassembly — 32
reassembly to crankshaft — 28
removal and renovation — 24
Contact breaker points — 67
Cooling system
components removal — 44
description — 43
fault diagnosis — 52
specifications — 43
torque wrench settings — 43
Crankcase
reassembly — 30
renovation — 28
Crankshaft
assembly of gears — 28
oil seal — removal — 27
oil seal — replacement — 36
pulley wheel — 21
reassembly — 30
removal and renovation — 27
Cylinder heads
dismantling — 64
reassembly — 34
removal — 22
replacement — 36
Cylinders
removal and renovation — 24
replacement — 34

D

Direction indicators — 152
Distributor
  driveshaft — 28, 70
  removal and replacement — 68
  repair — 70
Doors
  latch mechanism — 201
  latch striker plates — 203
  rattles — 199
  removal and replacement — 199
  trim panels — 201
Driveshafts
  constant velocity joints — 107
  removal and replacement — 107
  specifications — 106
Dynamo
  current output and reverse current test — 136
  dismantling — 138
  no load regulated voltage test — 135
  no load unregulated voltage test — 136
  removal and replacement — 138
  routine maintenance — 135
  testing in car — 135

E

Electrical system (charging and starting systems)
  description — 134
  fault diagnosis — 143
  regulator — 138
  specifications — 134
  torque wrench settings — 134
Electrical system (lighting, facia board and electrical accessories)
  description — 145
  specifications — 144
Engine
  ancillary components refitment — 38
  ancillary components removal — 20
  assembly of Nos. 3 and 4 main bearings — 28
  bearings — removal and renovation — 24
  description — 16
  dismantling — 20
  fault diagnosis — 42
  main bearings — removal and renovation — 27
  maintenance procedure — 16
  numbers — 16
  reassembly — 28
  removal — 18
  removal preparation — 16
  repair procedure — 16
  replacement and starting-up — 40
  specifications — 12
  torque wrench settings — 14
Emission control equipment — 63
Exhaust system
  description — 43
  removal and replacement — 52

F

Facia board — 149
Fan belt — 44
Fan
  housing removal — 20, 46
  housing replacement — 35, 46
  removal and replacement — 44
Fault diagnosis
  braking system — 133
  carburation — 64
  clutch — 81
  cooling system — 52

  engine — 42
  electrical system — 143
  front suspension — 194
  fuel system — 64
  heating system — 52
  ignition system — 74
  steering — 194
  transmission — 99
Final drive
  description — 84
  specifications — 82
  torque wrench settings — 82
Flywheel
  removal and renovation — 25
  replacement — 36
Fog lights — 155
Front suspension
  description — 176
  fault diagnosis — 194
  specifications — 174
  torque wrench settings — 175
Front suspension (MacPherson strut)
  ball joint — 181
  modification — 184
  stabilizer bar — 184
  strut — 183, 184
  track control arms and bushes — 184
Front suspension (torsion bar)
  ball joints — 182
  front axle assembly — 182
  shock absorbers — 182
  stabilizer bar — 184
  torsion arm — 182
  torsion bars — 182
Fuel pump
  cleaning filter and checking — 62
  recent modifications — 60
Fuel system
  description — 53
  fault diagnosis — 64
  inlet manifold — 62
  specifications — 53
Fuel tank and gauge unit transmitter — 62
Fuses — 149

G

Generator
  removal and replacement — 44

H

Headlamps — 145
Heated rear windows — 155
Heating system
  components removal — 44
  description — 43
  fault diagnosis — 52
  heat exchanger controls — 50
  heat exchangers — 49
Horn — 149

I

Ignition key warning device — 155
Ignition system
  coil — 72
  description — 66
  examination — 66
  fault diagnosis — 74
  specifications — 65
  timing — 70

L

Lamps — 145, 147, 149

O

Oil cooler
    removal and renovation — 21
    replacement — 38
Oil pressure relief and control valves — 21
Oil pump
    automatic transmission — 105
    removal and renovation — 21
    replacement — 38

P

Piston rings
    reassembly — 32
    removal and renovation — 24
Pistons
    reassembly — 32
    removal and renovation — 24

R

Radio sets — 155
Rear suspension
    description — 107
    diagonal arm — 115
    shock absorbers — 115
    specifications — 106
    torque wrench settings — 106
    torsion bars and spring plates — 116
Rocker gear
    overhaul — 22
    reassembly — 36

S

Safety belt warning system — 153
Seats
    conversion to reclining type — 209
    removal and repair — 209
Spark plugs — 72
Speedometer — 152
Starter motor
    dismantling and reassembly — 139
    removal and replacement — 139
    testing — 139
Steering
    fault diagnosis — 194
    specifications — 175
    torque wrench settings — 175
Steering (Super Beetles and Sports Bug)
    damper — 193
    gear — 186
    tie rods and joints — 192
    wheel and column — 190
Steering (USA Basic Beetle and UK GT Beetle)
    gear — 190
    tie rods and joints — 192
    wheel and column — 190
Steering column
    steering lock and ignition switch — 149
    turn signal and wiper switch — 149
Steering gear
    adjustments — 193
    description — 186
    dismantling and overhaul — 189
Steering geometry — 193

Suspension — front — see 'Front suspension'
Suspension — rear — see 'Rear suspension'

T

Tappets
    reassembly — 30
    renovation — 25
    replacement — 30
Thermostat — 50
Transmission (Automatic) — see 'Automatic shift stick transmission'
Transmission (Manual)
    assembly — 89
    bearings and reverse gearshaft — 90
    components — inspection for wear — 87
    description — 84
    differential and side covers replacement — 94
    differential gears — 95
    dismantling — 84
    fault diagnosis — 99
    gear carrier — assembly to main casing — 92
    gear carrier — fitting bearings — 90
    gear carrier — refitting shafts and selector forks — 90
    gearchange — GT Beetle — 98
    gear shift housing — reassembly — 93
    gear shift mechanism and linkage — 97
    input shaft oil seal — 94
    input shaft reassembly — 89
    limited slip differential — 97
    main casing — installing needle bearings — 90
    pinion shaft reassembly — 89
    removal and replacement — 84
    shift linkage adjustment — 97
    specifications — 82
    synchromesh hub assemblies — 94
    torque wrench settings — 82
Tyres
    care and maintenance — 193
    sizes — 106, 175

U

Underframe
    description — 195
    maintenance — 195
Upholstery
    maintenance — 196

V

Valve/rocker
    clearances and adjustment — 38
Valves
    overhaul — 22
    reassembly — 34

W

Wheels
    balancing — 193
    front bearings — 181
    rear shafts and bearings — 111
    specifications — 106, 175
Window
    quarterlight — 209
    regulator mechanism — 209
    removal and replacement — 209
Windscreen
    removal and replacement — 207
Windscreen washer — 151
Windscreen wipers — 151
Wiring diagrams — 156/173